Tactics and the Experience of Battle in the Age of Napoleon

Tactics
and the
Experience of Battle
in the
Age of Napoleon

Rory Muir

Yale University Press
New Haven and London

Set in Ehrhardt by Best-set Typesetter Ltd., Hong Kong
Printed in Great Britain by St Edmundsbury Press

Library of Congress Cataloging-in-Publication Data

Muir, Rory, 1962–
    Tactics and the experience of battle in the age of Napoleon/Rory
Muir.
    Includes bibliographical references
    ISBN 0–300–07385–2 (cloth)
    1. Napoleonic Wars, 1800–1815–Campaigns.   2. Military art and
science – France – History – 19th century.   3. Tactics.   I. Title.
DC151.M9   1998
940.2'7 – dc21   97-44386
                                                                                     CIP

A catalogue record for this book is available from the British Library.

10 9 8 7 6 5 4 3 2 1

Illustration acknowledgements:
Part One: Daily life with Wellington's army, from J.H. Pyne's *Camp Scenes*, 1803.
Part Two: Infantry in Italy, 1796, artist and source unknown. Part Three: Officer and Privates of the 52nd Light Infantry by Charles Hamilton Smith (National Army Museum). Part Four: Charge of Le Marchant's brigade at Salamanca, artist and source unknown.

Contents

Preface

Battles played a large and important part in the Napoleonic Wars and have
figured prominently in subsequent accounts. Innumerable books have been
written about individual battles and campaigns, with Waterloo and the
Hundred Days being easily the favourite subject. But these works are primarily
narratives and are designed to explain what happened in a particular battle,
rather than to draw conclusions about the nature of battles in general; so that
despite all that has been written about Napoleonic warfare, there has been little
serious analysis of what actually happened on the battlefield. Some of the
leading historians in the field, including Sir Charles Oman and David Chandler,
paused in their main work to devote a chapter or two, or an essay, to the tactics
employed in the battles they were describing. Drawing on their vast knowledge
of the subject, these discussions were far superior to the generally arid accounts
to be found in earlier specialist works on tactics, but they were limited in both
space and scope, and told only part of the story.

In 1976 John Keegan, in *The Face of Battle*, pioneered an original approach
to the subject by concentrating on the experience of individual soldiers in battle,
while in 1981 Paddy Griffith analysed infantry combat with a new and convincing emphasis on psychological factors. These studies marked the final stage
of a shift in approach from a late nineteenth-century view of tactics, which often
took the blind obedience of soldiers for granted and attributed any failure to a
lack of 'gallantry', to an approach which acknowledges the humanity of soldiers,
and places more emphasis on the intangible bonds of morale and cohesion
which held units together under the immense stresses and strains of battle.
However neither Keegan nor Griffith pretended to give a full account of the
subject: both wrote only single chapters on the Napoleonic period as part
of larger works; Keegan's limited to the British experience at Waterloo, and
Griffith's to Wellington's infantry.

The Anglocentrism of their approach was not simply the product of national
bias – Griffith's research expertise is in the French, not the British, archives.
Rather it reflects the fact that for the period of the Napoleonic Wars there is an

extraordinarily rich collection of first-hand British accounts of combat, which appears to be unmatched in any other language. Griffith has written elsewhere (*Age of Napoleon*, no. 12) of his frustration at being unable to uncover comparable sources in other languages despite looking for almost thirty years; while Charles Esdaile confirms the rarity of Spanish accounts – published or unpublished – which shed much light on the details of combat and tactics in their battles in the Peninsula. Only John Lynn, with much laborious work in the French archives, has uncovered significant new material, and that relates to the Armée du Nord between 1792 and 1794, a decade before the Napoleonic Wars began; and while this evidence is most interesting, it is fair to say that it is seldom as rich and detailed as the British literature.

The impression that any analysis of what actually happened in Napoleonic battles must rely largely, though certainly not exclusively, on British accounts is, paradoxically, confirmed by Brent Nosworthy's *Battle Tactics of Napoleon and His Enemies*. This excellent new work, the first full-length study of the subject, concentrates on the French perspective, and the lack of detailed accounts of combat constantly drives Nosworthy back to drill manuals and theoretical accounts of how battles ought to be waged, with many assumptions and much doubt and uncertainty as to the extent to which these were ever put into practice.

However it is precisely the practice of what actually happened in battle that I wish to study: how soldiers reacted on coming under fire; what they felt like before the battle began and after it finished; how the different arms, infantry, cavalry and artillery, interacted on the battlefield; what it was like to ride in a cavalry charge and see the enemy run before you; what a general actually did in a battle, and what roles his subordinate commanders and staff officers played; how did regimental officers help sustain the morale and discipline of their units; and what happened when a unit finally broke? In search of answers to these and similar questions I have read hundreds of first-hand accounts of combat in memoirs, diaries and letters, most, though by no means all, by British soldiers, with a large proportion of the remainder being French. This Anglo – or to some eyes 'Franglo' – bias in the sources may disappoint some readers, especially those admirers of Napoleon who still hold the snobbish view that the only 'real' fighting was in central Europe, and that the war in the Peninsula was no more than a tiresome sideshow. However I doubt that this emphasis in the sources greatly affects the result, for at this level of combat national differences mattered comparatively little: Russian, Scot or Portuguese, a line of horsemen galloping straight at you looks much the same, and the steadiness of your unit will depend on its confidence and training, its recent experiences and losses, not on its mother tongue.

This is not to say that warfare was completely homogeneous across the whole period, for clearly there were great differences between, for example, Austerlitz and Leipzig, and such variations have been noted and discussed where appropriate. But these differences are less clear-cut or aligned with national experiences than one might expect: on most criteria, Waterloo has more in common with Borodino than with Fuentes de Oñoro, and Austerlitz is closer to Salamanca than to Leipzig. Furthermore, beneath the diversity there were great similarities – whatever the colour of their coat, most soldiers were armed, equipped, manoeuvred and handled in action in much the same way; they employed similar tactical formations, though some armies might prefer one to another; and their generals faced much the same problems.

Many of the questions which I raise in this study cannot be answered definitively, for the emphasis in any discussion of experiences and emotions will depend upon the choice of passages quoted and sources employed, so that the subjective judgement of the author will determine the tone and colouring of the treatment. The same is true to a lesser extent even in the more objective field of tactics, for if one can cite a dozen examples to prove a point, there are sure to be a couple of exceptions to cast doubt upon it, and naturally it is the tales of extraordinary accomplishments which are told and retold most often by veterans. Faced with such uncertain evidence I have tried to be reasonable and balanced, though not, I hope, insipid. I have not advanced dogmatic theses in an attempt to appear bold or original, and while some readers will naturally differ with my interpretation and conclusions, I hope they will not find me wilfully wrong-headed.

This book has grown over many years, with two main periods of activity. I first became interested in the subject in the mid-1970s, read widely and was particularly encouraged by the lively discussion of these topics in a number of amateur magazines such as the *Courier* and *Empires, Eagles and Lions*. This period culminated in 1983 when, as part of my honours year at the University of Adelaide, I wrote a long (15,000 word) essay on the subject. Then, as a postgraduate student, I turned from the details of combat to grand strategy and began the research which ultimately led to *Britain and the Defeat of Napoleon, 1807–1815* (Yale University Press, 1996). When, in the middle of 1994, I finished writing *Britain and the Defeat of Napoleon* I returned to the old interest, went through my notes, and decided to pursue the subject in more detail. Much reading followed, and as I read my concept of the subject broadened so that more than half this book is devoted to topics either totally ignored or barely touched on in the original essay.

After so many years, I naturally have many people to thank for their help. Professor Austin Gough of the University of Adelaide must come first as the supervisor of both the honours essay and my doctoral thesis, and the source of much excellent advice. Professor Trevor Wilson and Dr Robin Prior, also of the University of Adelaide (though the latter is now at the Australian Defence Force Academy), gave me much encouragement and set me an example of how military history should be both intellectually rigorous and innovative in its approach. Dr Charles Esdaile of the University of Liverpool is both a good friend and an admirable correspondent. His knowledge of the subject is immense, and I have not only greatly benefited from his reading of the manuscript but also enormously enjoyed his marginal comments, many of which were informed by his personal experience in the Sealed Knot re-enactment society. He has greatly enriched the book, and I suspect that many of its remaining flaws are due to my occasional refusal to take his advice!

I must thank another good friend, Dr Christopher Woolgar of the Hartley Centre at the University of Southampton, for his advice concerning the Wellington Papers, and Mrs Marion Harding of the National Army Museum in London for her assistance in trying to track down the original source for the story of Colonel Mainwaring and the colours of the 51st at Fuentes de Oñoro. In the early 1980s I learnt much from extended correspondence with John Koontz of Boulder, Colorado, and Joe Park of Austin, Texas, which covered a multitude of subjects. The staff of the National Army Museum, British Library and Public Record Office in London, and the National Library of Scotland and the Scottish Record Office in Edinburgh were most helpful, although I should add that this book was only one of several lines of research that I was pursuing on these visits. At home I constantly rely upon the Barr Smith Library of the University of Adelaide and the State Library of South Australia. Nor should I forget Ms Rebekah Marks of the State Library of Victoria who was able to track down a precise reference for some twelve-year-old photocopies.

The path to publication was made easy by the encouragement, discernment and efficiency of Dr Robert Baldock, Ms Candida Brazil and all the other staff at Yale University Press's London Office.

Finally, I must thank my mother for her constant encouragement and interest, her keen eye for a good story, her rigorous scholarly standards, and her appreciation of the, sometimes mixed, joys of research and writing.

Part I
Introduction

Chapter One
The Eve of Battle

On the night before Austerlitz Napoleon visited the outposts of his army with some of his staff. There was no moon and the darkness of the night was increased by fog which made progress difficult. The Imperial party accidentally brushed into a detachment of Cossacks and there was a brief flurry of activity before they made their escape, with Yvan, Napoleon's personal surgeon, having to be rescued from a marshy stream. The chasseurs of the escort then had the idea of lighting the way with improvised torches made from pine boughs and straw. The troops, dozing in front of their camp-fires on the chill December night, recognized the party and, twisting the straw which was their only bedding into thousands more torches, illuminated Napoleon's path as he moved through the army, accompanied on all sides by cries of 'Vive l'Empereur!' It was the eve of the anniversary of his coronation, and Napoleon was moved by the spontaneous demonstration of loyalty and affection, saying as he returned to his bivouac, 'This is the finest evening of my life.' That night he slept little.

One of the officers on Marshal Berthier's staff recalled that earlier in the evening

the soldiers merrily talked over past successes or those which they counted on achieving in the future. . . . [Our bivouac] was a very lively one, for one of our comrades, M. Longchamps, who had been detained in France, had only been able to join us that day, and during his journey he had composed some verses which very aptly hit off the rapidity of our march. The arrival of this merry companion, who brought letters from home for each of us, was the most charming episode of the day.

The letters from our families, the portraits, and in some cases the love letters brought by the friendly singer, the Tokay wine which we drank straight from the casks through straws, the crackling of the bivouac fire, with the presentiment of a victory on the morrow, combined to raise our spirits to the highest pitch. By degrees, however, one after the other fell asleep, the songs ceased, and we were all closely wrapped in our cloaks and stretched comfortably on a little straw beneath the twinkling stars, when we were aroused by shouts of joy and the glare of brilliant illuminations.[1]

It is a lyrical evocation touched equally by nostalgia for lost youth and by the romance of the Napoleonic legend: hard stones, short commons, petty quarrels and the nagging dread of what the morning would bring are all forgotten, driven out of mind by the knowledge that this was the eve of the most famous and glorious of all Napoleon's victories.

A Westphalian officer, Captain von Linsingen, reveals a more dour, and perhaps a more realistic outlook, in his description of the night before Borodino: 'I could not escape the feeling that something huge and destructive was hanging over all of us. This mood led me to look at my men. There they were, sleeping around me on the cold, hard ground. I knew them all very well . . . and I was aware that many of these brave troops would not survive until tomorrow evening, but would be lying torn and bloody on the field of battle. For a moment it was all too easy to wish that the Russians would simply steal away again during the night, but then I remembered how we had suffered over the last few weeks. Better an horrific end than a horror without end! Our only salvation lay in battle and victory!'[2]

Such feelings were common and the evidence suggests that soldiers usually welcomed the prospect of action despite the risk it brought of death and mutilation. A soldier in the ranks of Sir John Moore's army recalled that, 'On the 24th of December [1808] our headquarters were at Sahagun. Every heart beat with joy. We were all under arms and formed to attack the enemy. Every mouth breathed hope: "We will beat them to pieces and have our ease and enjoy ourselves", said my comrades. I even preferred any short struggle, however severe, to the dreadful way of life we were, at this time, pursuing.'[3]

The hardships of campaigning can best be appreciated by following one young soldier, the nineteen-year-old Jean-Baptiste Barrès, a private in the Imperial Guard, through the advance to Austerlitz. At first Barrès was enthusiastic:

We left Paris quite content to go campaigning rather than march to Boulogne. I was especially so, for war was the one thing I wanted. I was young, full of health and courage, and I thought one could wish for nothing better than to fight against all possible odds; moreover, I was broken to marching; everything conspired to make me regard a campaign as a pleasant excursion, on which, even if one lost one's head, arms, or legs, one should at least find some diversion. I wanted, too, to see the country, the siege of a fortress, a battlefield. I reasoned, in those days, like a child. And at the moment of writing this, the boredom which is consuming me in cantonments (at Schönbrunn) and four months of marching about, months of fatigue and wretchedness, have proved to me that nothing is more hideous, more miserable, than war. And yet our sufferings in the Guard are not to be compared with those of the line.

The march to Strasbourg 'was beautiful, but long' and the weather was almost constantly fine. Yet Barrès fell ill, lost his appetite and suffered from a fever. However, he refused to go into hospital, or even ride in the carts accompanying the column, and reached Strasbourg 'still intoxicated with glory'. 'Several of my colleagues,' he noted, 'not more unwell than I was, stayed behind in the hospitals and there found their deaths. . . . Woe to those who go into hospital on campaign! They are isolated and forgotten, and tedium slays them rather than their sickness.'

At Strasbourg the troops were issued with fifty cartridges, four days' supplies and their campaigning equipment. Crossing the Rhine Barrès had 'a secret feeling of contentment when I recalled to memory all the noble feats of arms which its banks had seen. Then warlike reminiscences made me long for a few glorious encounters in which I might satisfy my eager impatience'. But by ten o'clock that night after a long march, 'I was so weary that I could neither eat nor sleep. I began to regret Paris.'

A few days later he briefly fell out on the march and could not find his unit for several days: a dismal time without food or comrades to cheer him; the only consolation being the warm welcome he got when he finally rejoined his regiment. 'Ah, it is a nasty thing to be lost in the midst of an army on the march!'

The army was now approaching the Austrian positions at Elchingen and Ulm. For two hours he and an Austrian sentry eyed each other across a ravine, but neither fired at the other. Soon Barrès was shocked at his first sight of the destructiveness of war when he saw a farm thoroughly plundered and half demolished for firewood to keep the troops warm. 'I shed tears over the fate of these poor villagers, who had in a moment lost all their possessions. But what I saw later caused me to regard them as still happy in their misfortune. As I was a novice in the military art, all that was contrary to the principles in which I had been trained surprised me; but I had time, afterwards, to become accustomed to such things.'

Barrès did not take part in the fighting before the Austrian capitulation at Ulm although 'I should have been glad if we had fought, in order to prove that even if one were new to such work one had as much love of glory as the veterans.' Instead there were more marches as the army advanced up the valley of the Danube, and for the first time Barrès camped in the open in bad weather: 'I did not find it very fascinating; it is a dismal way of going to bed', 'no straw on which to lie, little wood for burning, and a north wind that was like a wind of Lapland. I passed a wretched night; roasted on one side, frozen on the other. That was all the rest I got.' It was the middle of October.

A few weeks later they arrived in Vienna, only to be disappointed at being ordered to camp in the grounds of the Schönbrunn Palace and forbidden to enter the city without special leave. They expected peace, but were soon ordered to cross the Danube to carry on the war. The Russian army retreated and 'drew us perforce into the most frightful country, and this, above all, at a time of the year unsuitable for marching. I confess frankly that this departure displeased me sorely.' And so the campaign continued for another fortnight, the only consolation being 'the many cellars filled with Moravian wine which were met with along our route'. By the time the army camped at Austerlitz Barrès had been on the move for three months, had marched about 1,000 miles, and had yet to fire a shot in anger.[4]

But not all soldiers disliked campaigning: Barrès was young and inexperienced while many veterans welcomed the relative freedom and excitement of life on the road, especially when compared to the boredom and discipline of garrison duty or peacetime soldiering. As Edward Costello of the 95th Rifles recalls, in 1814 the comforts of peace were briefly relished, but soon 'the old soldiers once more panted for fresh exploits; for their souls were strong for war, and peace became irksome to them'.[5] Nor did soldiers only welcome battle in the hope that it would offer a respite from the rigours of campaigning. Indeed many battles, although not Austerlitz, were followed by even greater exertions, so that the Prussian defeat at Jena-Auerstädt precipitated the *Grande Armée* into a ten-week advance through Germany and into central Poland.

Battle added an element of excitement, glamour and purpose to a soldier's life; it was the culmination of the campaign, and the chance to prove the man, the unit and the army. Confidence was vital to a soldier: confidence in himself, in his comrades, in his officers, and in his army's commander. The soldier who entered battle expecting defeat was already half beaten. One British officer recalls the mood in the army before the Battle of Salamanca in 1812: 'There assuredly never was an army so anxious as ours was to be brought into action on this occasion. They were a magnificent body of well-tried soldiers, highly equipped, and in the highest health and spirits, with the most devoted confidence in their leader, and an invincible confidence in themselves. The retreat of the four preceding days had annoyed us beyond measure, for we believed that we were nearly equal to the enemy in point of numbers; and the idea of our retiring before an equal number of any troops in the world was not to be endured with common patience.'[6]

This ebullient self-confidence, resting on past successes, *esprit de corps* and faith in the general commanding, normally counted for far more than such background factors as love of country, ideological commitment or hatred of the enemy. But individual soldiers also had their own private views, which differed widely according to their circumstances. The dashing *beau sabreur* of twenty-three anticipating his third battle might hope for honour, glory and promotion; while the 'grizzled veteran' nudging forty and still, thanks to insubordination and drunkenness, a private, would look first to his own survival and then to some hope of plunder – even if only new boots, some provisions or a bottle of brandy! Most young soldiers would be anxious to prove their courage in order to retain their self-respect and the respect of their comrades, without which life in their rough 'military family' would be much more difficult.

Naturally all would feel a nagging apprehension of being killed or horribly wounded, for the 'soldier who pretends that he never felt fear is a humbug and not to be believed', as one British officer of indisputable courage emphatically declared.[7] This was worst just before the battle began, when

> time appears to move upon leaden wings; every minute seems an hour, and every hour a day. Then there is a strange commingling of levity and seriousness within himself – a levity which prompts him to laugh he scarce knows why, and a seriousness which urges him from time to time to lift up a mental prayer to the Throne of Grace. On such occasions little or no conversation passes. The privates generally lean upon their firelocks, the officers upon their swords; and few words, except monosyllables, at least in answer to questions put, are wasted. On these occasions, too, the faces of the bravest often change colour, and the limbs of the most resolute tremble, not with fear, but with anxiety; while watches are consulted, till the individuals who consult them grow weary of the employment. On the whole, it is a situation of higher excitement, and darker and deeper feeling, than any other in human life; nor can he be said to have felt all which man is capable of feeling who has not gone through it.[8]

And all the soldiers, whatever their position, would hope for victory, both for its own sake and as the surest route to their own private objectives. For the *beau sabreur* would be unlikely to make his name in defeat, the grizzled veteran would risk losing his own knapsack rather than gaining that of an enemy, and the raw conscript was far more likely to be put under intolerable pressure and to panic if the army as a whole was thrown into confusion and retreat. They were also safer, for the victorious army usually, though not invariably, suffered fewer casualties than its opponent; while a rout was an occasion of misery, fear and disorder, with soldiers separated from their units, wounded comrades abandoned, rations thrown away in flight, and the only common purpose being the desire to escape the enemy's pursuit. Wellington is said to have remarked that the only thing worse than a battle won was a battle lost; but the difference between the two could be dramatic.[9]

It is a commonplace to say that the Revolutionary and Napoleonic Wars was an age of battles when commanders were willing to risk defeat in the hope of gaining a decisive victory, in contrast to the cautious manoeuvring which is supposed to characterize eighteenth-century warfare. One modern authority even states that there were no fewer than 713 battles in Europe in the thirty years 1790–1820,[10] but on closer examination it is obvious that the great majority of these were partial combats between detached forces, advance and rearguards and the like, rather than pitched battles between the main bodies of opposing armies. In fact, actual fighting was comparatively rare in the life of a Napoleonic soldier, and Barrès was not unusual in not having fired a shot in the whole campaign until Austerlitz.

When the battle came it could be very bloody, though even here we must not exaggerate. At Austerlitz the French army as a whole lost about 8,800 casualties (including some men taken prisoner) from a total strength of perhaps 65,000 men. Of these casualties 1,305 were killed. In other words forty-nine of every fifty French soldiers present at Austerlitz survived the battle (though some would have died subsequently of their wounds), and six out of seven emerged unscathed. These losses were spread unevenly through the army: for example only a single officer (Surgeon Maugra) in the infantry of the Guard was wounded and none were killed; while the 24th *Léger* in Vandamme's division of Soult's corps lost no fewer than 126 men killed and 364 wounded.[11] At Salamanca, in 1812, the 30,562 British and German troops in Wellington's army lost 3,129 casualties (just over one in ten), and only 388 men, or one in seventy-nine of those present, killed. Austerlitz and Salamanca were triumphant victories and other battles were more bloody. At the terrible, bungled Battle of Albuera no fewer than four in every ten of the British and German infantry under Beresford's command were killed, wounded and missing; one in twelve of those present being killed.[12] Similarly, at Waterloo the British contingent of the allied army lost 30 per cent of its strength as casualties, about 5 per cent or one man in twenty being killed.[13] Defeat at Waterloo cost the French dearly: 40 per cent of the officers in the Imperial Guard were casualties, 7 per cent of those present being killed; while d'Erlon's corps suffered even more, with over half of its officers being casualties (395 of 788), and no fewer than 10.9 per cent, or almost one officer in nine, killed.[14] However such very heavy losses were rare, and the average over the whole period for battles fought by the British was a mortality rate of 3.3 per cent, or one man in thirty.[15]

Moreover these figures are based on the number of soldiers actually present at the battle, and this was usually only a part, often a small part, of the total army. Napoleon was the great apostle of concentrating his forces against the main body of the enemy. He began the campaign of 1805 with 210,000 men in the *Grande Armée*, with a further 70,000 men in Italy, 30,000 left at Boulogne, and many thousands more in garrisons and depots throughout France, while during the campaign he was joined by some 25,000 Bavarians, and by substantial contingents from other German allies. Thus his total force probably approached, or even exceeded, 400,000 men, yet he had only 65,000 troops at Austerlitz. Even the Imperial Guard had fewer than 7,000 of its 11,500 men present on the day of battle, many of the rest being on duty in palaces or in depots far to the rear.[16] Some of the other troops went into battles of their own – most obviously Masséna's army at Caldiero – but nonetheless it seems likely that fewer than half of Napoleon's soldiers took part in any serious fighting in 1805. This was not due to incompetence. Some of these men, though in the army, were not fit to take the field, while others had taken the field only to fall ill. Large detachments were made to occupy important positions and to guard the army's flanks and lines of communication. Such troops were not wasted even if they never came within sight of the enemy. The essence of strategy did not consist simply of collecting every man in the army together and marching straight at the enemy, and Napoleon's genius was much more subtle than is implied by some of his aphorisms.

Wellington faced the same drains on his resources, and the 30,562 British and German troops at Salamanca were only part of a much larger army, there being 62,000 British and German other ranks in the Peninsula in July 1812, while the total British army, with its garrisons scattered across the globe, included 243,885 rank and file.[17] Again some of the British troops in the Peninsula but not at Salamanca, and even some of those outside the Peninsula, saw combat in 1812, but even so, only a minority of the army as a whole would have smelt the smoke of battle in their nostrils in that, or any other year of the long war.

Given this, it is not surprising that the greatest killer of soldiers in the age of Napoleon was not the enemy, but disease and privation. Nor does this simply reflect British garrisons rotting in fever-soaked islands in the Caribbean, for it applies almost equally to armies engaged in active operations in Europe. The most obvious example is Napoleon's invasion of Russia where, although there are no reliable figures, it seems that of every twelve soldiers who crossed the Niemen, two returned alive, one fell in action or died from wounds, two were taken prisoner, and the remaining seven succumbed to the rigours of the campaign (as many in the advance to Moscow as in the famous retreat). The Russian campaign was unique, but other operations also produced huge numbers of sick. Between October 1806 and October 1808 French military hospitals treated over 421,000 patients, and of those admitted in 1807 (when there was most fighting) less than one-quarter were wounded, the remainder being ill, mostly with fever.[18] Things were no better for the British troops in the Peninsula where, for much of the war, between one-fifth and one-third of Wellington's rank and file were sick at any one time; and where, between January 1811 and May 1814, two-thirds of all the British soldiers who died succumbed to illness and disease. Probably about 240,000 officers and men in the British army died between 1793 and 1815: of these only about 27,000 fell in battle or died from their wounds.[19]

The bloody carnage of the battlefield may not have equalled the steady attrition of the hospitals, but nonetheless it was the climax of the campaign. Not all battles were decisive: Eylau and Aspern-Essling left the strategic balance unchanged; while on other occasions a tactical victory might prove fruitless, when other considerations intervened and forced the victorious army to retreat, as after Talavera and Busaco. Nor were all campaigns decided by battles: for example, the Austrian capitulation at Ulm showed how an army could be manoeuvred into surrender with relatively little fighting; while Wellington defeated Masséna's invasion of Portugal by a combination of defensive works so formidable that the French refused to attack them, and a scorched earth policy which deprived the invaders of supplies and ultimately forced them to retreat with the loss of some 15,000 men dead from disease and malnutrition.

But despite these exceptions most campaigns of the period were decided in a final dramatic battle. Marengo, Austerlitz, Jena-Auerstädt, Friedland, Wagram, Leipzig and Waterloo all transformed the strategic balance and led to diplomatic negotiations, though not always to peace. In 1800 Marengo led to an armistice by which the Austrians evacuated northern Italy, but it took Moreau's victory at Hohenlinden to force them to make peace. In 1809 the confused fighting at Eckmühl saw the initiative pass from the Austrians to the French, Aspern-Essling created a strategic stalemate, which was then shattered by Napoleon's victory at Wagram. Seeing that no real hope of victory remained, the Austrian emperor agreed to peace talks, and finding that Napoleon's terms, though severe, were not intolerable, he accepted defeat and made peace. This pattern was repeated in many campaigns: an initial victory such as Marengo, Ulm, Eckmühl, or even Jena-Auerstädt would give one side an advantage, but did not deprive the other of all hope of victory. In some cases tentative peace overtures were made at this stage, as after Jena-Auerstädt and during the campaign of 1813, but without success; so the campaign continued until a further action or series of actions produced a decisive shift in the balance of forces, the vanquished conceded defeat, and peace was made. The strategic situation at the end of the campaign would greatly affect the peace terms: thus with Vienna and a considerable part of their territory occupied, the Austrians were in a weak negotiating position in both 1805 and 1809, while the Russians were able to continue the war in 1805 and to make peace in 1807, if not as equals, then at least not as suppliants.

But a battlefield victory was not always enough to bring a war to an end. The long struggle between Britain and France dragged on because neither was strong enough to strike at the vital interests of the other. In 1812, Borodino was far from an overwhelming victory, but even if it had been a second Austerlitz, it is not clear that Alexander would have accepted defeat and made peace. His prestige had suffered enormously from the French advance and he might well have preferred to continue the war rather than risk the domestic consequences of admitting defeat. In Spain, repeated defeats in battle proved unable to break the will of the people to resist Napoleon's occupation of their country; indeed the presence and misbehaviour of French troops provided a constant stimulus to fresh resistance. This was a particularly hard war to end, for by overthrowing the Bourbons, Napoleon had removed the only government with the legitimacy and authority to survive making a compromise peace; while by seeking to impose his own brother on Spain as king, Napoleon had left himself little or no room to manoeuvre. The war could thus end only with one side or the other accepting complete defeat: with Ferdinand restored and all the French troops withdrawn, or with Joseph Bonaparte accepted as King of Spain.

These were great exceptions, but battles had proved decisive in forcing Austria, Prussia and Russia to make peace, and in establishing Napoleon's hegemony in central Europe. The failure to consolidate and make permanent that hegemony owed more to his restless ambition, constant search for fresh conquests, and determination to defeat, rather than ignore, Britain, than to any incompleteness in his earlier victories.

Chapter Two
Battles and Battlefields

Leipzig was the largest battle of the Napoleonic Wars with more than half a million combatants and fighting on four successive days (16–19 October 1813), although the heaviest fighting was limited to two days (16 and 18 October). The smallest actions of the period which can properly be called battles were probably Barrosa and Maida with around 10,000 combatants in each; but there is no clear-cut distinction between a 'battle' and a 'combat'. A hard-fought action between the main bodies of two armies was almost certainly a battle, even when the armies were as small as at Maida and Barrosa, while most engagements between rear and advance guards were combats even if the number of troops engaged was considerable. In this context the term 'combat' is likely to imply an engagement between parts of the opposing armies rather than their main bodies, although if large forces were involved and the fighting was fierce, it might sometimes still be described as a battle. Thus Auerstädt was certainly a battle though only one French corps was present, and the fighting at Wavre on 18 June 1815 is also usually described as a battle, if only because the combined losses of both sides amounted to about 5,000 casualties.

A number of Napoleon's battles saw one or both armies bring 100,000 men or more into action, but a figure of between 50,000 and 100,000 on each side was more common. Significantly, all Napoleon's greatest victories – Marengo, Austerlitz, Jena and Friedland – were won with armies of fewer than 100,000 men on the field of battle: for larger armies were less flexible and harder to control, while their opponents, if equally large, were less vulnerable to a sudden stroke. In subsidiary theatres such as Italy and the Peninsula armies were generally smaller, and most battles were fought with fewer than 60,000 men on each side. Vitoria, in June 1813, was the first battle in which Wellington commanded more than 60,000 men in action, and it revealed problems in co-ordinating the movements of such a large force, admittedly in very difficult country.

The great majority of battles were completed in a single day of fighting, sometimes just an afternoon. A few others, such as Talavera and Fuentes de

Oñoro, saw a preliminary attack on one day with the main fighting on the following or on a subsequent day. Only very rarely did full-scale fighting extend over more than one day – as at Wagram and Leipzig – and most of these instances occurred between 1809 and 1813, reflecting the great increase in the size of armies in that period. On other occasions there might be a number of separate but closely related combats and battles fought in rapid succession within a few days, for example the Battles of the Pyrenees, the Battles of the Nive, the fighting around Eckmühl in 1809, the series of operations beginning with Napoleon's victory at Champaubert on 10 February 1814, and even the Waterloo campaign. The trend to larger armies and more prolonged engagements points to the future of warfare in the middle of the century (particularly the American Civil War) and beyond, but it was not typical of Napoleonic warfare.

Campaigning was naturally easiest in summer and early autumn when forage for the horses and food for the troops was plentiful and the roads were hard and dry. Marengo, Friedland, Vitoria and Waterloo were all fought in June; Ulm, Jena-Auerstädt and Leipzig in October, and many other battles fell in the months in between. But sometimes, as at Austerlitz and Coruña, operations extended into winter, while the winter campaign in Poland in 1807 led to Eylau (7–8 February). At the beginning of 1814 the allies decided to launch an immediate invasion of France rather than wait for the spring. It proved an exceptionally severe winter and troops on both sides and the civilian population suffered enormously, but the decision denied Napoleon four months in which to raise and organize a new army, and so shortened the war and kept suffering to a minimum. Just as battles could be fought at any time of the year, they were fought on any day of the week: Waterloo was fought on a Sunday, Toulouse on Easter Sunday.

Fine weather suited armies best: gunpowder would not ignite if wet and both cavalry and artillery preferred to manoeuvre on firm dry ground. Yet the weather played a significant part in a number of battles: both Gross-Beeren (23 August 1813) and the Katzbach (26 August 1813) were fought in heavy rain which greatly increased the confusion and disorder of the actions. A snowstorm at Eylau reduced visibility so much that Augereau's corps took the wrong direction in its advance and was almost destroyed by the Russian artillery. A sudden rain squall at Albuera is said to have concealed the advance of the Polish lancers who were then able to take Colborne's brigade in the flank and roll it up, inflicting terrible losses. In general poor weather, particularly heavy rain, tended to encourage bloody battles of attrition with little manoeuvring or subtlety. The finest battles of the period were all fought in good weather and 'the sun of Austerlitz' became part of the Napoleonic legend.

There was no standard pattern to Napoleonic battles and they varied widely according to circumstances. The simplest form was a pitched battle with both armies camping in position the night before, expecting to fight on the morrow. Each general could get some idea of the enemy's deployment and from it attempt to guess their plans. At Austerlitz the allies totally misjudged Napoleon's intentions, while he anticipated and countered theirs, even though some parts of his attack were unsuccessful. On this occasion both armies took the offensive in different parts of the field, but in many battles, such as Talavera, Busaco and Borodino, one army remained firmly on the defensive at the outset. Waterloo presents a more complicated but by no means untypical picture, for while the French launched a series of frontal attacks against Wellington's army, they were seeking to check the unexpected advance of the Prussians in their flank and rear, and the battle ended with a general advance by Wellington's army which, with the subsequent Prussian pursuit, converted the French defeat into a rout.

Outflanking manoeuvres resulting in fresh troops arriving more or less unexpectedly in one army's flank or rear were common. At their best they could disrupt the enemy army and deplete its reserves by forcing the hasty improvisation of a new defensive line, demoralize the enemy troops who would naturally be unnerved to hear firing in their rear, and magnify the scale of their defeat by disrupting their retreat. However it was not easy to co-ordinate the arrival of the outflanking force with the actions of the main army, and as the years passed generals became more aware of the danger and took precautions against it. Spectacularly successful at its best, it was more often only a partial success, and sometimes it failed completely.

Few battles were totally unanticipated by both sides, but there were occasions when armies, knowing that the enemy were in the region, still collided unexpectedly, and an encounter battle developed as each side fed fresh troops into the fray as soon as they came up, Auerstädt being the most obvious example. More common were battles where one general attacked what he believed was a detached body of the enemy, only to find that his opponents were able to concentrate on the field of battle, as at Friedland, Lützen and Dresden. Then there was Salamanca, where the two armies had been manoeuvring at very close quarters for several days. Neither general expected a battle on 22 July: Wellington made preparations to retire into Portugal, and Marmont intended to harass his retreat. But in the early afternoon Wellington saw that the French were over-extending their forces, and having watched this continue for some time, he suddenly launched his army into an attack which carried all before it. But such spontaneous battles were rare.

Whatever their form, all battles of the period in Europe had much in common, for they were all fought by largely similar types of troops armed with much the same array of weapons. More than twenty years of warfare saw remarkably little technical innovation: a few light infantry were armed with a muzzle-loading rifle, but against this some light cavalry reverted to the lance, a weapon whose design (though not its use) was of the utmost simplicity, and which had been largely abandoned in western Europe more than a century before. Equally, if not more, significant was steady progress in making artillery equipment lighter, simpler and more mobile; an improvement which was complemented by bringing artillery drivers under military discipline. But by far the greatest change in the period was the increase in the size of armies, which reflected both the increasing productivity of European agriculture, and the greater authority and efficiency of the state in enforcing its demands on its citizens – a development seen first in Revolutionary France which was then imitated by its enemies.

The great majority of men raised, whether by conscription, 'voluntary' enlistment or levy on the owners of serfs, became infantrymen, the backbone of every army. Infantry were the most versatile troops on the battlefield: they could operate in virtually any terrain and both attack and defend positions. Most fighting in almost every battle was between the infantry of the two armies, and compared to infantry the other arms were little more than auxiliaries. Nonetheless, cavalry were very important. On campaign light cavalry screened the army's advance while searching for the enemy, while in battle they were often deployed on the army's flanks where they could give early warning of any enemy threat. Light cavalry could also be used for a shock role in battle, but this was best performed by medium and heavy cavalry – dragoons, cuirassiers and the like – whose primary function was to break the enemy line once it had been shaken by earlier fighting. Cavalry was best used offensively either as part of a wider attack or, if the army as a whole were on the defensive, in a limited counter-attack; although sometimes, as at Talavera and Ligny, relatively small numbers of cavalry could successfully 'contain' a much larger enemy force which was reluctant or unable to leave a strong defensive position to attack it. Artillery by contrast was best used in defence where it could fire steadily at an advancing enemy until either the attack was repulsed or the guns had to be withdrawn or abandoned. Its role was to wear down both the physical strength and moral cohesion of enemy units by inflicting casualties and by the psychological strain of remaining, often inactive, under fire. The way these three arms combined and interacted on the battlefield constituted the elements of combat and these remained largely similar throughout the period.

Battles were shaped by the wider strategic situation, by the plans of commanding generals, by the size and composition of the armies and, not least, by the ground on which they were fought. As well as being the largest battle of the period, Leipzig may also have been fought on the largest battlefield, although it is hard to tell for there was fighting on several fronts within an area about ten miles square. Wagram was probably the next-largest battlefield, for there the armies stretched over a continuous front some eleven miles long. At the other end of the scale Maida, with a front of barely a mile, may have been the smallest battlefield. Borodino probably saw the highest density of troops of any battle of the period: about 44,000 men per mile in the French army, and nearly 36,000 for the Russians, which goes a long way to explaining why it was such a hard-fought, bloody battle of attrition. Tactical finesse and brilliance required more space, at least in attack: there were only 8,000 men per mile at both Austerlitz and Salamanca. By contrast at Waterloo Wellington had some 24,000 men per mile: not that a general could guarantee a successful defence simply by crowd-ing his troops closely together, for a narrow front merely invited a turning movement unless both flanks rested on impassable obstacles.

Most battles of the period were fought in relatively open, gentle country-side where both armies could manoeuvre with ease. The hills and ridges so fre-quently referred to in accounts of battles were often no more than slight rises and falls in the ground, of considerable tactical significance, but offering little obstacle to man, horse or gun. Of course there were exceptions: the Serra do Busaco is a mountain ridge rising some 300 to 500 feet from the valley below; the two Arapiles at Salamanca are steep isolated hills rising abruptly from the surrounding countryside; while the Cerro de Medellin, the key to Wellington's position at Talavera, falls on its eastern side down to the Portina brook too steeply to be passable for cavalry, and is difficult ground even for infantry.

Being uphill offered great advantages to defending troops: there was the psychological advantage of literally looking down on their opponents and the practical advantage of improved visibility which greatly reduced the risk of being surprised. Even a gentle slope would slow advancing troops, exposing them to fire for longer, while steeper, rougher ground would leave them breath-less and disordered with little or no momentum. They would also be vulnerable to a counter-attack which would gain impetus by coming downhill. This was the key to Wellington's defensive tactics, but he added to the advantage by not deploying his troops on the actual crest of the hill where they could be observed and fired upon by French artillery, but slightly on the reverse slope where they were safer and where their counter-attack would benefit from an element of surprise. The volley or volleys preceding the counter-attack would be fired slightly uphill which, according to one veteran, 'is far more destructive than firing down, as the balls in the latter case fly over'.[1] Rough ground afforded protection against cavalry – and Wellington's cavalry was usually outmatched by the French – while if the hill was steep and high, as at Busaco, it made the task of the enemy artillery difficult or impossible. Artillery benefited from being deployed on hills, chiefly from the improved visibility and the protection this gave from cavalry. If the ground fell steeply away in front it might create dangerous dead ground, while if it fell away in the rear it would make the withdrawal of the guns difficult; nonetheless, both French and British guns were deployed on each of the Arapiles at Salamanca, and on similar heights in many other battles.

Given their size, it was inevitable that many battlefields would contain villages and these often became the scene of heavy fighting. A village was a tangible, recognizable prize men would struggle and die for with far more determination than for an open ploughed field or stretch of barren hillside. It also had consider-able tactical significance, for once a village was firmly secured, artillery could be moved in and it could normally command the ground for hundreds of yards beyond. So villages tended to become the focal point of a defensive line and the prime object of an attacker. Cavalry had little or no place in fighting in villages, and artillery was generally deployed behind and to one side of the village so as to sweep its approaches and exits. The fighting in the streets and houses was normally the preserve of infantry, and such struggles frequently ebbed and flowed as first one side and then the other threw in fresh troops. General Langeron, the *émigré* French soldier in the Russian service, describes how at Leipzig he captured the village of Schönefeld for the second time:

> I believed the position was assured, and went forward of the village to establish a chain of outposts. At this moment Ney . . . launched against me so unexpected an attack, and so impetuous and well directed, that I was unable to withstand it. Five columns, advancing at the charge and with fixed bayonets, rushed at the village and at my troops who were still scattered and whom I was trying to re-form. They were overthrown and forced to retire in a hurry. I was swept along by the fugitives, but I really cannot blame their sudden retreat because it was impossible to hold out, and I must confess that they moved as fast as I could manage. . . .
>
> . . . Fortunately I still had considerable reserves, and after letting the regiments which had been expelled from Schönefeld pass through the gaps between them, I soon did to the enemy what he had done to me, because my columns were in good order and his troops were by this time scattered.[2]

But this was not the end of the contest, and the struggle for Schönefeld was to last most of the day, with repeated attacks and counter-attacks, until the French reserves were finally depleted.

House-to-house fighting had a reputation for particular savagery. Soldiers quickly became confused and dispersed in a village so that officers could exercise only minimal control. Often no quarter was given and soldiers could become trapped in houses, gardens or blocked roads with no escape; bayonets were frequently used, although not between formed bodies of troops. Wounded men would seek the illusory security of a house rather than try to escape into the open fields beyond the village. Almost inevitably fire would spread from house to house, adding to the chaos. At Schönefeld,

> Many wounded of both sides were burnt to death and in the manor-farm all the cattle perished, even the huge black bull of Swiss stock. Maddened by all the firing and yelling, and by burns, the bull had broken loose, taken the part of Friedrich August [King of Saxony] and France, and run, bellowing and with fearful violence of a 'roasted-beef' [*sic*] stuck alive on a spit, against the attacking Russians so irresistibly that on his own he scattered an entire column.
>
> The burning church-tower made common cause with the raging bull to defeat the Russians. It collapsed and buried a large number of these soldiers beneath its ruins. . . . the noise and shouting of the troops, the sound of artillery and small-arms fire, the landing and explosion of shells, the howling, moaning and lowing of human beings and cattle, the whimpering and calls for help from the wounded

and those who lay half-buried alive under the masonry, blazing planks and beams was hideous. The smoke, dust and fumes made the day so dark that nobody could tell what time of day it was.[3]

This was written by a relatively dispassionate observer; the individual experience of storming a village, in this case Ligny, is well conveyed, though with some heightening of details, by a novelist:

At this moment our batteries on the road below opened their fire on Ligny, the roofs in the village tumbled, and the walls sank, and we rushed forward with the generals at our head with their swords drawn, the drums beating the charge. We shouted '*Vive l'Empereur*.' The Prussian bullets swept us away by dozens, and shot fell like hail, and the drums kept up their 'pan-pan-pan'. We saw nothing, heard nothing, as we crossed the orchards, nobody paid any attention to those who fell, and in two minutes after, we entered the village, broke in the doors with the butts of our muskets, while the Prussians fired upon us from the windows.

It was a thousand times worse in-doors, because yells of rage mingled in the uproar; we rushed into the houses with fixed bayonets and massacred each other without mercy. On every side the cry rose, 'No quarter!'

The Prussians who were surprised in the first houses we entered, were old soldiers and asked for nothing better. They perfectly understood what 'No quarter' meant, and made a most desperate defense.

As we reached the third or fourth house on a tolerably wide street on which was a church, and a little bridge further on, the air was full of smoke from the fires caused by our bombs; great broken tiles and slate were raining down upon us, and every thing roared and whistled and cracked, when Zébédé, with a terrible look in his eyes, seized me by the arm, shouting, 'Come!'

We rushed into a large room already filled with soldiers, on the first floor of a house; it was dark, as they had covered the windows with sacks of earth, but we could see a steep wooden stair-way at one end, down which the blood was running. We heard musket-shots from above and the flashes each moment showed us five or six of our men sunk in a heap against the balustrade with their arms hanging down, and the others running over their bodies with their bayonets fixed, trying to force their way into the loft.

It was horrible to see those men with their bristling mustaches, and brown cheeks, every wrinkle expressing the fury which possessed them, determined to force a passage at any cost. The sight made me furious, and I shouted, 'Forward! No quarter!'

If I had been near the stair-way, I might have been cut to pieces in mounting, but fortunately for me, others were ahead and not one would give up his place.

An old fellow, covered with wounds, succeeded in reaching the top of the stairs under the bayonets. As he gained the loft he let go his musket, and seized the balustrade with both hands. Two balls from muskets touching his breast did not make him let go his hold. Three or four others rushed up behind him striving each to be first, and leaped over the top stairs into the loft above.

Then followed such an uproar as is impossible to describe, shots followed each other in quick succession, and the shouts and trampling of feet made us think the house was coming down over our heads. Others followed, and when I reached the scene behind Zébédé, the room was full of dead and wounded men, the windows were all blown out, the walls splashed with blood, and not a Prussian was left on his feet. Five or six of our men were supporting themselves against the different pieces of furniture, smiling ferociously. Nearly all of them had balls or bayonet thrusts in their bodies, but the pleasure of revenge was greater than the pain of their wounds. My hair stands on end when I recall that scene.[4]

Yet if one British account of similar fighting at Fuentes de Oñoro can be believed, no sooner had the firing died down at the end of the day than soldiers of both nations mingled amicably, carrying away their wounded and distributing whatever provisions and plunder could be found with complete disregard to previous hostility.[5] However, fraternization between British and French in the Peninsula went beyond the normal 'live and let live' toleration of other armies into a rather bizarre camaraderie.

Even if not in the actual fighting line, villages and the fields and enclosures which frequently surrounded them could affect operations by creating a serious obstacle to the rapid movement of troops. The allied advance at Austerlitz was brought to a halt as much by the congestion and defiles of Sokolnitz and Tellnitz as by the strength of the French defence, while the whole Prussian advance to Waterloo on 18 June 1815 was delayed by the need to pass through Wavre. At Salamanca even the miserable little village of Arapiles delayed the advance of Cole's division despite the fact that the fusilier brigade, which actually passed through the village, did so with great regularity, forming up promptly on the further side.

Strongly built, isolated farmhouses and châteaux were less common than the examples of La Haye Sainte and Hougoumont at Waterloo and Sokolnitz Castle at Austerlitz would suggest. At their best they could be a great asset to the defence, requiring a smaller garrison than a village but being much less vulnerable to attack. Wellington's line at Waterloo was immensely strengthened by his two outposts, which channelled French attacks into a narrow front and which absorbed the energy of a large number of French infantry. Indeed probably Napoleon's greatest tactical mistake at Waterloo was to permit so much of Reille's corps to be committed to the struggle for Hougoumont, which even if it had succeeded would not have made Wellington's main line untenable. By contrast the fall of La Haye Sainte posed a serious threat to the allied position, for it happened when few reserves were available to fill the gap, and because it was so close to the allied line that French infantry and artillery there could pour effective fire into the allied troops.

Fortunately large towns were seldom involved in the fighting, though of course they might be besieged. Street fighting in a large town would absorb too many troops too rapidly, producing nothing but a shapeless slaughter without purpose, and an army beyond the control of its general. At the Battles of Dresden, Leipzig, Toulouse and New Orleans the main fighting took place outside the town, while at Smolensk the Russians attempted to defend the ancient fortifications of the city. The British defeat at Buenos Aires and the appalling scenes of rapine and murder which followed their success in storming Ciudad Rodrigo, Badajoz and San Sebastian showed what might happen to an army let loose to wage war in a strange city. But while the populations of cities were generally spared the worst ravages of war, the poor civilian residents of villages and farms on what became a battlefield had little choice but to flee while their homes were destroyed. Still, as battles were brief and infrequent the damage they did was trifling compared to the broad sweep of devastation caused by a large army on campaign.

In addition to the farms and villages found on the field of battle, armies sometimes constructed earthworks and other field fortifications to strengthen weak points in their line. Wellington made extensive use of them in his preparations for the defence of Portugal in 1810, both at Ponte de Murcella near Busaco, and in the formidable Lines of Torres Vedras. After the Battle of Albuera the position was strengthened by the construction of three redoubts in case another battle had to be fought there to cover the siege of Badajoz.[6] Soult used earthworks extensively to increase the already great natural advantages of his positions in the Pyrenees in 1813, and built a large entrenched camp outside Bayonne. Earlier in the same year Napoleon had strengthened the defences of Dresden with earthworks, and these saw some fighting in the battle of 26–27 August 1813. And it is said that the British wanted to make some entrenchments for their guns on the morning of Waterloo, but were unable to do so due to lack of tools and time.[7] The Russians had the reputation of being particularly fond of field fortifications, and with the 'Raevsky Redoubt' and the 'Bagration Flèches' at Borodino they constructed the largest and most important earthworks to be tested in battle in the period. The former was unusually elaborate: 'Originally a simple V-shaped earth rampart, with a large battery behind a parapet, it had been strengthened by wolf pits dug some 100 paces in front of its ditch, and was protected by breast works extending laterally in its rear. In addition, a double row of palisades was erected across the back, providing additional protection.'[8]

These field fortifications served several functions: they protected their garrisons – usually artillery, but sometimes only infantry – from enemy fire and enemy cavalry, thus encouraging them to make a more spirited defence. And as with villages, they gave the soldiers something tangible to fight over. Often the garrison had themselves constructed and slept in the earthwork, and a sense of proprietorial pride added vigour to their defence. Also they felt – often irrationally – safe in the earthwork, and resisted being driven out into the exposed open. Ideally fieldworks would be constructed a little in advance of the main line, so that they would absorb or break up enemy attacks much as La Haye Sainte and Hougoumont did. They were particularly useful in open country, especially if the defending army was weak in cavalry.

Marshal Ney advised that,

> For the attack of an intrenched [*sic*] camp with two divisions of eight battalions each: the troops shall arrive in columns, and form into line out of the reach of the enemy's shot.
>
> The first line, which is that of attack, shall detach about a company from each battalion as tirailleurs [i.e. skirmishers]; to these volunteers, shall be added the sappers of the battalions and of the division, with hatchets, a few hoes, fascines, and light ladders. . . .
>
> . . . As soon as the troops are within half a cannon range of the enemy, the tirailleurs shall advance at a run, and leap into the ditches of the works attacked, in order to cut the palisades and make openings through which they may penetrate the interior. Meanwhile, the line of attack shall advance in good order. . . .
>
> The tirailleurs must carry the redoubts attacked; if they are not strong enough they shall be reinforced by a few companies of grenadiers. In no case must the line of attack be broken, in order that it may always be ready to face the enemy's second line and reserve.[9]

Reality was seldom as regular and orderly as these instructions, though the British attack on La Petite Rhune at Nivelle in November 1813 conformed surprisingly closely to Ney's views, albeit with a smaller force: 'Sir James Kempt, who commanded the 1st Brigade of the Light Division, ordered that two companies of the regiment should lead in skirmishing order, followed by a support of four in line under Lieut.-Colonel [William] Napier, and a reserve of three companies under Lieut.-Colonel Duffy.' The British faced not one but a series of earthworks and redoubts which were, however, occupied not by artillery, but by rather demoralized French infantry. The leading companies stormed the first entrenchment with little difficulty and took cover while waiting for their supports to come up.

> Captain Murchison and myself got alongside of a flat piece of rock within about forty yards of the redoubt, and as they [the French] could see part of us, they made the rock smoke with their shots. . . . A sergeant pointed out better cover about twenty-five yards nearer the redoubt, to which we both went; and I borrowed his fusee and fired several shots at the heads of the French, the sergeant loading for me. While so employed, Colonel Napier and the support came sweeping up behind us, on which I gave the order to advance, and we all dashed forward with a cheer. Napier, boiling with courage, and being withal very active, attempted to scale the walls without observing the bayonet points over his head; and, being rather short-sighted, would certainly have been very roughly handled had not James Considine and myself laid hold of the skirts of his jacket and pulled

him back, for which we received anything but thanks. We of course apologised to Colonel Napier for the liberty we had taken, for he was very wrath at the time. We then pointed out an easier ascent for him, and assisted each other over the wall. To show the danger he was in at the moment, I was even under the necessity of striking a bayonet up with my sword, though they were giving way, as a hint that we were coming over in spite of them. The hint was taken, and a free passage left.

On getting inside I saw a French officer kneeling with his arm raised begging for quarter, and his head and face covered with blood. I told one of the men to take care of him, and proceeded through the gate at the rear, following the retiring enemy towards the second redoubt on the ridge of rocks, similarly constructed to the one we had just taken.[10]

The second redoubt was taken with similar *élan*, but the men were now out of hand and it was only with considerable difficulty that the officers regained control, halting the pursuit and re-forming their units. This was the moment of danger when a counter-attack might have swept the British back, but there were no fresh French troops in the area to take advantage of the opportunity.

The struggle for the Raevsky Redoubt at Borodino was much more fiercely contested, and here the first French assault which reached the redoubt was driven back by a Russian counter-attack before the French could consolidate their hold. This was followed by a prolonged artillery bombardment before the French mounted a second attack, this time, most unusually, led by two corps of heavy cavalry supported by three divisions of infantry who were to hold the redoubt once it fell and prevent any repetition of the earlier setback. The cavalry lost heavily in their advance and many men and horses fell as they tried to scramble through the ditch and over the breastwork, all the while under heavy fire. Wathier's division of cuirassiers was driven off by Russian infantry as it attempted to sweep round the redoubt and attack it in the rear, while General Caulaincourt was killed at the head of his men. Nonetheless the Saxon, Polish and Westphalian cuirassiers of Lorge's division succeeded in entering the redoubt where 'the cramped interior space . . . was [soon] filled with a frightful press of murderously-intentioned cavalry and Russian infantry [*sic*: actually gunners], thrown pell-mell together and doing their best to throttle and mangle one another'. The redoubt was captured, though the Russians managed to bring off some of their guns and yielded remarkably few prisoners. The use of cavalry for the attack was an extraordinary decision and while it may have been justified, despite its cost, by the circumstances of the day, it certainly does not form an economical model of how to drive an enemy from his position.[11]

Extensive woods and forests were not common on battlefields for much the same reason as generals avoided fighting in cities, but copses, orchards, olive groves and even small woods were not infrequent, having much the same effect as other rough ground: checking the momentum of attacking troops and giving cover to the defenders. Cavalry and artillery were at a great disadvantage in such conditions, which were best handled by light infantry who were used to acting independently. Fighting could soon slide into indecisive skirmishing if the attacking force lacked the momentum to press home, and the defenders failed to counter-attack. Occasionally a general would rest the flank of his army on a wood, as Wellington did at Quatre Bras, and Villars had done at Malplaquet in 1709. At Waterloo Wellington fought in front of the Forest of Soignes, and it has long been debated whether this would have seriously impeded his retreat in the event of defeat, or whether he would have retired obliquely in a north-westerly direction avoiding the forest but uncovering Brussels.

Many battles were fought over cultivated ground and in summer the tall crops (higher than modern varieties) could sometimes impede the passage of the troops. Sergeant Anton, of the 42nd Highlanders, remembers that at Quatre Bras:

> The stalks of rye, like the reeds that grow on the margin of some swamp, opposed our advance; the tops were up to our bonnets, and we strode and groped our way through as fast as we could. By the time we reached a field of clover on the other side we were very much straggled; however, we united in line as fast as time and our speedy advance would permit.[12]

Such grain could also conceal the presence or advance of hostile troops – even cavalry on occasions – leading to disastrous surprises, while it provided good cover for skirmishers.

In late summer, crops or even dry grass could pose another menace if it caught fire, ignited by shells, burning wadding from artillery or some other chance. Such a grass fire would naturally cause disorder among even the best-disciplined troops. Major Roverea, Lowry Cole's aide-de-camp, writes that at Maida, 'a shell exploded quite close to us and set fire to the dried grass of the field in which we were, and very soon the whole was in flames, and this accident caused some confusion in the centre of the 27th Regiment'.[13] Such fires added another horror to the battlefield, for some of the wounded were too badly hurt to escape and so were burnt alive, while dead men and horses were incinerated, causing sights and smells which nauseated even the most callous veterans.

Hedges could also conceal troops, and if well maintained might be a serious obstacle to the passage of infantry and cavalry alike. Even a slight straggling hedge or low stone wall was a psychological barrier, checking an advance and encouraging a more determined defence; while one Highlander is emphatic in describing the reluctance of men in kilts to push their way through thorns![14]

Rivers and streams were quite common and often had a major effect in shaping the course of a battle. One of the worst positions an army could find itself in was with a river immediately in its rear and a stream cutting at right angles through its front: this was just what happened to the Russians at

Friedland and it largely accounts for the severity of their defeat. Crossing a river in the face of the enemy posed great risks as Napoleon found at Aspern-Essling. Here and at Wagram the Archduke Charles did not attempt to defend the actual river line, but let part of the French army cross and then tried to destroy it before it could be either reinforced or withdrawn. Most commentators agreed in preferring this method to a more passive linear defence of the riverbank, where the attacker could almost always concentrate sufficient force at a single point to break through. Two of Wellington's most elegant and least costly victories – the crossing of the Douro at Oporto in 1809, and the passage of the Bidassoa in 1813 – tend to support their opinion.

Streams on the actual field of battle could also have a significant effect. At Ligny the Prussian position appeared very strong: a winding, marshy stream ran along the foot of the valley passing through a number of villages. But there were disadvantages: as Wellington pointed out, the Prussian reserves on the slopes behind the villages were exposed to French observation and artillery fire; even more seriously, the stream was an obstacle to movement in either direction and this enabled Napoleon to 'contain' Thielemann's corps on the Prussian left for much of the day with only a few thousand men. But at Vitoria stubborn French defence of the line of the Zadorra succeeded in delaying Graham's turning movement for some hours, although it could not keep the Royal Highway to Bayonne open for the army's retreat. Even a dry creek bed running in a depression – or, as some British accounts would have it, a 'ravine' – brought disaster on the 23rd Light Dragoons in a famous incident at Talavera. But cavalry were always vulnerable to unexpected inequalities of the ground, and experienced officers usually tried to reconnoitre their path in advance.

Every battlefield had its own special features, from the sand pit near La Haye Sainte to the frozen lakes at Austerlitz. But as well as these natural features of the terrain there were some created by the battle itself: the smoke, the noise and the carpet of dead and wounded littering the field. Accounts of Waterloo frequently state that the 'smoke hung so thick about, that, although not more than eighty yards asunder, we could only distinguish each other by the flashes of the pieces', or 'We breathed a new atmosphere – the air was suffocatingly hot, resembling that issuing from an oven. We were enveloped in thick smoke', or 'we every instant expecting through the smoke to see the Enemy appearing under our noses, for the smoke was literally so thick that we could not see ten yards off'.[15] But this cannot be regarded as typical. Waterloo was an unusually small battlefield with a high density of soldiers and particularly intense fighting on positions which scarcely changed throughout the day. Evidently there was little or no wind, and both Hougoumont and La Haye Sainte caught fire, adding to the murk. Rather than the norm it represents an extreme occasionally matched on other battlefields especially in and around contested villages such as Schönefeld at Leipzig.[16]

First-hand accounts of fighting in other battles do sometimes mention the smoke produced by heavy firing even when the troops were in open order. Thus Rifleman Harris describing Vimeiro writes, 'I myself was very soon so hotly engaged, loading and firing away, enveloped in the smoke I created, and the cloud which hung about me from the continued fire of my comrades, that I could see nothing for a few minutes but the red flash of my own piece amongst the white vapour clinging to my very clothes . . . until some friendly breeze of wind clears the space around, a soldier knows no more of his position and what is about to happen in his front, or what *has* happened (even amongst his own companions) than the very dead lying around.'[17] And there is no doubt that when battalions of infantry became locked in an indecisive firefight they would soon surround themselves with a dense cloud of smoke through which they could scarcely see their target, and which greatly contributed to the stunned daze into which they often sank. But what are we to make of all the accounts which make little or no mention of smoke on the battlefield – did they simply take it for granted, or was it usually not a serious problem? While it would be unwise to be too dogmatic, it seems unlikely that many battles were fought in the equivalent of a late Victorian pea-souper fog.

Just as with smoke, the noise of battle varied considerably and was naturally worst on small crowded battlefields such as Waterloo and Borodino. Nadezhda Durova describes the latter as 'A hellish day! I have gone almost deaf from the savage, unceasing roar of both artilleries. Nobody paid any attention to the bullets which were whistling, whining, hissing and showering down on us like hail. Even those wounded by them did not hear them; we had other worries!' And William Verner noted that at Waterloo 'The shots and shells from artillery are discernible at a distance whereas bullets from musketry produce a whistling noise not very agreeable to the ear. It is a remarkable fact that horses soon become reconciled to the noise of Cannon, but never to the whistling of bullets.' Even lesser battles could be deafening to troops closely engaged, and this could create command problems. Lieutenant Charles Booth recalled that at Busaco, 'Orders . . . could only be communicated by sound of bugle, or by the stentorian voice of a company officer. Great was the screech set on foot by our fellows during the charge.' This is confirmed by Rifleman William Green who writes that at Coruña, 'The roar of the cannon and the roll of musketry was so loud, that without great attention the word of command could scarcely be given, and the sound of the bugle hardly heard.' But again we must remember all the accounts which make little or no mention of noise and accept that orders were normally heard and obeyed even when issued by officers not endowed by nature with a stentorian voice.[18]

Nonetheless a battlefield was a truly horrible place. As well as the smoke and noise of weapons, there were the screams of wounded men and horses, the noise of drums and trumpets, of men cheering, cursing and weeping, exploding shells, bouncing cannon-balls, dazed men wandering in search of their units or for treatment of their wounds, riderless and sometimes horribly injured horses galloping about out of control, and the smell of gunpowder, blood, vomit and human excreta. All this acting on men raised to a high pitch of excitement by the prospect of action was enough to overwhelm some soldiers who would take any opportunity to slip away to safety in the rear; but most remained, consoled by the reassuring presence of their comrades, sustained by pride, and determined to see the battle through to the end.

Part II
The Elements of Combat

Chapter Three
Artillery

Artillery was the smallest of the three arms which comprised the bulk of a Napoleonic army, and it was something of a poor relation compared to fashionable regiments of cavalry and infantry. Its officers were often bourgeois in origin or the sons of artillery officers, for the service required a level of technical and mathematical knowledge which made it unappealing for many young gentlemen. Nonetheless one poor young artillery officer, from a remote and wild province of France, rose to make his mark upon the times.

Gunners were an indispensable part of an army, but their numbers varied considerably. Wellington's armies in the Peninsula suffered from a shortage of artillery: at Salamanca he had only fifty-four guns manned by 1,186 gunners in an army of nearly 52,000 men (including Portuguese and Spanish), a ratio of just over one gun per 1,000 men. This compared to the French at Wagram and Waterloo who had a ratio of about 3.3 guns per 1,000 and where gunners and supporting services amounted to between 11 and 12 per cent of the army (it was 2.3 per cent for the allies at Salamanca). The Russians at Borodino had more than five pieces of artillery per 1,000 troops, although gunners still only amounted to around 11 per cent of the army. Napoleon constantly tried to increase the proportion of artillery in his army and had some success, although the great increase in the size of armies themselves made the task difficult. Marshal Marmont, himself a gunner, stated that the ideal proportion was four guns per 1,000 at the outset of a campaign, pointing out that this proportion would rise of its own accord as men suffered more than ordnance for the attrition of operations. But this proportion was seldom reached even on the day of battle, and at Salamanca Marmont had fewer than two guns per 1,000 men. In any case, as Philip Haythornthwaite has pointed out, there was no simple correlation between superior artillery and victory; indeed far more depended on the way in which the guns were used than on their total number.[1]

The heaviest guns were used only for sieges, being too slow to manoeuvre in battle or to bring off in the event of defeat. They and their ammunition and associated equipment composed the 'siege-trains' which were normally kept well in the rear until they were needed to attack an enemy fortress. Field artillery was divided into horse and foot. Horse artillery generally consisted of lighter pieces and all the crews were mounted to give it greater mobility. Originally it was intended to support cavalry with firepower, without which the cavalry could be unable to defeat even small numbers of resolute infantry. But it increasingly came to be used in battle as a mobile reserve, while on campaign its place was often with the advance and rearguards, whether they comprised infantry or cavalry. Horse artillery had dash and glamour: its uniforms were modelled on those of hussars and other light cavalry, while the gunners 'rapidly developed something of the *panache* and *élitism* of the cavalry, and would regard their companions of the foot artillery as boring stick-in-the-muds'.[2] Nonetheless the great bulk of artillery was normally foot, not horse. They were unromantic, plodding slowly into battle, doing their work, then plodding on or back again as the fortunes of the day dictated. They produced few memoirists or diarists to preserve their fame, but one contemporary authority compared them favourably to their mounted comrades: 'these troops are more patient in their duties and works, more careful of their equipages and implements, and the effects of their efforts are more certain'.[3]

All artillery, horse and foot, was organized into batteries (called troops, companies or brigades), most commonly of six or eight guns. A few of these guns, usually one or two per battery, were howitzers: short-barrelled pieces capable of high-angle indirect fire which, except at short ranges, fired 'common shells' – a hollow metal sphere filled with gunpowder which would be set to explode with a fuse, when the shell would disintegrate killing or maiming anyone hit by the pieces. Most of the guns, however, were long-barrelled smooth-bore cannon which would fire directly at a target which had to be within line of sight. Their main ammunition was round-shot: a solid metal ball between 3 and 4.25 inches in diameter – rather larger than a tennis ball. This would fly through the air on a nearly flat trajectory for hundreds of yards, and once it hit the ground (unless the soil was very soft or steeply sloping) it would bounce or skid onwards almost as far as it had already travelled, remaining extremely dangerous. Cannon were categorized by the weight of the shot they fired: three- and four-pounders were becoming obsolete; six-, eight- and nine-pounders composed the great bulk of field artillery; while twelve-pounders were the heaviest cannon commonly used in the field. The heavier the shot, the greater the accuracy, range, and noise of the cannon, and the impact of the ball. But any cannon-ball hitting an individual would kill or seriously wound him, unless it was at such extreme range that the ball had lost almost all its kinetic energy, while at close ranges even the wind of a ball passing close by could stun and bruise a man or horse.[4] Some hits, particularly those from heavier pieces, might inflict more than one casualty, and heavy artillery was much more widely esteemed – and feared – than lighter guns.

All guns fired canister or case at short ranges. This consisted of a thin metal box filled with musket balls. On being fired these spread in a cone, many striking the ground or passing over the heads of attacking troops, but others would hit their target. One type of canister, with fewer, heavier balls for use at slightly longer ranges, was sometimes referred to as 'grape', although properly speaking this was a different type of ammunition used only at sea. British artillery also had two 'secret weapons': Congreve Rockets and shrapnel shells. Colonel Sir William Congreve's rockets had great theoretical advantages, being far more portable than conventional artillery, carrying a powerful charge, and, by their loud hissing, erratic movements and novelty, terrifying troops who had not encountered them before. But they were also extraordinarily inaccurate, sometimes even turning full-circle in flight and exploding in front of friendly troops. Consequently they saw little service in the field and their potential was never fully developed. Shrapnel, or spherical case as it was officially known, was far less revolutionary, but much more practical. It consisted of shells which could be fired by cannon as well as howitzers, and in which bullets were mixed with gunpowder. Wellington initially had some doubts about its effectiveness, complaining after Busaco that the wounds it inflicted were 'of a very trifling description'. At his suggestion the gunners substituted musket balls inside the shells for the carbine balls which had previously been used, and this evidently solved the problem for shrapnel soon became well established in the British army, being used extensively at long ranges. Thus at Waterloo Whinyates's troop of horse artillery fired 236 rounds of shrapnel and 309 of round-shot, although this proportion was unusually high. The British maintained the secret of its manufacture throughout the war, and while certainly not a 'battle-winner' it gave them an advantage which partly offset the fact that their artillery was usually lighter and less numerous than that of the French.[5] Between 70 and 80 per cent of ammunition carried for both British and French cannon was round-shot, although the British proportion may have fallen in later years as shrapnel became more widely used. Of the remainder, at least half was the heavier form of canister, which implies that artillery was not normally expected to do much fighting at very close range.[6]

Batteries typically had a strength of about half a dozen officers and between 100 and 150 men, which made them the smallest tactical unit on the battlefield, apart from independent companies of light infantry such as those Wellington attached to his divisions. This placed great responsibility on the comparatively junior officers who commanded batteries, although in the British artillery at least, promotion was so slow (being solely by seniority) that a captain in the artillery might easily be older and more experienced than a lieutenant-colonel in the line. Despite their lack of rank, commanders of batteries often demanded and obtained great tactical independence, for while they would generally be attached to a division of infantry and answerable to its commander, they would also be under the general supervision of senior artillery officers, and the two authorities could be played off against each other. According to Wellington's official dispatch on the Battle of Vitoria, 'The Artillery was most judiciously placed by Lieut. Colonel Dickson [commander of the allied artillery] and well served.' On reading this Lieutenant-General Lord Dalhousie, commander of the Seventh Division, asked 2nd Captain R. M. Cairnes, RA, who commanded the battery attached to his division,

> 'Pray, Cairnes, did you see any thing of Dickson or receive any orders from him during the action?' Answer. No, to both questions. He added: – 'I should use very plain words to any Commanding Officer of Artillery who would venture to interrupt or hinder the arrangements I had concerted with the Commanding Officer of my Artillery, as they can only be in unison with the movements of my Division.'

Cairnes himself believed that

> The Commanding Officer of Artillery of an Army has less probably to say to the placing of the guns in a general action than any subaltern of the Corps. A Brigade [i.e. battery] of Artillery is attached to each Division of Cavalry or Infantry: the remaining Brigades are in reserve under a Field Officer. With these the Commanding Officer *may* interfere, but with the Divisional Artillery he *cannot* without telling the General Officer Commanding that he knows nothing of the matter.[7]

Dickson's own account of battles and his general correspondence indicates that Cairnes's comments are only slightly exaggerated; and while Sir Augustus Frazer played a very active role at Waterloo, it was in the direction of those batteries of horse artillery which had been kept in reserve at the outset of the battle. Senior artillery officers played an important role in administration and organization on campaign, and came into their own in a siege, but in battle their role was limited and depended largely on the discretion granted to them by the general.

But officers commanding divisions, and indeed armies, usually had no expertise in artillery matters, and battery commanders were likely to resent any interference by them which went beyond giving a general indication of the role which the battery should fill in the division's operations. In June 1813 Lieutenant Swabey commanded his own troop of horse artillery against the French rearguard under the eyes of the headquarters staff and wrote in his diary with some surprise, 'All this time the staff stood by me, but I was permitted to choose my own ground and was in no way interfered with. . . . Lord Wellington sent me a message to go down into the high road, where indeed I should have been glad to be, but it was then too late and on my representation it was left to my discretion.' Nonetheless senior officers at all levels often did intervene, bringing a battery up to a threatened point or even directing its fire. At Lodi Napoleon proved his professional expertise by personally siting and aiming thirty guns, thus earning the nickname *le petit caporal*, for the task of laying each gun was normally performed by a corporal of the artillery. But few generals had Napoleon's training and their involvement could easily be counter-productive. Thus in March 1812 when General Graham ordered Bull's troop to fire on some retreating French when they were already out of range Swabey wrote, 'It is ridiculous that general officers should not be better informed on these subjects.' Nor was this a new problem, or even one limited to British officers, for Frederick the Great had conceded many years before that senior officers of other arms would often place great pressure on the gunners to open fire prematurely.[8]

The weakness of Wellington's artillery in the Peninsula ensured that it was more decentralized than in other armies, for after allocating batteries to each division Wellington was generally left with few in reserve. The French, by contrast, typically had one or more batteries of medium field artillery attached to each infantry division in a corps, a battery of horse artillery might be attached to the brigade of cavalry belonging to the corps, and in addition, the corps would have a substantial reserve of artillery probably including a battery of twelve-pounders. The army as a whole had a further reserve of artillery to which could be added the artillery of the Guard which often was brought into action even when the rest of the Guard was held back. The guns attached to the infantry divisions usually remained with them to provide close support, but the corps, reserve and Guard guns could be collected into a grand battery which would bombard a selected part of the enemy line in preparation for the decisive attack. These grand batteries were most common in the later years of the Napoleonic Wars (from 1809 onwards) reflecting the increasing proportion of artillery in the army and perhaps also more stubborn resistance – for if Napoleon's victories became bloodier and less decisive over the years, the cause lies more in the growing skill of his opponents than in any decline in his own powers. Other armies also employed grand batteries – indeed the Russians had long been known to favour heavy concentrations of artillery.

Serving in these batteries must have been most unpleasant: the constant roar of the guns was deafening, the black powder produced choking clouds of smoke, and the heat must have been tremendous. Captain Parquin noticed that even the gunners of the Guard took off their coats to work in greater freedom during the Battle of Wagram. The work was hard: continually carrying up fresh supplies of ammunition, pushing the guns back into position after each discharge – for the recoil sent them several yards to the rear – handling the horses, and keeping watch lest a burning piece of wadding, or an enemy shell, set fire to the dry grass and caused an explosion. But in some ways it was less bad than we might imagine. Batteries generally began the battle with more men than were really needed to crew the guns and look after the horses, so there were spare hands to replace any casualties or men who disappeared to the rear. The guns were normally deployed between twelve and twenty yards apart, and though they were sometimes packed a little more closely in grand batteries, they were usually not crowded together as they are shown in many films and nineteenth-century paintings. Nor did their rate of fire approach its theoretical maximum of two, three or more rounds per minute: had it, the guns would soon have become overheated and unusable, the gunners and the ammunition would both have been exhausted, and the smoke surrounding the battery would have been impenetrable. Between twenty and thirty rounds per hour was probably the norm for sustained fire, with the tempo increasing before an attack was launched. Napoleon regarded 150 rounds per gun as ample for a major battle, and while some batteries occasionally exceeded this, the average across the whole of an army was generally lower.[9]

These grand batteries could have a devastating effect, battering at the enemy's line, overwhelming his attempts to return their fire, and shaking and demoralizing his men. The sheer quantity of fire concentrated on a selected part of the enemy's line was unprecedented, and unless the ground gave some cover it was not only the men in the front line but also the supports and reserves who suffered. The effects were psychological as well as physical, for the men in the target area were battered and bruised by the constancy of the fire, and recognized that their own guns could make no adequate response. Even a battery of forty guns – far fewer than in some of Napoleon's largest batteries – occupying a front of about 600 yards might throw 1,000 rounds an hour into the enemy position facing them – and still increase their rate of fire in the minutes before an attack. At Waterloo, Wellington carefully positioned his men on the reverse slope, so that they were protected from the worst of the French fire, but even so, the mental strain of waiting passive under this fire is a constant theme in almost all the Waterloo memoirs and letters.

Grand batteries were typically used to support attacks at longish ranges, but artillery could also be used very effectively to provide close support for infantry, or, more rarely, cavalry, at short or medium range. This support was mutual, for despite an odd heroic exception, it was generally accepted that unaided artillery could not maintain a position on its own; while infantry gained enormous encouragement from the close co-operation of friendly artillery, over and above the material damage it did to the enemy. Lieutenant-Colonel Dickson recognized this when he wrote home about some very light guns intended for use among the mountains of the Pyrenees:

As yet we have not tried them much, but for general purposes I think it may be said, they are more useful from the confidence they give men, than from their own effect, which it is evident must be very uncertain except when employed at very short ranges; soldiers like the noise of Artillery; it gives them confidence when employed in their support, with however little effect, and in like manner it disquiets them when brought against them, and although perhaps the shot only pass over their heads, still they are not well able to judge how high, and feel that if they remain in the same position the practice may become more annoying. Were armies from a peculiarity of Mountain Country, obliged to wage war for a length of time without being able to employ any other ordnance than the small pieces termed Mountain Guns, I have no doubt that the soldiers would very soon learn the inefficacy and uncertainty of these pieces when employed at a distance, and would grow indifferent about them, but when a country is diversified, and in one action a Corps is fired upon by 9 P[ounde]rs, in the next by 6 P[ounde]rs, and in another by 3 P[ounde]rs, or *vice versa*, the Soldiers know that it is Artillery that is employed against them, the effect of which they have frequently felt, and will not in the hurry of their occupation make any observation as to its quality, and they will, in the different instances, attribute the success or failure to Ordnance being well or ill directed, more than the real cause.[10]

In the eighteenth century each infantry regiment in most armies had had two light cannon permanently attached to it, to provide this kind of direct support, but the guns proved an encumbrance, slowing the infantry and discouraging risks. Napoleon abolished them in the French army during the Peace of Amiens (1802–3); he attempted to restore them in 1809–10 in response to the declining quality of French infantry, but few if any saw service in Spain, and when he was rebuilding his army in 1813 after the Russian débâcle other claims rightly gained priority.

Gunners sometimes performed prodigies of valour while providing close support to hard-pressed infantry – Mercer's battery at Waterloo is probably the best-known example; while at Auerstädt Davout skilfully used his artillery to strengthen threatened points in his line. But most engagements were less dramatic, and Thomas Dyneley's account of his part in the Battle of Salamanca describes a more typical experience. It began strikingly enough when a staff officer, Colonel Sturgeon, brought orders directly from Wellington that Dyneley with two of his guns was to occupy the summit of the Lesser Arapile and defend it 'as long as you have a man left to your guns'. As Dyneley wrote to his brother John, 'From these orders I made sure of an "ex" or "dis" – tinguish.' But the expected French attack never came, and a few hours later Dyneley was joined by the remaining four guns of his battery as the allies went on the attack. For some time his task was to bombard French troops on the Greater Arapile 700 or 800 yards away (which was medium to long range for his six-pounders), and he takes credit for silencing some French guns which attempted to return his fire. Then Pack's Portuguese brigade attacked the French position and almost reached the summit, only to be driven back in confusion. As the French counter-attack swept towards the Lesser Arapile Dyneley's guns redoubled their efforts, opening with canister at 300 yards which effectively checked the French advance. The tide of battle in the centre had already turned against the French and soon they were in full retreat. The allies occupied the Greater Arapile but Dyneley's guns do not seem to have moved, or taken part in the pursuit until the following day. During the battle the battery fired a total of 492 rounds or an average of eighty-two rounds per gun, but unfortunately there is no way of telling the number of casualties they inflicted.[11]

Not all fighting was so satisfying or so famous. Both Swabey and Dyneley have left accounts of a relatively obscure rearguard action on 17 November 1812 when the British army was nearing the end of its retreat to Portugal after the failure of the siege of Burgos. Their troop of horse artillery, then under the command of Captain Macdonald, was ordered to support the Seventh and Light Divisions in checking the French advance at the River Huebra (or Huelva) between Salamanca and Ciudad Rodrigo near the village of San Muñoz. According to Swabey,

we crossed a rivulet, and took up a position to check the enemy. At the place where our rear-guard forded there was a height that entirely commanded us. On it the enemy brought up their guns with astonishing rapidity, and from thence fired with great execution on the light division as it boldly dashed through the water. When all had crossed they turned their fire upon Whinyates' and our guns which were immediately under their muzzles, and unable on account of their height above us to return the compliment. Almost the first shot wounded poor Macdonald and three men at my gun; Macdonald being so close to me that we touched, I supported him till he was carried off. We remained four hours calmly receiving the enemy's fire, and occasionally checking their infantry and keeping the passage of the river; Lord Wellington gave no orders but to reserve our fire for formed bodies, none of which appeared. Many were the hair-breadth escapes of men and horses; the wet state of the ground, which kept the shot from rising, and the mercy of Providence, alone saved us from certain destruction. At 11 o'clock we got to a wet camp in the rain and broiled some beef.[12]

Dyneley, writing a week later to his sister, confirms Swabey's account, adding some details:

On the 17th, between one and two o'clock, we came into action and the second or third round of the enemy's fire disabled Macdonald. Of this I knew nothing until a few minutes afterwards when, enquiring for him, I was told he had been carried very severely wounded to the rear. In the course of half-an-hour a man returned bringing with him the piece of shell about an inch and a half square, just as it was cut out of the wound, and begged to know if I wished to have it, which I declined, thinking it was more than probable I should have a bit to take care of for myself before the day was over. For we remained on the same spot from that time till dark with five guns playing from a hill on our right flank and four in our front ploughing the ground up in beautiful style, the troop standing counting the shots on their fingers. As we had received orders from his Lordship not to fire at artillery, or anything but formed columns, which latter did not trouble us much, we [the battery] only expended 140 rounds the whole day and our loss was very trifling, only four men wounded. The poor infantry, who were immediately in front and directly behind us, suffered dreadfully. When our men were not actually firing, I made them get behind some trees near us.[13]

These accounts show the different ways artillery could be used in action: defending an important position against – in Dyneley's case – an attack that never came; supporting an attack at longish range, and then helping to repel the enemy's counter-attack; or, as in the last example, helping to deter an attack and so gain time for the main body to make an unmolested, although still miserable, retreat. They also reveal some of the more technical factors which affected the performance of artillery, particularly the terrain. At the Huebra Swabey says that the British could not have returned the French fire effectively, even if Wellington had not forbidden it, because of the height on which the French guns were deployed. On the other hand the soft ground caused by recent rain meant that the French cannon-balls stuck in the mud rather than bouncing along for hundreds of yards inflicting further casualties. A more famous example of this was at Waterloo where a combination of rain-soaked fields and Wellington's use of the reverse slope minimized the effects of Napoleon's greatly superior artillery.

Captain Adye's *Bombardier and Pocket Gunner* offered much useful advice for a battery commander in selecting a position:

The guns should be placed as much as possible under cover; this is easily done upon heights, by keeping them so far back that the muzzles are only to be seen over them: by proper attention many situations may be found of which advantage may be taken for this purpose, such as banks, ditches, &c every where to be met with.

A battery in the field should never be discovered by the enemy till the very moment it is to open [fire]. The guns may be masked by being a little retired; or by being covered by troops, particularly cavalry.

To enable the commanding officer of artillery to choose the proper positions for his field batteries, he should of course be made acquainted, with the effect intended to be produced; with the troops that are to be supported; that he may place his artillery so as to support, but not incommode the infantry; nor take up such positions with his guns, as would be more advantageously occupied by the line. That he may not place his batteries too soon, nor too much exposed; that he may cover his front and his flanks, by taking advantage of the ground; and that he may not venture too far out of the protection of the troops, unless some very decided effect is to be obtained thereby.

The guns must be so placed as to produce a cross fire upon the position of the enemy, and upon all the ground which he must pass over in an attack. . . .

. . . The shot from artillery should always take an enemy in the direction of its greatest dimension; it should therefore take a line obliquely or in flank; but a column in front.[14]

The idea of oblique or enfilading fire was stressed by other authorities and backed by tales of a dozen or more men cut down by a single cannon-ball. Linear formations certainly appeared vulnerable to flanking fire, although in practice it may not always have been easy to hit the narrow target they presented from side on. But when successful, fire from the flanks or rear made troops far more uneasy than that from the front. Jomini stresses this psychological advantage of oblique fire, evidently regarding it as more important than any material benefit:

> The moral effect of a reverse fire upon a body of troops is inconceivable; and the best troops are generally put to flight by it. The fine movement of Ney on Preititz at Bautzen was neutralized by a few pieces of Kleist's artillery, which took his columns in flank, checked them, and decided the marshal to deviate from the excellent direction he was pursuing. A few pieces of light artillery, thrown at all hazards upon the enemy's flank, may produce most important results . . .[15]

However, there were dangers in trying to create an opportunity for enfilading fire: by deploying a battery at an angle to the main line of the army, an artillery officer risked exposing his own flank to attack, both by opposing artillery and more directly by enemy troops. Batteries normally deployed in a staggered, uneven line to minimize the danger of being caught by enfilade fire, while their own angle of fire was relatively limited: a battery with a frontage of eighty or a hundred yards could not simply or easily rotate through sixty or ninety degrees.

Adye also stresses the importance of close co-operation between artillery and the troops to which it was attached. Despite its firepower a battery could not normally defend itself without support: its flanks were too vulnerable, cavalry and skirmishers could threaten it, and the gunners lacked the cohesion of troops who fought in close order. Even Mercer's battery at Waterloo, which provides a famous example of artillery repulsing frontal attacks of cavalry through firepower alone, benefited from the close support of the Brunswick squares which protected its flanks and probably emboldened the gunners, if not their commander. A more typical example is provided by Lieutenant Reuter's experiences at Ligny:

> I suppose it was between two and three o'clock in the afternoon when I received an order to take four guns of my battery and accompany the 14th Regiment in its advance towards St. Amand, while the howitzers and two remaining guns took up a position opposite Ligny, so as to be able to shell the open ground beyond the village, and the village itself, too, in the event of our not being able to hold it. I halted my guns about six hundred paces from St. Amand, and opened fire on the enemy's artillery in position on the high ground opposite, which at once began to reply with a well-sustained fire of shells, and inflicted heavy losses on us. Meanwhile the 14th Regiment, without ever thinking of leaving an escort behind for us, pressed gallantly forward to St. Amand, and succeeded in gaining possession of a part of that village. I myself was under the impression that they had been able to occupy the whole of it. The battery had thus been engaged for some hours in its combat with the hostile guns, and were awaiting the order to follow up the

movement of the 14th Regiment, when suddenly I became aware of two strong lines of skirmishers which were apparently falling back on us from the village of St. Amand. Imagining that the skirmishers in front of us were our own countrymen, I hastened up to the battery and warned my layers not to direct their aim upon them, but to continue to engage the guns opposite. In the meanwhile the skirmishers in question had got within three hundred paces of the battery.

I had just returned to the right flank of my command, when our surgeon, Zinkernagel, called my attention to the red tufts on the shakos of the sharp-shooters. I at once bellowed out the order 'With grape on the skirmishers!' At the same moment both their lines turned upon us, gave us a volley, then flung themselves on the ground. By this volley, and the bursting of a shell or two, every horse, except one wheeler, belonging to the gun on my left flank, was either killed or wounded. I ordered the horses to be taken out of one of my ammunition waggons, which had been emptied, and thus intended to make my gun fit to move again, while I meanwhile kept up a slow fire of grape, that had the effect of keeping the marksmen in my front glued to the ground. But in another moment, all of a sudden, I saw my left flank taken in rear, from the direction of the Ligny brook, by a French staff officer and about fifty horsemen. As these rushed upon us the officer shouted to me in German, 'Surrender, gunners, for you are all prisoners!' With these words he charged down with his men on the flank gun on my left, and dealt a vicious cut at my wheel driver, Borchardt . . . who dodged it, however, by flinging himself over on his dead horse. The blow was delivered with such good will that the sabre cut deep into the saddle, and stuck fast there. Gunner Sieberg, however, availing himself of the chance the momentary delay afforded, snatched up the handspike of one of the 12-pounders, and with the words, 'I'll soon show him how to take prisoners!' dealt the officer such a blow on his bearskin that he rolled with a broken skull from the back of his grey charger, which galloped away into the line of skirmishers in our front.

The fifty horsemen, unable to control their horses which bounded after their companion, followed his lead in a moment, rode over the prostrate marksmen, and carried the utmost confusion into the enemy's ranks. I seized the opportunity to limber up all my guns except the unfortunate one on my left, and to retire on two of our cavalry regiments, which I saw drawn up about 600 paces to my rear. It was only when I had thus fallen back that the enemy's skirmishers ventured to approach my remaining gun. I could see from a distance how bravely its detach-ment defended themselves and it with handspikes and their side-arms, and some of them in the end succeeded in regaining the battery. The moment I got near our cavalry I rode up to them and entreated them to endeavour to recapture my gun again from the enemy, but they refused to comply with my request. I, therefore, returned sorrowfully to my battery, which had retired meanwhile behind the hill with the windmill on it near Ligny.[16]

The most famous occasion when artillery is credited, not merely with defending itself, but with taking the attack to the enemy, was at the Battle of

Friedland. Here General Senarmont, commander of the artillery of I Corps, acting on his own initiative, though with the approval of the corps commander General Victor, hastily collected most of the artillery in the corps, including divisional batteries, into a single force of thirty guns. With these he first checked the pursuit of Ney's corps, which had been broken, and then advanced against the Russian line, unlimbering his guns and opening fire at 450 yards. The Russians stood firm but could make no effective reply, and after a few rounds Senarmont again advanced, this time to within 250 yards. Even Napoleon was astounded at his audacity and sent an aide-de-camp, General Mouton (later Count Lobau), to ask for an explanation, but Senarmont replied, 'Leave me to do it with my Gunners, I will reply to all', and Napoleon let him have his way. Again the French guns advanced until they were only 150 yards from the Russian line; the Russian cavalry attempted to overrun them but were repulsed with terrible losses and the whole Russian left wing fell back in chaotic disorder.

Such at least is the traditional story, based on Senarmont's own account of the battle. In broad outline it is probably fairly accurate, but there are problems with it which suggest that the details are exaggerated, and in particular that the ranges quoted are far too short. Senarmont's thirty guns fired a total of 2,516 rounds (an average of eighty-four per gun), of which only 368 (roughly one seventh) were canister. It is hard to believe that his guns would really have closed to within 150 or 250 yards and continued to fire round-shot when canister was specifically designed for use at these and even longer ranges. Nor do Senarmont's casualties support the idea of his closing within musket range of the enemy, for he lost only one officer and ten men killed, three officers and forty-two men wounded. It may be that the Russians passively waited to be slaughtered, but it seems more likely that the tale of Senarmont's daring grew in the telling, encouraged no doubt by Napoleon, eager to inspire his gunners with a spirit of emulation. After all, 'to lie like a bulletin' was proverbial in the *Grande Armée*.[17]

Whatever the actual ranges, it is clear that Senarmont's target was the main body of the enemy troops facing him – the Russian infantry and cavalry. In this he was following the prevailing orthodoxy which strongly discouraged counter-battery fire. Adye firmly stated that 'Artillery should never fire against artillery', although he went on to add the qualification, 'unless the enemy's troops are covered, and his artillery exposed; or unless your troops suffer more from the fire of his guns than his troops do from yours'.[18] The usual explanation for this prohibition was that artillery made a poor target and that such fire was wasteful; but behind this we may glimpse an international camaraderie between gunners such as that which used to prevent fast bowlers in cricket from bowling intimidating bouncers at each other. In any case the convention soon broke down in practice. Lieutenant Reuter exchanged heavy fire with the French artillery at Ligny; Dyneley prided himself (whether accurately or not is another question) on having silenced the French guns opposite him on the Greater Arapile at Salamanca, and he and Swabey came under heavy French fire on the Huebra on 17 November 1812. On this occasion they would have liked to reply to the French guns but were prevented from doing so partly by orders from Wellington to reserve their fire for formed bodies of enemy troops, and partly because the French artillery was on a height which made it physically impossible for the British guns to respond effectively. The implication of this double explanation is that Wellington's order alone might not have sufficed, and this impression is strengthened by one of Mercer's stories of Waterloo. It was quite early in the day and Mercer's battery, then on the right flank beyond Hougoumont, was being annoyed, though not seriously harmed, by the fire of a light French battery:

> I ventured to commit a folly, for which I should have paid dearly had our Duke chanced to be in our part of the field. I ventured to disobey orders, and open a slow deliberate fire at the battery, thinking with my 9-pounders soon to silence his 4-pounders. My astonishment was great, however, when our very first gun was responded to by at least half-a-dozen gentlemen of very superior calibre, whose presence I had not even suspected, and whose superiority we immediately recognised by their rushing noise and long reach, for they flew far beyond us. I instantly saw my folly, and ceased firing, and they did the same – the 4-pounders alone continuing the cannonade as before. But this was not all. The first man of my troop touched was by one of these confounded long shot. I shall never forget the scream the poor lad gave when struck. It was one of the last they fired, and shattered his left arm to pieces as he stood between the waggons. That scream went to my very soul, for I accused myself as having caused his misfortune.[19]

This incident shows how effective artillery fire could be in suppressing the fire of enemy guns even when it did not inflict many casualties, and we may suspect that Dyneley and Swabey's guns might have fired more than the 140 rounds they actually used on 17 November 1812 if their gunners had not spent so much time sheltering behind trees from the French fire.

This does not mean that counter-battery fire did not sometimes inflict heavy casualties, for although a battery was a diffuse open target there was always a chance that a shot or shell might hit an ammunition cart and the resulting explosion could inflict many losses. Even without such a disaster, enemy fire could be heavy, and Swabey records that in one phase of the Battle of Vitoria he was hit in the knee and the battery lost 'one man killed and thirteen wounded, twenty-six horses killed and wounded, and a shot cut in two the axle-tree of the howitzer limber, killed four of its draught horses and left it a wreck'.[20]

This raises the vexed question of the overall effectiveness of artillery fire in battle. Unfortunately there seems to be little reliable evidence on which to base firm conclusions. According to Clausewitz:

> The fire of artillery produces greater effect than that of infantry. A battery of eight six-pounders does not occupy a third of the front of a battalion of infantry, is worked by an eighth of the number of men comprising a battalion, and does

certainly twice, if not three times, as much execution with its fire. . . . A great
battery of twenty or thirty guns is in most cases decisive at the point where it is
placed.[21]

Other authorities estimate that 'each well sited gun could be expected to have
inflicted between 60 and 120 casualties during each hour in which it was actively
engaged', and 'on average,well-sited and well-handled artillery could expect to
inflict between one and $1\frac{1}{2}$ casualties per shot'.[22]

But not even the bloodiest battles produced enough casualties to support
these estimates. In the two days of fighting at Wagram the 617 guns in Napoleon's army fired a total of 96,000 rounds: considerably more than double the
highest estimate of Austrian casualties. Indeed if each gun had fired for a single
hour and inflicted sixty casualties, 37,020 Austrians would have been killed and
wounded – which comes very close to the total Austrian casualties from all
causes during the battle. Figures for other battles, where they exist, confirm the
point. At Borodino 587 French guns fired 91,000 rounds, while the Russians
probably sustained around 44,000 casualties. Wellington's artillery was relatively weak and never dominated his battles, but at Vitoria his ninety guns fired
6,800 rounds and total French casualties, from all causes, were between 6,000
and 8,000; while at Waterloo the seventy-eight British guns alone (not counting
the Hanoverian, Dutch-Belgian, and other allied batteries) fired 10,400 rounds.
No wonder that when the French gunner Major Boulart walked over the
field of Wagram on the day after the battle 'he did not find that the damage done
was proportionate to the ammunition expended . . . yet never had such a
mass of artillery been assembled, producing such a brisk, continuous and
frightening noise'.[23]

The most probable explanation of this discrepancy is that much artillery fire
was at very long range, or directed at troops who were under cover. Most
modern authorities agree that the maximum effective range in battle conditions
of even the heaviest field pieces (twelve-pounders) was not much more than
1,000 yards, and the Russian artillery commander Major-General Kutaisov was
even more pessimistic, declaring that at 1,000 paces it was worth chancing a shot
only to check the range or to interfere with enemy movements and that it was
best to wait until the enemy were within 600 paces before opening sustained
fire. But at the Battle of Vimeiro Colonel Landmann – an engineer officer and
so, presumably, capable of judging ranges reasonably accurately – observed
British guns opening fire on French cavalry at 2,000 yards. At Salamanca,
before the main battle began, there were prolonged exchanges of artillery fire,
not only between the batteries on the two Arapiles, but also further west where
the two lines were separated by nearly a mile (1,760 yards). William Müller, in
his theoretical calculations of the number of casualties inflicted by artillery,
assumed that the guns would commence firing at 1,700 yards, while Captain
Webber, serving in a battery of British nine-pounder foot artillery, recorded in
his journal for 14 November 1812 that his guns had fired successfully on French

cavalry at 1,500 yards forcing them to retreat, although the range had proved too long for the six-pounders of the horse artillery.[24]

Fire at these ranges cannot normally have been very effective at inflicting casualties, for even visibility was strained. (According to the *Artillerist's Manual*, 'Good eyesight recognizes masses of troops at 1,700 yards: beyond this distance the glitter of arms may be observed. At 1,300 yards infantry may be distinguished from cavalry, and the movement of troops may be seen; the horses of cavalry are not, however, quite distinct but that the men are on horseback is clear. A single individual detached from the rest of the corps may be seen at 1,000 yards. . . .')[25] Even under the perfect conditions of a peacetime test-firing at a large canvas screen, only 26 per cent of rounds fired by a twelve-pounder hit the target at 950 yards, falling to 15 per cent at 1,300 yards.[26] Ordinary gunners firing in the flurry and confusion of action would presumably do far less well; while their target, instead of being a passive uniform screen, might be moving or partly under cover. Plainly the test figures need to be heavily discounted to obtain a credible figure for battlefield conditions, but there is no evidence to judge how great that discount should be.

As ranges reduced, guns normally became more accurate, although the pressure on the gunners would have increased as the enemy approached. Unfortunately the test results here are virtually useless, for they quickly produce perfect results of 100 per cent of shots hitting the target (at 600 yards for a twelve-pounder and 520 yards for a six-pounder) which have almost nothing to do with artillery in real action.

When the target came within close range round-shot would be replaced by canister. Test results show canister being effective at quite absurd ranges: 600, 700 or even 800 yards. If it had been, why was it not used more often? It amounted to only 15 to 30 per cent of the ammunition carried by artillery, and as the weapon of last resort would be the type of ammunition gunners made most sure they retained in reserve supply in case they were suddenly threatened. At Salamanca Dyneley waited until the French were within 300 yards before opening fire on them with canister; but his guns were light six-pounders, and heavier pieces would have had a longer effective range. It seems probable that canister was generally used at under 450 or 500 yards at most, but again there is too little evidence for certaintly.[27]

Test results of its effectiveness are equally implausible, giving figures of twenty to twenty-five hits on a screen at 600 yards, rising to forty or more hits at 400 yards. Major-General B. P. Hughes, the modern authority, suggests that we reduce these figures to allow for the practical problems of operating in action and 'for the many eccentricities which must have occurred', and concludes that a battery of six six-pounders firing a single salvo of case shot at 200 yards could be expected to have inflicted 150 casualties.[28] But even this seems much too high, for if just ten British batteries had each fired just ten rounds this well at Waterloo, they would have inflicted 15,000 French casualties – more than half the total French losses in the whole day, including those inflicted by the

Prussians. But Wellington had 157 guns at Waterloo not sixty, many were nine-pounders not six-pounders, and they fired, not 600 rounds, but over 10,000! Similarly, if the 368 rounds of canister fired by Senarmont at Friedland had been this effective, they alone would have caused 9,200 Russian casualties, not to mention the more than 2,000 cannon-balls his batteries fired, or the casualties inflicted by the rest of the French army.

Gunners were always urged: 'Never abandon your guns till the last extremity. The last discharges are the most destructive; they may perhaps be your salvation, and crown you with glory.'[29] But gunners were no more universal heroes than infantry or cavalry, and it was no part of their job to engage in hand-to-hand fighting except in extraordinary circumstances such as when defending a redoubt. They lacked the cohesion of the close-packed ranks of infantry or cavalry, and their officers and NCOs were stationed further apart, and so were less able to check signs of panic among the men. It has always been regarded as a point of honour among artillerymen not to let their guns fall into the hands of the enemy, and this naturally inclined them to withdraw when the enemy approached unless they were very well supported by friendly troops. A complicating factor was the generally poor reputation of artillery drivers who in many services (including the French and British foot, though not horse, artillery) belonged to separate units from the batteries to which they were attached. In late 1813 Colonel Dickson wrote that 'the discipline and arrangements of this corps is so bad that I despair of ever seeing matters properly put to rights. . . . Many of the Officers are negligent, and indifferent to their duty.' While Sir Robert Wilson said of the Russian drivers that they were 'stout men'; however, 'like all other drivers, they require superintendence in times of danger, to prevent their escape with the horses'.[30]

Major-General Kutaisov, commander of much of the Russian artillery at Borodino, issued orders before the battle which, by their very insistence, suggest what might commonly happen in action. He told his subordinates to

> remind the companies from me that they are not to make off before the enemy are actually sitting on the guns. Tell the commanders and all the officers that they must stand their ground until the enemy are within the closest possible canister range, which is the only way to ensure that we do not cede a yard of our position. The artillery must be prepared to sacrifice itself. Let the anger of your guns roar out! Fire your last charge of canister at point-blank range! A battery which is captured after this will have inflicted casualties on the enemy which will more than compensate for the loss of the guns.[31]

While Wellington complained that at Waterloo

> The French cavalry charged, and were formed on the same ground with our artillery, in general within a few yards of our guns. In some instances they were actually in possession of our guns. We could not expect the artillery-men to

remain at their guns in such a case. But I had a right to expect that the officers and men of the artillery would do as I did, and as all the staff did, that is to take shelter in the squares of the infantry till the French cavalry should be driven off the ground, either by our cavalry or infantry. But they did no such thing; they ran off the field entirely, taking with them limbers, ammunition, and everything; and when, in a few minutes, we had driven off the French cavalry, and had regained our ground and our guns, and could have made good use of our artillery, we had no artillerymen to fire them; and, in point of fact, I should have had no artillery during the whole of the latter part of the action, if I had not kept a reserve in the commencement.[32]

This letter, written with all the intemperance which characterizes Wellington's private correspondence, is certainly exaggerated, but it is hardly credible to dismiss it entirely, and it is notable that most of the best recorded achievements of the allied artillery at Waterloo were performed by batteries of horse artillery (such as Mercer's) which were held in reserve at the commencement of the action, and whose drivers were an integral part of the unit.

The idea that artillery was generally, though not invariably, disinclined to stand firm if the enemy came within close range is supported by the low casualties usually suffered by the gunners. There are difficulties with the figures for both the strength and losses of the British artillery at Waterloo; however, the thirteen batteries individually listed in Duncan's *History* lost 253 casualties from a strength of 1,869 officers and men, or 13.5 per cent, compared to 30 per cent for the British contingent as a whole.[33] We know that there were about 287 French artillery officers present at Waterloo, and of these only twenty-nine are recorded as killed or wounded in Martinien's lists – or marginally more than one in ten – compared to losses of four in ten for the army as a whole.[34] At Talavera the British and King's German Legion artillery sustained 6.7 per cent casualties, compared to 22 per cent for the whole army; at Busaco it was 0.9 per cent compared to 2.4 per cent; at Fuentes de Oñoro it was 2.8 per cent compared to 4.8 per cent; at Albuera the Anglo-German contingent as a whole had almost 40 per cent casualties, but the artillery had less than 12 per cent; while at Salamanca the entire Anglo-Portuguese artillery (which was admittedly very weak) suffered only fifteen casualties (four men killed and eleven wounded) out of total losses of 4,756 men (the ratios were 1.2 per cent for the artillery compared to 9.8 per cent for the army). Put another way, the artillery at Salamanca made up 2.7 per cent of the army, but suffered only 0.32 per cent of its losses. Detailed figures for other armies are less readily available, but at Austerlitz only one officer of the French artillery was killed and six were wounded – fewer than in many individual battalions of infantry.[35]

These figures, of course, prove nothing, other than that it was normally much safer to be in the artillery than in the infantry or the cavalry. It might even be argued that they show that gunners largely obeyed orders and concentrated their fire on enemy infantry and cavalry, rather than on counter-battery fire; and that artillery officers generally knew their business and placed their guns in good positions where they were able to keep the enemy at a distance. There is the legitimate objection that most of these figures refer to victorious armies, and that gunners were most likely to perish defending their guns to the last in a defeat. (The explanation is that there are few reliable figures for the casualties suffered by defeated armies.) And there is the point that to fight effectively infantry and cavalry had to come to close quarters, while artillery by its nature was perhaps not most effective, but at least at its greatest advantage, when the enemy was beyond musket range. But despite all this, and despite Mercer at Waterloo, it does seem reasonable to conclude that artillery in general was inclined to withdraw rather than let the enemy come to close quarters. And from this it follows that relatively few rounds would normally have been fired at ranges much less than, say, 300 yards, and that this is the principal reason why estimates based on the theoretical performance of artillery produce excessive totals of casualties inflicted.

If this seems a negative conclusion it is worth pausing to consider one last set of figures before quitting the statistical side of the subject. Unfortunately there seem to be no figures breaking down the casualties suffered in any Napoleonic action by cause, that is, whether the death or wound was caused by round-shot, canister, shell, musketry or cavalry, but two estimates from outside the period, while imperfect, are at least suggestive. The first is for admissions to the Invalides in Paris in 1762 where 68.8 per cent had been wounded by small arms, 13.4 per cent by artillery, 14.7 per cent by swords and 2.4 per cent by bayonets.[36] These were, by definition, survivable wounds, and there is good reason to believe that this means that artillery – whose effects were usually serious, and often mortal – is under-represented; and that sword and bayonet wounds, which were less often mortal, are over-represented. But even if, to correct this, we allow that half of all men killed in action (who seldom amounted to more than one-fifth of all casualties) fell to artillery fire, this still means that only just over 20 per cent of all casualties were the result of artillery.[37]

The second breakdown of casualties comes from the American Civil War, a century later than the Invalides figures. These show that 94 per cent of wounds were attributable to bullets and only 5.5 per cent to artillery.[38] Again we must allow for the greater lethality of artillery fire, but after making every allowance we are left with an upper limit of 12 to 15 per cent of casualties being inflicted by artillery.

It can however be argued that the figures would be higher for the Napoleonic period. Infantry firefights were less common and intense than during the Seven Years War; while compared to the American Civil War troops manoeuvred in close formations taking little cover, which made them very vulnerable to artillery fire. Although these arguments smack of special pleading, we might give them sufficient credence to consider a figure of between 20 and 25 per cent as being the maximum normal proportion of casualties caused by the fire of artillery. But immediately we must enter cautious caveats: neither the figures for 1762 nor for the American Civil War are completely reliable, nor can our adjustments to them be rigorously justified. More important still, the proportion of casualties caused by artillery in the Napoleonic period would have varied enormously between battles. It would have been highest at battles such as Borodino, Wagram and Waterloo, where it may have exceeded 25 per cent, and very much lower at Salamanca, where it may have been less than 10 per cent; though we really do not know. It would also, other things being equal, have been higher in the attacking rather than the defending army, so that Marmont's army at Salamanca would be at the bottom end of the scale. No generalized estimate of the role of artillery in inflicting casualties can sufficiently allow for this variation, nor can any calculation of the number of casualties produced on average by each gun or each round. The most we can say is that where we have evidence of the ammunition consumed and the losses suffered by the opposing army, it took, on average, a number of rounds of artillery fire to inflict one enemy casualty; though of course, individual batteries firing at close quarters would have been much more effective.

But as well as inflicting casualties, artillery had another role. It frightened and disturbed soldiers, wearing down their courage, sapping their morale and disrupting the cohesion of their units. George Hennell writes of the Battle of Vitoria, 'Several of our officers remarked, & I think it just, that cannon make more noise and alarm than they do mischief. Many shots were fired at us but we suffered little from them. A young soldier is much more alarmed at a nine pounder shot passing within 4 y[ar]ds of his head than he is of a bullet at a distance of as many inches, although one would settle him as effectively as the other.' Soldiers of all nations agreed that 'The standing to be cannonaded, and having nothing else to do, is about the most unpleasant thing that can happen to soldiers in an engagement' (Ensign Leeke on Waterloo), or 'There is no possible suffering greater than to expect to be killed without being allowed to defend one's self [*sic*]' (Captain Coignet on Eylau).[39] In such a position there was nothing to occupy men's minds, nothing to do and no way of striking back at the enemy, while around them their comrades who had been hit died in agony or were assisted to the rear.

> There is no part of an action more disagreeable than looking on. When engaged, the mind is employed and the attention is taken up with what is going forward; to be exposed to fire without being able to return it, is like receiving a personal insult, and not having the power to resent it. Such was our position during the first part of the day, and until the action became more general, we were all the time exposed to a Fire of the most galling description. Everybody knows that for one shot which takes effect, several go over the object fired at.
>
> At the commencement of the action we were mostly exposed to the fire of artillery, consisting chiefly of shots which were aimed at Troops in front of us, but from their being directed too high, many passed over us, or fell amongst us. . . .

Captain Wildman belonging to the Regiment was serving on the Staff of Ld. Uxbridge; seeing the danger of our position, he rode up to Colonel Kerrison and said he thought we would be less exposed to the fire by moving a little to the right. This advice was acted upon by the Colonel. I have always entertained a strong feeling, that where I was placed was the proper place, there I was willing to remain and take my chance on the result, and so it proved in this Instance. . . .

Hardly had we taken up the new ground, when a shot came, went thro' the Breast of the man beside me, passed thro' the knee of a Sergeant close behind, and broke the leg of a horse in his rear, all of which took place in less time than it takes to write it. The Sergeant was lifted off his horse, and there being no assistance at hand and no means of taking him to the rear, he bled to death. The death of the soldier was instantaneous, the poor horse's sufferings were soon put to an end by shooting him thro' the head. I could not help wishing that Wildman had left us where we were.[40]

The sight of the wounded could be unnerving though officers did their best to maintain morale. At Coruña a cannon-ball

had torn off the leg of a 42nd man, who screamed horribly, and rolled about so as to excite agitation and alarm with others. The general [Sir John Moore] said, This is nothing my lads, keep your ranks, take that man away: my good fellow don't make such a noise, we must bear these things better. He spoke sharply, but it had a good effect; for this man's cries had made an opening in the ranks, and the men shrunk from the spot, although they had not done so when others had been hit who did not cry out.[41]

Within a few hours Moore himself received his mortal wound and lived up to his own precepts, ignoring the pain while directing his attention first to the success of the army as a whole, and then to the safety and prospects of his staff.

Officers often urged their men not to duck when cannon-balls whizzed past. Colonel Lepic of the Grenadiers à Cheval at Eylau is recorded to have used language less polite but more plausible than that which usually appears in memoirs, when he shouted to his men 'Heads up! Those are bullets, not turds!'[42] But such injunctions could backfire, as is shown by a story told by Colonel Landmann relating to the Battle of Vimeiro:

I was walking my horse along the right of that regiment [the 9th Foot], when a shot having tickled the feather of one of the men, about the centre of a division, he stooped, or, as is usually called, bobbed. The officer on the right, who was standing a pace or two in advance, and whose vigilant eye was directed along the front of his division, was greatly offended at this involuntary movement, and called out with a stern voice, and great severity of aspect, 'Who is that I see bobbing there? What are you bobbing about, sir? Let me see you bob again, sir, and I'll—' This severe rebuke was exceedingly proper, and would have had its desired effect, had not a cannon shot, or howitzer shell, I know not which, at this most critical moment, just as he had commenced his threat with 'I'll—' whizzed over the officer's head. The noise made by such a missile, when passing within a yard or so of a person's head, is, to say the least of it, exceedingly disagreeable, and the stoutest nerves would not always save the individual from this highly reprehensible bobbing; so down went my officer a yard at least, but in an instant he had recovered his original erect position, having neither looked to the right nor to the left, his face the colour of his coat, his heart beating, ready to burst with rage at his own conduct, and wishing most sincerely that the shot or shell had taken off his head, and so have spared him the anguish he felt at being the first to deserve the mysterious punishment which he had, but three seconds before, half pronounced against the next bobber. By the rapidity with which he had recovered his position, he may at the instant have entertained a hope, his bob had not been noticed; if so, how keenly must he have felt his disappointment, for the whole of the front rank of the division in his rear had seen it, and also many men in his own company, which was instantly manifested by each of them muttering, 'Who is that I see bobbing there? What are you bobbing about, sir?' and then adding, 'Who bobs now?'[43]

As this suggests, bobbing or ducking was all but universal, and many memoirists and letter writers refer quite naturally to it without the least hint of shame. One British officer even tells of pulling a near-sighted comrade out of the way of an approaching ball, while so vain a man as Captain François has no hesitation in writing that 'Despite my wounded leg I did as well as my *voltigeurs* in jumping out of the way of round-shot which ricocheted into our ranks.'[44]

Skirmishers naturally suffered least from artillery fire: their loose order made them a difficult target and meant that they could duck and seek cover without reproach. Cavalry presented the largest target and were hit by many balls which flew over the heads of infantry, but their greater speed when moving must sometimes have protected them, and it seems likely that gunners would grow uneasy and perhaps limber up and go to the rear when cavalry were further away than infantry. It is often said that infantry in square or column offered a far better target for the guns than infantry in line, but this seems an oversimplification. At long or even medium ranges columns and squares presented small targets which must have been quite difficult to hit, while lines, being almost continuous, actually offered a better target.[45] On the other hand it was relatively easy for men in a two- or three-deep line to duck out of the way of an approaching cannon-ball (at long range their approach could be seen quite clearly), but those in an eight- or twelve-deep column – let alone on the rear side of a square – would have had little chance of escape. Furthermore, columns and squares were so compact that every man in the unit was likely to be at least vaguely aware when anyone was hit, while the greater frontage of a battalion in line meant that soldiers were much less conscious of what was happening to men not in their own or adjacent companies.

Artillery played many roles in battle: providing close support for beleaguered infantry, bombarding an enemy-held village, being rushed from reserve to fill a gap in the line, silencing troublesome enemy guns or giving cavalry an element of firepower. But the broadest, most consistent role was to begin the process of eroding the enemy's strength both by inflicting casualties and by wearing away the morale and cohesion of enemy units. 'Softening up the enemy' – curiously gentle words for a brutal, bloody reality.

Chapter Four
Light Infantry

No section of the army attracted such attention and controversy in the late eighteenth and early nineteenth centuries as light infantry. Their extensive use in the American War of Independence aroused professional interest in Britain and on the Continent. This was heightened by the success of French armies in the early years of the Revolutionary War which was often attributed to their use of skirmishers, who were supposed to have overwhelmed the slow rigid formations of the armies of the *ancien régime* which opposed them. Always a crude oversimplification, recent research has further undermined this explanation by showing both that it exaggerated the importance of French skirmishers, and that the best skirmishers were not untrained recruits fired by revolutionary doctrines and adept at using their initiative, but experienced soldiers, preferably specialist light infantry. Yet it remains true that French armies in the 1790s pioneered the use of very large numbers of skirmishers acting independently or in co-operation with close-order infantry, and that this was one ingredient in their success.[1]

The allied armies attempted to respond by developing light infantry of their own, but with only mixed success. By 1813 the Austrians had virtually given up, believing that the great bulk of their infantry lacked the training and aptitude needed for the role. As Radetzky observed in September 1813, 'fighting *en tirailleure* [skirmishing] should be done only in very restricted fashion because neither the Russians nor we have mastered the *manière de tirailler*'.[2] The Prussians, however, were much less despairing, for after the catastrophic defeat of 1806 their reform party had taken up the question with vigour. Many of their reformers were light infantry officers or had a long-standing interest in light tactics; they were convinced that French superiority in this field had contributed largely to their defeat; and the ethos of light infantry, with its emphasis on individual initiative and on inspiring soldiers with patriotism rather than controlling them with draconian discipline, was in harmony with their political views. Between 1807 and 1812 they made considerable progress both in reforming the regulations and tactics of the army, and in ensuring that up to half the infantry received some training in skirmishing. But the great expansion of the army in 1813 led to an influx of recruits who could receive only a few weeks' training before being sent into battle, and this seriously diluted the work of the reformers. Fortunately for the allies Napoleon's army in 1813 was also full of raw troops, so the two sides were well matched.[3]

There was equal interest in Britain, especially in the years around 1800 when numerous books of guidance and instruction for light infantry officers were published. The author of one of these, Captain T. H. Cooper, was not unusual in setting out his claims for the importance of light infantry with some fervour:

> the services of Light Infantry . . . are of the utmost utility, and may be ranked as next to those of Riflemen: they conceal from the enemy the most important manoeuvres of a battalion. As the fore-runners of an army, Light Infantry are vigilant night and day, and alert in the extremest degree; they are accustomed to the opposites of concealment in ambush, and exposure in open plains; have double the advantage of a battalion, from the excellent simplicity of their manoeuvres. In the open plain, they can act as a compact body; in coppices and woods, as light troops; and in the line, as regulars: they can pursue the course with order and regularity over steep hills, and rugged precipices; and through woods and thickets, relying upon the activity and gallantry of their files; they seize upon elevated positions and important posts, with a rapidity peculiar to themselves. . . .
>
> . . . When an army advances in the presence of the enemy, the Light Infantry are in front; retreating, they are in the rear; foraging, they protect; landing, they are the first to jump out of the boats; embarking, they are the last to leave the shore.[4]

Surprisingly, some British light infantry of the period – the famous Light Division of the Peninsular War – made good Cooper's extravagant claims. Firing 'the first and last shot in almost every battle, siege, and skirmish in which the army was engaged during the war' – as one veteran put it with characteristic modesty[5] – they were an elite corps who excelled not only in the particular functions of light infantry but in anything which required daring and initiative, as is shown by their prominence in the storming of Ciudad Rodrigo and Badajoz. But it is the distinctive functions of light infantry, and in particular skirmishing, which are the subject of this chapter.

In battle light infantry, fighting in open order and relying on the initiative of individual soldiers, would occupy rough terrain, woods and even villages; they would harass enemy formations, sniping at officers, distracting and unsettling the men by their fire. Ideally they acted like a cloud of midges, giving way in the face of any determined enemy advance but quickly returning if the enemy halted, and constantly biting. Their loose formation enabled the men to take cover so that if their close-order target returned their fire it would do them little harm. And this produced their other major role: to protect their own close-order formation from enemy light infantry, so that a bickering fight against opposing skirmishers was the most characteristic of all their activities.

Effective skirmishing needed a high degree of skill, training and experience for, as Napoleon declared, the duty was 'the most fatiguing and the most deadly'.[6] By far the best skirmishers were specialists who relished their distinctive function, often wearing a dark green uniform, and sometimes equipped with a rifle rather than the normal smooth-bore musket. Units such as the British 95th and 60th Regiments, the light battalions of the King's German Legion and German *Jäger* regiments, were quintessential skirmishers – although they were perfectly capable of operating in close order: indeed the 2nd battalion 95th Rifles spent the entire Battle of Waterloo in close order.[7] Not all these skirmishers came near to matching the high reputation of the 95th. For example, the Brunswick Oels Regiment in Wellington's army was notorious for indiscipline and desertion – problems which must certainly have been exacerbated by its being distributed, a company or two to a division, throughout the army. Next came units designated as 'light infantry' or 'chasseurs' or 'tirailleurs', 'caçadores' or 'grenzer', some of which, such as the British 43rd and 52nd Regiments, had received intensive training and were adept at skirmishing, although they most commonly fought in close order. Others, however, were termed light infantry 'merely by terminological accident' and were distinguished from their comrades in the line 'only by some tailor's flourish in the cut of the jacket, or by an unconventionally coloured plume'.[8] This was the case with many British light regiments, and with most if not all of the large number of French and Russian units which bore the title. Finally there were the light companies of line regiments (or, in some armies, men from the third rank), who were used extensively as skirmishers but who seldom had much, if any, specialist training or enthusiasm for the task. One admirer of the 95th gives an idea of these gradations in action:

> Our rifles were immediately sent to dislodge the French from the hills on our left, and our battalion was sent to support them. Nothing could exceed the manner in which the ninety-fifth set about the business. . . . Certainly I never saw such skirmishers as the ninety-fifth, now the rifle brigade. They could do the work much better and with infinitely less loss than any other of our best light troops. They possessed an individual boldness, a mutual understanding, and a quickness of eye, in taking advantage of the ground, which, taken altogether, I never saw equalled. They were, in fact, as much superior to the French *voltigeurs*, as the latter were to our skirmishers in general. As our regiment was often employed in supporting them, I think I am fairly qualified to speak of their merits.[9]

The 95th were armed with the Baker rifle, which was much more accurate, but slower to load, than a conventional musket. Equally important and unusual, the regiment took marksmanship seriously. Recruits were given plenty of target practice and success was rewarded with badges and other distinctions. The slow rate of fire mattered less in skirmishing, where fire was usually slow (otherwise a man would exhaust his fifty or sixty rounds in less than an hour), while the greater accuracy was invaluable, for much skirmishing was conducted at long ranges or against other skirmishers who presented a difficult target. The rifle was shorter than a musket, which made it easier to load when lying down; and rather than the made-up cartridges used by the rest of the army the riflemen carried loose powder and balls – although they also had a few cartridges for use in an emergency. All these characteristics made it an excellent weapon for specialist skirmishers, but not for the bulk of the infantry, for whom speed of fire was regarded as more important than accuracy; who had to be firmly discouraged from firing at long ranges; and who lacked the training of riflemen.[10]

Nonetheless the 95th owed their success less to their rifle than to their *esprit de corps*, and to the training which taught each private soldier that in skirmishing 'he must act for himself, and on his own judgment, in taking advantage of the ground on which it may be his lot to engage the enemy; and that, in the desultory nature of our warfare, it is impossible that an officer or sergeant can always be at his elbow to set him right'.[11] The Prussian General Yorck agreed with this, and stressed the need for accurate shooting and teamwork:

> The rifle was not made for drill, and drilling is not the *Jäger*'s purpose. . . . It is an irrevocable basic rule that the *Jäger* never hurries his fire, but always shoots with effect. It is an equally irrevocable rule that two *Jäger* always defend one another, that is, always act in groups of two – front and rear man. These two *Jäger* must at all times consider themselves as one body; one defends the other, so that when one man has fired and therefore is defenseless, the other has loaded and is capable of defensive action. This rule must be an unbreakable law to every *Jäger*, since his honor and life depend on it.[12]

Other armies also taught their light infantry to operate in pairs, but experience forced Yorck to admit that 'in reality situations often occur in which this cannot be followed slavishly'. The essential point was that the skirmisher 'should hit, and not [just] make noise'.[13]

While light infantry were encouraged to use their initiative, they remained under the control of their officers who conveyed orders such as 'advance', 'halt', 'cease firing', or 'retire', either by shouting or using whistles, horns or bugles. In the Prussian army eight different horn signals proved too few, and after a period of near chaos when the number multiplied beyond reason, it was fixed at twenty different calls for twenty-two distinct commands – which in the noise and confusion of battle must have proved a taxing repertoire for musician and audience alike.[14] As with all troops, orders were sometimes ignored or wilfully disobeyed, and men dispersed in open order, particularly when taking cover, could not be supervised as closely as those in the line. For poor troops, skirmishing provided a perfect opportunity to go to ground or try to slip to the rear, perhaps with the pretence of having received a wound. The British government responded to this danger by giving its light regiments an additional lieutenant, sergeant and corporal per company.[15]

While the battalion was the basic tactical unit for close-order operations, in skirmishing a company and its commander often had to act independently, as the Prussian regulations of 1812 made clear:

> The battalion commander arranges the disposition of the companies and guides their movements in general. The company commanders use the specific advantages that the terrain affords their purpose, they decide which squads or sections are to skirmish, they reinforce or reduce the skirmish line according to the course of the action, choose an advantageous position for the closed sections from which these can easily support the skirmish line.[16]

As this implies, only some of the light infantry would normally be sent forward to skirmish at any one time, with the rest held back in close formation to act as supports and a reserve. In the Prussian system the skirmishing line of a brigade (equivalent to any other army's division) would at first be made up of a few companies of the two battalions of fusiliers: 100 paces or so to their rear would be two sections in close order acting as supports, while further back lay the main body of the fusilier battalions, and behind them the main strength of the brigade. The skirmishing line would be reinforced from the fusilier battalions, or even from the rest of the brigade, just as the skirmishing sections could be withdrawn to rest and receive fresh supplies of ammunition. Although up to half the Prussian infantry had – at least in theory – been trained to skirmish, this does not mean that it fought largely in open order.[17]

A British officer, writing in *Colburn's United Service Magazine* in 1829, explains in more detail the role and importance of these supporting troops, while advocating some changes in the way a battalion deployed to skirmish:

> The battalion now consists of ten companies: – when required to engage in a skirmish, the companies 1 and 2, 7 and 8 advance, extending obliquely to their right and left, until they have obtained the necessary distance in an extended line equal to the front of the regiment. The grenadiers and light infantry [companies] follow as supports in columns of sections in the rear of the advanced line, and in the positions marked down. The reserve consists of the four remaining companies, formed in column at quarter distance, the colours and a serjeant coverer *from each detached* company in the centre. If the *supports* are obliged to take a share in the skirmish, numbers 3 and 6 are moved on to occupy the vacated positions; but the two centre companies are not under any circumstances to act on the offensive; although the other eight companies may be cut to pieces, *they* may bear off their colours and secure an honourable retreat in a grand division square.

The advantages of my proposed arrangement are, that each section column can follow the advance of the skirmishers with facility, and can, if necessary, defend itself in a small square by closing to the head section and facing outwards; it likewise forms a nucleus for a rallying square, should the skirmishers be assailed by cavalry: but should the skirmishers and *supports* be obliged to retire in confusion on the reserve, the serjeant coverers who have remained with the latter, immediately step out and take up quarter distance in column for their companies, and every man running to his respective serjeant, the companies are instantly formed, and the column stands in readiness to form square, to deploy, or to act in any manner that may be requisite.[18]

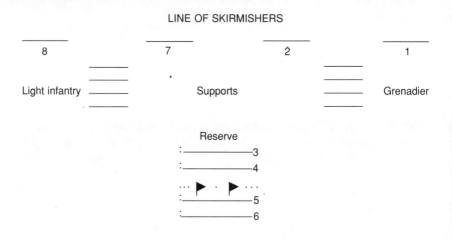

This proposal went further than many other plans by having as many as four in ten men in the skirmish line. By comparison the Prussian reformer Tiedeman was cautious in suggesting that no more than one-sixth of the unit be allowed to skirmish, with a further sixth in close support. He also stipulated that there should be between 100 and 200 paces between the skirmishers and their supports, and that the main body be between 300 and 400 paces behind the skirmishers.[19]

These supports played a vital role in sustaining the skirmishing line. Prolonged skirmishing typically saw a succession of rushes forwards and back as the troops competed for minor points in the terrain which gave them some advantage, or when one side or the other took the initiative. Without supporting troops to rally behind, the retreat of the dispersed and unsettled men might easily get out of control. It also allowed the companies in the skirmish line to be replaced by fresh troops, for after an hour or two, even if the men had not lost heavily, they would be physically and mentally tired, and their ammunition would be depleted.

Skirmishers were particularly vulnerable to cavalry. Scattered footsoldiers, they could offer no resistance to even the most disorderly charge unless rough terrain gave them protection. If there was time they would fall back on their supports, who in turn would fall back on the reserve, for safety lay in numbers, and while a single company of good soldiers might defy a cavalry charge if the men kept their nerve and formed square, it was asking a lot of the soldiers, and accidents were likely to happen. If caught in the open beyond their supports the best the men could do was band together in little knots (sometimes called 'hiving') thrusting their bayonets outwards in all directions and hoping that the horsemen would sweep past. Even so they could lose heavily: at Fuentes de Oñoro the light companies of the British First Division were taken by surprise by French cavalry, caught 'in the flank, rolled up, and very badly mauled' losing sixty or eighty casualties and twenty prisoners in a few minutes, the survivors being those who had clubbed together and held the French at bay until the British cavalry advanced to their relief.[20]

This raises the interesting, but unanswerable, question of whether skirmishers generally went into action with fixed bayonets. Few sources mention the point, and Cooper's *Guide*, which does, is ambiguous: 'The arms in general are to be carried sloped, with bayonets fixed. Flanking and advanced parties may carry them trailed without bayonets, both for ease and for purpose of taking cooler and more deliberate aim. . . .'[21] It seems probable that skirmishers would normally only fix bayonets when close to the enemy or when operating in open country where enemy cavalry might suddenly threaten them, but it was the type of question where practice might evolve quite differently from the the rules laid down in regulations.

In most cases the skirmishers, their supports and reserves either came from the same unit, or – as was generally the case in Wellington's army – were a composite body made up of the light companies of each battalion in a division together with a company or two of specialist light infantry (from the 5th/60th, Brunswick Oels, or similar regiment), and often also a battalion of caçadores. This heterogeneous mixture would gradually gain confidence and *esprit de corps* as the men gained experience in serving together in battles and petty combats, but it could not hope to equal the self-confidence of the Light Division. As one officer of the 95th wrote in his memoirs,

> I beg to be understood as identifying our old and gallant associates, the forty-third and fifty-second, as a part of ourselves, for they bore their share in everything, and I love them as I hope to do my better half (when I come to be divided); wherever *we* were, *they* were; and although the nature of our arm generally gave us more employment in the way of skirmishing, yet, whenever it came to a pinch, independent of a suitable mixture of them among us, we had only to look behind to see a line, in which we might place a degree of confidence, almost equal to our hopes in heaven; nor were we ever disappointed. There never was a corps of riflemen in the hands of such supporters![22]

In battle, skirmishing often took one of two forms: the bickering between opposing light infantry in the no man's land between the two armies when neither side was intent on a determined advance; and more serious fighting when either the light infantry themselves, or the troops they were covering, were intent on coming to close quarters. A good example of the first type of fighting occurred on the morning of the Battle of Salamanca when, according to Oman, Marmont ordered the voltigeurs of Foy's division

> to push back the English pickets on the height of Nuestra Señora de la Peña. These belonged to the 7th Division, which was occupying the wood behind. Not wishing his position to be too closely examined, Wellington sent out two whole battalions, the 68th and the 2nd Caçadores, who formed a very powerful screen of light troops, and pushed back the French from the hill and the ruined chapel on top of it. Marmont then strengthened his firing line, and brought up a battery, which checked the further advance of the allied skirmishers. The two screens continued to exchange shots for several hours, half a mile in front of Wellington's position. The *tiraillade* had many episodes, in one of which General Victor Alten, leading a squadron of his hussars to protect the flank of the British skirmishers, received a ball in the knee, which put him out of action. . . . After much bickering, and when noon had long passed, the 68th and Caçadores were relieved by some companies of the 95th from the Light Division, as Wellington wished to employ the 7th Division elsewhere.[23]

What were the losses suffered during these hours of skirmishing? The Seventh Division was scarcely engaged later in the day, though it probably lost a few men to stray shots and distant artillery fire. The total loss for the 68th that day was one officer and three men killed, two officers and fourteen men wounded: twenty casualties from an initial strength of 338 officers and men. Oman does not differentiate the losses of the 2nd Caçadores from the rest of the Portuguese brigade, but as the whole brigade lost only five men killed, one officer and ten men wounded, and one man missing, seventeen casualties in all, it hardly matters.[24]

These trifling losses suggest that this skirmish was not pressed with any urgency. The two allied battalions probably amounted to about 700 men (Oman does not give the strength of the caçadores), but of these, presumably only a couple of hundred would have been in the actual firing line at any one time, the rest acting as supports and reserves. Even so, the fact that no more than thirty-seven casualties were suffered (and probably a similar number inflicted) in several hours of fighting, needs explanation. Both sides were deployed in open order, taking advantage of every scrap of cover, and so presenting a poor target for their opponents. Contemporary muskets were notoriously inaccurate even against massed targets at more than 100 or 150 yards. Unfortunately there is no evidence for the ranges in this particular fight, but George Hennell's satisfaction in describing another skirmish suggests that ranges were often longer than we might expect: 'I then had as fine a fire upon them as I possibly could have. We were upon a hill . . . [and] they were crowding into a narrow pass to get into a wood. . . . I had this fire upon the men in the gateway for about $\frac{3}{4}$ of an hour at 300 yards.'[25]

Not that all skirmishing was this bloodless. Later in the affair which Hennell was describing, his company and another advanced too far and came under very heavy fire from the main French position only '90 or 100 yards' distant. Although they took cover under a slight bank, they lost three officers, two sergeants and seventy-six men killed, wounded and missing from what Hennell described as 'the hottest fire I ever saw, Badajoz not excepted'. But the losses in this case, as in many others, were due to a mistake, the decision to advance too far, which Hennell blames on hearing the bugles sound '*Advance*' (although this may be an attempt to shift the blame for his own or others' impetuosity). Without this mistake Hennell believed that the whole day's skirmishing would have cost his regiment only ten men wounded.[26]

At Vitoria, O'Callaghan's brigade of Hill's Division captured the village of Subijana with little opposition and was then instructed to occupy the French troops facing it, without pressing home an attack. According to Edward Macarthur of the 39th:

The companies of the brigade were ordered independently to the front, to skirmish with the Enemy. The ground on which they stood was open, and exposed to the Artillery of the Enemy who had lined the opposite coverts with a swarm of light troops. In the short space of ten minutes my company lost in killed and wounded two Officers, and twenty-nine men. Every Company maintained its ground till its ammunition was exhausted, when it was succeeded by another.[27]

Moyle Sherer of the 34th, which was in the same brigade, reports a similar experience and offers an alternative explanation for the heavy losses:

Not a soul . . . was in the village, but a wood a few hundred yards to its left, and the ravines above it, were filled with French light infantry. I, with my company, was soon engaged in smart skirmishing among the ravines, and lost about eleven men, killed and wounded, out of thirty-eight. The English do not skirmish so well as the Germans or the French; and it is really hard work to make them preserve their proper extended order, cover themselves, and not throw away their fire; and in the performance of this duty, an officer is, I think, far more exposed than in line fighting.[28]

O'Callaghan's three battalions lost forty-eight men killed and no fewer than 443 officers and men wounded in the battle, most of them, apparently, in this episode.[29] Lack of skirmishing skills may have contributed to these casualties, but the brigade was performing an important role in the battle and was bound to suffer considerably.

In general, however, heavy losses were more likely to occur when one side or the other was screening the advance of troops in close order, intent on making a serious attack, for then the advancing skirmishers could not take their time and advance cautiously, but had to drive off their opponents without delaying the advance of the main body and so prolonging its exposure to the enemy's artillery fire and allowing its momentum to slacken. The defending skirmishers equally needed good judgement: they had to make sure that the enemy's attack was serious and not a feint, and to make their opponents pay for their hasty advance; while at the same time avoiding the risk of being cut off or forced to fall back so quickly that their retreat became disorderly. Inevitably mistakes were made: Captain Douglas of the British 79th Regiment describes the consequences of one such incident at Busaco:

> a message came up to say that our Picquet was nearly cut off, and I was sent with my Company to endeavour to extricate them. When I got to the brow I saw our men fighting close to the French and a Party running down the Valley with the intention of turning their right and so cutting them off. This party I immediately attacked, & soon forced to retire. The Picquet then drew off & I began to retreat but was attacked by very superior numbers which issued out of the wood and obliged me to keep up a sort of running fight of it, but I had the greatest difficulty in getting my men to come away, many of them begging hard to be allowed to charge them. When we got nearly to the top of the hill I was looking at a Battalion of Portuguese charging a French column and was in the act of cheering them, when I received a shot in the Left Shoulder. . . . My Company was immediately relieved and it was found that there were three killed and 25 wounded, making including myself a total of 29 out of 64.[30]

But in general Busaco provided a fine opportunity for the British and Portuguese skirmishers, for the ground was so steep and rough that there was no danger from the French cavalry. The Light Division was deployed with the 43rd and 52nd Regiments and the 1st Caçadores (about 2,300 men in all) near the summit of the ridge, and a very strong skirmishing line consisting of the 1st/95th, the 3rd Caçadores and a company of the King's German Legion light infantry – altogether nearly 1,500 men – on the lower slopes. Unfortunately the normally very full sources for the Light Division give few details of the activities of the skirmishers as the French advanced, although according to one account, 'Whenever the Caçadores got a successful shot, they laughed uproariously as if skirmishing were a source of great amusement to them.'[31] It seems that the light troops defended first the woods below the village of Sula, then the village itself, and finally a third position higher up the ridge. At some point Craufurd sent the 1st Caçadores down to join them, so that half the men in the Light Division were opposing the French advance, although the 1,800 officers and men of the 43rd and 52nd remained in reserve, out of sight and in perfect order. Were all the light infantry on the forward slope deployed in open order and skirmishing, or were some held back in close order under patches of cover to act as supports and reserves? We do not know, but it seems likely that they were deployed in a succession of positions up the hillside, so that as one line was forced to give way under French pressure, it could fall back and rally on the next. As cavalry presented no threat these supports may well have already been deployed in open order, though it is equally likely that at least some companies were kept in close order in case they were required to move suddenly, either to lead a local counter-attack or to check an unexpected threat to one flank or the other. It is said that the French had to deploy whole battalions of their attacking force as skirmishers to drive the allied light infantry back, and even if the entire 26th *Ligne* had been extended it would not have matched the number of allied skirmishers. But of course it was not the role of skirmishers to attempt to halt the advance of a French division of more than 6,000 men; rather they were to delay and disrupt its progress, inflicting as many casualties as possible, and this they evidently did. For while it is impossible to discover which French losses were due to the allied skirmishers; which to the allied artillery; which to the final confrontation at the summit of the slope, when the 43rd and 52nd broke the French attack; and which were suffered in the flight down the slope, the total French loss was enough for each allied element to have performed well. In Loison's division 162 men were killed and 1,091 wounded: 1,253 casualties in all – as many as the entire allied army suffered in the whole battle. The contrast with the Light Division's losses is striking. In the 95th nine were men killed and thirty-two wounded; in the 3rd Caçadores ten men were killed, and three officers and seventy-six men were wounded; while the in 1st Caçadores two men were killed, twenty wounded and one went missing. Altogether the skirmishing battalions sustained 153 casualties, while the losses of the 43rd and 52nd were even lower–only twenty-four casualties between them. Whether the caçadores lost more men than the 95th because they occupied a more exposed position or purely because of their lack of experience is unclear. One officer of the 95th comments with surprise on the fact that none of its officers was hit, which he explains partly as a result of the fact that they were rather short of officers on the day due to losses in the action on the Coa two months before; and 'In the second place the hills occupied by the Light Division were extremely high and the approach to them near the summit full of craggy rocks. Amongst these and some fir trees our Companies lay scattered and had such excellent cover that I am puzzled to conceive how we contrived to lose forty-one men.'[32]

On few if any other occasions was such a high proportion of a defending force committed to the skirmishing line, but whatever its strength its task was much the same and was well expressed in the orders given to the commander of a composite force of light companies drawn from the Third Division at Waterloo:

To cover and protect our Batteries. To establish ourselves at all times as much in advance as might be compatible with prudence. To preserve considerable intervals between our extended files for greater security from the fire of the Enemy's Batteries. To show obstinate resistance against Infantry of the same description, but to attempt no formation or offer useless opposition to charges of Cavalry, but to retire in time upon the Squares in our rear, moving in a direct line without any reference to Regiments or Nations. When the charge was repulsed, to resume our ground.[33]

The role of light infantry in attack naturally mirrored these tasks. They were to drive back the enemy's skirmishers and seek to fire on the enemy's main body, picking off officers, unsettling the men, and if possible provoking a response which might disrupt and disorganize the enemy. If the defenders could be led into beginning firing before the main attack was launched, they would be far more vulnerable when it came, while their fire was unlikely to do the skirmishers much harm. Enemy batteries were a particular object of attention, for if the gunners could be persuaded to withdraw before the main body of attacking troops approached, its chances of success would be greatly strengthened. The advance of the British Fifth Division, commanded by Major General James Leith, at Salamanca illustrates many of these points. The division consisted of two British and one Portuguese brigades, amounting to nearly 6,700 men in thirteen battalions. Some time before the division began its advance (probably between thirty minutes and an hour), the light companies of all the British battalions, the two companies of Brunswick Oels light infantry attached to the division, and the 8th battalion of caçadores from the Portuguese brigade, were sent forward to skirmish. This force amounted to about 1,000 men, or nearly one-sixth of the division, which was probably a rather higher proportion than was normal. They advanced across the mile or more of open country which separated them from the main line of Maucune's division and soon encountered French skirmishers. There is no evidence as to how the allied skirmishers were deployed, but the front of Leith's division was about 750 yards long and they seem to have extended beyond it for some distance to the right where there was a gap in the allied line, later to be filled by the British heavy cavalry. So they had roughly one man per yard of front to cover, but presumably (again the sources are silent) a considerable portion was retained as supports and reserves – for this was open country and Marmont's cavalry, though weaker than Wellington's, could not be discounted. Leith's nephew and aide-de-camp Andrew Leith Hay writes that

the ground between the advancing force and that to be assailed was also crowded with light troops in extended order, carrying on a very incessant tiraillade. The General desired me to ride forward, make the light infantry press up the heights to clear his line of march, and, if practicable, make a rush at the enemy's cannon. . . . the light troops soon drove back those opposed; the French cannon were removed to the rear; every obstruction to the regular advance of the line had vanished.[34]

Although forced to retreat, the French artillery was not silenced: it rede-
ployed in the gaps between the French battalions which were arrayed in a line
of squares or columns, and other British memoirs refer to its destructive fire.[35]
Nonetheless by driving it back the British skirmishers had silenced it for a time
during one of the most dangerous stages of Leith's advance, while the French
gunners had no time to settle into their new position and were probably rather
flurried. There is no suggestion in the British accounts that their skirmishers
were able to do much damage to the main line of French infantry before Leith's
leading brigade launched its attack. Presumably the skirmishers allowed their
main line to sweep past them to make its attack and collected together ready to
resume skirmishing if necessary. At least, this is what they were meant to do
when the attack was made in line, as Leith's was – had it been in column, the
skirmishers could have advanced on either side of the column (or, if there was
more than one column, in the gaps between them), partially compensating for
the column's lack of firepower. But again the sources are silent, except for a
confusing claim that the light infantry of Leith's second brigade (Pringle's)
broke a French battalion, not of Maucune's, but of Thomières's division, just as
Le Marchant's cavalry made their charge. The issue is unresolved, but the claim
at least suggests that some of Leith's light infantry extended well beyond
his right flank and ultimately linked up with the advance of Pakenham's Third
Division.[36]

The broad role, if not the details, of the skirmishers screening Leith's attack
is thus fairly clear, but this account gives little impression of how the combat
looked through the eyes of participants. Given the innumerable memoirists and
diarists in the Light Division it is surprising that there are not more good
descriptions of skirmishing from these veterans: but all too often their accounts
are vague and generalized, taking for granted all that we most wish to know.
Perhaps the problem is inherent in the nature of skirmishing, for John Lynn
in his excellent study of the motivation and tactics of the *Armée du Nord*
writes, 'Unfortunately, a detailed knowledge of light infantry tactics as prac-
ticed early in the wars of the French Revolution must largely elude the present-
day scholar. This is a most embarrassing but necessary admission, since
official directives were few, and contemporary descriptions are vague and
unreliable.'[37]

However occasional anecdotes give glimpses of a reality far removed from the
orderly world of regulations and drill manuals. At Talavera, on the morning of
28 July 1809, the light companies of Hill's division were retreating before
Victor's second attack. They fell back slowly and reluctantly, often turning to
fire at the French and keeping their order 'with the regularity of a field day'.
But far from inspiring official praise, their coolness drove Hill – normally
the mildest of generals – to furious impatience. He wanted to get his front clear
and sounded the bugles to hasten the retreat, swearing (on only one of two
recorded occasions during the whole war), 'D—n their filing, let them come in
anyhow.'[38]

Opposing skirmishers often engaged in personal duels with each other, and neither their tactics nor their motives were always entirely above board: 'after a trifling skirmish', one British officer records,

> when the firing had ceased on both sides . . . we observed a Portuguese . . . amusing himself by fighting a sort of duel with the French sentry in his front. After they had exchanged three or four shots, down dropped the Portuguese to all appearance dead; and the Frenchman, without waiting to reload his musket, ran up in the hope of securing the dead man's knapsack before any one could reach the spot from our side. But the Portuguese proved too cunning a fellow for 'Johnny Crapaud'! He allowed him to come within a few yards of him, when, jumping up, he shot him dead, and then quietly resumed his duty.[39]

Captain Mercer describes the experience of being the target of skirmisher fire with his customary skill, although in his case the skirmishers were cavalry not infantry – which probably explains how he lived to tell the tale:

> a cloud of skirmishers . . . galled us terribly by a fire of carbines and pistols at scarcely forty yards from our front. We were obliged to stand with port-fires lighted, so that it was not without a little difficulty that I succeeded in restraining the people from firing, for they grew impatient under such fatal results. Seeing some exertion beyond words necessary for this purpose, I leaped my horse up the little bank, and began a promenade (by no means agreeable) up and down our front, without even drawing my sword, though these fellows were within speaking distance of me. This quieted my men; but the tall blue gentlemen, seeing me thus dare them, immediately made a target of me, and commenced a very deliberate practice, to show us what very bad shots they were. . . . One fellow certainly made me flinch, but it was a miss; so I shook my finger at him, and called him *coquin*, etc. The rogue grinned as he reloaded, and again took aim. I certainly felt rather foolish at that moment, but was ashamed, after such bravado, to let him see it, and therefore continued my promenade. As if to prolong my torment, he was a terrible time about it. To me it seemed an age. Whenever I turned, the muzzle of his infernal carbine still followed me. At length bang it went, and whiz came the ball close to the back of my neck, and at the same instant down dropped the leading driver of one of my guns (Miller), into whose forehead the cursed missile had penetrated.[40]

In this case Mercer's guns were holding their fire for the next French cavalry charge which was already being prepared. At Ligny Lieutenant Reuter's guns managed to keep enemy skirmishers at bay with their heads down, by a slow and deliberate fire of canister (see above pp. 38–9), but it is clear that skirmishers could often discompose gunners, who felt themselves sitting targets, while the open formation and use of cover of light infantry largely protected them from the battery's fire. (Whether the light infantry felt so confident of this protection is more doubtful.)

For close-order infantry assailed by skirmishers the best solution was to detach a company or more to keep the enemy at a respectable distance by skirmishing against them. But sometimes, especially where enemy cavalry were nearby, this proved impossible, or the troops so detached proved unable to drive off the enemy skirmishers. This left few choices – the infantry could stoically endure the enemy fire, which seldom inflicted very many casualties but which imposed a great psychological strain, or the whole battalion might fire or advance in the hope of driving the skirmishers back. This seldom brought any lasting benefit and was full of danger for it disrupted the broader line, and by advancing the battalion might expose its flank, while once the men began firing it could be difficult to make them stop, which left them much more vulnerable to a serious attack. The experiences of the 79th Cameron Highlanders in Kempt's brigade of Picton's division at Quatre Bras illustrate the problem.

Scarcely had the division got into position when the enemy advanced to the attack. The light companies of the first brigade, with the 8th company and marksmen of the 79th, were ordered out to skirmish and keep down the fire of the enemy's sharp-shooters, which was causing a heavy loss particularly amongst the officers. It was now a quarter to three o'clock. The light companies in front maintained their ground for an hour against the ever-increasing number of the enemy; but as his sharp-shooters had by this time picked off nearly all the artillerymen who were serving the only two British guns which had as yet come into action, and as he was becoming very threatening in front, the Duke of Wellington, who was present with his staff, directed Sir Thomas Picton to detach a regiment to the front, in order to cover the guns, and drive the enemy from his advanced position. Sir James Kempt thereupon rode up to Colonel Douglas and said that the honour of executing his grace's orders would devolve on the Cameron Highlanders.

The regiment accordingly cleared the bank in front, fired a volley as it advanced, and, charging with the bayonet, drove the French advanced troops with great precipitation and in disorder to a hedge about one hundred yards in rear, where they attempted to re-form, but were followed with such alacrity that they again gave way, pursued to another hedge about the same distance, from which they were again driven in great confusion upon their main column, which was formed on the rising ground opposite. The regiment, now joined by number 8 company, halted and formed up behind the last hedge and fired volleys at the enemy until all the ammunition was expended. Whilst in this critical position it was ordered to retire, which it accomplished without confusion, although it had to re-pass the first hedge and cross a deep ditch, and formed line about fifty yards in front of its original position. Here it was ordered to lie down as it was much exposed to the enemy's fire, and it remained lying down for about an hour, when it was again ordered to its original position in the Namur road.[41]

In this case the losses inflicted by the French skirmishers were unusually heavy, for the Camerons lost two officers and twenty-eight men killed, sixteen officers and 259 men wounded, while all the mounted officers had their horses shot under them. But it is clear that the regiment's advance had failed to drive off the skirmishers, though it may have brought at least temporary relief to the other units in the division. It was fortunate that it made its advance and subsequent retreat without interference from enemy cavalry: probably the hedges and ditch helped to protect it, although it was repeatedly threatened later in the day.[42]

But even the presence of a strong force of friendly skirmishers did not always provide protection, as Colonel Landmann found at Vimeiro:

falling in with Fane's Light Infantry, who were actively engaged in driving back the enemy's Voltigeurs, I joined my old friends, and in a very few minutes I observed a Frenchman amongst the bushes, not more than sixty to eighty yards distant, shifting about from one concealing place to another, and at length I perceived him taking up a convenient position for giving me a proof of his abilities as a marksman. At the same moment I perceived just under my horse's nose a man of the 5th battalion of the 60th Regiment, belonging to Fane's brigade, and whose German countenance I recognized. Upon this, I called to him, 'Do you not see that rascal taking his aim at me? Fire at him quickly, if you do not, he will hit me to a certainty.'

A mounted officer amidst a parcel of riflemen stands but a bad chance of escaping, for he alone is visible, and seems to be put up as a target for the enemy to shoot at, whilst the privates or riflemen are all creeping about with so much industry in trying to conceal themselves, particularly the foreigners; and it has been observed that a German or a Prussian *jäger* will make himself quite comfortable behind a cabbage, a pumpkin, or even a large turnip, and there remain for hours, if he have the opportunity, dogging his prey, and that, too, without the least chance of being seen.

My friend of the 60th, however, had other views of greater interest to him than my life; for after repeatedly pressing and then ordering him to knock off the Voltigeur, who was taking so much pains to prevent me from becoming grey-headed in the service, he pettishly and half turning round, said, 'Silence! ton't tisturp me; I want de officeer [*sic*].'

'Why do you want to kill the officer,' cried I, 'you rascal?' with as much vexation as he had manifested.

'Pecaus ter pe more plunder,' muttered the wretch, keeping his eyes fixed on the object of his ambition.

It now immediately occurred to my mind, that, as we were rapidly driving back the enemy, this worthy had calculated on permitting the Voltigeur to pick me off, whilst he should return the compliment on the French officer; and thus secure the advantage of plundering me first, trusting to the almost certainty of getting up to the enemy before the French officer's carcase should be stripped by his friends, whose life he was unwilling to endanger.[43]

As this shows, not all light infantry were the paragons of military virtue depicted in some Light Division memoirs. Nonetheless they played several important roles on the battlefield and were also immensely useful on campaign, manning the outposts and constituting advance and rearguards. In battle their foremost role was negative: to screen and protect their own close-order troops from enemy skirmishers. Their secondary role, whether in attack or defence, was to harass and unsettle the enemy line: even distant and relatively ineffective fire was unpleasant for waiting troops. If possible, they were to press closer, sniping at enemy officers and gunners, hoping to force the enemy artillery to retreat and to provoke a response from the main enemy line. Their function, though not their methods, was thus similar to that of artillery: to begin to wear down the physical and psychological strength of the enemy, preparing the way for the decisive attack.

Chapter Five
Infantry Combat

ORGANIZATION, FORMATIONS, DRILL AND TRAINING

Infantry was the predominant and most important element in every European army of the period. It usually formed between 60 and 90 per cent of an army in battle, and was both the cheapest and the most versatile type of troops. Generals might crave more cavalry or more artillery, but most fighting in almost every battle was between opposing infantry; and when an army was short of infantry, as was Napoleon's at Waterloo, it suffered accordingly.

The basic tactical unit of infantry was the battalion, whose strength in battle ranged widely from fewer than 300 men to more than 1,200 but was most commonly between 500 and 700. At Salamanca the strongest British battalion was the 1/42nd with 1,079 all ranks; the weakest was the 2/44th with 251 all ranks. Of forty-four British and German battalions present (excluding some detachments), five had 800 or more of all ranks, and nine had fewer than 400 with the average strength being 572. Coincidentally a return of Marmont's army dated a week before the battle gives an average strength of 568 officers and men, but this is rather misleading – other battles would show a wider variation in the average strength of battalions in opposing armies, depending on the circumstances of the campaign.[1]

Within the battalion, men were organized into companies: nine per battalion in the French army until 1808, when a reorganization reduced it to six (one grenadier, one light, four line). In the Austrian army battalions had six companies; in the Prussian, four; and in the British, ten. Confusingly a pair of companies were often referred to as a division, so that a battalion in a 'column of divisions' had a front of two companies. This had nothing to do with the higher formation of a division (which usually contained several brigades: ten or a dozen battalions), though it has been suggested – not very plausibly – that confusion over the terms was responsible for d'Erlon's monstrous formation at Waterloo.

In the British army some regiments had only one battalion and few more than two. Ideally the second battalion was to remain in the home garrison and supply drafts of trained men to the first battalion in the field, though there were many exceptions to this neat formula. Thus at Salamanca four British regiments had more than one battalion present: the 4th, 5th, 38th and 95th. The 95th had detachments of the 2nd and 3rd battalions, amounting to a rather weak battalion between them, serving in one brigade of the Light Division, and the 1st battalion serving in the other brigade. The three line regiments each had their two battalions brigaded together.

In other armies, regiments generally put a number of battalions into the field – four was the French standard – with a weak 'depot battalion' to collect, train and forward recruits. These battalions could serve on widely separate fronts: some French regiments had battalions fighting in Spain and Russia at the same time, but when present in the one army, battalions of the same regiment usually fought together. Thus almost every regiment in Marmont's army at Salamanca had two or three battalions present, and the regiment formed an intermediate level of command between the battalion and the brigade. Marmont's army had eight infantry divisions each consisting of some artillery, and two brigades of infantry, each brigade in turn having two regiments, giving an average of nine battalions of infantry, or just over 5,000 men, per division (including the artillery). Wellington's army had seven divisions of infantry, generally with three brigades (including one Portuguese), each with between three and five battalions. There were also two independent brigades of Portuguese infantry and a Spanish division – though the latter took little part in the battle. The relatively small size of armies in the Peninsula meant that there was seldom any need for organization above the level of divisions, but in central Europe several infantry divisions were commonly grouped together, with a brigade or division of light cavalry and a reserve of artillery, to form an army corps. Such corps varied widely in size from fewer than 10,000 men to Davout's corps in the invasion of Russia, which was a substantial army in its own right. The divisions comprising these corps might also be larger than in the Peninsula: the three divisions in Davout's III Corps in 1806 averaged almost 9,000 men each.

Most of these infantry usually fought in close order: only the light companies and a few specialist units were normally sent out to skirmish, although circumstances sometimes demanded that whole battalions act as light infantry. But in general infantry formed in line or in column, in a variation on these such as *l'ordre mixte* or, when threatened by cavalry, in square (which will be considered in the next chapter). In all these formations each company formed in line, two or three deep, with a front of thirty or forty men – more in a strong battalion, fewer in a weak one, depending also on the number of companies in the battalion. How these companies were arranged determined the formation of the battalion.

Line had been the standard formation for infantry in the eighteenth century and remained widely used during the Revolutionary and Napoleonic Wars. The companies were deployed side by side, making a single line two or three men deep: a battalion of 600 rank and file formed two deep would have a frontage of about 200 yards, or 133 yards if three deep. The obvious advantage of the line was that every musket could be brought to bear (although there were great doubts of the effectiveness of men in the third rank firing). It was also felt to be less vulnerable to artillery fire (see above, pp. 49–50), and certainly casualties were distributed more evenly throughout the unit and over a greater area. But against this the line was liable to confusion and disorder if it attempted to advance rapidly over rough terrain. It was hard enough to maintain the alignment of a single battalion with a front of 200 yards as it advanced under fire, but normally the battalion would be taking part in the advance of a larger formation, so that the front to be dressed might be 700 or 800 yards long. If just one battalion advanced at a slight angle to ninety degrees, confusion would quickly arise as it crowded its neighbour on one side, and a gap opened on the other. Such confusion could be deadly in the face of an enterprising enemy (particularly cavalry), while at best it would delay the advance, cooling the men's confidence and exposing them for longer to enemy fire, and perhaps destroying the co-ordination between the brigade's advance and that of other units. For this reason advancing in line was dangerous except for very well trained and disciplined troops; using line on the defensive, however, was much less risky.

Nonetheless, the line had other disadvantages, which again affected poor troops disproportionately more than good units. Officers and NCOs were spread far more thinly when a battalion was deployed in line, than in a more compact column or square, and their influence and control was consequently lessened. The flanks of a line were also extremely vulnerable, and if they were unprotected a whole brigade, or even more, could be rolled up by a sudden attack which it was powerless to resist. This danger could be minimized by having a substantial body of supporting troops behind the first line: such deployment in depth was always desirable, though not always possible. If this could not be done, and if the terrain offered no protection, the battalions at each end of the line might be formed in column or in square, as they were in Ferey's division when it covered the French retreat at Salamanca.[2]

The question of whether infantry were best deployed in two or three ranks caused considerable debate at the time. According to Marshal Marmont, 'Nothing justifies a third rank', while his colleague Gouvion St Cyr was equally emphatic:

> It is not an exaggeration to say that the third rank places *hors de combat* a quarter of the men who are wounded in an affair. This statement is not carried high enough, if it is a question of a troop composed of recruits. It is said that the first rank should kneel on one knee in the fire of three ranks, and that in the fire by file the third rank should not fire, but should pass its arm loaded to the men in the second rank. All this can be executed only in drill, but in war soldiers fire as they can without passing their muskets to their comrades, and without kneeling.[3]

Despite such criticism most armies in Europe retained the third rank in the belief that it added stability to the line, even if its fire was largely ineffective – though it was increasingly trained to act independently in some circumstances, either as skirmishers or as a local reserve.

Two plausible arguments support the idea that the third rank strengthened the line: it brought officers and NCOs much closer together, and it provided an immediate pool of replacements for casualties in the front ranks. This was the argument David Dundas used in defending the third rank in his *Rules and Regulations*: 'In no service is the fire and consistency of the third rank [to be] given up; it serves to fill up the vacancies made in the others in action; without it the battalion would soon be in single rank.'[4] Against this there is the probability that the fire of the third rank – even if it did less damage than St Cyr claimed – unsettled and discomposed the men in front; and the fact that the great users of line – whether in attack or defence – were the British, who consistently used only two ranks. Finally there is the point that the third rank absorbed large numbers of men who might have been better employed elsewhere – perhaps with fewer units in the front line and more in reserve. And yet, it may be that the Continental armies knew their own needs best, and that in the heavy fire and prolonged attrition of many battles in central Europe the two-deep line would have left their infantry dangerously fragile.

While the line was inherited from the eighteenth century, the use of columns was largely an innovation of the Revolutionary Wars, although French theorists had discussed it for decades. A battalion would form column on a front of one, or more commonly two, companies, giving it a front of around fifty to eighty men, and a depth of nine to twelve men, depending on the number and strength of the companies in the battalion. It would thus be thirty to sixty yards wide and between twelve and fifteen yards deep, when the companies were closed up for an attack, making it more a stubby line than a 'column'. Sometimes, however, a number of battalions – perhaps a whole regiment, or even more – were deployed one behind the other, greatly increasing the depth of the column while its front remained limited to two companies. Such a formation had little to recommend it, except in a defile or when the terrain otherwise compelled the advancing troops to attack on a very narrow front. Open columns, with large gaps between successive companies enabling them to easily swing out and deploy into line or square, were widely used for manoeuvring at a distance from the enemy, even by the British; but they were not suitable for close combat, having none of the compactness and cohesion of a closed column, nor the firepower of a line.

In general the column – particularly smaller battalion columns – had many advantages. With their narrow front and without the need to maintain perfect alignment with their neighbours, they could advance far more rapidly and over much rougher ground than infantry in line. Their officers and NCOs were concentrated so that they could more easily set their men a prominent example or maintain pressure from behind as circumstances required, while the press of comrades to front and rear must have encouraged the men, far fewer of whom were in the exposed front ranks immediately facing the enemy. The flanks of the column were far less vulnerable, for by filling the gaps between companies with officers and NCOs, while men on the outer edge of each company faced out-wards, it could quickly convert into a solid block, less secure than a properly formed square but still capable of resisting all but the most determined cavalry. Alternatively a proper square could be formed more quickly and easily from a column than from line. For all these reasons columns were ideally suited for use by poorly trained troops making an attack.

But they were not without disadvantages: their vulnerability to artillery fire may have been exaggerated, but the disproportionate damage done by those round-shot which hit the unit was unnerving. Casualties from canister and small arms fire, including enemy skirmishers, were concentrated on the compa-nies at the head of the column, which consequently suffered more heavily than if the unit had advanced in line. And the assumption that the greater depth of the column gave it greater impetus and moral cohesion has been strongly questioned by Ardant du Picq, who argues that it was the men in the rear of the unit who were under the greatest psychological strain, and who were most likely to give way first.[5]

Less debatably there is the obvious fact that a column had very little firepow-er and that it would suffer severely in a prolonged contest against a steady opponent in line. In theory an attacking column would advance to about 300 yards from the enemy: if its opponents showed signs of wavering it would push its attack home in the reasonable expectation that they would break in the face of a determined attack. But if the enemy appeared steady and well ordered, the column would deploy into line and meet it on equal terms. Practice was seldom this neat, or the enemy so obligingly passive. Deploying from column into line took time, and if the enemy counter-attacked it might catch the column in a state of confusion and disorder. Even if it did not, the attack-ing troops would be exposed to enemy fire (including supporting artillery fire) while they deployed, and lose all the physical and psychological mo-mentum of their advance. This does not mean that the manoeuvre could not be successfully performed, but it needed good troops, and was certainly not a universal solution for the problems columns encountered when attacking steady opponents.[6]

Napoleon sometimes recommended the use of a formation – *l'ordre mixte* – which was supposed to combine the advantages of line and column by deploying three battalions, one in line with one on each side in column. This had advan-tages, for it had some firepower, the flanks of the battalion in line were well protected, and it concentrated a strong body in a relatively small area; but it was slower and less flexible than battalion columns, and extravagant with man-power. Despite its Imperial patronage, it never became the customary mode of fighting in the French army, nor does it seem to have been copied widely by Napoleon's enemies.

But other, less formal, combinations of line and column were very widely used. In the later years of the war (from about 1808) the armies of the Continental Powers used columns extensively; indeed they had little choice, for they were rapidly expanded by the influx of large numbers of partly trained men. When standing on the defensive they continued to use the line however, though often with a second line of troops in columns, deployed well behind the first. If the first line broke, these supporting troops could lead the counter-attack and the wide gaps between the columns ensured that the fleeing men of the first line would not disrupt their formation. The role of such supporting troops was equally important in attack, where, ideally at least, the assault would be made with two lines of columns placed 'chequerboard', i.e. with those in the second line forming behind the gaps in the first, the whole preceded by a cloud of skirmishers and followed by a substantial reserve. Thus even if the first wave of columns was repulsed, it would unsettle and disrupt the enemy, creating an opportunity for the second line. But again it was easier to perfect the theory than to implement it, and few battlefields proved so tidy and convenient.

Underlying all these formations and manoeuvres was drill, which enabled soldiers to operate effectively in close order. The use of drill in training today is justified as inculcating instinctive obedience and encouraging group cohesion. No doubt it performed similar functions equally well 200 years ago, but its primary purpose then was to carry soldiers through the complicated evolutions necessary to change formation and to load and fire their weapons, amidst the noise, confusion and fear of battle. Details of drill make extremely dry reading, but a single example should convey the complexity of the movements involved and the need for automatic and unhesitating obedience where a single mistake could sow confusion and reduce a unit to chaos. Here a modern authority explains as simply as possible how a battalion of eight companies (numbered one to eight) forms from line into square: a full account, giving all the mechanics involved, would be much longer.

The inner sub-divisions of numbers 4 and 5 companies stood fast, but their outer sub-divisions faced inwards. Numbers 2 and 3 companies wheeled back slightly by sub-divisions pivoting on their left; numbers 6 and 7 wheeled back similarly on their right; all eight sub-divisions then turned about. Numbers 1 and 8 companies turned inwards.

The outer sub-divisions of numbers 4 and 5 companies marched behind their inner sub-divisions, halted and fronted.

Numbers 2, 3, 6 and 7 companies stepped off wheeling inwards, their outer sub-divisions gradually falling into position behind their inner ones. When they reached their proper places on the flank faces of the square they halted and turned about. Numbers 1 and 8 companies wheeled left and right respectively, their outer sub-divisions gradually coming up on the outside of the inner sub-divisions, as they marched to their places on the rear face where they faced outwards. Front ranks knelt.[7]

And this was a movement carried out under imminent threat of enemy cavalry, with every need for haste, and yet when confusion would spell ruin. No wonder Colonel Wallace of the 88th exhorted his men,

> Mind the square; you know I often told you that if you ever had to form it from line, in the face of an enemy, you'd be in a d——d ugly way, and have plenty of noise about you; mind the tellings off, and don't give the *false touch* to your right or left hand man; for by G——d, if you are once broken, you'll be running here and their like a parcel of frightened pullets![8]

Drill manuals survive in abundance, but there is only fragmentary evidence of how closely they were followed in the field. The officer of the 88th already quoted stated that,

> Perhaps in the whole British army there was not one regiment *so* severely drilled. If a man coughed in the ranks, he was punished; if the sling of the firelock, for an instant, left the hollow of the shoulder when it should not, he was punished; and if he moved his knapsack when standing at *ease*, he was punished, more or less, of course, according to the offence. The consequence of this system, exclusively Colonel Wallace's, was that the men never had the appearance of being fatigued upon a march. . . .

But he also says, in praising Wallace, that 'by a good commanding officer, I do not mean one too fond of *quackery* – quite the contrary. Too much training is as bad as too little; we had no fuss with our men.' And 'At drill our manoeuvres were chiefly confined to line marching, echellon [*sic*] movements and formation of the square in every possible way; and in all these we excelled.'[9]

When Sir Ralph Abercromby was preparing for his campaign in Egypt in 1801 he decided that Dundas's *Regulations* with its eighteen manoeuvres – the official drill of the British army – was too complicated for use in the field. He therefore introduced a simplified version which concentrated on a few basic manoeuvres, while adding several new types of square to counter the anticipated French predominance of cavalry.[10] While in 1813 Wellington commented on the difference between what was expected of soldiers in England, and his veterans.

> [He] observed that his men were now all so round-shouldered and slouching in their gait, that he was sure, if his regiment here was in its present state to pass in review in Wimbledon Common, the whole would be sent to drill immediately, and declared quite unfit for service. Indeed, he added, that the men had now got into such a way of doing everything in the easiest manner, that he was often quite ashamed of the sentries before his own quarter. He did not mention this by way of complaint, but as showing how ideas here and at home differed.[11]

The difference between parade ground theory and battlefield reality was just as great in other armies. For example, in the 1820s there was great pressure from veteran officers in the French army for the *Ordonnance* (i.e. drill regulations) of 1791 to be completely revised and drastically simplified – the reformers arguing from experience that 'few of the complex drills of the Ordonnance were ever executed in war'.[12]

Nor is it clear whether soldiers always maintained their stately marching rate of about 90 (ordinary), 105 (quick step) or 120 (double quick) steps per minute, though obviously confusion could arise if a battalion's advance became ragged, especially if it was in line. According to a Prussian officer at Ligny, 'About two o'clock we started; double time soon became a run, which at the order of the brigade commander, Major General von Tippelskirchen, grew faster minute by minute.' Two French accounts, one admittedly fictional, report the same experience: 'We advance, carry arms, in readiness for a charge, at a quick step and in good order, but it always ends in double quick, because the shot makes you impatient.' And, 'the men became excited, called out to one another, and hastened their march; the column began to become a little confused . . . soon we got nearer, crying "*Vive l'Empereur! En avant! A la Baionnette!*" Shakos were raised on the muzzles of muskets; the column began to double, the ranks got into confusion, the agitation produced a tumult . . .'[13] Columns could afford to give the men their heads and accelerate their advance for their success depended on their dash and impetuosity, and confusion threatened them far less than troops in line. Nonetheless, no commander wanted his troops to get completely out of hand, even if they had just broken their enemy with a charge.

Yet although armies might not always follow their drill book to the letter, there is no doubt that proficiency at drill was immensely important on the battlefield in giving battalions the confidence and tactical flexibility which distinguished good troops. This proficiency was not readily acquired. William Napier estimated that it took three years to make infantry completely disciplined – as opposed to just fit to take the field, which might take only a few weeks – and other authorities largely agreed.[14] Wellington's success in the Peninsula owed much to the years 1803–5 when most of the British army was concentrated at home, and was able to train without the disruption of frequent expeditions overseas. Beresford worked for over a year reforming the Portuguese army before it first saw action in the brief Busaco campaign and this was followed by months of further training. The *Grande Armée* of 1805–7 was the finest force Napoleon ever commanded – a superb mixture of veterans and well-trained new troops led by officers who were young but experienced, enterprising and ambitious; but the foundation of its success was the two years it had spent in the Camp at Boulogne and other camps on the North Sea coast, training for the invasion of England. These camps permitted not only constant repetition of the basic evolutions of a battalion, but provided the much rarer advantage of regular practice manoeuvring in larger formations – brigades, divisions and even whole corps took part in mock operations. Men, and particularly officers, gained valuable experience, and a sense of collective identity and camaraderie which extended beyond the battalion or regiment to the whole corps.

Still, training and discipline alone were not enough, as the Prussian army discovered in 1806. Its battalions were as well trained and strictly disciplined as any in the world, maintaining much of the tradition of Frederick the Great. It failed because, after a decade at peace, it was unready for war; because of deficiencies in command, not just at the apex but at many intermediate levels; and because its tactics could not match the flexibility and enterprise of the French. The new Prussian army of 1813 was much less well trained than its predecessor, though over the course of the year it gained plenty of experience in battle. Its great virtue was not its drill, nor its tactics, but its fighting spirit: it was repeatedly defeated, but did not break. However, it had three great advantages over the army of 1806: it was far better led, at all levels; the broad strategic position was much more favourable, and grew still more so after the armistice; and it was not facing the *Grande Armée* of 1806, but an army cobbled together with as much haste and improvisation as it had been.

MUSKETRY

Apart from those few soldiers armed with rifles, all Napoleonic infantry carried a smooth-bore muzzle-loading musket, about five feet long (not counting the bayonet) and with a bore of around 0.7 of an inch. As the bore of the British musket was slightly larger than that of the French, British infantry could, in an emergency, use captured ammunition. None of the standard muskets of the period was particularly well designed or made. They were produced in enormous quantities and economy, not precision, was the overriding concern. Contemporaries differed in their opinion of the relative virtues of muskets of different armies, often believing that their enemy's weapon was the best, while a Prussian test produced inconclusive, indeed contradictory, results. It seems likely that no musket was markedly superior to the rest, and certain that the quality of the musket mattered far less than the quality of the troops who wielded it.[15]

Both the design of the musket and the training infantry received discouraged them from deliberate aiming; rather they were taught to load as quickly as possible, level the musket in the general direction of the enemy and – at least in theory – fire in simultaneous volleys. This approach naturally aroused the ire of the reformers. Thus Kenneth Mackenzie, who played a large role in training the Light Brigade at Shorncliffe, wrote that

> The present method of bringing the firelocks from the recover to a certain level, and there remaining till the Drill Serjeant has aligned them before he gives the

word 'Fire', and his criterion of perfection being their having acquired this habit, and pulling their triggers together, is the greatest possible preventative to the means of correctly aiming at or killing his enemy.[16]

Scharnhorst was equally decided: 'Good marksmanship is always the most important thing for the infantry – it always decides the action. Before the war we taught the men to load quickly, but not well, to fire quickly, but without aiming. This was very ill-considered; we must therefore work with all our might to root out this error.'[17]

Such views had some success in ensuring that many light infantry were taught the value of aimed fire, but most other infantry continued to be trained in the old way and to have virtually no target practice with live ammunition. While regrettable, this was not completely senseless. Muskets were dreadfully inaccurate. Even in perfect test conditions barely half the rounds fired at a large canvas screen 150 yards away hit the target, while at half this range a third or a quarter of the shots still missed.[18] Training troops to aim with care might have improved these figures, but it might also have revealed to the men the inefficiency of their weapons and so undermined their confidence. Battlefield conditions for close-order infantry did not encourage aimed fire: men were distracted by the movements and noise of their comrades (including the fall of those hit by enemy fire); and after the first round vision was likely to be obscured by smoke; while the target might be moving or, having itself fired, be wreathed in its own smoke. By concentrating training on the complicated mechanical process of loading, the infantry were given a task which they could master and which would divert their attention from the enemy.

Infantry were trained to fire in regular volleys, but there is good evidence that in action this quickly degenerated into individual fire-at-will. Even in the eighteenth century, when infantry was better trained and disciplined, a British officer wrote of the 1st Foot Guards at Dettingen,

> They were under no command by way of Hyde Park firing, but the whole three ranks made a running fire of their own accord. . . . The French fired in the same manner, without waiting for words of command and Lord Stair [the allied commander] did often say he had seen many a battle, and never saw the infantry engage in any other manner.

While G. H. Berenhorst described how, in Frederick the Great's army,

> You began by firing by platoons, and perhaps two or three would get off orderly volleys. But then would follow a general blazing away – the usual rolling fire when everybody blasted off as soon as he had loaded, when ranks and files became intermingled, when the first rank was incapable of kneeling, even if it wanted to. . . .[19]

Similarly, although the French *Règlement* of 1791 laid down four methods of fire, the three which stipulated volleys at command were generally disregarded in favour of the fourth where fire-at-will followed an initial volley.[20] And yet many memoirists and other eyewitnesses refer to orderly volleys, and while this may often be a rhetorical device, it seems that some well-trained battalions – especially those with little combat experience – were able to maintain their fire discipline, providing the combat was not too prolonged. Thus an observer describes the 18th Royal Irish at Mandara (1801): 'No impression was to be made upon infantry which coolly waited for the words of command, ready, present, fire, and this the 18th Regiment did; much greater proof of steadiness, coolness and discipline could not be given.'[21] But such exceptions were rare.

By far the most effective round of fire was the first – not necessarily of the battle, but of any engagement within it. It would normally have been loaded carefully when the men were calm and unhurried, and fired at the word of command, without the troops or probably the target being obscured by smoke. The quality of subsequent rounds would continue to decline steadily. The coarse gunpowder clogged the muskets, flints needed frequent changing, men would make mistakes in loading, sometimes even shooting off their ramrods, or fail to notice a misfire and double-load their piece, which might then explode in their face. One authority estimates that 15 per cent of shots misfired in dry weather, rising to 25 per cent in wet conditions.[22] Some old soldiers deliberately spilt their powder on the ground, or failed to ram the charge home in order to lessen the recoil of their musket. Constant fire made the barrel too hot to touch, and one French veteran claims – not altogether plausibly – that at Marengo, 'Our musket-barrels were so hot that it became impossible to load for fear of igniting the cartridges. There was nothing for it but to piss into the barrels to cool them, and then to dry them by pouring in loose powder and setting it alight unrammed.'[23] Meanwhile the men would grow first more nervous and excited as their fire failed to drive off the enemy, and then, if the firefight continued, sink into a stupefied daze compounded of the incessant noise, the smoke and fear. They would mechanically load and fire, but with far from mechanical precision; some would fire off their ammunition as quickly as possible and then try to hurry to the rear, as would others using the pretext of helping a wounded comrade, or being wounded themselves, or their musket being broken.

The effectiveness of the first volley led officers to seek to hoard it until the enemy were within close range, when it might be decisive and break their resolve. But this placed great strain on discipline, as Humphrey Bland recognized as early as 1727:

> In advancing towards the enemy, it is with great difficulty that the officers can prevent the men (but more particularly when they are fired at) from taking their arms, without orders, off from their shoulders, and firing at too great a distance.

How much more difficult must it be to prevent their firing, when they have their arms in their hands already cocked, and their fingers on the triggers? I won't say it is impossible though I look upon it to be almost so.[24]

Frederick the Great wanted his men to advance without firing at all, but found that this was asking too much even of his infantry. Many commanders believed that it was an advantage to let the enemy fire first 'for a psychological reason . . . men were never so likely to break as when they received a shattering volley from the enemy while they fumbled in haste to reload empty weapons they had themselves just fired; in that moment they felt helpless, and the havoc of their own volley was, of course, hidden from them by clouds of smoke their own crude powder had created in the instant of firing'.[25]

Once infantry began firing it was very difficult (Marshal Ney described the problem as 'almost insurmountable') to get them to stop and advance against the enemy. At Coruña, when Charles Napier led his regiment, the 50th, forward without orders, he forbade firing 'and to prevent it and occupy the men's attention, made them slope and carry arms by word of command. Many of them cried out, Major let us fire! Not yet was my answer, for having advanced without orders, I thought to have them more under command if we were wrong, whereas, firing once begun, we could not change.'[26] At Roliça, the previous year, officers on both sides had vainly tried to stop their men from firing. The British 29th had advanced up a steep narrow path and were endeavouring to form on the summit in the face of the French, who

suddenly rose up and opened their fire, which their officers seemed endeavouring to restrain, and apparently urging them on to the charge, as we observed them knocking down the men's firelocks with their swords. But they did not advance.

Colonel Lake called out, 'don't fire, men; don't fire; wait a little, we shall soon charge,' (meaning when more companies should come up,) adding 'the bayonet is the true weapon for a British soldier' . . . [but he was killed, and the companies on the right] opened their fire and a desperate engagement ensued.[27]

Sometimes the officers themselves were to blame, as another British veteran observed:

Inexperienced officers have repeatedly given orders to commence a fire, without either judgment or consideration as to whether or not it was the proper time to open a fusillade. This was their fault and not the men's. However, the mischief to which it tended was, that after the first command was given, the soldiers of themselves, taking out a sort of carte blanche, blazed away, in the most independent manner, in all directions, until at length the utmost skill and energy of the most active officers was baffled, in their efforts to controul [*sic*] them; and when the ammunition was most required they found it was expended to little purpose, beyond that of raising noise and smoke.[28]

Occasionally orders would be given that an attack should be made with unloaded muskets if the only hope of success was to carry the enemy position in a single rush. Thus in his attack on the Greater Arapile at Salamanca, 'Sir Denis Pack . . . ordered that none should load, but that the Hill should be carried with the bayonet (knowing well that if once such troops as we had began firing they would never get to the top).'[29] But this was a desperate measure, and Pack's attack did not succeed.

More typically a combat would involve a test of nerve, especially if both parties were clearly visible to each other. Officers on both sides would be trying to prevent their men from opening fire, while those in the attacking force would be endeavouring to combine a reasonably rapid rate of advance with the maintenance of good order. If the defenders were poor troops or already shaken, they were likely to open fire prematurely at long range. Such fire would be ineffective and this would encourage the attackers to press on with emboldened spirits. The defenders, already shaken, struggling to reload, and seeing that their fire had failed to halt the attack, grew more and more likely to break, the closer the attacking troops pressed. Even if they managed to let off another round they were likely to shoot wildly, losing any advantage brought by the shorter range, while the enhanced confidence of the attackers would make them disregard losses (unless severe) and press on. But if the defenders' morale was better and they held their initial fire as the attackers approached, the advancing troops would become increasingly apprehensive and fire into the air or even halt and seek to deploy (if in column) or to fire (if in line). At this point the initiative had clearly passed to the defenders and if they fired a volley and charged, the attacking troops were likely to fall back in confusion. If the resolution of both sides was nearly equal, or some other factor, such as the presence of enemy cavalry, prevented the superior party from bringing the combat to a crisis by charging, a protracted firefight might develop, which was likely to continue until some fresh element entered the equation, breaking the stalemate.

This does not mean that the result was predetermined by the underlying quality of the troops, for many other factors influenced their performance in combat. Fire from skirmishers could unsettle troops on either side and perhaps even lead them to begin firing prematurely. Earlier fighting, artillery and skirmisher fire could weaken the unit both through casualties and by the gradual erosion of the troops' courage and physical energy. The broader tactical situation played an important part – soldiers were naturally encouraged if they believed that their army was winning the battle – while the relative numbers of troops, and the presence of supporting units, affected morale. The sight of a friendly unit fleeing by in disorder could completely unnerve inexperienced troops – panic was infectious – though good troops might sometimes be roused to avenge the ill-treatment of their comrades. The presence of a trusted senior officer would inspire confidence while an incompetent general might fill his soldiers with forebodings of defeat. Anything which affected the good order and discipline of the unit was most disadvantageous, whether it was the need to cross rough terrain, or to open ranks to allow friendly troops to pass through to the rear, or some mistake in the unit's evolutions. Above all a surprise – such as the sudden appearance of fresh enemy troops or an unexpected threat to a flank – could shatter a unit's confidence and deprive it of the psychological initiative at the decisive moment.

Two examples from Stutterheim's account of the Battle of Austerlitz illustrate some of these points:

> The action then became very warm, and it was attempted to regain the ground that had been lost by the advanced guard. The Russians made an attack; opened their fire at too great a distance, and without much effect, while the French columns continued to advance without firing a shot; but when at a distance of about a hundred paces, they opened a fire of musketry which became general, and very destructive . . .

> There was no other chance of turning the fate of the day but a general and desperate attack at the point of the bayonet. The Austrian Brigades, with that of General Kamensky, charged the enemy; the Russians shouting, according to their usual custom; but the French received them with steadiness, and a well-supported fire, which made a dreadful carnage in the compact ranks of the Russians. General Miloradovich, on his side, advanced upon the right; but the Generals Berg and Repninsky being wounded, their troops had lost that confidence in themselves, without which nothing is to be done in war. The ardour of this attack soon evaporated. The superior numbers of the enemy, and his steadiness, soon changed it to a slow uncertain pace, accompanied by an ill-directed fire of musketry.[30]

Unfortunately neither of these cases specifies the range at which the allies opened fire, but Paddy Griffith has collected nineteen examples involving British troops where a figure is given. Of these only four mention a range of 100 yards or more, while the average is seventy-five yards.[31] These are very short ranges and may be distorted by the exaggeration of memoirists writing for effect – after all, in the heat of action few officers or men would make an accurate calculation of their distance from the enemy when they opened fire, let alone remember it years later. But even if the specific figures are doubtful, it is clear from all accounts that thanks to Wellington's tactics and their own good discipline, British troops were unusually good at holding their fire. Other armies placed less emphasis on close-range musketry. Clausewitz put the effective range of musketry at '150 to 200 yards', while in October 1813 a British officer commented, with a tinge of contempt, that the French, who were long past their prime, 'delight in a long shot (the Spaniards & they are well matched at this – famous ammunition wasters)'.[32] An incident in the Battle of Vitoria shows the French opening fire at long range, and the British responding while still well over 100 yards away. Edward Costello, rifleman in the 95th, watched the advance of the British 88th:

The 88th next deployed into line, advancing all the time towards their opponents, who seemed to wait very coolly for them. When they had approached to within three or four hundred yards, the French poured in a volley or I should say a running fire from right to left. As soon as the British regiment had recovered the first shock, and closed their files on the gap it had made, they commenced advancing at double time until fifty yards nearer to the enemy [but still at least 250 yards away], when they halted and in turn gave a running fire from their whole line, and without a moment's pause cheered and charged up the hill against them. The French meanwhile were attempting to reload. But being hard pressed by the British, who allowed them no time to give a second volley, came immediately to the right about, making the best of their way to the village.[33]

The impression that much infantry firing was at long range is supported by the fragmentary evidence of the ratio of ammunition consumption to casualties inflicted. There is far less evidence for the expenditure of small arms ammunition in battle than for artillery, and one of the most frequently cited figures – Henegan's calculations for Vitoria – contains faulty assumptions which make it almost worthless.[34] Nonetheless a wide range of authorities accept estimates that for every bullet which caused a casualty between 200 and 500 had been fired, and their view is supported by contemporary comments on the high consumption of ammunition for the results obtained. At the Battle of Saalfeld in 1806 the French infantry is said to have used 200,000 cartridges. The Prussians suffered 900 casualties: if we boldly assume that two-thirds of these were caused by French musketry, this produces a figure of 600 casualties, or one for every 333 rounds fired. This is encouraging, but obviously further examples would be needed to establish the estimate securely.[35]

A very rough check of these figures can be made by comparing them to the results of actual battles. If we say that Wellington had 50,000 infantry at Waterloo who each averaged eighty rounds (both figures are deliberately on the high side), they would have fired a total of four million rounds. At 200 rounds per casualty that would have produced 20,000 casualties – which is rather too high, being about 80 per cent of all the French losses in the battle, including those caused by the Prussians. At 500 rounds per casualty it would produce 8,000 casualties, which is probably too low, especially given the high assumptions behind the figure. A third estimate sometimes quoted – that 10,000 rounds were needed to produce a casualty – would mean that all of Wellington's infantry inflicted only 400 casualties through their fire in the entire battle, which is obviously absurd. Waterloo is perhaps not the best example, but other battles produce similar results, supporting the range of 200 to 500 shots fired per casualty, and with a hint that the lower end of the scale may be more accurate. But the assumptions on which these calculations are based are too arbitrary for the results to have any precision.

Of course this did not mean that a battalion of 600 men firing a volley at 100 or even 200 yards would inflict only one to three casualties; indeed Costello's account, quoted above, implies that even at over 300 yards the French volley inflicted quite a few casualties on the 88th – or why did they need to recover from the shock and close their files on the gap it had made? Rather it means that much ammunition was fired at ludicrously long ranges, much was wasted in bickering between skirmishers, and much was probably thrown away by broken troops or deliberately squandered by soldiers who were only anxious to empty their pouches as quickly as possible and then hurry to the rear.

Troops who were heavily engaged could quickly exhaust their ammunition. On the parade ground, rates of fire of four or even five rounds per minute were achieved, but in action a figure of between one and two rounds is more plausible, and this would probably fall as the action went on. Yet even at these rates the sixty rounds which most infantry carried (fifty in some armies) would be exhausted in less than an hour. References to units running short of ammunition are not uncommon, and Henegan claims that the British field train issued 1.35 million cartridges to Wellington's infantry during the Battle of Vitoria – about twenty rounds per man, or a full sixty rounds to one third of the army. There are few accounts of how this worked in practice. Henegan simply says that 'As near as possible to the divisions of the army, were brigades of small-arm ammunition to feed the expenditure.' At Waterloo, according to an officer of the 40th, 'boxes of ammunition were placed at intervals along our rear, from about fifty to one hundred paces from us, so that the men could help themselves when they required it'.[36] This must have created an excellent opportunity for reluctant heroes to leave the ranks, on the pretext of replenishing their ammunition, and not return, but at least it was better than the confusion implied by stories of men scrabbling in the cartridge boxes of the dead and wounded for fresh supplies. Sergeant Cooper of the 7th Fusiliers recalled a near disaster at Sorauren in 1813 when the colonel ordered him to

'go up the hill and tell the brigade-major to send down ammunition immediately, or we must retire.' This was necessary, as our men were taking cartridges out of the wounded men's pouches. I scrambled up the steep and performed my duty. . . . I then dragged a Spaniard, with his mule laden with ball cartridge, down to my company. . . . Having unladen his beast, he disappeared in an instant. Throwing off my knapsack, I smashed the casks, and served out the cartridges as fast as possible, while my comrades blazed away.[37]

There must have been many other occasions on which fresh ammunition did not arrive in time, and a unit was forced to fall back which might otherwise have held its position. Conversely there were limits to the physical endurance of even veteran troops and the anonymous memoirist of the 71st Light Infantry mentions the firing of 107 rounds on the first day of Fuentes de Oñoro, and 108 at Vitoria, as remarkable feats which took their toll: 'Next morning we awoke dull, stiff, and weary. I could scarce touch my head with my right hand; my shoulder was as black as coal.'[38]

Musketry inflicted many casualties – probably well over half those inflicted in most battles (see above, pp. 46–7) – but it was a poor way of resolving a combat. If neither side had the resolution to force a decision by attempting to charge, a protracted firefight was the most likely result. The effectiveness of each round would fall, but casualties would still accumulate. If both sides were good troops the result could be a bloody battle of attrition which destroyed the effectiveness of both units. This is what happened at Salamanca when, late in the day, Ferey's division tried to cover the French retreat and was attacked by the British and Portuguese troops of Clinton's Sixth Division.

> It was half-past seven [writes a British officer who was present] when the sixth division, under General Clinton, was ordered to advance a second time and attack the enemy's line in front, supported by the third and fifth divisions. The ground over which we had to pass was a remarkably clear slope, like the glacis of a fortification – most favourable for the defensive fire of the enemy, and disadvantageous to the assailants, but the division advanced towards the position with perfect steadiness and confidence. A craggy ridge, on which the French infantry was drawn up, rose so abruptly that they could fire four or five deep; but we had approached within two hundred yards of them before the fire of musketry began, which was by far the heaviest that I have ever witnessed, and was accompanied by constant discharges of grape. An uninterrupted blaze was then maintained, so that the crest of the hill seemed to be one long streak of flame. Our men came down to the charging position, and commenced firing from that level, at the same time keeping their touch to the right, so that the gaps opened by the enemy's fire were instantly filled up.[39]

It is worth noting that although the French opened fire at relatively long range, 'within two hundred yards' (which our author, significantly, regards as surprisingly short), the British were unable to press on with their attack, resulting in a prolonged firefight. A French officer continues the tale:

> the cruel fire cost us many lives, and at last, slowly, and after having given nearly an hour's respite to the remainder of the army, Ferey gave back, still protected by his flanking squares, to the very edge of the forest, where he halted our half-destroyed division. Formed in line it still presented a respectable front, and halted, despite the English batteries, which enfiladed us with a thundering fire.[40]

Clinton attacked this second position, not with his British brigades which had been shattered in the earlier contest, but with Rezende's Portuguese brigade (which was almost as strong as the two British brigades combined), supported by troops from other divisions and some cavalry. The French were now shaken and the officer already quoted admits that 'We fired first, the moment they got within range', but though he claims that this fire was enough to break the attack, he cannot conceal that the division soon fell back in confusion.[41] The British losses were extremely heavy although some, at least in Hulse's brigade, had probably been incurred earlier in the battle. This brigade entered the battle with 1,464 officers and men, and lost 115 killed and 729 wounded: 844 casualties in all, or more than 60 per cent of its strength. Neither of the other brigades lost nearly as heavily: Hinde's brigade had 51 killed, 282 wounded, and 12 missing, totalling 345 casualties from 1,446 present or nearly 24 per cent; while Rezende's brigade lost 121 killed, 346 wounded and 20 missing, a total of 487 from 2,631 present or 18.5 per cent. Thus the division as a whole lost 1,676 casualties or 30 per cent of its strength. Ferey's losses are less certain, but Oman, extrapolating from French officer casualties (which are known), puts them at about 1,200, or 22.3 per cent.[42] Neither division was in a fit state to take any further part in the battle, which in any case was in its last gasp as the long summer day finally drew to an end.

The experience of such a sustained firefight is unimaginable, but one modern writer does manage to convey, not the sight and sound of the wounded, nor the fear, but at least the raw discomfort involved:

> An infantry fire fight was a brutal, jostling, deafening affair. When your priming sparked, you got a small shower of half-burnt powder grains and flint particles in your face. Your musket kicked savagely; with three ranks of men firing, the centre rank would be jostled, with many shots going wild. Every so often a front-rank man, bobbing about as he reloaded, got hit by a third-rank comrade, a fate that unpopular NCOs were wise to ponder. It was dry, harried work; muskets slamming all around you, smoke in your eyes. Biting cartridges dried out your mouth and throat and left your teeth and tongue gritty and hating each other. At the end, your shoulder might be bruised black, your head ached and rang, your voice was a croak, and your thirst was intolerable.[43]

And a British officer describes the confusion which would engulf even the best infantry in a sustained firefight:

> What precision of aim can be expected from soldiers when firing in line? One man is priming; another coming to the present; a third taking, what is called aim; a fourth ramming down his cartridge. After a few shots, the whole body are closely enveloped in smoke, and the enemy is totally invisible; some of the soldiers step out a pace or two, in order to get a better shot; others kneel down; and some have no objection to retire a step or two. The doomed begin to fall, dreadfully mutilated perhaps, and even bold men shrink from the sight; others are wounded, and assisted to the rear by their comrades; so that the whole becomes a line of utter confusion, in which the mass only think of getting their shot fired, they hardly care how [or] in what direction.[44]

BAYONETS AND HAND-TO-HAND FIGHTING

As well as their muskets or rifles, all infantry were armed with a bayonet – usually about fifteen inches long – which fitted around the muzzle of their gun, and hindered, but did not prevent, loading and firing. This gave them a crude six-foot-long improvised spear, one of the most important functions of which was to deter enemy cavalry from charging home (see below, Chapter 6). But the bayonet was also meant to be used in combat with other infantry, and this aroused much debate, for there was good evidence that few men were ever wounded by enemy bayonets. Thus Surgeon Larrey, studying the wounds inflicted in a mêlée, found 119 bullet wounds and only five caused by a bayonet, while the Invalides figures for 1762 quoted in Chapter 3 show that only 2.4 per cent of survivable wounds were made by bayonets.[45]

But this does not mean that the bayonet was useless, for its primary function – at least against infantry – was not to inflict casualties, but to inspire fear which would lead the enemy to break, thus resolving the combat between two units quickly and relatively cheaply. Infantry in formed bodies almost never fought each other with bayonets on open ground: either one side would break before contact was made, or the attack would falter and the troops would begin firing while still some yards apart. Most alleged instances to the contrary appear on closer inspection to be mere hyperbole. Sir John Stuart, the British commander at Maida, wrote home that

> The two corps at the distance of about 100 yards fired reciprocally a few rounds, when, as if by mutual agreement, the firing was suspended, and in close compact order and awful silence, they advanced towards each other, until their bayonets began to cross. At this momentous crisis the enemy became appalled. They broke, and endeavoured to fly, but it was too late; they were overtaken with the most dreadful slaughter.[46]

However, a British veteran who was present denies the story:

> I have heard that in Lieut.-General Sir John Stewart's [sic] official dispatch concerning the battle of Maida it is stated that the bayonets of the contending forces actually crossed during the charge. They may have done so, in some parts of the line – but *so far as I could see* they did not do so, and I have never heard any one who was in the action say that 'the bayonets actually crossed.'[47]

Another soldier declares baldly:

> No two lines have ever crossed bayonets in battle. I was often assured that it was done at the battle of Maida, but I did not believe it. Long after the battle, Sir James Kempt, who commanded our battalion of the 49th Regiment making that charge, declared in my presence that the bayonets did not cross. The French

while advancing hesitated, and at last turned and ran away; but they delayed too long in doing so; the British rushed in and laid upwards of 300 of them on their faces with the bayonet.[48]

And this account is broadly confirmed by a letter written a few weeks after the battle by Lieutenant Dyneley:

> The French advanced firmly towards us, keeping up a tremendous fire of musketry which either fell short or went over our heads. When we were about 100 yards apart, Colonel Kempt, who commanded the light infantry, with incredible coolness gave the order 'Halt!' 'Throw down your blankets, shoes,' etc; then the order 'Forward!' and in a few seconds after 'Charge!' Our men reserved their fire until within a few yards of the enemy and then fired in their faces. The French turned tail and those who could run fast enough escaped the bayonet, the whole of the rest were either killed, wounded or taken prisoner.[49]

Sir Charles Oman, nearing the end of his great history in which he had closely studied scores if not hundreds of battles and combats, discovered a brief example of 'one of the rarest things in the Peninsular War, a real hand-to-hand fight with the white weapon'. This was at the Combat of Roncesvalles on 25 July 1813 when British and French forces, both advancing, unexpectedly came across each other only ten yards apart on a narrow path. 'The French instinctively stepped back a pace,' according to the Brunswick officer whose account of the affair Oman quotes:

> several of them made a half turn, as if about to give way; but their officers, some with appeals, some with threats, and some with curses, kept them to their work. They stood firm, and their bayonets came down to the charge: so did those of Tovey's company. For a few seconds the two sides surveyed each other at a distance of two paces: then one French company officer sprang forward into the middle of the British, and began cutting right and left. He was at once bayoneted, and then the two sides began to fence cautiously with each other, keeping their line and not breaking forward into the enemy's ranks; it was more like bayonet drill than a charge. I do not think that more than a dozen men fell on either side. After a minute the English captain saw that the French supports were closing in – he shouted 'right about face,' and his men trotted back.[50]

This evidently is the exception which proves the general rule, while the account suggests that the men were reluctant to leave the security of their ranks to join in a general scrimmage, unless the enemy had already begun to flee, when there was little danger.

Infantry mêlées were much more common in close country – woods, villages, earthworks and other terrain which inspired desperate resistance from defending troops, or reduced visibility to such ranges that hand-to-hand fighting was unavoidable. Not that such fighting involved bayonet fencing between regular bodies of orderly infantry; rather it was a chaotic brawl where musket butts, pieces of wood or tree branches, fists, teeth and knees to the groin were as useful as the ill-made, unreliable bayonet. Here too the advantage generally lay with the fresher, more orderly troops, still under the control of their officers and with some forward momentum, and this explains why such contests often swayed back and forth as each side fed fresh reserves into the fray.

Although hand-to-hand fighting in the open was rare, bayonet charges were common: one side or the other almost always broke before contact, though, as at Maida, it could not always escape unscathed. One British soldier of Picton's division, describing Waterloo, writes, 'With regard to any "*bayonet conflict*", I saw none. We appeared to charge, and disperse, and *make a road* through the columns, – the usual result of the British charge. This accounts for the absence of bayonet wounds. . . . The weaker body generally gives way: after which, what British soldier would bayonet a flying enemy?'[51] Many soldiers – British and foreign – had, of course, little compunction in striking at a fleeing foe, as innumerable first-hand accounts proudly testify. But the letter of one officer, written on the day after Barrosa, rings true, while showing that his scruples were not widely shared:

> The French waited until we came within about 25 paces of them, before they broke, and as they were in column when they did, they could not get away. It was therefore a scene of most dreadful carnage. I will own to you my weakness. As of course I was in front of the regiment, therefore in the middle of them, I could not, confused and flying as they were, cut down an[y] one, although I might have twenty, they seemed so confounded and so frightened. They made, while we were amongst them (about Quarter of an hour), little or no opposition. We could have taken or destroyed the whole regiment, but at this moment the 47th French regiment came down on our right. . . .[52]

In essence a bayonet charge was a test of will and resolution: whose nerve would break first. Initially the advantage probably lay with the aggressor, for he held the initiative and the momentum of his advance would carry him forward. But if the defenders' fire was sufficiently heavy to check the advance and make it falter, the initiative could quickly pass, especially if the defenders were able to exploit the moment with a counter-attack. The use of column offered advantages of speed and greater concentration of officers and NCOs to the attackers, while line maximized the firepower of the defenders, but any simple opposition between 'shock' and 'fire' tactics is essentially misleading. An attack relied on the fire of skirmishers and artillery to prepare its way, and might well mean resorting to musketry if the enemy appeared resolute; while defenders who relied solely on fire – not supporting it with a ready counter-attack with the bayonet – might halt the enemy's attack only to produce a prolonged firefight. Far more important than the formations employed or calculations of casualties inflicted by musketry, was the underlying quality and confidence of the troops, their coolness and good order, the leadership of their officers and all the other factors which influenced their morale at the moment.

INFANTRY IN ACTION

The way these elements combined in action can best be seen by examining a few combats in some detail. The decisive French attack at Austerlitz was the advance on to the Pratzen plateau led by the divisions of Saint-Hilaire and Vandamme in Soult's corps. Brigadier Thiébault, who commanded one of the three brigades in Saint-Hilaire's division, has given us a full account of his part in the early stages of the battle. It is rather vainglorious and not all its details agree with other contemporary accounts, but the broad outline seems to be accurate, and it gives an interesting picture of French tactics at their best.

Thiébault's brigade consisted of two regiments of infantry: the 14th and 36th *Ligne*, each of two battalions. Their strength on the day of battle is not known, but it was probably approaching 3,000 men, of whom a good half were veterans, and all had drilled together for years at Boulogne, developing great *esprit de corps*. Of the other two brigades, one, commanded by General Varé, was detached to support Vandamme's division; the other was a weak brigade of a single regiment – the 10th *Léger*, perhaps 1,500 men in two battalions – under General Morand.

At daybreak on 2 December Soult gave the order to advance. Morand, advancing on Thiébault's right, was instructed to occupy the plateau while Thiébault drove the enemy out of the village of Pratzen before joining him. The French thought that the village would only be occupied by allied pickets and seem to have advanced rather carelessly, the 1/14th leading the way in line, supported some distance to the rear by the remaining three battalions in column. Strangely, neither skirmishers nor scouts preceded their advance. As Colonel Mazas and the 1/14th were approaching the village, a Russian battalion suddenly sprang to its feet 'and poured such a murderous fire almost point blank into him that in their surprise and alarm the whole 1st battalion of the 14th broke and fled'. Thiébault quickly ordered the two battalions of the 36th to attack the village, thus presumably threatening the Russians' retreat, while he attacked frontally with the 2nd battalion of the 14th, which deployed into line as it ran forward. This attack was completely successful, though it is not clear if it involved any real fighting, or if the outnumbered Russians withdrew in the face of the renewed French advance. Among other points worth noting are the effectiveness of surprise – which largely accounts for the 1/14th's panic – and the French use of line.

The attack on the village had delayed Thiébault's advance, leaving Morand to face superior enemy forces. General Saint-Hilaire, commander of the division, who had been with Morand, now arrived in search of reinforcements, and left with the 1/14th which had rallied quickly after its discomfiture. (It had not been pursued, could rally behind friendly troops and had probably not sustained many casualties despite the 'murderous fire' of the Russians: Thiébault was fond of extravagant language.) The rest of the brigade followed as soon as the three successful battalions had been restored to order.

As he approached Morand's position, Thiébault noticed a large unidentified force – which he estimated as 'four regiments in close order' – approaching Morand's exposed flank. Neither he nor Saint-Hilaire could identify these troops, and their suspicions were not allayed when a mounted officer galloped to within shouting distance and called out, 'Do not fire; we are Bavarians,' but did not join them. Thiébault quickly deployed his men so that they joined Morand's line at an angle and protected his flank. The 36th deployed into line with three guns from the divisional battery between the two battalions. The 2/14th remained in column so as to protect the open flank of the 36th, and be ready to mount a counter-attack. Just at this moment Major Fontenay arrived with six twelve-pounders sent, Thiébault insists, by the Emperor, though other sources give the credit to Marshal Soult. The battery was divided with three guns at each end of the 36th's line; they were screened by some infantry and 'double-shotted', that is, loaded with both canister and round-shot simultaneously. The unidentified force was still approaching slowly without firing a shot, and as his preparations were now complete, Thiébault rode out to reconnoitre them – and met Morand who had the same idea. What they saw convinced them that the approaching troops were indeed hostile, and both commanders hurried back to their brigades, where Thiébault instructed his men 'to take good aim before firing, and to aim at the men's belts and the centre of the sections, so as to waste no shots'.

According to Thiébault, he let the enemy approach to within 'thirty or forty yards' before suddenly opening fire, though it seems highly unlikely that the range was really this short. Whatever the range, the sudden fire, unexpectedly supported by nine cannon 'served with incredible smartness', may well have been devastating. Thiébault says that the allied troops broke and fled, and tests our credulity by adding, 'I had not lost a single man, and if I had had a brigade of cavalry at my disposal not one of my assailants would have escaped.' Austrian sources identify Thiébault's opponents as two brigades of very poor troops – invalids and untrained recruits – so it is possible that they did break at the first attack, although they seem to have rallied and fought well later on. For the battle was far from over, and Thiébault's brigade still had its hardest fighting to come. Saint-Hilaire's division was repeatedly attacked from two sides and had to give ground slowly in the face of superior numbers. Unfortunately Thiébault gives us few details of this fighting, although he expresses some of the feeling of the moment when he writes, 'we had no news either of the imperial headquarters nor of Marshal Soult, and it was with a certain anxiety that we became convinced of our isolation'. But at last the allied attacks slackened, and the battered French battalions were able to drive them back.

Thiébault is inclined to exaggerate the losses of his brigade, claiming that his two regiments 'had two-thirds of their officers killed or wounded; while of the 236 grenadiers of the 36th, seventeen only remained with the colours in the evening'. Martinien's lists confirm that the officers lost heavily: two were killed, a third died of his wounds two days after the battle, and no fewer than forty more were wounded. Evidently the brigade suffered severely, though without better figures for its strength that morning it is difficult to make an estimate of its overall losses.[53]

Thiébault's experiences at Austerlitz act as a useful corrective to oversimplified accounts of French tactics. He used a mixture of column and line, shock and firepower, according to the circumstances of the moment. Not everything went well: the initial advance on the village of Pratzen was careless, the absence of any mention of skirmishers is surprising, and, on a wider view, the lack of supporting troops advancing behind Saint-Hilaire suggests a flaw in Napoleon's dispositions. But these criticisms are completely outweighed by the credit side of the ledger, above all by the great flexibility of the French forces. This reflected both the high quality of the infantry and a very effective command structure. At every point the French showed an ability to react quickly to events without confusion or disorder, Saint-Hilaire co-operating well with his brigadiers. The close support provided by the artillery was evidently crucial, and is another sign of how well the army as a whole was working. The contrast between the smooth functioning of the French commanders and the confusion in allied ranks is striking, and represents probably the greatest advantage the French had over their adversaries in these years. For the allies were very slow to develop effective systems of higher command, and as a result their attacks tended to be slow, awkward and poorly co-ordinated.

The French army declined in the years after 1807. Too many new conscripts were added, with insufficient training; experienced and capable officers were spread too thinly, and more reliance was placed on allied contingents, mainly from the small German and Italian states. Some of these units were individually good, but it was difficult to integrate them into the army and their presence led to a loss of cohesion and flexibility. The high standards set at Boulogne slowly faded, as did the early enthusiasm and zest for war. French tactics reflected the decline, becoming less supple and precise and relying more on heavier formations and weight of numbers. Yet this decline should not be overstated: it was not uniform throughout the army, and as late as 1812 many of Marmont's divisions manoeuvred with skill and fought with tenacity at Salamanca, despite being taken at a great disadvantage. But the disaster in Russia destroyed Napoleon's main army, while the forces in Spain were deprived of many thousands of experienced officers, NCOs and soldiers – who were used to form the cadre of new units – and as a result fought poorly in 1813.

This decline in the French army was one factor in the failure of Masséna's attack on Wellington's position at Busaco (27 September 1810). One episode in the battle – Loison's attack on the Light Division – is often regarded as the

archetypal case of 'column versus line in the Peninsula', although it was complicated by a number of other influences. Loison's division had around 6,700
officers and men (6,826 in a return dated 15 September), who were mostly
either foreign troops – the Légion du Midi (Piedmontese) and the Hanoverian
Legion – or 4th, 5th, 6th or even 7th battalions of French regiments. They were
not veterans of the *Grande Armée* or the Camp at Boulogne, though some had
served in that unhappy army of raw conscripts which Junot had led into
Portugal in 1807 and the British had defeated at Roliça and Vimeiro.

Loison's men pushed up the high, steep slopes of the Serra do Busaco under
heavy fire from Craufurd's skirmishers (see above, pp. 60–61). Little is known
of their formation – one early account speaks of two columns, others of only one
– but the distribution of their casualties strongly suggests that Simon's brigade
was in the lead, possibly a good distance ahead of Ferey's brigade. Clambering
up such a steep slope under heavy fire, it is likely that they became strung out,
perhaps with gaps opening between regiments. Many skirmishers were sent out
to drive back the British riflemen and Portuguese caçadores – possibly the
whole of the 26th *Ligne* (three battalions) which would normally be the leading
regiment in Simon's brigade. One battalion of Ferey's brigade (the 2/32nd
Léger) took a divergent path and was eventually repulsed by Coleman's
Portuguese, quite separately from the rest of the division.

As the French approached the summit they came under heavy fire from
Ross's guns which, according to George Napier, 'threw such a heavy fire of
shrapnel-shells, and so quick, that their column . . . was put into a good deal of
confusion and lost great numbers'. Nonetheless the French pressed on and the
British gunners fell back, though it is not clear whether they temporarily
abandoned their guns or were able to withdraw them. As the total losses of all
the British artillery (not including King's German Legion or Portuguese) in the
whole battle were one man killed and seven wounded, it is evident that they
withdrew in good time and did not persist to the last.[54]

Craufurd kept his main line – the strong battalions of the 43rd and 52nd,
1,800 officers and men – on a protected shelf of level ground on the forward
slope of the ridge, some way from its summit. After the French had driven off
the British artillery, they halted for a few moments to catch their breath and
restore some order to their leading ranks before making the final ascent. According to Captain Leach, there were signs that they were about to form line at this
point, but none of the other sources mentions this, and it seems unlikely if, as
Leach goes on to say, the French were convinced that they were facing nothing
more than skirmishers.[55]

In any case, they seem to have resumed their advance in one, or possibly two,
columns; certainly not in line. As they approached the spot where Craufurd was
observing their progress, 'he turned round, came up to the 52nd, and called out,
"Now, 52nd, revenge the death of Sir John Moore! Charge, charge! Huzza!"
and waving his hat in the air he was answered by a shout that appalled the
enemy.' This at least is the account of George Napier, who was present on the

day, but who wrote his memoirs many years later. His brother William, the historian, was also present, and he supports the story in general terms, though he does not repeat the words. The sequence of events which followed is rather confused and surprising, but it seems that all the British infantry advanced to the edge of the shelf on which they were standing, and that the four companies immediately facing the head of the French column (or columns) charged without firing. George Napier, whose company was one of these four, explicitly says that he formed his company in column of sections 'in order to give more force to our rush'. The French, shocked at the sudden appearance of the British, and daunted by their confident cheer and charge, broke and were pursued for a short distance. Then the four companies were halted – with difficulty – and some of the other companies which had swept forward on each flank of the French fired, in William Napier's words, 'three terrible discharges at five yards' distance' before the four companies again charged forward, pursuing the French to the bottom of the hill.[56]

The earliest and best account of these few minutes of intense action comes in a letter written by Lieutenant Charles Booth of the 43rd, written only a few weeks after the battle. It is worth quoting at length, both for the interesting details he adds, and to show the difficulty of reconstructing the exact sequence of events. He is, incidentally, the only witness to state that the French were in two columns.

In the part of the line occupied by the Light Division and about 200 yards immediately to its front two columns of the enemy – supposed about 5,000 each – were met by the two left-hand companies of the 43rd, and the right two of the 52nd. The front of their columns alone – chiefly composed of officers – stood the charge; the rest took to their heels, throwing away their arms, pouches, &c. Our men did not stand to take prisoners; what were taken were those left in our rear in the hurry of pressing forward in the charge. The flanks of the 43rd and 52nd in their charge met only the enemy's skirmishers who had by superior numbers driven in the 95th Rifles but a few seconds before the charge of the division. These poor fellows were all glad enough to give themselves up as prisoners, our men not being allowed to fire a shot at them. The advanced part of the charging line – the four companies first mentioned – after throwing themselves into the midst of the enemy's retreating columns, killing, wounding, and in short felling to the ground lots of them, were with great difficulty halted, and then commenced from the flanks of the whole division the most destructive flanking fire that I believe was ever witnessed. Not a tenth part of their whole force would have escaped had not the four companies, by precipitating themselves too far in front of the general line, exposed themselves to the fire of their comrades, and thus prevented more than 300 firelocks on each flank of the division from being brought into action. The flanks, and in fact every other part of the division (except the four centre companies), had to pass over in the charge some very steep rugged ground, where, not meeting anything but the enemy's skirmishers, they pushed on head-over-heels, until the descent became almost perpendicular. At this time they were halted, and had a fine view of what was going on in the centre.[57]

Loison's division sustained 1,253 casualties during the battle – or 1,140 if those of the 2/32nd *Léger*, which fought separately, are deducted. Of these 1,140, 812 were from Simon's brigade, which lost over 24 per cent of its strength, compared to under 11 per cent in Ferey's brigade. The single battalion of the Légion du Midi in Simon's brigade lost over 50 per cent of its strength, suggesting that it bore the brunt of the British counter-attack. Further, these returns seem to make no allowance for the men captured, which British estimates put at between 150 and 300, including General Simon himself, although it is possible that the missing men were listed as wounded (the proportion of killed is rather low). By contrast the 43rd and the 52nd sustained only twenty-four casualties between them (three men killed, three officers and eighteen men wounded), while the Light Division as a whole had 177 casualties.[58]

The defeat of Loison's division was so comprehensive because many ingredients contributed to it. There was the yawning gap in quality between the elite of Wellington's army and the rag-tag odds and ends which made up the French division. There was the immense strength of the position which slowed the French advance and ensured that when their men finally approached the summit, they would be out of breath and in disorder. And there was Craufurd's skilful use of skirmishers and the excellent close support provided by the artillery. Compared to these factors, the disadvantages of the French formation in column seem almost irrelevant. Loison could hardly have advanced up such a slope in line, for this would have required constant halts to dress the ranks, thus depriving his men of all forward momentum and exposing them for much longer to skirmisher and artillery fire. He might have advanced in column and intended to deploy into line if he encountered serious opposition, but the British kept their main line well hidden, and any attempt to change formation close to the enemy was fraught with risk – inviting a counter-attack which would catch the French neither in column nor in line. And even if the French succeeded in forming line, it would not ensure success. Suppose Simon's brigade, out of breath from its climb and having already suffered heavily, had managed to form line, would it then have held its nerve when faced by 1,800 fresh British infantry charging downhill at short range, and expressing their confidence in three raucous cheers? It seems much more likely that its men would have fired a ragged volley – more effective than that which they actually fired, but still not nearly effective enough to halt the British – and then taken to their heels. Loison's defeat was far from being the result of a simple confrontation between column and line on equal terms.

Busaco showed Wellington's defensive tactics at their best: the choice of battlefield, the skilful occupation of the ground, and the vigorous counter-attack based on surprise which drove the French back in disorder. But not all his battles were so one-sided, and at Talavera, the previous year, the French had come close to victory. Here, on 27 and 28 July 1809, a French army of about 45,000 men (46,138 on 15 July) confronted Wellington's 20,000 British and King's German Legion troops, together with Cuesta's 32,000 Spaniards. The allied position ran from the town of Talavera through olive groves and enclosures then open country to the steep hill of the Cerro de Medellin, with the British army occupying the hill and open ground, while Cuesta defended the more broken terrain nearer the town. On the evening of the 27th, and again early on the 28th, Victor made two partial attacks on the Cerro de Medellin which were beaten back with heavy loss after some confused fighting. There followed a lull in the battle. King Joseph and his advisers were at first reluctant to renew the action, but the arrival of news that Venegas was threatening Madrid and that Soult's march against Wellington's communications had been delayed forced their hand, and they decided on an attack all along the line.

Wellington prepared for a new French attack by strengthening his left wing beyond the Cerro de Medellin, borrowing a division of infantry, a battery of twelve-pounders and, later, Alburquerque's cavalry from Cuesta. But the main blow was to fall in the centre, in the open ground between the lower slopes of the hill and the olive groves. This part of the allied line was held by Sherbrooke's division: Low and Langwerth's brigades of the King's German Legion closest to the hill, then Cameron's British brigade (1/61st and 2/83rd), and Campbell's brigade of Guards (1/Coldstreams, 1/3rd Guards – both very strong battalions), altogether almost 6,000 men, although Low's brigade had suffered quite badly in the earlier French attacks. Beyond Sherbrooke to the south lay another, weaker British division, and then the Spanish army, while to the rear, acting as supports, lay Mackenzie's brigade of infantry and two regiments of Light Dragoons. There were two batteries of artillery in the front line – each comprising five six-pounders – in front of Langwerth's and Cameron's brigades, and a third battery in reserve behind Langwerth's brigade.

Attacking Sherbrooke's position were two strong divisions – about 15,000 men in twenty-four battalions commanded by Lapisse and Sebastiani. These were good troops, veterans of the *Grande Armée* who had served in the campaigns of 1805–7 and entered Spain in late 1808. Four years of hard service had taken their toll: they were not as fresh, flexible or enthusiastic as they had been in 1805 or 1806 when they had campaigned under the Emperor's eye, but they were hardy veterans, much tougher than Loison's men at Busaco. Further south, Leval's division (nine battalions of German infantry) made a supporting attack.

The French attack began with a sustained artillery bombardment from eighty guns lasting about an hour which completely overwhelmed the allied artillery. Sherbrooke's men had little cover but endured the ordeal stoically, leading an ensign in the 3rd Guards to write home:

I witnessed courage beyond what I could have conceived . . . a tremendous cannonade – shots and shells were falling in every direction – but none of the enemy were to be seen – the men were all the while lying in the ranks, and except at the very spot where a shot or shell fell, there was not the least motion – I have seen men killed in the ranks by cannon shots – those immediately round the spot would remove the mutilated corpse to the rear, they would then lie down as if nothing had occurred and remain in the ranks, steady as before. That common men could be brought to face the greatest danger, there is a spirit which tells me it is possible, but I could not believe that they could be brought to remain without emotion, when attacked, not knowing from whence. Such, however, was the conduct of our men (I speak particularly of the Brigade [of Guards]) on 28 July, and from this steadiness so few suffered as by remaining quiet the shots bounded over their heads.[59]

Unfortunately there is no way of assessing the losses inflicted by this bombardment, though the final comment quoted suggests that they may have been less than we might otherwise expect. This impression receives some independent confirmation from the regimental history of the 24th; in Mackenzie's brigade: 'The men fell fast from shot and shell. The brigade was therefore ordered to lie down, and then the roundshot did little damage, but the shells annoyed the men much.' However the German Legion brigades, which were closer to the French guns on the Cascajal heights opposite the Cerro de Medellin, probably lost more heavily. Whatever the casualties, the strain of remaining quiet under fire was considerable, and the allied troops probably felt some relief when the guns fell silent as the French infantry moved forward.[60]

There is some uncertainty about how the French were formed for their attack, though most sources are agreed that each division was divided into two equal waves. The first wave of twelve battalions (six from each division) was probably formed by a line of individual battalion columns, each with a frontage of two companies. They were screened and supported by skirmishers, and there was enough space for the columns to have sufficient intervals to enable them to deploy into three-deep line – although there is no suggestion that they did so. The second wave of twelve battalions was held well back, acting as the support or reserve for the attack. It may also have been formed in individual battalion columns, though some sources suggest a heavier formation – perhaps regimental columns.

The French advanced across open ground and then the gully of the Portina brook, driving the British light infantry before them. Sherbrooke had given orders that his men were not to fire until the enemy came within fifty yards, and then were to give a single volley and immediately charge. According to John Aitchison, the Guards ensign already quoted, the neighbouring brigades obeyed this order, but the Guards did not. In a letter written three days after the battle he says, 'On their approaching within two hundred yards we were ordered to advance without firing a shot and afterwards to charge this *we* did as became British officers.' And he repeats the point a few weeks later with a slight variation: 'In the centre where at last the enemy made his grand push, we charged when he was within 100 yards, and our fire was reserved until they were flying.' Faced with such explicit contemporary testimony from both Talavera and Busaco, it is hard to doubt that the British sometimes relied entirely on their charge to break the French, and did not fire until after they had broken. But Sherbrooke's orders, which were apparently followed by the other brigades in his division – though they may have fired more than the single volley he specified – show that the more customary pattern of firing before charging was also used.[61]

The French line was broken despite the fact that they were good troops who had suffered few if any casualties before they began their attack. The ground was not unfavourable to them, nor were they taken by surprise by the appearance of the British troops. Rather they seem to have been intimidated by the cool discipline and steadiness of Sherbrooke's line which impassively watched their approach. A French account, published in 1824, describes events from their perspective:

> The French charged with shouldered arms as was their custom. When they arrived at short range, and the English line remained motionless, some hesitation was seen in the march. The officers and NCOs shouted at the soldiers, 'Forward; March; don't fire'. Some even cried, 'They're surrendering'. The forward movement was therefore resumed; but it was not until extremely close range of the English line that the latter started a two rank fire which carried destruction into the heart of the French line, stopped its movement, and produced some disorder. While the officers shouted to the soldiers 'Forward: Don't fire' (although firing set in nevertheless), the English suddenly stopped their own fire and charged with the bayonet. Everything was favourable to them; orderliness, impetus, and the resolution to fight with the bayonet. Among the French, on the other hand, there was no longer any impetus, but disorder and surprise caused by the enemy's unexpected resolve: flight was inevitable.[62]

But this was not the end of the fighting in the centre, for Sherbrooke's men pursued the French with wild enthusiasm. Only Cameron's brigade halted just beyond the Portina brook: the other three brigades continued the chase in complete disorder, and were soon vulnerable to a counter-attack. The French artillery on the Cascajal heights opened a heavy enfilading fire on Low and Langwerth's brigades, inflicting very heavy casualties, while Latour-Maubourg's dragoons threatened the right flank of the Guards. The second wave of Lapisse and Sebastiani's divisions now moved against the scattered, breathless men, and the hunters became the hunted.[63]

According to Aitchison, the Guards fell back in fairly good order: 'we faced about, retired to the ravine, slower and in better order than we advanced. Here we made a stand and did considerable execution' before being again forced to retreat. Other sources disagree, but there is no doubt that the Guards did not lose as heavily as the German Legion, which was completely routed:

the whole of their infantry ran fairly away. Poor Langwerth seized the colours and, planting them, called to the men to form. He was killed in attempting to rally them. Colonel Derenham was equally unsuccessful. He got 40 or 50 round the colours but the instant he went to collect others these set up. Had not the 16th [Light Dragoons] been moved up opportunely there would have been a gap left in the line. The Germans formed in our rear.[64]

The breaking of Sherbrooke's division left Wellington with a yawning hole in his line and the entire battle in jeopardy. He had to find troops to fill the gap temporarily, in order to give Sherbrooke's men time to rally. Behind the Guards was Mackenzie's brigade which was supported by two battalions of Spanish infantry.[65] Cameron's brigade had not advanced so far, and may have remained in reasonable order. The greatest problem was to replace the four battalions of the King's German Legion, which had suffered most in the impetuous advance. Wellington did not dare detach a whole brigade from the Cerro de Medellin, but sent down a single strong battalion, the 1/48th, which had begun the day with nearly 800 men, though it had seen some fighting in the earlier French attack. Otherwise there were the two regiments of Light Dragoons who covered the last stages of the Germans' retreat, three batteries (fifteen guns) in the immediate area, and the possibility of enfilade fire and flanking attacks from the troops on the Cerro de Medellin. Evidently this was enough, for Lapisse's division does not seem to have pressed its second attack. The two regiments of cavalry suffered only fourteen and fifteen casualties in the whole battle, and Cocks, who was with the 16th Light Dragoons, makes no mention of them coming under heavy fire or charging. Even the 1/48th had only 168 casualties in the day, some of them in the morning, which does not suggest that it engaged in repulsing a determined attack from six French battalions.[66]

Mackenzie's brigade however was seriously engaged, for Sebastiani's second line pursued the Guards with great enthusiasm. Once protected, the Guards rallied quickly, but the task of checking Sebastiani fell mainly on Mackenzie's 2,000 infantry. The French attacked in column, but were halted by the British fire, and, as neither side could summon the resolution to charge, a furious firefight developed which is said to have lasted for about twenty minutes. In such a situation, as Oman remarks, the line always had an advantage over troops in column, but it seems that the deadlock was only broken when a regiment of Spanish cavalry charged the left flank of Sebastiani's division, inflicting some 150 casualties.[67]

The losses on both sides were heavy. 'The gallant General Mackenzie, the man who did more than anyone towards our victory, is killed', as Cocks wrote home. In his brigade, seventy-four men had been killed, 519 wounded and thirty-nine were missing – a total of 632 casualties, to which must be added the 153 sustained on the previous day, bringing its combined losses to more than one-third of its strength. The Guards lost equally heavily, and Cameron's brigade more so as a proportion of its strength, though this amounted to fewer actual casualties. The two German brigades suffered even more: Langwerth's brigade lost 106 killed, 590 wounded and twenty-five missing: 721 in all, or over 50 per cent of its strength, on the 28th, while Low's situation was nearly as severe, with heavy losses on the 27th as well as on the 28th, including large numbers of men missing on both days. Altogether the five brigades in Wellington's centre sustained 2,881 casualties, or 36.7 per cent of their strength, on 28 July alone.

The French suffered even higher losses, though distributed among larger forces. Lapisse was mortally wounded, and in Sebastiani's division all four colonels and seven of the twelve battalion-chiefs were killed or wounded. Altogether, in the two divisions 403 men were killed, 3,481 wounded and sixty-three missing: a total of 3,947 casualties, or 26.3 per cent of the force.[68]

The failure of the French attack reflected no discredit on their troops, who had fought extremely well. It might be argued that they would have been more successful if they had attacked in line, but at Maida in 1806, when good French infantry did attack in line, it was defeated in just the same way. At Talavera, the French came near to success because their initial attack was well supported by a large number of troops kept back in the second wave, who were able to take advantage of the confusion in Sherbrooke's line when his men pursued too far. This, rather than the decision to attack in column, points to the real flaws in other French attacks in the Peninsula: they advanced without proper reconnaissance, without overcoming the allied light infantry, or shaking the allied line through skirmisher or artillery fire, and without adequate support, so that when the first wave of columns was broken they had no troops available to strike a second blow before the British could recover their poise. It is hard not to believe that these mistakes were due to arrogance and carelessness born from years of victory. But they did not last long, for after the battles of 1808–10 French generals learnt their lesson and repeatedly refused to attack Wellington frontally in positions of his choosing: at Fuentes de Oñoro, the Caya, the heights of San Cristobal, and, on the retreat from Burgos, at Salamanca. In 1813, Sorauren and the Nive were partial exceptions, but in each case Soult was trying to use large numbers of poor troops to overwhelm an isolated portion of Wellington's army. This leaves only Waterloo, where Napoleon left the tactical conduct of the battle to subordinates – Ney, d'Erlon, and Reille – who were rich in experience of the difficulties of fighting the British, but who nonetheless repeated all the old errors and devised some new ones.

The fighting at Busaco and Talavera shows how both firepower and the threatened shock of a charge were integral to British tactics. Loison's leading unit was broken by the British charge, but the rout of the whole force was assisted by the 'three terrible discharges' fired into its flanks. At Talavera the Guards charged their opponents without firing, but the other brigades fired at least one round before they charged – and the French account quoted above shows how important this fire was in undermining French cohesion and resolve. Mackenzie's brigade halted the renewed French advance by the use of fire alone, but its heavy losses show the cost of a sustained firefight. The relative importance of fire and shock varied according to the circumstances of each individual encounter, and an exclusive reliance on either element would have opened the way for defeat. Wellington's infantry was successful because it was so good at both, ever ready, even when on the defensive, to charge forward with the bayonet, but just as capable of withholding its fire until the enemy was within devastatingly short range.

Many of Wellington's later battles proved that these qualities were equally useful in attack. Indeed Wellington's offensive tactics share many elements with his methods of defence. There was the same careful appreciation of the ground, the same use of a heavy screen of skirmishers, and the same reliance on infantry in line. Not that the British invariably advanced in line: at Vitoria in 1813 Robinson's brigade of Picton's division attacked and carried a village in column, while as dedicated a light infantry officer as Harry Smith felt that the British attack in line at Redhina in 1811 'was heavy, slow, and not half so destructive as a rush of many contiguous columns would have been'.[69] But in general the British were well satisfied with their tactics, believing that they had mastered the art of advancing rapidly in line, even over rough ground, without too much disorder. In part this reflected the quality of their troops, thorough discipline, good training, and underlying confidence. But equally important was the development of effective larger units – particularly divisions – which could manoeuvre independently of each other on a front of a few battalions while still providing mutual support. Jomini asked rhetorically, 'Can an immense deployed line be moved up into action while firing?' and responded:

> I think no one will answer affirmatively. Suppose the attempt made to bring up twenty or thirty battalions in line, while firing either by file or by company, to the assault of a well-defended position: it is not very probable that they would ever reach the desired point, or if they did, it would be in about as good order as a flock of sheep.[70]

But Wellington achieved this in many of his later battles by making two crucial changes to Jomini's formula. He broke down his line into a series of sub-units – usually divisions – which supported each other while moving relatively independently. These divisions, wherever possible, were formed in two separate lines, so that supports were immediately on hand if their flanks were threatened, or if the first line was disrupted, whether by success or by failure. And he expected his men to withhold their fire as they advanced for as long as possible, and then – if they could be brought to do it – to fire a single volley, or at most a few rounds, and then to charge while they still retained some of their forward momentum and were in reasonable order.

The attack of Leith's division at Salamanca provides a good example of how this worked in practice. The activity of its skirmishers has already been described (see above, pp. 62–3). The main body of the division was formed in two long lines, each of two-deep infantry. The first line comprised Greville's brigade (3/1st, 1/9th, 1 and 2/38th) and part of the 1/4th from Pringle's brigade brought forward to equalize the lines – about 2,600 rank and file after deducting the light companies. The second line contained the remainder of Pringle's brigade and the four line battalions of Spry's Portuguese brigade – about 2,800 rank and file. According to Andrew Leith Hay this second line was about 100 yards behind the first – closer than one would expect, for if the first line were broken, its flight would surely have disrupted the second. His account of the attack is worth quoting at length:

> The confident presence of the enemy was now exchanged for the quiet formation proceeding in his ranks, as preparatives for resisting the evidently approaching shock. His columns, retired from the crest of the height, were formed in squares, about fifty yards removed from the ground, on which, when arrived, the British regiments would become visible. The French artillery, although placed more to the rear, still poured its fire on the advancing troops. . . .
>
> . . . We were now near the summit of the ridge. The men marched with the same orderly steadiness as at first: no advance in line at a review was ever more correctly executed: the dressing was admirable, and spaces were no sooner formed by casualties than closed up with the most perfect regularity, and without the slightest deviation from the order of march.
>
> General Leith, and the officers of his staff, being on horseback, first perceived the enemy, and had time to observe his formation, previous to the infantry line becoming so visible, as to induce him to commence firing. He was drawn up in contiguous columns, the front rank kneeling, and prepared to fire when the drum beat for its commencement. All was still and quiet in these columns; – not a musket was discharged until the whole opened. Nearly at the same moment General Leith ordered the line to fire, and charge: the roll of musketry was succeeded by that proud cheer that has become habitual to British soldiers on similar occasions – that to an enemy tremendous sound, which may without doubt be termed the note of victory. . . . In an instant every individual present was enveloped in smoke and obscurity. No struggle for ascendency now took place; resistance was vain; the French squares were penetrated, broken and discomfited; the victorious division pressed forward, not against troops opposed, but a mass of disorganized men, overpowered and flying in all directions.[71]

The destruction of Maucune's division was completed by the magnificent charge of the British heavy cavalry under General Le Marchant. Leith's division seems to have halted and re-formed soon after its attack; it collected many prisoners, and when it resumed its advance it appears (the sources are rather vague on the point) that the second line – Pringle's brigade and the Portuguese – now led the way. It saw little further fighting in the battle.

Why did this British attack succeed where French attacks had failed? Wellington had attacked suddenly, catching the French at a disadvantage. Maucune's division was unsupported and occupied a longer front than it could hold. Its battalions were probably deployed in squares, as Leith Hay says, to protect them from Le Marchant's cavalry, although some other British accounts state that they were in column. In either case they were not in line and so could not maximize the advantages of being on the defensive. Nonetheless their fire was not insignificant: in Leith's first line fifty-one officers and men were killed; 367 were wounded and one went missing: 419 casualties in all or 14 per cent of its strength. This was for the whole battle, but the great bulk of the casualties were probably incurred in this advance and attack. Nor were the losses spread evenly: two of the battalions in the front line lost lightly (1/9th lost 6.9 per cent; 1/4th only 3.9 per cent), while the brunt of the losses were borne by just three battalions (1 and 2/38th lost 17.9 and 17.3 per cent respectively, 3/1st lost 21 per cent). Although the troops in the second line would have suffered from French artillery and stray shots in their advance, and their light companies had joined in the skirmishing, they sustained less than half the casualties of the first line (6.9 per cent for the remainder of Pringle's brigade, 5.3 per cent for the Portuguese).[72]

This fire might have caused lesser troops to hesitate, but Leith's division – and the whole of Wellington's army – was in excellent condition and full of confidence. Most of the troops were veterans (though the 1/38th had only just joined the army) and their officers and commanders had learnt much in the years of campaigning. Wellington's care during four years in the Peninsula had given his army an unbroken record of success, adding wonderfully to the sound foundations laid in 1803–5. But though very good, his infantry was not invincible. Ferey's division, properly deployed in a good position, checked Clinton's advance. And Cole's division, deployed in a single line on Leith's left, was initially successful, but became disordered and was broken by a French counter-attack.

The quality of Leith's infantry was shown by their ability to advance rapidly in line while retaining good order; possibly in the effectiveness of their fire (though by taking a position a little behind the crest of the – very gentle – slope, the French ensured that the first volley for both sides would be at short range); and by the confident cheer and willingness to charge as soon as they had fired. This quality underpinned all Wellington's tactics and explains their most distinctive characteristic: the search for a sharp decisive combat at short range, rather than a long-drawn-out battle of attrition. At its best this produced excellent results very cheaply: the Light Division sustained only 177 casualties at Busaco; Leith only 629 at Salamanca, and in each case the opposing division was rendered incapable of any further serious fighting in the battle. Defence, in Wellington's capable hands at least, was both more certain and cheaper than attack, especially in the early years of the war when his cavalry was weak and his infantry was still building its confidence. For, like any good general, Wellington tailored his tactics to suit his army, taking risks in 1813–14 which he would not have considered in earlier years.

Napoleon was equally quick to adjust to the changes in his army, though in his case the troops were declining rather than improving in quality. The French army at Wagram was not as good as the army at Austerlitz and could not be expected to perform to the same standard, while the army at Dresden was still worse. This decline in quality led to a loss of tactical flexibility and greater deployment in depth, as well as increasing emphasis on the use of artillery.

At the same time the allied armies were also changing. They developed more effective higher formations, and their intermediate and senior officers – particularly at the brigade, divisional and corps level – improved with experience. But on the other hand, the quality of the ordinary soldiers actually declined, especially in 1813–14, as the well-drilled veterans were swamped by a huge influx of raw conscripts. Radetzky, the Austrian chief of staff, complained in 1813 that barely one-third of the army was properly trained, the remainder being no more than 'peasants in uniform'.[73] Such troops were clearly incapable of complicated evolutions, rapid changes of formation or advances in line: their tactics had to be kept brutally simple and direct. They were also, inevitably, unreliable, and in these campaigns the allies copied the French in forming their divisions and corps in great depth, so that if one layer of troops broke and fled there was a second, third and even fourth layer behind them to contain the damage. This in turn led to protracted battles of attrition as both sides sought to wear down the enemy army. Soldiers are not uniform automata, and the heart of tactics lies not in formations or drill, but in understanding what any particular army can achieve.

Any analysis of Napoleonic combat inevitably and necessarily simplifies it in order to make it comprehensible, just as most first-hand accounts play down the confusion of the moment in order to produce a readily understood narrative. The reality was more messy. Infantry formations were less perfect than they appear on paper, men were frightened, shouted, perhaps abused their officers or tried to fall out of the ranks. Even the relatively sharp, decisive fighting in the Peninsula was less simple than it appears at first – and our sources contain frequent contradictions and anomalies. Most battles – though not all – contained a great deal of indecisive fighting: skirmishing at long range, or half-hearted advances which petered out while still hundreds of yards from the enemy. An officer in d'Erlon's corps at Waterloo describes the later stages of the battle:

> we again descended into the hollow to renew our attack on the plateau where we had been already so roughly handled. We there found our old antagonists as much weakened as ourselves, so ere long the attack resolved itself into a desultory skirmishing fight, which continued for some time with no serious results, for the vital question was destined to be decided on another part of the ground.[74]

But although these troops were not engaged in making or resisting the final critical attack which would decide the fate of the battle, their actions were not irrelevant, for their fighting wore away at the cohesion of both armies, exhausting the troops and absorbing the reserves, preparing the way for the collapse of purpose and discipline, as one army or the other accepted defeat and disintegrated in a rout.

Chapter Six
Cavalry Combat

ORGANIZATION, EQUIPMENT AND TRAINING

The third element in every army of the period was cavalry – the most expensive and prestigious of the three arms – powerful, sometimes decisive on the battle-field, and indispensable on campaign. In the main theatre of operations – commonly the battlefields of central Europe, but extending as far west as France and Belgium and as far east as Moscow – cavalry generally amounted to between 10 and 20 per cent of an army's effective strength. In the Peninsula, especially after 1809, the figure was lower, between 5 and 15 per cent, although in each case there were exceptions in both directions.

Cavalry formed in regiments which brought a number of squadrons (most commonly three or four) into the field, each squadron in turn being divided into several troops, companies or platoons. Squadrons had considerably more tactical independence than infantry companies, and were often detached on quite separate duties, so that it becomes a debatable point whether they or the regiment were the basic tactical unit. Higher organization mirrored that of infantry, although the number of sub-units and men at each level was generally smaller. Two or three regiments formed a brigade, two (or rarely three) brigades formed a cavalry division, and two or three divisions might be grouped into a corps of cavalry. The structure was not rigid, and sometimes one layer might be left out: for example, in Napoleon's army at Wagram, both Grouchy and Pully commanded divisions of dragoons which each consisted of three regiments not organized into brigades. Many, but not all, brigades or divisions of cavalry had a battery of horse artillery attached to them. Not all armies followed the pattern precisely, with neither the Prussians nor the British making much use of any units higher than brigades for their cavalry.

The nominal strength of cavalry regiments varied widely from army to army, and year to year, from fewer than 800 men to more than 1,500. The effective strength in battle was much lower, commonly averaging around 500 in central Europe, and between 300 and 400 in the Peninsula after 1809 – though these figures are only rough approximations. At Wagram Napoleon's strongest line regiment was the 9th Cuirassiers with 776 officers and men – but the Chasseurs à Cheval of the Imperial Guard had 1,109. His weakest independent unit seems to have been the single squadron of the Prince Albert Chevauleger – 142 officers and men – in the Saxon corps. Similarly, at Waterloo, Wellington's strongest regiment was the 3rd Hussars of the King's German Legion with 875 all ranks, and his weakest was the 2nd Life Guards with 265. By contrast, at Salamanca, Wellington's strongest regiment – 2nd Dragoons, King's German Legion – had only 407 officers and men, and the average strength of his ten regiments of British and German cavalry was only 354 all ranks, while his two regiments of Portuguese cavalry did not amount to 500 men between them.[1]

Cavalry was divided into different types much more distinctly than infantry, although the roles and functions of the types showed considerable overlap. The principal, almost the only, function of heavy cavalry was to charge in battle. The epitome of the type was the French cuirassiers, perhaps the most famous cavalry of the period. 'Big men on big horses', they received the tallest and strongest of each year's conscripts and were an elite force second only to the Imperial Guard. A shortage of good horses meant that they were not at their best until 1807 when Napoleon's victories gave them access to the stud-farms of Germany and Poland. The privations of the Russian campaign (the advance as much as the retreat) dealt them a terrible blow, but the year's peace in 1814–15 allowed a recovery, and they performed well in 1815. Their armour – heavy steel breast and back plates, with a helmet, tough leather gauntlets and high boots – gave them considerable protection against swords, lances and pistols, although even the breast plate was not proof against musketry at short range. It required strength and experience to move freely while carrying this burden, and at Waterloo Captain Mercer noted that wounded (or thrown?) cuirassiers would take off some of their armour before hurrying to the rear.[2] Heavy though the armour was, it brought both practical and psychological advantages, protecting its wearer in a mêlée with other cavalry, and giving him more confidence to charge against infantry. Thus Marshal Marmont declared, 'To engage infantry, heavy and iron-clad cavalry is necessary, which is sufficiently protected and sheltered from the fire, so as to confront it fearlessly.' Some critics disagreed, with Captain Nolan, the famous advocate of light cavalry, arguing that the protection afforded by the armour was no compensation for the reduction of speed – and hence longer exposure to enemy fire – it caused. But their views failed to convince their contemporaries.[3]

Not all heavy cavalry wore armour: in the French army the two regiments of carabineers – who always regarded themselves as even more of an elite than the cuirassiers – did not get their distinctive gilt armour until 1809–10; while the *crème de la crème*, the Grenadiers à Cheval of the Imperial Guard, never wore armour at all, but permitted no doubts about the magnificence of their appearance, their effectiveness in action, or their weight. Most Continental armies equipped their heavy cavalry with cuirasses; the Austrians wore only a breast plate, and suffered severely from the lack of all-round protection in a famous engagement in 1809.[4] But no British cavalry wore armour until after Waterloo, when it was adopted by the Life Guards to the lasting delight of tourists in London.

The essence of heavy cavalry was not armour but the size and strength of the men and horses, and the confidence which went with it. Their task was simple: to plough their way across the battlefield regardless of any enemy in their path. They were superbly good at it, their size, appearance and reputation enabling them to deliver a more fearsome psychological, as well as physical, blow than any other troops.

Heavy cavalry were not for everyday use – they were too expensive and hard to replace to be used for anything other than their main role. Although Napoleon condemned a miserly attitude to cavalry and could use it with great extravagance in battle, he recognized – at least in theory – the need to protect it on campaign. With this in mind, he decided after the 1809 campaign to attach a regiment of light cavalry to each division of cuirassiers to take over the wearing tasks of scouting, skirmishing, providing escorts and orderlies for commanders and, in battle, pursuing the broken enemy, while the heavy cavalry rested their horses. This plan was adopted in 1812, but it may have proved less effective than it sounds, for it was not followed in 1815.

French heavy cavalry were almost unknown in the Peninsula. After Napoleon's departure, only a single regiment of cuirassiers served south of the Pyrenees: the 13th Cuirassiers in Suchet's army on the east coast where they performed extremely well, winning many battle honours, most notably at Saguntum (25 October 1811), where a brilliant charge secured the fortunes of the day. But in general the heaviest French cavalry in the Peninsula were dragoons, those jacks of all trades, or 'amphibious animals' as Jomini called them. Their past as mounted infantry long behind them, dragoons of the Napoleonic period were no more willing to dismount in action than any other cavalry. They were medium cavalry: expected to charge in battle, but not spared multifarious other tasks on campaign; they got the first pick of neither men nor horses. But though not an elite force like the cuirassiers, and without the dash and glamour of the light horsemen, they were not – generally – despicable, but useful all-rounders, typical line troops. Napoleon was dissatisfied with their performance in 1805–7, particularly at Austerlitz, and thereafter they were concentrated in secondary theatres such as the Peninsula, until he was glad to have them to draw upon when he was rebuilding his cavalry in 1813.[5]

But the commonest of all cavalry was light: hussars, chasseurs à cheval, light dragoons and numerous other distinctions signifying no real difference. Where cuirassiers had weight and splendour, light cavalry had panache and an air of raffish romance, with colourful uniforms and outrageous tales of adventure. They loved their image: 'in every land, dearly beloved by the wife, hated by the husband'; but as one French hussar officer was forced to admit, the rest of the army accused them 'of being, in the main, plunderers, wasters, and drinkers; and of taking every license in the presence of an enemy'.[6]

A brigade of light cavalry was normally attached to each infantry corps in Napoleon's army, while the heavy cavalry and sometimes the dragoons were concentrated in their own divisions for use on the battlefield. At Wagram, heavy cavalry amounted to about a third of Napoleon's cavalry, the dragoons and the Guard cavalry to about 10 per cent each, and light cavalry to just under half the total.[7] But Napoleon had concentrated his best troops for the battle: heavy cavalry and the Guard were not nearly such a large proportion of the army as a whole, while dragoons and light cavalry are under-represented in these figures.

Rather more typical were the Austrian figures for Wagram, where they had five regiments of cuirassiers, four of dragoons and no fewer than sixteen of assorted light cavalry. Yet even this overstates the proportion of heavy and medium cavalry, for their regiments were, on average, smaller. The Prussian army in 1815 had thirty-six regiments of regular cavalry: four Guard, four of cuirassiers, eight of dragoons and twenty of hussars and uhlans, while there were a further thirty-three regiments of Landwehr cavalry.[8]

Light cavalry were expected to be extremely flexible: capable of skirmishing with the enemy both on and off the battlefield, mounting patrols and manning the outposts on campaign, but also taking part in full-scale charges in pitched battles. This last was at least as important as their campaign functions: light cavalry were expected to take their place on the field of battle, providing close support to the infantry to whom they were attached, or being brought up from reserve to plug a hole in the line, as well as leading the pursuit of a broken enemy or covering the retreat if their army was defeated. Their charge lacked the force of heavy cavalry, but on most battlefields heavy cavalry was scarce or held back until the closing stages, and in its absence light and medium cavalry were a vital ingredient. The only exception was the Cossacks – irregular cavalry who specialized in skirmishing and harassing an enemy, but who would normally only close when the odds were heavily in their favour.

All cavalry were armed with a sword or sabre, but many were dissatisfied with it. One British officer declared that 'A Light Dragoon's sabre was hardly capable of killing', while another stated that the sword of the heavy cavalry was 'too heavy, too short, too broad, too much like the sort of weapon with which we have seen Grimaldi cut off the heads of a line of urchins on the stage'.[9] Most modern authorities agree, but Captain Parquin put the blame on British lack of skill:

> they [British cavalry] found us very dangerous when we attacked with our sabres. We always thrust with the point of our sabres, whereas they always cut with their blade which was three inches wide. Consequently, out of every twenty blows aimed by them, nineteen missed. If, however, the edge of the blade found its mark only once, it was a terrible blow, and it was not unusual to see an arm cut clean from the body.[10]

Yet the French heavy cavalry were equally unhappy with their 'long cumbersome swords' which 'were virtually useless in hand-to-hand cavalry fighting, and whose power of penetration was not improved by having the point on the upper edge of the blade. Most cuirassier colonels had them re-ground until the point was in the centre.'[11]

There are many reports of individuals surviving multiple sword and lance wounds: one man of the Royal Horse Guards at Waterloo is said to have suffered no fewer than sixteen such wounds, including a fractured skull, and still recovered! Andrew Leith Hay saw 'wounded dragoons and captured soldiers . . . arriving from the front in rapid succession, the former exhibiting, in the cuts they had received, the comparatively harmless effect of sabre encounters, when contrasted with the more deadly working of musketry, or thrusts from the straight sword of the French dragoon'.[12]

It is not surprising that the wounds inflicted by cavalry should be less lethal than those inflicted by firearms, for most cavalrymen were preoccupied with controlling their horses and defending themselves, rather than ensuring that they struck home. Indeed it seems highly likely that most casualties actually caused by cavalry, and especially the more serious wounds, were inflicted when the enemy had already broken and was making no resistance. But focusing on casualties distracts attention from the prime function of cavalry, which was to break enemy units by a sudden, severe test of their morale and cohesion, and to spread fear and panic throughout an opposing force.

As well as their swords, cavalry were encumbered with an array of firearms: two pistols and a carbine was not an uncommon allowance, although in practice some surplus weapons were often thrown away. Yet some firearms were useful: both for light cavalry or dragoons skirmishing at the outposts or on campaign, or – more rarely – allowing limited dismounted action if no infantry support was available; and, in some circumstances, in action against other cavalry (see below, pp. 122–3). British regulations discouraged firing from the ranks, but permitted skirmishers, who were to be sent about 200 yards in front of the regiment, to fire. They 'can take the surest aim with their carbines to the left; but can also fire occasionally to the front or to the right; but must take the greatest care not to hit or burn the horse's head; or at this time to spur the horse. Firings are best performed on the move, and it is unnecessary to halt for that purpose alone.' Mercer describes just such a scene during the Waterloo campaign:

Two double lines of skirmishers extended all along the bottom – the foremost of each line were within a few yards of each other – constantly in motion, riding backwards and forwards, firing their carbines or pistols, and then reloading, still on the move. This fire seemed to me more dangerous for those on the hills above than for us below; for all, both French and English, generally stuck out their carbines or pistols as they continued to move backwards and forwards, and discharged them without taking any particular aim, and mostly in the air. I did not see a man fall on either side; the thing appeared quite ridiculous; and but for hearing the bullets whizzing overhead, one might have fancied it no more than a sham-fight.

Yet as we have seen, Mercer himself found the fire of mounted skirmishers far from ridiculous when they were aiming at him (see above, p. 64). Nonetheless, cavalry officers recognized that their skirmishing was often ineffectual: late in the Battle of Waterloo when the surviving Royal Dragoons were under unpleasant musketry fire they 'sent out a few skirmishers to meet those of the Enemy, more for the purpose of occupying the men than from any good they could do'.[13]

A few regiments of cavalry in the Napoleonic era were also armed with a lance: roughly nine feet long and weighing about seven pounds, it had a steel point (a flat blade about nine inches long), and metal-sheathed butt. This ancient weapon had fallen out of favour in western Europe in the seventeenth and eighteenth centuries, but Napoleon was so impressed with the performance of his Polish lancers that in 1811 he ordered six regiments of dragoons to adopt the weapon, beginning an unexpected revival in its use which was to last for the rest of the century. There was always much debate about the effectiveness of lancers in action. They had some notable successes, such as at Albuera when they caught Colborne's brigade in the flank and inflicted terrible losses, and – according to one of Marbot's stories – at the Katzbach, when they broke a Prussian square which had defied other French cavalry despite being unable to fire due to the rain. A voice from the British ranks – Sergeant Anton – declared that 'Of all descriptions of cavalry, certainly the lancers seem the most formidable to infantry'; but Swabey strongly disagreed, writing in his diary that 'They owe their reputation to having destroyed a great many of our infantry when their ranks were broken at Albuera, but as to their being formidable to formed troops it is quite ridiculous; a dragoon with his broadsword is worth two of them.'[14]

There were even more doubts about the practical use of the lance in combat with other cavalry, for being so long and cumbersome it was difficult to handle in the confused fighting of a mêlée. For this reason, and in order to reduce the inordinate weight of weapons which Napoleon piled on them, the French lancers soon copied the Poles, with the front rank discarding the carbine but retaining the lance, while the rear rank relied on their swords for close combat but kept their carbines. A Prussian account of a mêlée in 1741 suggests the experiences which lay behind this compromise: 'the lance was no help to us in the press, in fact it acted to our disadvantage. Our uhlans found that they were skewering one another with these long weapons, stabbing the next man's horse, or sticking them in the ground in the general confusion and heaving themselves from the saddle.' But a couple of British accounts indicate that the French found unexpected ways of using their lances to advantage. James Smithies saw that at Waterloo the French had the lance resting on their foot and 'when we neared them, they sent it out with all their might; and if a man at which they aimed did not manage to parry the blow, it was all over with him'; while according to Dyneley, 'They are armed with a long lance, at the end of which a flag is fixed so that, when our dragoons make a stand to receive them, the flags frighten their horses, and they go about and the lancers have them through the body in the "twinkling of an eye".'[15]

Faced with such contradictory evidence, firm conclusions are difficult, but it does seem that the lance gave its user a distinct advantage against broken, fleeing opponents and perhaps also infantry in general – for if Anton's view was widely shared the lancers began with a considerable psychological advantage. Conversely the lancers may well have felt themselves to be at a disadvantage when facing well-formed enemy cavalry, and if so they were already half beaten. To be effective in any circumstances, however, the lancers needed to be well trained, for the weapon was difficult to handle in the tumult and jostling of a charge.

But if lancers needed special training in the use of their weapon, and cuirassiers needed experience to feel at home in their armour, all cavalry needed far more training than infantry before they were fit to take the field. One French expert – admittedly overstating his case – declared in 1793 that cavalry needed three or four years of drill before they could be risked in action whereas infantry recruits could take their place after only six weeks' training providing they were well mixed with veterans.[16] There were several reasons for this discrepancy. First the recruit had to be taught to ride, and then to keep his horse in the ranks and handle it amid all the noise and distractions of a battlefield. Second, there was the intrinsic difficulty of evolutions and drill, particularly turns and wheels, for mounted men, due to the fact that their horse was so much longer than wide. This was compounded by a natural inclination to manoeuvre at a trot or canter, although this almost inevitably spread confusion through the ranks. Such confusion was at least as dangerous for cavalry as for infantry, especially as little of the cavalry of the period was really well trained.

Because it was so difficult to keep cavalry aligned and in good order, squadrons often manoeuvred on their own or with some independence even if the regiment was acting as a whole. A strong squadron of 160 men in two ranks would have a frontage of just over 100 yards – which was difficult enough to manoeuvre. Regiments often attacked in echelon, that is, with one squadron leading and the others behind and to one side. This enabled them to protect the flanks of the leading squadron and deliver a succession of shocks to the enemy without risking the confusion which was likely to arise if a whole regiment, let alone a brigade, attempted to charge in a single line. The commanders of squadrons had far more tactical independence than the captains of infantry companies, for they would often need to hasten or delay their attack, or react to some sudden threat or opportunity, on their own responsibility.

Horses as well as men had to be trained. French regulations stipulated that

Horses will be habituated to fire by firing pistols at the stable doors when they are being fed their oats. Take care to dwell for a pause between the shots at first, but as the young horses become accustomed to the fire, repeat the pistol shots more frequently. If among the young horses, there are some who are sufficiently upset to affect the troupe [*sic*], you must lead them to the stable before beginning the lesson, which should be continued, morning and evening, while they are eating their oats, and to habituate them, separately and little by little, to the noise of firearms. In this way the horses will also become accustomed to the movement and the flapping of the standards and, when in company with the infantry, to the noise of their drums.[17]

Whether these steps were ever routinely implemented may be doubted, and whatever the preparation, a horse's reaction to its baptism of real fire was always a moment of great anxiety to its rider. Thus Colonel Landmann was

much pleased and surprised at the readiness with which my horse's nerves had been reconciled to the violent explosions of Artillery, for after a few shots had been fired, he became perfectly steady; but as soon as the 50th Regiment, behind which I happened to be in conversation . . . began a running fire, the poor animal was greatly agitated, and made various attempts to run off with me towards the rear.

Even this was better than the borrowed troop horse which Nadezhda Durova was riding in some simple training exercises, which became quite uncontrollable when she fired her pistol.[18]

The number of horses used by the armies was extraordinary. A single British regiment, the 14th Light Dragoons, lost 1,564 horses in five and a half years of campaigning: more than double its strength when it arrived in the Peninsula, and three or four times its strength for most of its service. In other words its horses lasted only two or three years on average. The British, serving in the Peninsula, may have been particularly hard task-masters, but even though he had all Europe to draw on, Napoleon could never find enough horses for his cavalry.[19]

With such a turnover, the combination of a well-trained horse and a good rider must have been relatively rare in the ranks. Officers were more fortunate and could develop a relationship with their horse marked by mutual affection and regard – feelings which are unconcealed in Captain (later General) Thomas Brotherton's reminiscences:

The charger I rode during most of the Peninsular War was bought by my father (who was a great judge of horses) at the sale of the King's stud, at three years old, and her name was Fatima. She was of the purest Arabian blood, and perfect symmetry, fifteen hands high, dark brown, a perfect picture, most graceful in all her movements, but very conceited. As she walked along she looked to the right and to the left, as if to see who was admiring her. She was the admiration of the whole army. She was so sagacious that marvellous stories were told of her. She always wore a silken net to protect her from the flies that maddened her when she hadn't it on. She was wounded several times. At Salamanca a shell shattered her stifle or thigh, and I was nearly advised to shoot her as incurable, but the stud groom of Lord Charles Manners effected a perfect cure after a long time, only leaving an immense scar and dent. She was twice wounded by sabre-cuts on the head. The last time was in the *mêlée* on 13th December 1813, when I was taken prisoner, when she actually reared and pawed my antagonists, as if to defend me. She had her head cut open in a dreadful way. I tried to recover her, and offered any sum to get her back, but in vain; she was sent to one of the Imperial studs. I was often tempted, by large offers, to sell her. Sir Charles Stewart, since Lord Londonderry, had offered me 300 guineas for her. She was, though of excellent temper, difficult to ride, from her fiery disposition. In bivouac, when lying down beside me, she would lift up her head to see if I was sleeping, and if she saw I was she would immediately lie down again, for fear of disturbing me. She was particularly fond of raw beef-steaks, and it was difficult to keep the men's rations from her, even if suspended on trees as they usually were, by way of safety.[20]

CAVALRY IN ACTION

For most cavalrymen, battle meant hours of sitting quietly on their horses or lounging beside them, perhaps under distant artillery fire, waiting for orders to move forward. It was a nerve-racking, anxious time, made worse by the sight of wounded men struggling to the rear, and by the difficulty which even veteran troops had of guessing which way the battle was going. Sometimes they would play no greater part in the battle than this, acting as a reserve which was never drawn upon. Of the eight brigades of British cavalry at Vitoria, only two suffered more than ten casualties.[21] On other occasions they would be brought forward but never actually committed to the fray, the danger or opportunity having passed before they could arrive. Or their mere presence might be enough to deter an enemy attack, or to encourage the enemy to abandon an untenable position. They might be sent forward into the front line to drive off enemy skirmishers or disordered enemy cavalry, not by an all-out charge, but by an orderly advance at a gentle pace which would force the enemy to withdraw before it. They might lose a few men in the process, but the cohesion of the unit as a whole would not be threatened. Where cavalrymen talk of having charged a dozen or more times in a day, it seems likely that they are usually referring to partial charges such as these. For example, the remains of the British heavy cavalry at Waterloo, after their great charge against d'Erlon's corps, made numerous partial charges later in the day to drive back the French cavalry once it had spent its momentum against the British squares.

But the essence of cavalry fighting, its most distinctive feature, was the headlong charge designed to break the enemy's resistance and terrify him into submission. General Seidlitz, the great Prussian cavalry commander, said that 'In the charge, it is a matter of indifference what weapon a soldier carries. The chief thing is that he should be well mounted, and that he should bear in mind the unshakable resolution to ride the enemy down with his horse's breast.' A century and a half later the military writer F. N. Maude agreed:

> success was decided, not primarily by the actual collision, but by the moral effect of the appearance of an absolutely closed wall of horsemen approaching the adversary at full speed. If the necessary degree of cohesion was attained, the other side was morally beaten before the collision took place, and either turned to flight, or met the shock with so little resolution that it was ridden over without difficulty.[22]

Maude's formula was unrealistic in one respect, for experience showed that if cavalry galloped at full speed the men would invariably open their ranks slightly despite all the efforts of their officers and NCOs. Contemporaries recognized that a choice had to be made between speed and good order, but there was no consensus on which was the more important. It is no surprise that Captain Nolan favoured rapidity, and Marmont agreed with him, urging that troops 'be instructed to charge thoroughly, without occupying themselves par- ticularly with preserving order, which this impetuous manner of movement would render impossible', though he went on to stress the importance of training the men to rally at the first signal. But Napoleon warned that 'it is not only its velocity that insures success; it is order, formation and proper employ- ment of reserves'. While Jomini claimed that 'The only advantage of the gallop is its apparent boldness and the moral effect it produces; but, if this is estimated at its true value by the enemy' his firm compact mass will be more effective than the disordered gallopers. Even Ardant du Picq, the great exponent of psycho- logical factors in war, argued that a slow, orderly advance was more intimidating to an opponent than a premature charge. Yet Ardant du Picq agreed that the final stage of an advance should be at a gallop, for 'it is the winning, intoxicating gait, for men and horses'.[23]

In practice, much depended on the circumstances of any particular encounter, but it does seem that the French cavalry was more inclined than its opponents to maintain a steady trot – and so good order – up until almost the last moment, when it might suddenly accelerate. Paradoxically one of the great exponents of these tactics was General Lasalle, the epitome of the dashing, romantic *beau sabreur*, but whose cool head in action made him a divisional commander at only thirty-three.[24]

Such tactics required good discipline, and Ardant du Picq argues that 'strong men, moved by pride or fear, by taking up too soon the charge against a firm enemy, have caused more charges to fail than to succeed. Keeping men in hand

until the command "charge", [and] seizing the precise instant for this command, are both difficult.' A story of the Brandenburg Hussars in 1814, commanded by General Sohr, illustrates the difficulties that could be caused by an
impetuous officer:

> The gallop was sounded; Count v. d. S., a lieutenant who had lately joined from
> the Saxon cavalry, wishing to distinguish himself, brandished his sword on high,
> called to the men to follow him, and dashed forward at speed. The second
> squadron, which began to follow him, lost its place in line. Sohr immediately
> ordered the trot to be sounded, and then, waiting till the whole regiment was
> steady, he sounded the gallop and the charge, the only means by which he could
> hope to break through the enemy's line. When the engagement was over, Sohr
> called the officers together, and addressing himself to Lieutenant v. S., said, 'You
> proved to us this day that you have lots of pluck, and I honour those who have,
> but I am myself no "Hundsfott" and if you again forget yourself as you did this
> day, and dare to interfere with me in the leading of the regiment, I shall cut you
> down in front of the line.'[25]

An even greater danger, of course, was cavalry who, so far from increasing
their speed as they approached the enemy, gradually slowed down until their
courage altogether evaporated and they turned tail. Lieutenant William Light –
later to win lasting fame as the first Surveyor-General of South Australia and
founder of Adelaide – describes such an incident at Albuera: 'we all started, as
I thought, to do the thing well; but when within a few paces of the enemy the
whole pulled up, and there was no getting them farther; and in a few moments
after I was left alone to run the gauntlet as well as I could'.[26]

The experience of a successful cavalry charge was much more exhilarating,
though the rapid sequence of thoughts and emotions could never be precisely
recalled and recorded, so that even a detailed account written a few days after
the event gives a blurred and confused picture. On 25 July 1812 Lieutenant
William Bragge of the 3rd King's Own Dragoons wrote home describing his
part in the charge of Le Marchant's brigade at Salamanca three days before:

> My dear Father,
>   Knowing the Anxiety you and my Mother will feel upon hearing of a great
> and sanguinary Battle, in which the Third Dragoons bore no inconsiderable
> share, I take the earliest possible opportunity of informing you that I escaped
> perfectly sound, Wind and Limb, together with the Little Bay Mare who
> carried me through the Day delightfully and I believe to her Speed and
> Activity I may in a great measure attribute my marvellous escape, as I at one
> Time had to gallop along the whole Front of a French Brigade retreating in
> double quick step.
>   . . . Lord Wellington gave the Signal for a general Attack. . . . Immediately
> upon this, our Right and Left turned theirs, the Enemy were driven from the
> Hills and the Cavalry advanced upon the Backs of the Infantry. Our Brigade

literally rode over the Regiments in their Front and dashed through the Wood at a Gallop, the Infantry cheering us in all Directions. We quickly came up with the French Columns and charged their Rear. Hundreds threw down their Arms, their Cavalry ran away, and most of the Artillery jumped upon the Horses and followed the Cavalry. One or two charges mixed up the whole Brigade, it being impossible to see for Dust and Smoak, but this kind of Attack – so novel and unexpected – threw the French into confusion and gave our Infantry Time to get another Battle at them, when they served it out nicely, making them fly in all directions. We lost our General in a square of Infantry and in him we have experienced a severe Loss. One Lieut. was killed by his side, but in other respects our Loss is trifling considering we were solely engaged with Infantry and Artillery. The Brigade marched off nine Pieces of Artillery and about 500 Prisoners.[27]

Another officer, Lieutenant Norcliffe Norcliffe of the 4th Dragoons, tells a similar story of the same charge in a letter dated 10 August 1812:

We were pursuing the French Infantry, which were broken and running in all directions. I was cutting them down as well as I could, when in the hurry and confusion I lost my regiment and got with some soldiers of the 5th Dragoon Guards; on looking behind me, I could only see a few of the 5th, and we were in the centre of the enemy's infantry, amongst whom were a few Chasseurs and Dragoons. Nothing now remained but to go on, as we were in as much danger by going any other way.

I rode up to a French officer, who was, like the rest, taking to his heels, and cut him just behind his neck; I saw the blood flow, and he lost his balance, and fell from his horse. I perceived my sword was giving way in the handle, so I said to the officer who lay on the ground: '*Donnez-moi votre épée*' – I really believe he was more frightened than hurt; I sheathed my sword and went on with his. I had not gone 10 yards further before my horse was wounded in the ear by a gun shot; he turned sharp round, and the same instant I was shot in the head. I turned giddy and fell off. I can recollect a French Dragoon taking away my horse.[28]

He lay for some time, wounded and incapable of moving, and was ill-treated by the French cavalry; but then some French infantry came up who looked after him with great kindness until the approach of British troops forced them to hurry away. The British soldiers got him to a surgeon, and at the time of writing the letter he was recovering well, and had no regrets:

It was a glorious day for our Brigade. They behaved nobly; 4 men killed of the troop I commanded, and several men and horses wounded. It was a fine sight to see the fellows running, and as we held our swords over their heads fall down on their knees, drop their muskets, and cry: '*Prisonnier, monsieur.*'

British cavalry were notorious for their lack of restraint: once they charged, their officers seemed to lose control completely, but all nations suffered from this to some extent, as the French Rocca admits: 'When a regiment or squadron of cavalry charges, either in line or column, the exact order in which it commenced to gallop cannot long be preserved; for the horses incite each other, and their ardour increases, till he who is best mounted finds himself foremost, and the line of battle is broken.'[29] Lieutenant Roth von Schreckenstein of the Saxon Zastrow Cuirassiers explicitly endorsed such impetuosity:

> To control and halt a regiment under such circumstances is a pious hope. Men who are imbued with true cavalry courage pursue and attack the enemy for as long as they can . . . and anybody who imagines that one can invariably control and direct a cavalry regiment just as one pleases by means of one's voice or a trumpet, as if on peacetime manoeuvres, has never been in an action where all arms of the service co-operated.

Schreckenstein's own experiences at Borodino were similar to those of Norcliffe Norcliffe. His horse had been killed.

> I looked about for another horse, but those nearest to me had been wounded. One Russian horse which I did mount refused to move, even when I clapped spurs to it, so I was on the point of moving off on foot, pistol in hand, without really knowing which way to flee, because, owing either to an illusion stemming from fear or else because they were really there, I could see enemies on all sides.
>   The thought of being captured and ill-treated overwhelmed me, and I gripped my pistol in much the same way as a person who is drowning clutches at the nearest straw. At very best this weapon would enable me to sell my liberty or my life more dearly. By some fortunate chance a riderless horse came past with a troop of Life Guards, so close that I was able to grab hold of it and escape with a swarm of horsemen who were withdrawing. Skill at vaulting stood me in very good stead, because I had no time left in which to mount in the normal way, and I was thankful when I eventually managed to reach the middle of the saddle.[30]

But if it was almost inevitable that cavalry would get out of hand during the charge, it was essential that they be trained to rally when it was over and their impetus was spent. Lack of experience and inadequate training for this lay behind many of the embarrassing misadventures suffered by the British cavalry in the period. Captain Tomkinson, that assiduous soldier diarist, wrote in 1812: 'In England I never saw nor heard of cavalry taught to charge, disperse, and form, which, if I only taught a regiment one thing, I think it should be that.' Seven years later he added a note to this passage:

> We never teach our men to disperse and form again, which of all things, before an enemy, is the most essential . . . they should be taught to disperse as if in pursuit of a broken enemy, with as much confusion as possible, but to form

instantly on hearing the bugle, or rather retreat at that sound, and for fear anything should happen to the trumpeter, to return by word.[31]

The ill-effects of this were felt in the aftermath of the charge of the Union and Household Brigades at Waterloo when, again according to Tomkinson, 'the men did not know where to assemble after the charge, and this being the first action they had ever been in, they, I suppose, fancied that nothing remained for them to attend to after this one attack, and many went in consequence to the rear'. This view is supported by the story of an officer of the Royal Dragoons who, seeing a party of British cavalry near him at the end of the charge, 'called out to them, "Royals form on me"', only to receive the reply, '"We are King's Dragoon Guards, not Royals", and they passed on'.[32]

A writer in the *Royal Military Chronicle* put much of the blame for the problem on the British horses which 'in every charge . . . run away with their riders'. This was due partly 'from the peculiar breed of our native horse; partly from his ill breaking; and partly from his unskilful riding'.[33] But whether the British cavalry were, like John Gilpin, carried away by their steeds, or whether they were inflamed with the excitement of battle, this was only part of the problem. Lord Uxbridge's account of the aftermath of the charge at Waterloo suggests the other elements:

> After the overthrow of the Cuirassiers I had in vain attempted to stop my people by sounding the Rally, but neither voice nor trumpet availed; so I went back to seek the support of the 2nd Line, which unhappily had not followed the movements of the Heavy Cavalry.
>
> Had I, when I sounded the Rally, found only four well-formed Squadrons coming steadily along at an easy trot, I feel certain that the loss the first line suffered when they were finally forced back would have been avoided, and most of these Guns might have been secured.[34]

Once cavalry were committed to the charge it was almost inevitable that they would get out of hand and, at the end of their charge be extremely vulnerable to a counter-stroke from the enemy. It was therefore important that their commanders kept part of their force as a reserve to cover their withdrawal or – if the enemy's army as a whole was broken – to begin the pursuit. This plainly did not happen at Waterloo. At least one regiment in each brigade should have been held back as a reserve, following their comrades at no more than a trot. There is some evidence that the Scots Greys and the Royal Horse Guards were intended for this role, but either the orders never reached them or they were ignored, for they took a leading part in the fighting from the earliest stages of the charge. Equally the attack should have been supported by several further brigades of cavalry, whereas only Vandeleur's advanced, belatedly and on its commander's own initiative, to cover the retreat. The charge of the British heavy cavalry at Waterloo was far from a failure: it was perfectly timed and succeeded in driving back d'Erlon's corps, breaking its attack, inflicting heavy losses and capturing thousands of prisoners, nor was the French right wing able to make a serious attack again during the battle. But the cost was high, for the two brigades were virtually destroyed[35]: these losses were not inevitable, but the result of indiscipline among the men, and, more seriously, failures of command. Uxbridge himself admitted this years later, telling Siborne,

> This forces from me the remark that I committed a great mistake in having myself led the attack. The *carrière* once begun, the leader is no better than any other man; whereas, if I had placed myself at the head of the 2nd line, there is no saying what great advantages might not have accrued from it. I am less pardonable in having deviated from a principle I had laid down for myself, that I had already suffered from a similar error in an affair at Irtragau [?], where my reserve, instead of steadily following as I had ordered, chose to join in the attack, and at the end of it I had no formed body to take advantage with.[36]

Similar mistakes lay behind two famous defeats for British cavalry in the Peninsula: at Campo Mayor in March 1811 and Maguilla in June 1812. In both these small combats the British cavalry charged boldly and broke their opponents, and then pursued them recklessly – at Campo Mayor for seven miles! – before being put to flight by fresh French forces. Both affairs could have been minor triumphs for the British cavalry if only they had halted and rallied after a moderate pursuit. Instead the fruits of victory were squandered – which at Campo Mayor included a train of sixteen heavy fortress guns – and the triumph became a rout. Much of the blame was rightly put on the commanders who had failed to keep a reserve intact, but as Brigadier Long – the culprit at Campo Mayor – explained in a letter commenting on Maguilla, this was not always easy:

> The failure is, in my opinion, decidedly to be attributed to the indiscreet manner in which the reserve or supporting body was conducted, for they cease to fulfil that character the moment they join in the attack or pursuit of an Enemy's rearguard, and in doing so advance so far and with such speed, as to destroy all order, blow their horses, and necessarily become the prey of fresh Troops brought against them. General Slade it appears observed this error, and endeavoured to provide against the consequences by directing a squadron on the right of his line to halt and stand fast, but by some fatality the order was not complied with, and consequently the men, when obliged to turn about, found nothing to rally upon, and therefore continued their flight to what may be considered an unfortunate and perhaps disgraceful distance. Thus you see how much depends with us upon the Chapter of Accidents, and how much we are the creatures of chance. A day that promised to be a brilliant one, and if successful would have established Slade's fame for ever, has turned against him, and left only recollections of the most painful description.

I know from experience how difficult it is to contain a British victorious Cavalry in sight of a fugitive Enemy, and I know equally well how much better the Enemy has his men under his hands than we. Knowing this, although I must lament with others the result of this unfortunate day, I do not see what Slade could do more to prevent it than he did, for in all such affairs, which are more or less extensive, one man cannot be everywhere to control every individual, and of course something must be left to, and depend upon, the discretion of others. . . .[37]

What Slade could and should have done, of course, was to ride at the head of the reserve squadron or squadrons, using all his personal authority to keep them in check. Instead he joined in the charge and when the men broke he

rode in every direction begging the men to form and rally, but it was in vain that he threatened them, entreated them, and finally offered any man fifty pounds if he would rally. It was also quite in vain that the other officers did all that they could. The men continued galloping hard to the rear, leaving their officers to follow or stand and fight alone.[38]

Such incidents explain Wellington's well-known comment: 'I considered our cavalry so inferior to the French from want of order, that although I considered one of our squadrons a match for two French, yet I did not care to see four British opposed to four French, and still more so as the numbers increased, and order (of course) became more necessary. They could gallop, but could not preserve their order.' But it is only fair to add that the British cavalry had a number of triumphs in the Peninsula to set against their disasters, ranging from well-executed combats such as Sahagun, Benavente and Villagarcia, to Le Marchant's great charge at Salamanca. Nor were foreign cavalry totally without their Campo Mayors and Maguillas, for Rocca describes just such an incident occurring to his comrades in Spain.[39]

In 1816 Wellinton explained in some detail his views about cavalry reserves in some instructions to the Army of Occupation in France. He emphasized the importance of reserves, whether to exploit success, cover the retreat after a failure, or even to convert a failure into a success by attacking the enemy when they were disordered. Ideally the reserve should amount to between half and two thirds of the cavalry involved in an operation, depending on the ground and the strength of the enemy. The second line of cavalry should be deployed in line, but the third line – if there were enough troops available to form a third line – might be in column. Ample intervals were to be left between lines when facing cavalry, so that if one line fell back in disorder it would not disrupt the line behind. Wellington stipulated 400 to 500 yards as a suitable interval, arguing that as the supporting cavalry could cover it in a little over a minute they could readily 'improve and secure any success' achieved by the first line. Against infantry and artillery, where there was less danger of a counter-attack, he suggested that the interval be reduced to 200 yards so that the second line could strike as soon as possible after the first.

He then addressed the perennial problem of how to contain the enthusiasm which swept British reserves into the charge with the first line:

> so much in the cavalry depends upon the preservation of order in the second line or reserve, where the *first* charges, that more precautions ought to be taken to secure it. The rule should be, then, for the second line invariably to pull up to a walk when the first line charges, and in case of the failure of the charge, to continue at that pace till the first line will have passed through the intervals. In case the charge should be successful, the second line would then preserve its pace, and its settled distance of 450 yards from the first. If there should be a third line, it should follow the movement of the second, keeping its distance from it, till the second should become *first*, by the retreat of the *first*, and it should then act as above detailed for the *second* line.[40]

Cavalry reserves also protected the front line's rear by preventing the enemy it had broken from rallying. In this way they would often take numerous prisoners, though it was important that they did not allow themselves to become distracted or to fall too far behind. Supporting infantry could fill this function very well: at both Salamanca and Waterloo British infantry, advancing in the wake of the cavalry charges, collected thousands of prisoners who might otherwise have escaped or perhaps even re-formed and opposed the retreat of the British cavalry. Well-handled support from infantry and artillery could also be invaluable against stubborn resistance, but it was difficult to achieve, and the great French charges at both Eylau and Waterloo suffered from the lack of it.

Reserves protected the flanks as well as the rear of the front line by moving to counter any threat to them. Cavalry's flanks were particularly vulnerable, for once committed to a line of advance it was almost impossible to change direction, as Captain Nolan explains:

> when the line is formed and launched forward on the enemy, if he is suddenly found to be on the right or left front instead of straight before the advancing line, it is too late to alter the direction on the move, and to halt is dangerous; what with the difficulty of hearing words of command, particularly when under fire, and the impossibility of seeing what the base squadron is doing, the cavalry cannot easily be brought to bear straight down upon the foe.[41]

The psychological impact of an unexpected threat to one flank was just as great, so that a strong force of cavalry might be broken by a much weaker force which attacked it in the flank.

All this placed great demands on cavalry commanders, who had to be able to anticipate problems long before they became obvious. They also had to have a very good eye for the ground, for a sunken road, dry stream bed or patch of

marsh or bog could destroy the momentum of advancing cavalry, and sometimes, as at Talavera, cause considerable casualties. At Salamanca Le Marchant
had to advance over more than a mile of open ground before approaching the
French position, and in front of the brigade he 'sent Lieutenant-Colonel
Dalbiac, of the 4th Dragoons, and Lieutenant [William] Light of the Staff, to
reconnoitre the ground in front, and to post vedettes at the difficult points, a
precaution that facilitated his march and prevented confusion; and by skilfully
availing himself of the inequalities of the ground, he suffered few casualties
from the cannonade'.[42] Such precautions were not always possible, but the risks
of advancing over unknown ground only strengthened the arguments for keeping firm control over the men and retaining a strong reserve.

    The heart of cavalry tactics, as with much else in the period, lay in the basic,
mundane points: preserving a reserve, maintaining proper intervals, guarding
against flank attacks, reconnoitring the ground and such like; simple, obvious
things in theory, but often very difficult to achieve in practice. They were one
half of the equation; the other, equally necessary, was the courage and *élan* to
charge with confidence, combined with the discipline to maintain order and to
rally when the charge was spent.

CAVALRY VS CAVALRY

Between the charge and the rally lay the moments of decision, and whatever
fighting the combat contained. The dynamics of the contest varied considerably
depending on whether the opponents were cavalry or infantry or artillery.
When facing other cavalry, both sides usually charged, although sometimes
one would remain halted and rely on carbine fire to break the opponent's
momentum. This placed great strain on men who had been taught to despise the
fire of infantry and rely on the *arme blanche*, who had little practice with their
carbines, and who knew that their fire could not equal that of infantry, if only
because they could bring fewer guns to bear on any given frontage. The Austrian regulations of 1806 went so far as to prohibit their cavalry from receiving
any attack at the halt, while the British seldom if ever did so. But there are many
references to the French using their firearms in this way, usually with unhappy
results. At Sahagun, where Debelle's brigade had been taken by surprise, its
leading regiment formed up along a road with a ditch separating them from the
approaching British. According to one eyewitness, they opened fire at 400
yards, but only had time to fire a few ineffectual shots before the British were
among them. A rare example of the tactic succeeding occurred at Eylau where
the snow and marshy ground slowed the Russian advance to a walk, which in
turn allowed the French to hold their fire to very close range ('six yards', if
Parquin is to be believed). Yet even in this case the Russian advance, though
disrupted, was not halted and a mêlée followed. Given that military opinion
since the middle of the eighteenth century had warned against cavalry relying

on their firearms, and that its record of success was unimpressive, it is perplexing that the French persisted in the tactic.[43]

Even so, such encounters were relatively rare: the normal response of cavalry, when attacked by enemy horsemen, was to counter-attack with a charge of their own. The two charging bodies did not always meet, for one side might lose heart and give way before contact was made. Thus Colonel D'Urban, commanding a brigade of Portuguese cavalry, describes his experiences at Majadahonda – a small combat a few weeks after Salamanca – in a rueful letter to a friend:

> My poor fellows are still a most daily and uncertain sort of fighting people. At Salamanca they followed me into the enemy's ranks like British dragoons; yesterday they were so far from doing their duty that in their first charge they just went far enough to land me in the enemy's ranks. In the second, which (having got them rallied) I rashly attempted, I could not get them within 20 yards of the enemy – they left me alone, and vanished before the French helmets like leaves before the autumn wind. They require a little incentive of shouts, and the inspiring cheers of a British line advancing near them. I am afraid they will never be quite *safe* by themselves, or in silence.[44]

Rocca descibes a similar event – with a little Gallic exaggeration – from the other side of the fence. It was at the Battle of Medellin in 1809:

> The Spaniards had sent against our single squadron six of their best, who advanced in close column with the Xeres lancers at their head. This solid mass all at once began to trot, with the intention of charging us while we made our retrograde movement. The captain of our squadron commanded his four platoons, which did not in all exceed 120 men, to wheel half round, at walking pace, to the right. This being done, he straightened his line with as much self-possession as if no enemy had been near. The Spanish horse, struck with astonishment at his coolness, insensibly slackened their pace. The leader of the squadron took advantage of their surprise, and immediately gave the signal to charge.
>
> Our hussars, who had hitherto preserved, amid the incessant threats and abuses of the enemy, a deep unbroken silence, now drowned the shrill clangour of the trumpet, as they dashed forward with one tremendous shout of joy and rage. The Spanish lancers, horror struck, stopped short, and, turning round at half pistol-shot, overturned their own cavalry behind them. Terror so impaired their judgment, that they could not look at each other, but believed every one to be their enemy. Our hussars rushed pell-mell among them, and hewed them down without opposition. We chased them to the rear of their army, when the trumpets sounded a recall, and we returned, to form our squadron once more in order of battle.[45]

Nor were such scenes limited to poor, ill-mounted troops such as D'Urban's Portuguese dragoons or the Spanish cavalry. At Waterloo, William Verner of the 7th Hussars noticed a party of disordered cuirassiers passing nearby. Calling to his men, 'Come along, now is the time to cut them off', he charged at the French only to find that he was alone except for one other officer. In his reminiscences he indulges in no recriminations or accusations, but gently wonders whether 'the men had not heard me, or whether they did not understand what I said'.[46]

After eighteen months in the Peninsula Captain Tomkinson wrote in his diary after the first day's fighting at Fuentes de Oñoro: 'This is the only instance I ever met with of two bodies of cavalry coming in opposition, and both standing, as invariably, as I have observed it, one or the other runs away.' Marmont agreed: 'Cavalry is destined to fight body to body; it must cross swords with the enemy, dash at him, overthrow, and pursue him. The pursuit of the enemy is its habitual office; for but rarely two parties engage in a hand-to-hand encounter. At the moment of their meeting the less confident one stops and flies.' Nolan offers an explanation:

> Cavalry seldom meet each other in a charge executed at speed; the one party generally turns before joining issue with the enemy, and this often happens when their line is still unbroken and no obstacles of any sort intervene.
>
> The fact is, every cavalry soldier approaching another at speed must feel that if they come in contact at that pace they both go down, and probably break every limb in their bodies.
>
> To strike down his adversary, the dragoon must close, and the chances are he receives a blow in return for the one he deals out.
>
> There is a natural repugnance to close in deadly strife . . . and cavalry soldiers, unless they feel confident in their riding, can trust to their horse, and know that their weapons are formidable, will not readily plunge into the midst of the enemy's ranks.[47]

Yet there certainly were occasions when neither side broke before contact. What happened then was *not* that 'two solid walls of cavalry came together with a crash like thunder which could be heard all over the field', as some more rhetorical accounts state. Neither the men nor the horses were so foolish: if they had been, the casualties from falls alone would have been enormous, far exceeding the light casualties normally produced by such encounters. What actually happened is rather less clear. Mercer describes one incident at Waterloo:

> we saw the charge perfectly. There was no check, no hesitation, on either side; both parties seemed to dash on in a most reckless manner, and we fully expected to have seen a horrid crash – no such thing! Each, as if by mutual consent, opened their files on coming near, and passed rapidly through each other, cutting and pointing, much in the same manner one might pass the fingers of the right hand through those of the left. We saw but few fall.

An account of a similar episode describes how the cavalry, having passed through their opponents, wheeled about and charged back, while in other cases they charged on, leaving their supporting squadrons to deal with the scattered enemy they left in their rear. But such opening of the ranks was only feasible in some circumstances – mostly involving small, or already disordered bodies of cavalry (which fits the context of Mercer's description) – and so was probably not the norm.[48]

A sergeant in the Scots Greys at Waterloo describes how, late in the day, when his unit was exhausted and had already lost very heavily, it was ordered to charge some exhausted French cuirassiers. Neither side broke, but neither had the resolution to charge home, with 'both sides halting and exchanging carbine fire at 30 yards'. This ineffective firefight was ended only by the arrival of the fresh hussars of Vivian's brigade who relieved the Scots.[49]

Another form of encounter occurred when one side's resolution broke at the last moment, leaving them no time to escape. Tomkinson describes one such incident in October 1810:

> we charged them; they instantly went about and wished to retire. There was the greatest noise and confusion with the enemy, their front wishing to get away, and their rear, not seeing what was going on, stood [*sic*] still. They got so close together that it was impossible to get well at them. . . . The enemy . . . made not the least resistance, each striving to get the fastest out of the way.[50]

But, more commonly, both sides would hold their nerve: each would slow as it approached and the lines would become ragged as some men pressed forward while others held back. The result was a confused mêlée, well described by Francis Hall, an officer in the 14th Light Dragoons at Fuentes de Oñoro:

> I had been carrying a message when the first charge took place, and returned in the midst of the mêlée. It was literally '*auferre, trudidare, rapere.*' Horses whose riders had been killed or overthrown ran wildly across the field or lay panting in their blood. The general recontre was sub-divided into partial combats. Two heavy Dragoons were in the act of felling a Chasseur with their broad swords; his chaco [shako] resisted several blows, but he at length dropped. Another was hanging in the stirrup, while his horse was hurried off by a German Hussar, eager to plunder his valise. Some were driving two or three slashed prisoners to the rear: one wretch was dragged on foot between two Dragoons, but as he was unable to keep pace with their horses, and the enemy were now forming for a second charge, he was cut down.
>
> . . . we again formed in line, and a second charge was led on by Captain Brotherton. . . . He rode at the French officer, who was in front of his men, but the latter made a few steps on one side and politely let him pass. We were soon completely intermixed. Our men had *evidently* the advantage as individuals. Their broad sword, ably wielded, flashed over the Frenchmen's heads, and

obliged them to cower to their saddle bows. The alarm was, indeed, greater than the hurt, for their cloaks were so well rolled across their left shoulders, that it was no easy matter to give a mortal stroke with the broad edge of a sabre, whereas their swords, which were straight and pointed, though their effect on the eyes was less formidable, were capable of inflicting a much severer wound. Many, however, turned their horses, and our men shouted in the pursuit; but it was quite clear that, go which way they might, we were but scattered drops amid their host, and could not possibly arrest their progress. We again, therefore, went about, and retired towards the Guards, who were formed in squares on the right of our line of infantry.[51]

Casualties in such mêlées were generally light, for the men were preoccupied with defending themselves and controlling their horses: indeed most casualties were probably inflicted after one side broke, in the pursuit. In the whole day's fighting at Fuentes de Oñoro, Francis Hall's regiment lost only three men killed together with five officers and twenty-seven men wounded and three men missing (perhaps captured), or thirty-eight casualties in all from a total strength of 375 officers and men. Similarly, at Austerlitz there was a fierce mêlée with 'bitter hand-to-hand fighting' between Napoleon's Grenadiers à Cheval of the Imperial Guard and the Russian Chevalier Garde, but the former, who were victorious, had no officers killed and only six wounded during the whole battle, according to Martinien's invaluable lists. At Maguilla, the British suffered twenty-two killed, twenty (or twenty-six) wounded, and no fewer than 118 taken prisoner (many of whom were probably also wounded), from a total strength of around 700. (In addition, twelve horses were killed, twenty-one wounded, and 209 missing.) The French commander acknowledged the loss of fifty-one casualties from a force of similar size. Finally, at Sahagun, the British lost only a few men: two or four killed (depending on the source), and about twenty wounded, while the French lost 'several men killed', and about 157 officers and men taken prisoner, many of them wounded: a disparity which suggests that there was only a little fighting before the French broke.[52]

This was not unusual for it was during the pursuit that the real damage was done, not just in terms of casualties inflicted but, at least as importantly, to the morale of the broken cavalry. If they were not pursued, defeated cavalry – unless very bad indeed – would normally soon rally and return to the fray with only slightly diminished confidence. But a vigorous pursuit could destroy a regiment's cohesion and shatter its confidence for the rest of the day and even beyond, for once cavalry were intimidated by their opponents they could be at a disadvantage for the remainder of a campaign.

Here again, the importance of supporting troops and reserves can hardly be overstated: they would check the enemy's pursuit and provide secure cover behind which defeated cavalry could rally, catch their breath and regain their courage. This was normally the function of supporting squadrons, but sometimes infantry could perform it just as well. At Austerlitz Caffarelli's division opened its ranks allowing Kellermann's fleeing hussars to pass through, before re-forming in time to pursue their pursuers; while at Venta del Pozo two battalions of King's German Legion infantry covered the retreat of their cavalry with great coolness.[53]

The actual mêlée was not decided by the level of casualties suffered by each side, however, for amidst all the confusion no one could know whether more friends or enemies were falling, but by a sudden collapse of resolution. Most mêlées were very brief – a participant in the fighting at Venta del Pozo describes it as lasting 'perhaps a long minute' before one side broke.[54] Many factors could influence the result: at Fuentes, Francis Hall and his men gave way because they believed themselves to be outnumbered, even though some of the French were showing signs of wavering. Colonel D'Urban believed that his Portuguese dragoons had been inspired at Salamanca by the encouraging shouts of nearby British troops, and were unnerved at Majadahonda to be by themselves. On other occasions one side might feel – not necessarily accurately – that it was being physically pushed back by its opponents, especially if it was facing heavy cavalry or was downhill. Heavy cavalry had a double advantage facing lighter opponents: size, weight and equipment gave them a material advantage, which was compounded by the knowledge that they outclassed their enemy: this gave the heavy cavalry confidence and made the light horse anticipate defeat. But other factors might tip the psychological balance and offset the physical advantage. Fresh troops had a great advantage over those who were tired, who had already drawn on their courage and whose horses were blown. Similarly a unit in good order with the officers in full control was better placed than one which was ragged and disordered. On the other hand cavalry sweeping forward from one success might have such confidence and enthusiasm that they could brush aside cooler opponents. The general course of the battle and the campaign, and the regiment's individual experiences, might enhance or depress its confidence, as might the presence of an inspiring – or, conversely, a distrusted – commander. The list of potential influences is virtually endless, and the relative importance of each factor varied with every mêlée, so as to defy precise calculation or analysis; especially as some allowance must be made for luck, or at least the random accumulation of trifling details: this officer's horse going lame, that man dazzled by the sun, a sword breaking, or a pistol misfiring.

At Villagarcia (11 April 1812) the French cavalry were broken when they were unexpectedly attacked in the flank by a regiment of British heavy dragoons, at the same time as the British light cavalry, who had been slowly falling back before them, suddenly turned and charged. At Venta del Pozo (23 October 1812) the French succeeded in galloping over a narrow bridge and deploying in the face of a brigade of British light cavalry, a brigade of heavy dragoons of the King's German Legion, and a battery of horse artillery. The allies mismanaged the affair, the light cavalry accidentally preventing the guns from firing by passing in front of them as the French were crossing the bridge; the heavy dragoons charged with vigour but were not well supported, either because of a mistake in command, or because the light cavalry – who had already seen action that day – were exhausted or lacking in resolution. At Genappe, on the day before Waterloo, Uxbridge's 7th Hussars charged advancing French lancers as they were about to leave the streets of the town, but were foiled when the French remained cool and halted and lowered their lances, presenting a steady line of spear points. To Uxbridge's mortification the Hussars – his own regiment – broke, but he was soon consoled when the Life Guards in turn broke the lancers, when they advanced beyond the confines of the town.

Each of these combats, and the hundred others which could be described, was different. Some were decided by unique elements which no one could anticipate, but in most it was some variation on the basic elements of the number and type of cavalry involved, their good order, cohesion and discipline at the critical moment, and the skill of the commanders – mixed with luck – which created the tactical circumstances in which they fought. As Nolan remarked, 'The most difficult position a cavalry officer can be placed in is in command of cavalry against cavalry, for the slightest fault committed may be punished on the spot, and a reverse lead to the most disastrous consequences.'[55] Events moved quickly, while orders took an appreciable time to be transmitted and obeyed, requiring great foresight and coolness. But a good cavalry commander would not be intimidated by the risks he faced; rather he would welcome the opportunity and inspire his men to share his confidence.

CAVALRY VS ARTILLERY AND INFANTRY

Cavalry and artillery each had good reason to fear the other: artillery feared cavalry's speed and mobility, while cavalry feared artillery's firepower. There was some debate in cavalry circles about how best to attack artillery; Captain Brotherton recounts the upshot of one such discussion:

> At Fuentes d'Onor [*sic*] we had a very fine fellow, Captain Knipe, killed through his gallant *obstinacy*, if I may call it so. We had the night before been discussing the best mode for cavalry to attack batteries in the open field. He maintained, contrary to us all, that they ought to be charged in front, instead of the usual way of gaining their flanks, and thereby avoiding their fire. Poor fellow, the experiment next day, in support of his argument, was fatal to him. He had the opportunity of charging one of the enemy's batteries, which he did by attacking it immediately in front, and got through the discharge of round-shot with little loss; but the enemy having most rapidly reloaded with grape, let fly at his party, at a close and murderous distance, almost entirely destroying it; he himself receiving a grape-shot, passing through his body. The shot went through his lungs. I was with the poor fellow next morning, as long as he survived. He could speak distinctly, and was most composed and resigned, and even argued the point over again.[56]

Captain Nolan also believed that cavalry could successfully charge a battery. He recommended using a weak force in open order, which would advance straight at the artillery until it reached canister range, then gallop forward as hard as possible while opening from the centre and making for the flanks of the battery.[57] He was, of course, the same Captain Nolan who brought the order from Lord Raglan which launched the Light Brigade on their fateful charge at Balaclava, and who was killed early in the charge. As that event showed, good cavalry could overrun artillery even charging frontally and in close order, but the cost was likely to be inordinate, and unless they were well supported they found it difficult to retain possession of the guns.

Cavalry are supposed to have charged at around twelve to fourteen miles per hour in the closing stages of their attack, meaning that they would cover about 350 or 400 yards in a minute. This would usually give artillery time to fire only one round of canister at effective range – for it would be unrealistic to expect the gunners to continue calmly to work their pieces when the cavalry were almost on top of them. And despite Captain Knipe's experience, one such round was not generally enough to break fresh, determined cavalry, charging over good ground. At Waterloo most British gunners retired from their batteries as the French cavalry approached, and took refuge in the cover of the squares. Captain Mercer's men did not, and repulsed the cavalry through fire alone, but they did not take up their position until after the early charges, when the French horses were tired, the ground was churned up, and the cavalry had lost their early confidence.

When cavalry did overrun a battery – whether by a frontal charge or by some more subtle attack – there would be confused fighting amidst the guns, as described by a French officer at Austerlitz:

> The soldiers threw themselves beneath the ammunition carts and the pieces, while the gunners defended themselves with their rammers. For a time the infantry was unable to shoot, because the mass of Kellermann's cavalry stood in the way, but once the field was clear they opened a rolling fire at thirty paces. At that moment I was at bay among my draught-horses, fighting hand to hand with a Russian officer. He had severed the little finger of my right hand with a blow of his sword, but all at once his horse collapsed, struck by a musket ball. The officer cast himself at my stirrups and cried out, 'We are heroes after all, aren't we?' He repeated these words several times and kept by my side, regarding himself as my prisoner.[58]

A few minutes of such fighting could do great damage to a battery and leave the survivors shaken and nervous for the remainder of the battle. But such scenes did not normally last long: either the cavalry would ride on in search of fresh prey, or the gunners would be rescued by supporting troops. Individual artillerymen might find refuge crouching under their guns or under the ammunition wagons, where the cavalry – unless armed with lances – could not reach them; but many stood and fought to defend themselves, perhaps reflecting that the cavalry were also armed with pistols.

Even more alarming for artillery was to be caught by hostile cavalry while limbered up. Foot artillery had little hope of escape unless they were saved by the intervention of friendly troops, but horse artillery could sometimes cut their way through to safety, as Norman Ramsay did with two guns in a famous exploit at Fuentes de Oñoro: though even he was helped by British cavalry.[59]

Direct conflict such as this between cavalry and artillery was comparatively rare because both sides had too much to lose, but the movement of each on the battlefield was often affected by the fear of the other. Artillery would be less bold and ready to advance if the enemy's cavalry was superior to its own, while cavalry officers – even those of unquestioned bravery such as Captain Brotherton – were wisely wary of launching themselves and their men at enemy batteries.

Cavalry was essentially a weapon of fear, and never was this so apparent as in its conflict with infantry. Cavalry would not charge home on steady well-formed infantry: its only hope of success was that the infantry would waver and give way when faced with the threat of its advance. In this case pace was indisputably more important than order for the cavalry – though a full gallop still must not be reached too soon. The speed of the charge excited the men and gave them the impetuous courage needed to disregard the infantry's fire. It also frightened the infantry and often made them fire too soon and inaccurately. Ineffective fire would in turn encourage the cavalry, as would any sign of wavering among the infantry. As the distance between them diminished the pressure on both sides increased until finally one or other lost their nerve.

The sight of a solid line of cavalry, especially heavy cavalry, bearing down at speed, would make the bravest man flinch:

> A considerable number of French cuirassiers made their appearance, on the rising ground just in our front, took the artillery we had placed there, and came at a gallop down upon us. Their appearance, as an enemy, was certainly enough to inspire a feeling of dread, – none of them under six feet; defended by steel helmets and breastplates, made pigeon-breasted to throw off the balls. Their appearance was of such a formidable nature, that I thought we could not have the slightest chance with them.[60]

If there was time, infantry's best defence against cavalry was to form a hollow square or oblong facing outwards. Each side of the square would be four or six ranks deep, with the front rank kneeling, holding their muskets out at a sharp angle, the butt resting on the ground, the bayonets making a hedge of sharp points. The officers, sergeants and colours were in the centre of the square where they were close to all the men and could move quickly to check any signs of disorder. This was one of the great advantages of a square: it so enhanced discipline that it 'would have taken a brave man to run away',[61] while the men's morale was helped by being packed tightly together. Another great advantage of a square was that it could not be attacked in the flank or rear, because it faced in all directions. Troops in other formations were probably always a little nervous about this even when no threat was visible, but in a square the men knew that their rear was protected by men of their own unit.

Squares were usually quite small, having a frontage of 100 feet or less, and with considerable gaps between them, so that approaching cavalry had to swerve only slightly to avoid a collision. This subjected the cavalry's resolution to much greater temptation than when charging a continuous line, where there was no easy or obvious alternative to a collision, or troops in open order (such as skirmishers, or even an artillery battery) where there was no fear of a collision to deter the cavalry from charging home.

Occasionally much larger squares might be used, most famously by the French in Egypt who formed squares from whole divisions; but such giant formations were inflexible, slow to form, and vulnerable to artillery. The combining of men from different units, while sometimes necessary (for example when two very weak battalions united to form a moderate sized square), weakened the psychological bonds holding the troops together. One veteran declared that:

> Squares have a moral strength in proportion to the mutual acquaintance of the men and officers who compose them. Men of the same company stand better together than those of mixed companies, and men of the same regiment better than those of different corps.[62]

But all squares, whether large or small, had several disadvantages: they were virtually immobile, or, at least, they lost much of their extra cohesion if they tried to move, and they could be vulnerable to attack by enemy infantry and artillery. Their small size made them a difficult target for guns at long range, but they were so dense that each round-shot which hit them did maximum damage, which was noticed by every man in the unit. They were even more vulnerable to infantry or canister fire, for their formation allowed them to bring only a small proportion of their muskets to bear. If the cavalry could establish a battery within canister range, or co-ordinate its attack with supporting infantry, the square would soon be reduced to a shambles, unable to make any resistance when cavalry attacked again. But in practice such co-ordination proved difficult.

Squares did not rely on their fire to repel the cavalry, but on their solidity. At the Katzbach the rain prevented the Prussian infantry from firing but they maintained their good order and formation until panicked by the appearance of French lancers. Good infantry would often hold their fire until the cavalry had turned aside, and at Waterloo isolated French horsemen sometimes taunted the

British infantry, even hitting at their bayonets with sabres, or firing into the square with pistols, in an effort to provoke them into firing. The British resisted partly to conserve ammunition, partly as an exercise in the discipline and order on which the square depended for its safety, and partly because the moments after firing were the most dangerous for the square. Then, if ever, there might be unsteadiness as the men hurried to reload. Parquin describes how an Austrian square was broken at Wagram when the French charged it twice in quick succession. The first attack was repulsed with a volley, but the second came before the Austrians could reload, and they broke, though if their nerve had held they would have been quite safe. The same sequence occurred to the 1/4th *Ligne* in Vandamme's division at Austerlitz. To guard against it the rear ranks might alternate their fire with those in front, so that some troops on each face of the square would always have their muskets loaded – though as with any form of controlled fire this could collapse in the pressure of the moment.[63]

The first attack on a square was normally the most dangerous: if it was repulsed the infantry would gain confidence. At Waterloo, one officer observed:

> The first time a body of cuirassiers approached the square . . . the men – all young soldiers – seemed to be alarmed. They fired high, and with little effect; and in one of the angles there was just as much hesitation as made me feel exceedingly uncomfortable; but it did not last long. No actual dash was made upon us. . . . Our men soon discovered that they had the best of it; and ever afterwards, when they heard the sound of cavalry approaching, appeared to consider the circumstance a pleasant change; for the enemy's guns suspended their fire.

This last, surprising point is supported by Gronow in his evocative description:

> During the battle our squares presented a shocking sight. Inside we were nearly suffocated by the smoke and smell from burnt cartridges. It was impossible to move a yard without treading upon a wounded comrade, or upon the bodies of the dead; and the loud groans of the wounded and dying were most appalling.
>
> At four o'clock our square was a perfect hospital, being full of dead, dying and mutilated soldiers. The charges of cavalry were in appearance very formidable, but in reality a great relief, as the artillery could no longer fire on us.[64]

So long as infantry held their nerve, a well-formed square was almost invulnerable. The only clearly established example of determined infantry in such a formation being broken was at Garcia Hernandez in 1812, when the French formation was thrown into confusion by a dying horse collapsing into its ranks. But the men did not always hold their nerve, particularly when they were attacked with some element of surprise; while forming square in the presence of the enemy was full of danger, requiring cool nerves and experience to execute the complicated drill without confusion. According to one correspondent to the *Royal Military Chronicle*, who may have overstated his case a little, for he was advocating reforms,

> almost everything depends on the perfect attention and recollection of twenty-four pivot men, the side faces of the square being formed from six companies, each composed of four sections, which sections having to wheel up half of them to the right, the remainder to the left: if any one of the twenty-four pivot men of these sections makes any mistake, such as turning to the wrong hand, or perhaps forgetting to face at all, considerable confusion must arise; and that such an event is not very improbable, even in the highest disciplined regiments, must be admitted, when we consider, that independent of the chances of pivot men being recently killed or disabled, this manoeuvre is performed at a moment when a body of cavalry is threatening to charge, and at such a moment the mind even of a British soldier may not be perfectly collected, particularly should it happen to be his first time in battle.

Nor was it only the pivot men who might make a mistake: at Quatre Bras, Major Lindsay of the 69th is said to have given the wrong order to two companies of his battalion, which as a consequence was ridden down by Kellermann's cuirassiers. At Waterloo, much of the British infantry was formed in four-deep line, which made the procedure for forming square much quicker and easier, by eliminating one step in the drill (see above, p. 73).[65]

Either because there was no time to form square, or for other reasons, infantry sometimes chose, or were compelled, to attempt to repulse cavalry when in line or column. This was difficult, but by no means impossible, especially if their flanks were well protected. At Albuera Harvey's Portuguese brigade of Cole's division, with steady nerves and regular fire, drove off four regiments of French dragoons which attacked them. This was especially impressive as the Portuguese had never been in battle before. It was their first action of the day, so they had suffered few, if any, casualties, and their muskets were clean and well loaded, but their confidence had not been bolstered by any earlier successes. Their flanks were protected by a battalion in column at each end of their line, and their advance was well supported by cavalry and artillery.[66]

In a case such as this the infantry needed both a steady demeanour to deter the cavalry from charging home and the effect of their fire to break the cavalry's momentum. The two were of course related, for it needed steady nerves to hold fire until the cavalry were within effective range. As they were in line every musket could be brought to bear, so that the fire would be much more effective than that of a square, provided the men remained calm. A cavalryman acknowledged: 'The sudden fall of men and horses, when it exceeds a certain proportion, entirely annuls the physical force of the squadron, and makes it continuing to dash forward, not a matter of will or courage, but a question of *possibility*.[67] But if the fire was ineffective, and the cavalry pressed on, the infantry were almost certain to break. Thus the encounter tested the resolution and discipline of each side: the greater the dash of the cavalry, the more likely they were to unnerve the infantry; the more determined the infantry, the more effective their fire and the better their chance of stopping the cavalry's charge.

Infantry were always cautious about advancing in the face of cavalry, especially in line. There would be no time to form square if the cavalry attacked, while any disorder – perhaps caused by rough ground – might give the cavalry the opportunity it needed. Columns were safer, for they were less likely to be disordered and could quickly form an improvised solid square. This formation was not nearly as strong as a regular square and its sides had little firepower, but it had a good chance of beating off any but the most determined cavalry charge. Even the British sometimes preferred to advance in column rather than line if the enemy's cavalry was in strength.[68]

Retreating was even more difficult, for the cavalry would be emboldened and the infantry more nervous, especially at having to turn their backs on the horsemen. The worst tactical mistake Wellington made in all his Peninsular battles was at Fuentes de Oñoro when he detached the newly formed Seventh Division too far on one flank and then had to bring them back in the face of a great concentration of French cavalry. But the men's nerve held and despite a few odd incidents they made their retreat in good order with the help of the British cavalry and the Light Division. At El Bodon later in 1811 French cavalry again pressed British and Portuguese infantry (this time the Third Division) as they retreated for six miles across flat open country. After one full-scale charge had been beaten off, the French tested the infantry's resolution with repeated half-charges, not pressing their attacks home when it was obvious that the infantry were steady. Long before Picton's men reached the safety of their entrenched camp at Fuente Guinaldo the psychological contest was over, for they had ceased to fear the cavalry, and the cavalry's confidence had evaporated.

Cavalry's main weapon may have been fear, but they were not immune to it themselves. Charging well-prepared infantry and artillery could be a terrifying experience, as Philippe de Segur found:

> We charged at full speed, I was about ten paces in front with my head bent down, uttering our war-cry by way of distracting my attention from the din of the enemy's fire which was all breaking out at once, and the infernal hiss of their bullets and grapeshot. Reckoning on the rapidity of our impetuous attack, I was hoping that in their astonishment at our audacity the enemy would aim badly; that we should have time to dash into the midst of their guns and bayonets and throw them into disorder. But they aimed only too well!

Very soon, in spite of our clamour and the detonation of so many arms, I could distinguish behind me the sound of smart reports followed by groans, with the thud of falling men and horses, which made me foresee defeat . . . I did not dare turn my head, fearing that the sad spectacle would cause me to give up. . . .

I was alone within thirty paces of the [enemy].[69]

Almost all cavalry's greatest successes occurred when their opponents were caught by surprise, or were already engaged with other troops, or were already wavering. But it took a good leader to recognize the fleeting opportunity and to seize it. At Marengo, it came late in the day, Desaix's counter-attack had faltered, and the Austrians were advancing, tired but confident of success. The French line broke, the Austrians rushed forward 'in all the disorder and security of victory', when suddenly Kellermann, at the head of 400 dragoons, burst from the cover of vines and into their flank. Panic spread throughout the Austrian lines: some were cut down, others fled, and many surrendered. With an exhausted army and no remaining reserves to counter the sudden threat, the Austrians could not avoid defeat.[70]

At Albuera Colborne's brigade of William Stewart's division was sent forward in line – against the wishes of its commander, who wanted the flanking battalion in column, but was overruled by Stewart. The brigade advanced against a heavy French column which was already engaged with Spanish infantry. The French moved a brigade of cavalry (including a regiment of Polish lancers) to support their infantry just as a rain squall swept across the battlefield. Out of the rain the unseen cavalry suddenly charged down on Colborne's unprotected flank. Three of the four British battalions were rolled up and destroyed in the space of a few minutes, only the fourth managing to form square in time. These three battalions entered the battle with 1,648 officers and men, and lost 1,258 casualties in all or 76 per cent: 319 killed, 460 wounded, and 479 missing (mostly prisoners). Five of their six colours were captured and a battery which accompanied them was overrun, though all but one of its guns were recovered when the cavalry were finally driven off by the arrival of the British cavalry. Of the 880 men in the French and Polish cavalry some 200 fell in the charge and subsequent fighting.[71]

At both Salamanca and Waterloo the British heavy cavalry broke French divisions when their attention was focused on the British infantry in their front. In all these cases the infantry offered little or no effective resistance. The cohesion of their units was broken and they became a mass of frightened individuals. 'The Enemy's Column', wrote one British officer, 'seemed very helpless, and had very little fire to give from its front or flanks . . . the front and flanks began to turn their backs inwards; the rear of the Columns had already begun to run away.' 'The Enemy fled as a flock of sheep across the valley – quite at the mercy of the Dragoons.' Another noticed men on the edge of the column 'with their backs towards me, and endeavouring to force their way into the crowd'. They were 'so jammed together that the men could not bring down their arms, or use them effectively, and we had nothing to do but to continue to press them down the slope'.[72]

Few infantry wrote much about the experience, though Private William Brown in the British 45th at Salamanca gives some idea what it must have been like, even though his regiment was saved before it could be completely broken:

> As our brigade was marching up to attack a strongly posted column of infantry, a furious charge was made by a body of cavalry upon our Regiment, and, not having time to form square, we suffered severely. Several times the enemy rode through us, cutting down with their sabres all that opposed them. Our ranks were broken and thrown into the utmost confusion. Repeatedly our men attempted to reform, but all in vain – they were as often cut down and trampled upon by their antagonists. At length, however, the enemy was driven off by some squadrons of our cavalry, who came up in time to save us from being totally destroyed. Numerous and severe were the wounds received on this occasion. Several had their arms dashed from their shoulders, and I saw more than one with their heads completely cloven. Among the rest I received a wound, but comparatively slight, although well aimed. Coming in contact with one of the enemy he brandished his sword over me, and standing in his stirrup-irons, prepared to strike; but, pricking his horse with my bayonet, it reared and pranced, when the sword fell, the point striking my forehead. He was, however, immediately brought down, falling with a groan to rise no more.[73]

In this situation infantrymen had few choices, and none of them was very attractive. They could, like William Brown, seek to defend themselves against the horsemen, though in such a fight they were at a great disadvantage and were likely to be knocked down by the press of cavalry if they were not first cut down. They could seek safety by burrowing and shoving their way into the centre of the unit – though they would have to struggle with many comrades if they were to succeed. Or they could try to run, and though men on foot had no hope of outpacing horsemen this might be their best chance if there were friendly troops or rough ground – a hill, a wood, or even a ditch – nearby which could provide shelter.

They might also lie down – or, more plausibly, trip and fall – and let the cavalry ride over them. Horses were generally reluctant to tread on a fallen man, even if their riders were actively urging them to do so, but in the press and confusion of a cavalry charge the horses might have no choice. At Waterloo, when the 69th were broken, Captain 'Barlow, and many others, lay down and escaped hurt, except from the trampling of horses. He was limping along, very sore and lame, and feelingly declaimed against the common notion, that a horse will not tread on a man lying on the ground. His jacket was blackened with the marks of horse shoes.'[74] Barlow, despite his soreness, had escaped serious injury – but then, if his skull had been crushed by a horse's hoof, we would never have known, for dead men tell no tales. Individuals might find safety by lying down, but the cohesion of the unit was broken and that, not the infliction of casualties, was the primary object of a cavalry charge.

At its best a successful cavalry charge – such as Kellermann's at Marengo – could alter the course of a battle, spreading destruction and fear throughout the enemy's army. Striking at the right moment cavalry could rout many times their own numbers of opposing infantry and even, by their impetuosity, sweep aside the enemy's supporting cavalry. They could inflict crippling casualties on a broken unit, shatter its morale, and send thousands of prisoners to the rear; but the cost, even of a successful charge, was likely to be high, not just in casualties received, but in men sent to the rear to guard the prisoners and others who, for one reason or another, never rejoined their unit, while the remainder were likely to be weary men on tired horses. Le Marchant's charge at Salamanca took only forty minutes and encountered little serious resistance, but at its end 'it was with difficulty that three squadrons could be collected and formed out of the whole brigade,' which had begun with nine.[75] Cavalry was a powerful but fragile weapon which needed an extraordinary mixture of caution and daring in its use.

Part III
Command and Control

Chapter Seven
The Role of the General

The responsibility for the success or failure of an army in battle rested entirely on the shoulders of the general commanding it. Nor was this just an abstract formality: during the height of the French and Spanish Revolutions unsuccessful generals paid with their lives, while the Austrian General Mack was sentenced to death for his failure at Ulm, and was actually imprisoned for several years in a fortress before he was pardoned. The rewards for success could be equally substantial: Napoleon rose to supreme power in France and his subordinates gained great wealth and prestige. Blücher emerged from provincial obscurity (one of nine sons of an infantry captain) to become a field marshal and Prince of Whalstadt, while Wellington advanced through every step of the British peerage, received vast sums in Parliamentary grants, together with a valuable estate in Spain, a fine collection of pictures captured at Vitoria (and now on display at Apsley House in London), and innumerable foreign titles and decorations. Even Bernadotte, despite having a relatively undistinguished career in the field, lived out his days as King of Sweden. As always, the punishments and rewards were not necessarily just or commensurate with real merit, but they emphasize the personal nature of the responsibility of commanding an army.

In a set-piece battle the general had usually done his most important work by the time the first shot was fired. The days or weeks of the campaign preceding the action determined its circumstances – which commander had managed to concentrate the greater force, whether one was able to fight on a battlefield of his choosing, or if one army had been unsettled by being forced to retreat. Wide turning movements may have been initiated which could bear fruit during the battle, or troops might have been detached too far to rejoin in time to take part in the fighting.

Long before the first clash of arms at Waterloo, the shape of the battle had been decided: Napoleon had detached Grouchy with 33,000 men to pursue the Prussians, leaving his main force dangerously weak. Wellington had received assurances of Prussian support, without which he would not have risked fighting: indeed the leading elements of the Prussian army were already approaching the battlefield, although it would be some hours before they arrived in strength. Wellington had also detached a force of 18,000 men to Hal, presumably to protect his right flank against a turning movement, and had given them no orders to march to the sound of the guns.

In a battle such as Waterloo the general standing on the defensive had considerable advantages. He, or his staff, could often choose the battlefield – which could require great skill. The Prussian position at Ligny appeared strong, but proved vulnerable, while the advantages of the position at Waterloo were far from obvious. The position not only had to be strong, it also had to suit his army: the high rocky ridge at Busaco was appropriate to Wellington's army, which was relatively weak in cavalry and artillery: had they been his strengths he would have preferred gently rolling open country. It also had to match the strength of his army, although exceptions can occasionally be found to this rule, as at Busaco and the Caya, where the great natural strength of the position compensated for it requiring more men to be held fully than Wellington had available. Having selected his battlefield, the defending general might seek to strengthen it with earthworks and other field fortifications, as at Borodino. Next he would deploy his army to occupy the position, allocating different sections of the line to different units and holding as many troops as possible in reserve. He would place his cavalry and artillery where they could operate most effectively and try to ensure that all his units could provide mutual support. If the ground would permit, he would be well advised to have most of his men out of sight of the enemy, who would then have to plan their attack guessing at his positions.

Once the defending general had deployed his army in his chosen position the initiative passed to his opponent, although if the latter committed a gross blunder the defender might suddenly move on to the attack, as Wellington was tempted to do, but did not, when Marmont dawdled invitingly in front of his San Cristobal position in June 1812. But usually he had to wait for his opponent to make the first moves before he could respond. On the night before Waterloo, Lord Uxbridge, Wellington's second-in-command, approached him in some anxiety complaining that if anything happened to the Duke, he, Uxbridge, would be left in command of the army and that he knew nothing of Wellington's plans.

> The Duke listened to him to the end, without saying a single word, and then asked: 'Who will attack the first tomorrow, I or Bonaparte?' 'Bonaparte,' was the reply. 'Well,' continued the Duke, 'Bonaparte has not given me any idea of his projects: and as my plans will depend upon his, how can you expect me to tell you what mine are?' The Duke then rose, and putting his hand on Uxbridge's shoulder, added, 'There is one thing certain, Uxbridge, that is, that whatever happens, you and I will do our duty.' The two men then shook hands, and Uxbridge retired.[1]

Wellington was always sensitive on the subject of his mortality, and greatly disliked the whole concept of having a second-in-command; nor did he have a great opinion of Uxbridge's ability, and the two men were not personally close. This accounts for the curtness of the interview, but there was in fact very little that Wellington could say, for, as he stated, his conduct of the battle would have to be extemporized in response to the French actions. Some gentle discussion of possible courses of action would however have done much to calm his deputy's nerves.

While the defending general could do little but wait, his attacking opponent would reconnoitre the position, perhaps launch a few probing attacks, make his plans, and issue his orders. This was when the attacking general had the advantage: he could choose the point or points at which he would strike, mask his intentions with a feint attack, concentrate his forces and prepare their way with artillery fire. His instructions were generally fairly simple, for the friction of war gave all military operations a tendency to go wrong, and the more complicated the plan the greater the danger of misunderstandings and confusion. Masséna's orders for Busaco are worth quoting almost in full (II Corps was commanded by Reynier, VI Corps including Loison's division was commanded by Ney, and VIII Corps by Junot):

II Corps will attack the enemy's right; it will endeavour to break through the enemy's line, after scaling the most accessible point of the mountain. It will reach its objective in one or two columns preceded by skirmishers. Once it has reached the crest at the point selected for attack, it will form up in close column and cross the mountain ridge to the Coimbra road beyond. It will halt at the Busaco monastery. . . .

VI Corps will attack by the two tracks leading to the Coimbra road; one of its divisions will be held in reserve, and its artillery will be distributed so as to give support as needed. Marshal Ney will dispose his two assault columns so as to launch them as soon as General Reynier has captured the ridge, and he will then advance on the Busaco monastery. It will be Marshal Ney's duty to press home his attack if he sees the enemy either trying to counter-attack General Reynier or retiring. . . . His attack will be preceded by skirmishers. On reaching the crest he will reorganize his troops in order to conform to the further movements of the army.

VIII Corps will concentrate behind Moura at 0600 hours. It will deploy and be ready to support the attacking corps as required and join in the forward advance. . . .

The cavalry reserve will be stationed on the Coimbra road, behind the centre of VIII Corps.[2]

These orders are a model of clarity and would surely win high marks in any staff college. Each corps was given a simple objective and the basic plan was elegant: Reynier's II Corps would break the British line where it was most accessible then advance along the ridge top rolling up the enemy forces; Ney would advance to attack the centre while Reynier threatened their flank; VIII Corps and the cavalry would provide an ample reserve and protection against any allied counter-attack. But, of course, the plan did not work. The French had not reconnoitred the allied position sufficiently, and Reynier encountered much more serious opposition than Masséna expected. The French marshal under-rated the fighting quality of Wellington's troops, and made his attacks with little preparation, while the stipulation that II and VI Corps should each attack in only one or two columns seems unwise. Still, his task was not easy. The great bulk of Wellington's men were concealed behind the crest of the ridge, whose height rendered the French artillery virtually ineffective. The allied skirmish-ing line was so strong that the French light infantry could not adequately prepare the way for their attacking columns. Hindsight suggests that Masséna would have been wiser to turn Wellington's flank and manoeuvre him out of his position, or, if he was determined to have a battle, that he should have placed more emphasis on overcoming the allied skirmishers, and ensured that each attacking column was supported by a second line a few hundred yards to the rear. But he was over-confident, dismissing the Portuguese troops as worthless, and underestimating both the British infantry and their commander. So he preferred to strike quickly and hard in the early morning, presuming that the local numerical superiority of each attack would ensure its success – and if his assessment of the allied army had been correct, the result would probably have been another French triumph.

Masséna's role once the fighting began was minimal and largely unimportant. He had committed two of his infantry corps to the attack and the success of the battle was now up to them and their commanders. Faced with their defeat all he could do was to advance his reserves to cover their retreat, and to decide whether it was worth throwing Junot's untouched corps into the battle in the hope of reversing the fortune of the day. Wisely he refrained and instead began to consider ways of manoeuvring the allies out of their position.

The simplicity of Masséna's orders for Busaco in part reflects the relatively simple shape of the battle: the British were occupying a clearly defined position which his men were to attack. But even in a more complex battle, such as Aspern-Essling or Austerlitz, where both sides were advancing to attack the other, the initial orders could not be too complicated. Thus the Austrian orders for Aspern-Essling run to only about 700 words, and are complicated only in that the army is divided into five columns whose movements sometimes depend on each other. For example:

The second column will consist of the troops of General Bellegarde; leaving Gerarsdorf to the left, it will march towards Leopoldau, endeavour to join the first column on the right, advance towards Kagrau, and then conjointly with the third column upon the left, push forward towards Hirschstetten.

These are the only orders specifically for Bellegarde's column but the instructions concluded with some directions for the whole army: the advance was to begin at noon, supporting troops were to follow at suitable distances and the order of march and deployment of the artillery were to be left to the column commanders, though to this discretion was added the rider that 'The whole will march by half divisions', and a few other specific instructions. The last two paragraphs are worth quoting:

> The principal objects are to drive back the enemy entirely over the first arm of the Danube, destroy the bridges he has thrown over it, and occupy the bank of the Lobau with a numerous body consisting especially of artillery.
>
> The Generalissimo recommends order, coolness, and a proper use of every species of arms during the advance. His station will be with the second column.[3]

These instructions convey much less of a sense of the shape of the battle which was to come than Masséna's: indeed they reveal no clear plan of how the Austrians hoped to break Napoleon's army, and amount to little more than instructions on how the army would deploy in the field. Subsequent actions would depend on how the French were deployed and the results of the early fighting. The Archduke Charles – the Austrian commander at Aspern-Essling – would play a far more active role in the battle than Masséna did at Busaco, reacting to events, seeking to exploit successes and contain local defeats, while trying to sense any shift in the overall pattern of the battle.

Brief though they were, these orders are perhaps overly elaborate: it is not hard to foresee the problems which would arise for the second column if either of its neighbours fell behind or got into difficulties. The Austrian staff were the most cerebral in Europe, and a famous clash of cultures occurred at Austerlitz where they prepared the plans for the advance of the predominantly Russian army. The Austrian General Weyrother addressed a meeting of the allied generals at Kutusov's headquarters on the night before the battle. According to General Langeron, who was present,

> General Weyrother came in. He had an immense map, showing the neighbourhood of Brünn and Austerlitz in the greatest precision and detail. He spread it on the large table, and read his dispositions to us in a loud voice, and with a boastful manner which betrayed smug self-satisfaction. He might have been a formmaster reading a lesson to his pupils, though he was far from being a good teacher. We had found Kutusov half asleep in a chair when we arrived at his house, and by the time we came to leave he had dozed off completely. Buxhöwden was standing. He listened to what was being said, though it must have gone in one ear and out the other. Miloradovich spoke not a word. Prebyshevsky kept in the background, and only Dokhturov examined the map with any attention.[4]

Langeron's jaundiced account may be exaggerated, but the chaos of the following morning as allied columns got in each other's way, causing untold delays and leading to a sense of dissatisfaction and uncertainty even before the fighting began, shows that Weyrother's plan was totally unsuited to the allied army.

Not all battles, of course, could be planned in advance. At Salamanca, Wellington took the decision to attack suddenly, when he concluded that Marmont's army had become irretrievably over-extended. He at once rode in person to the extreme right of the army, outpacing all of his staff on the way. Here he found Colonel D'Urban with his Portuguese dragoons, informed him that the Third Division was about to attack the French opposite, and ordered him to support them. He next arrived in front of the Third Division, commanded on that day by his brother-in-law Edward Pakenham, who was with a group of officers at the head of his troops. According to one account, Wellington appeared quite unruffled, though a little paler than usual. He tapped Pakenham on the shoulder and said, '"Edward, move on with the 3rd Division – take the heights in your front – and drive everything before you." – "I will, my lord" was the laconic reply of the gallant Sir Edward.'[5] Other versions differ slightly on the wording or insist upon a handshake, but all agree on the simplicity and lack of detail of the orders given, which left the entire arrangement of the attack to Pakenham's discretion, even though this was the first time he had commanded a large body in action.

Wellington's next move was probably to the cavalry where he is reported to have told Le Marchant to support Pakenham's attack, and to take the first favourable opportunity to charge the enemy's infantry. '"You must then charge," said Lord Wellington, "at all hazards."'[6] He is next sighted moving back towards the centre of the army and giving orders to Major-General Leith, commander of the Fifth Division. These instructions – according to Leith's nephew and aide-de-camp – were rather more detailed and specific:

> General Leith was directed to form his division in two lines, the first of which was composed of the Royal, 9th and 38th regiments, with part of the 4th regiment from General Pringle's brigade, necessarily brought forward for the purpose of equalising the lines, of which the second was formed by the remainder of General Pringle's, and the whole of General Spry's Portuguese infantry.
>
> When General Bradford's brigade came up, he division was to *appui* itself on his left, march directly up the heights, and attack the enemy's columns. Lord Wellington on this, as on all occasions, gave his orders in a clear, concise, and spirited manner: there was no appearance of contemplating a doubtful result; all he directed was as to time and formation, and his instructions concluded with commands that the enemy should be overthrown, and driven from the field. He then proceeded towards the 4th division. . . .[7]

And so Wellington went on, giving similar orders to each of the divisions in his front line. This level of personal involvement was unusual: the general's

orders would normally be carried by an aide-de-camp or orderly, but Wellington had embarked on a sudden and complete change of plan, and probably
felt that by delivering the orders in person he could avoid the risk of hesitation
or delay, and resolve any doubts on the spot. After all, it was much easier for
him to point out the troops he wished Pakenham to attack, rather than describe
them on paper or rely on the discretion of an assistant. It also suited the overall
shape of the battle he envisaged, where the British attack would be led by the
right flank and roll, in a slightly staggered sequence, along the line.

There are various mentions of Wellington once the battle began, watching
the progress of the attack and controlling his reserves. Private Wheeler
in the Seventh Division caught a typical glimpse of him towards the end of
the day:

> Lord Wellington rode up to us, and entered into conversation with Colonel
> Mitchell. He waited some time anxiously looking towards the hill, as the enemy's
> fire was very brisk. Colonel M—— said to Lord W—— that he should like to
> advance and drive them from the hill, but his Lordship looking as serious as a
> Judge going to pass sentence of death, shook his head and said it is not time yet.
> At length he called out '7th Division, Advance'; spurred his horse, rode to our
> left and in a few minutes was lost in dust and smoke.[8]

The informality, even casualness, of Wellington's battlefield orders does not
seem to have been unusual. At Wagram, Napoleon sent word to Oudinot, ' "to
push a little further forward" to "make some music before dark" '. At Ligny he
was overheard instructing Gérard, commander of the IV Corps, ' "You must go
toward that steeple, and drive the Prussians in as far as you can. I will support
you. Grouchy has my orders." ' While at Eylau, when the Russian counter-
attack was threatening the French centre, Napoleon turned to Murat and said
either: 'Take all your available cavalry and crush that column,' or, perhaps
more plausibly, 'Are you going to let those fellows eat us up?' Whatever the
wording, it was enough to send the reserve cavalry into a major attack, all of
whose details were left to Murat to organize, or to delegate further down the
chain of command.[9]

Napoleon normally seems to have left more to the discretion of his subordinates than Wellington, reflecting partly the larger armies which he commanded,
and perhaps also the greater experience of his subordinates. The long years of
the Revolutionary War gave French generals a level of experience and expertise
which the British did not match until the later campaigns of the Peninsular
War. Conversely, Napoleon himself had no experience of commanding infantry
or cavalry – as opposed to a whole army – in open battle; he seems to have had
little interest in the details of tactics, and his fighting commanders – men such
as Ney, Lannes, Davout and Murat – might well have resented interference
in the details of their operations (not that this stopped Masséna giving Ney
relatively detailed instructions at Busaco).

Written orders once the battle began seem to have been rare. If the general did not personally deliver his orders, he sent an aide-de-camp or staff officer with the message. Sometimes this could be embarrassing, and Marbot tells a characteristically highly coloured story of being sent by Marshal Lannes to Marshal Bessières with insulting orders to 'charge *home*'. More seriously, there was an obvious risk of the orders being confused in transmission, and a staff officer might sometimes jot down the gist of the orders in his pocket book, and read it back to the general before setting out. This seems a sensible precaution, yet Harry Smith, who had much experience as an aide-de-camp and staff officer in Wellington's army, explicitly says that he had never done so until an occasion in September 1813, at the action at Vera, when he strongly (and rightly) disagreed with the orders which he was being given by the officer in command, Colonel Skerret. A description of Napoleon at Wagram supports the point. When he wished to issue an order, Napoleon would summon an aide who 'was given the order slowly and clearly, then each time was required to repeat it. If this was not satisfactory, he was given the orders again, without an overbearing tone; then he was required to repeat them again. If the officer gave the order word perfect, he heard "Go"' and galloped off to his destination.[10]

But some orders were written, for two of Wellington's survive from Waterloo. They appear to be unique, partly at least because they were written in pencil on slips of asses' skin which could be wiped clear and used for a fresh order. Neither carries address or signature. The first was evidently to the commander of the troops defending Hougoumont:

> I see that the fire has communicated from the Hay stack to the roof of the Chateau. You must however still keep your Men in those parts to which the fire does not reach. Take care that no Men are lost by the falling in of the Roof or floors – After they both are fallen in occupy the Ruined walls inside the Garden; particularly if it should be possible for the Enemy to pass through the Embers in the inside of the House.

This all appears eminently sensible, though it is probable that the local commander would have taken these steps even without the instructions. Nor could Wellington devote equal attention to the whole battlefield. He is said not to have gone east of La Haye Sainte during all the fighting, while that vital post fell when its defenders ran out of ammunition. He was not unusual, however, in sometimes issuing orders directly to quite junior officers, bypassing the regular chain of command, and concerning himself with details such as the placement of a couple of guns or the withdrawal of a light company which might be thought to have been beneath his notice. This had obvious risks – a junior officer might be confused by contradictory orders from his august superiors, or the general might interfere in something of which he knew little, such as artillery – but with good commanders at least these risks were outweighed by the benefits of experience and an authority which could cut through many a Gordian knot.

The second surviving order may have been to Lord Uxbridge:

> We ought to have more of the Cavalry between the two high Roads. That is to say three Brigades at least besides the Brigade in observation on the Right; & besides the Belgian Cavalry & the D. of Cumberland's Hussars.
> One heavy & one light Brigade might remain on the left.[11]

It was probably as a result of this note that the light cavalry brigades of Vivian and Vandeleur were brought from the extreme left of the army to support the centre. The Prussian advance now protected the allied left, and these light cavalry led the advance of Wellington's army after the repulse of the Imperial Guard – indeed, according to Sir Hussey Vivian, his brigade virtually won the battle by itself, although this version of events has not gained wide acceptance.[12]

It was normally very difficult to withdraw troops even from a quiet sector of the battle line, in order to reinforce a threatened point. Once deployed in the front line troops largely passed beyond the control of their commander, although he could, as Wellington did at Waterloo, signal a simple order, such as to move from the defensive to a general advance, or, conversely, give the order to retreat. But for much of the time the general could only influence the course of the battle by committing fresh troops from his reserve, whether to exploit an advantage or to contain a local defeat. Such reserves were precious, and many hard-fought battles were decided by who retained the last uncommitted force. Consequently an important element in the art of generalship was the ability to judge the 'ripeness' of a battle; when to refuse to release any reinforcements, and when to dole out a few. Hence the image of Napoleon sitting slumped in a chair, or impassive on horseback, curtly waving aside the urgent pleas from his fighting marshals for more men, because the decisive moment had yet to come. Sometimes, as at Austerlitz, the reserves were not needed; sometimes, as at Borodino, the restraint was excessive and reserves which might have made victory complete remained unused; but usually the judgement was excellent, reflecting Napoleon's ability, his experience, and, not least, his strength of character.

What made a good general on the battlefield? It is easy to make lists of abstract virtues, although they tell us little:

> He must have imagination to originate plans, practical sense and energy to carry them through. He must be observant, untiring, shrewd; kindly and cruel; simple and crafty; a watchman and a robber; lavish and miserly; generous and stingy; rash and conservative. All these and many other qualities, natural and acquired, he must have. He should also, as a matter of course, know his tactics. . . .[13]

This sounds like Polonius, but in fact is Socrates; and it avoids the real problem, which is not finding a general who is both rash and conservative, kindly and cruel and so on, but finding one who knows when each quality is appropriate.

A modern description, though ostensibly of Wellington, is almost equally utopian: 'supreme confidence in himself, rapidity of decision, readiness to assume responsibility, sure judgment, sufficient imagination to "guess what was on the other side of the hill", intense energy, physical courage, painstaking care, stamina and tenacity'.[14] Such qualities would entitle their possessor to almost any job on earth and quite a few in Heaven; while Wellington was by no means devoid of two of the most notable absences from the list: compassion and wit.

Even when we move on from exalted descriptions of the characteristics of a perfect general to the more mundane question of what he actually did, it is difficult to formulate useful principles underlying success, for the results verge on being platitudes. Who can doubt that a general should inspire his men with confidence, look after their welfare, and understand their character? Or that he should study his enemies and learn to exploit their weaknesses? Or again, that he should be quick to seize the fleeting opportunity, yet careful to avoid traps; maintain firm control of his troops, but not dampen their natural impetuosity; have a fierce will to win, but know when to cut his losses, and so on? Such principles give little clue as to why Masséna failed at Busaco, and Napoleon triumphed at Austerlitz; for the same sudden attack which, when successful, is described as 'bold and daring' is condemned as 'rash and fool-hardy' in the event of failure; while a protracted defence is likely to earn applause as 'dogged determination' or be criticized as 'obstinate folly' according to the result.

There were no magic keys to success, which explains why the written testimony of successful generals is usually so unrevealing, and why few if any great captains have been able to train their subordinates and successors in their methods. The most that we can say seems to be that good generals made few serious mistakes on the battlefield and ruthlessly exploited the mistakes of their opponents; that they had a thorough knowledge of the practical mechanics of war: how long it would take for a division of, say, 8,000 men to advance across 1,000 yards, deploying under enemy fire, and if it would then be in a state to climb a hill and assault some enemy batteries; that they had something of the chess player's skill of seeing several steps in advance where the move of every piece had implications for all the others, and, unlike in chess, where every piece on both sides could move simultaneously and none responded immediately to their commander's orders; and, finally, that they had the mental toughness to bear the responsibilities of command, the coolness in action to deal with sudden setbacks, and the character to risk defeat in order to gain victory.

Even all this did not guarantee success: two generals with an abundance of these qualities might face each other, as Napoleon and Wellington did at Waterloo, and one would be defeated. A good general in command of a poor or weak army would not always triumph over an inferior opponent whose army was stronger: Napoleon was overwhelmed at Leipzig, and Soult defeated at Albuera. The quality of the general was just one important factor of several which together determined the success of the day; while even the ablest generals were not always at their best.

While explanations of victory remain elusive some factors inviting defeat are obvious. The most common was a lack of unity in command: Napoleon ben-efited enormously from unquestioned authority as commander-in-chief and head of state, while the allied armies he defeated often had a muddled command structure. Kutusov was the nominal commander of the allied army at Austerlitz, but his authority was undermined by the proximity of the Emperors Alexander and Francis, while General Weyrother drew up the plans for the allied attack. Frederick William of Prussia took the field in 1806, though his presence made a relatively minor contribution to the ineptitude displayed by the Prussian command during the campaign. Alexander was with his armies both in the 1807 and the early stages of the 1812 campaign, and his lack of discretion encouraged the caballing and intrigues which beset the Russian high command. This grew even worse in 1813 with both Alexander and, to a lesser extent, Frederick William actively interfering with the conduct of operations on and off the battlefield. The unhappy Wittgenstein – Kutusov's successor – resigned after the defeats of Lützen and Bautzen, although he had had little real control over how either battle was fought. The entry of Austria into the war placed some restraint on Alexander while bringing another monarch and his powerful min-ister into the field. When the Czar pressed his claim to be given the supreme command of the allied armies, Metternich threatened to withdraw from the Coalition, and the honour went to Schwarzenberg, who excelled in patience and diplomatic tact rather than strategy and tactics, but who fully earned Blücher's toast to 'the Commander-in-Chief who had three monarchs at his headquarters and still managed to beat the enemy'.[15]

Schwarzenberg's success shows that unity of command was not a *sine qua non*, and Wellington and Blücher co-operated well in 1815, but nonetheless it was a great advantage. In the Peninsula French commanders usually exercised com-plete authority over their army – though Masséna found Ney a difficult sub-ordinate and was finally driven to dismiss him – but they had to put up with the periodic arrival of out-of-date orders from Napoleon disrupting their plans, although these did not normally extend to the conduct of battles. Wellington was more fortunate. The British government gave him very broad discretion, and other than his supersession after Vimeiro he was able to conduct his operations with little interference. The one occasion he fought a battle with an independent ally not subordinated to him was Talavera, where he and Cuesta co-operated well, notwithstanding their acrimonious quarrels during the campaign.

One reason why unity of command was so important was that its absence undermined the confidence of the army. This was another significant but not absolute factor in determining success: confident armies were sometimes defeated, while armies which lacked confidence, in themselves and in their commanders, sometimes succeeded. It was usually wise to remove a general who had lost the confidence of his troops, but not always, for as the summer of 1810 dragged by and the French besieged and captured Ciudad Rodrigo without interference, discontent at all levels of the British army in Portugal rose, and faith in Wellington was at a low ebb, yet the troops fought well at Busaco, and that victory and the success of the Lines of Torres Vedras restored Wellington's reputation.

Nonetheless, confidence was important. A general who gained his men's affection or devotion would find it easier to inspire them in a period of privation or adversity; while if the troops trusted their commander to lead them to victory, they would be less likely to panic and more likely to rally and return to the fray. One of Blücher's great qualities as a general was the ability to inspire and maintain this faith, despite a record which contained as many defeats as victories.

Napoleon worked hard to maintain his men's loyalty, with grand reviews, decorations or instant promotion for deserving soldiers, the ability to recognize (or appear to recognize) men from the ranks and find the right words to say to each, tweaking one man painfully by the ear while tugging at the heartstrings of the multitude. After Ebelsberg in 1809 he inspected the 26th *Léger* which had lost heavily in the fighting, and stunned the soldiers by making Lieutenant Guyot, reputedly the regiment's bravest officer, a baron of the Empire with a fortune to support his rank; and the appropriately named Corporal Bayonnette – the bravest non-commissioned man – a Chevalier in the Légion d'honneur with a handsome pension. The story of such lavish rewards spread through the army and gave many poor soldiers, who could never hope to rise through regular promotion, a faint, if misleading, hope of fame and a comfortable future.

Napoleon's charisma was immense and he used it to the full, amplifying it through the lying, flattering bulletins which the troops simultaneously loved and derided. The soldiers both idolized him, and grumbled incessantly. At many reviews the cries of 'Vive l'empereur' were half-hearted and accompanied by murmurs of 'Let him give me my discharge, and I'll cheer as much as they please!', and 'We have no bread; when my stomach is empty, I cannot cheer.' But when he was slightly wounded at Ratisbon (he was hit in the heel, but not much hurt), 'The news spread immediately throughout the army, causing a great sensation. Staff officers were despatched in all directions from the Emperor's headquarters to reassure the army. General Lauriston, one of the Emperor's aides-de-camp . . . came in person to tell us that the Emperor's wound was not serious.'[16]

Wellington's style was quite different: without the least hint of courting popularity among his troops, he was sparing of praise and quick to blame – especially his officers. His objects were different: he wanted, not devotion or loyalty, but discipline, duty and attention to detail. He thoroughly understood his army and knew that his troops would behave as badly or worse than the French if given a chance, arousing local resentment which would cripple his campaign, and he relied on his officers to hold them in check. He could be heartless and unjust, as in the sweeping condemnation of the army and its officers after the retreat from Burgos, or the arrest of Norman Ramsay – incidents which aroused resentment which still burned strong decades later. But he achieved his ends, and in time the army came to have the greatest faith in his ability, so that when he arrived on the field at Sorauren he was greeted with cheers and universal relief by the previously dispirited soldiers.[17]

Personal bravery under fire was an essential but commonplace virtue for a general. Its absence would quickly destroy the faith of an army in its commander, but only rarely was the question even hinted at: most generals had seen considerable action as junior officers, and risen in part through their gallantry. Yet while scores of senior officers in subordinate positions were killed in action during the period, it was rare for a general commanding an army to be disabled during a battle. Sir Ralph Abercromby, who was renowned for his rash bravery, was mortally wounded at Mandara; the Duke of Brunswick, commanding the Prussian army, was killed at Auerstädt; Sir John Moore was killed at Coruña; Marmont was seriously wounded at Salamanca; and Blücher was thrown from his horse and shaken, though not seriously hurt, at Ligny, as was Cuesta at Medellin. Wellington was hit a few times by spent bullets, usually late in the day, and never really hurt – the closest he came to serious injury was at Orthez, where he was left with a nasty bruise which made walking and riding painful for a few days. Napoleon was equally immune, and it seems likely that most generals did not expose themselves recklessly, knowing that their fall would risk paralysing their army. This does not mean that they observed the battle from afar in comfortable security – Wellington's behaviour at Waterloo points to the absurdity of the idea – but rather that they understood the progress of the battle, and did not normally plunge in where the fighting was thickest. Stray shots and cannon-balls remained a danger – and they account for most of the commanders who did fall – but the general was less exposed than his staff, who were dispatched to all quarters to deliver orders or to observe, and who prided themselves on their courage. This theory at least helps to explain how Wellington emerged unscathed from Waterloo, where so many of his staff were killed or wounded; the only alternative explanations being blind luck or his own, uncharacteristic if natural remark: 'The finger of Providence was upon me, and I escaped unhurt.'[18]

But a good general needed moral as well as physical courage. Sir John Murray was an experienced soldier when he was given command of the British expedition sent to besiege Tarragona on the east coast of Spain in 1812. He disliked the plan for the expedition, which had been imposed on him by Wellington, and had not long been in command of the army. Once landed he soon began to fear the worst, imagining that French armies were closing in on him from all sides, and feeding these fears by the blackest interpretation of every report and scrap of news which reached him. After ten days his frayed nerves finally snapped and he ordered his army to re-embark, abandoning his siege guns and equipment and leaving his Spanish allies in the lurch. His panic was groundless: the approaching French forces were still distant, and were too weak to pose a serious threat. He was relieved of his command and court-martialled, but escaped serious punishment.[19]

Although he outnumbered Soult by three to two, Beresford did not expect or want to fight at Albuera. Only a third of his army were British, the remainder being Spanish and Portuguese, and he was intimidated by Soult's powerful cavalry. When the French advance made a battle inevitable, he occupied the ground poorly and was chiefly concerned with protecting his line of retreat. According to a staff officer, once the fighting began, 'Our Marshal bravely exposed himself, but gave no orders, and the officers on his Staff acted as they thought best.' And though he later denied the fact, it is fairly clear that he actually issued orders for the army to retreat; orders which were only counter-manded when he realized that – thanks to the fighting qualities of his men – the battle was won. Beresford never commanded an army in action again, and suffered a breakdown after the battle; but he later resumed his duties in com-mand of the Portuguese army, and had some claim to command the whole allied force if anything happened to Wellington.[20]

Sir John Stuart gained the first British victory on the European mainland in the Napoleonic Wars at Maida in 1806, but according to the acerbic pen of his staff officer Henry Bunbury, the general's part in the victory was minimal:

But where was Sir John Stuart? and what great part did he play in this brilliant action? In truth, he seemed to be rather a spectator than a person much, or *the* person *most*, interested in the result of the conflict. He formed no plan; declared no intention, and scarcely did he trouble himself to give an order. Perfectly regardless of personal danger, he was cantering about, indulging in little pleas-antries as was his wont; and he launched forth with particular glee when a Sicilian marquis, whom he had brought with him as an extra aide-de-camp, betook himself to shelter from fire behind a haystack. But after the charge of Kempt's Light Infantry, and the utter rout of the French left wing, a change came over the spirit of Sir John Stuart. Still he dawdled about, breaking into passionate excla-mations: 'Begad, I never saw anything so glorious as this! There was nothing in Egypt to equal it! It is the finest thing I ever witnessed.' From that moment he was an altered man, and full of visions of coming greatness. As I found that I could get no orders from him, I made it my business to go round to the leaders of our several brigades, to give them what information I could, and try to supply their wants.[21]

Such incompetence was rare, and it is unfortunate that these three examples all involve British officers, whose collective record in the war was excellent. But nor is it fair that Sir John Stuart – assuming that Bunbury's account is not a complete libel – became a celebrated hero, having done nothing to deserve it. The sins of most defeated commanders were venial in comparison. At Salamanca Marmont grew careless and over-confident after a week's close manoeuvring which had required intense concentration. He had forced Wellington back and correctly guessed that the allies were ready to abandon Salamanca and retreat towards Portugal. Impatient, arrogant, desiring to give the retiring foe a parting blow, Marmont over-extended his army, moving Thomières's and Maucune's divisions too far to the left before other divisions were ready to support them. A trifling mistake, but it cost him the battle, for Wellington pounced and the French were caught in disarray.

Bennigsen's error at Friedland was scarcely worse: he saw an isolated French corps and crossed the River Alle to crush it. But Lannes was less isolated than he appeared, and the Russians were soon fighting with their backs to the river the little hope of escape.

Napoleon did not devise the trap at Friedland, but he does seem to have deliberately induced the allies to attack him in a way which suited him at Austerlitz. Weyrother's plan was not only ill-suited to the allied army, it was intrinsically bad, concentrating too many men in the broken ground at the southern end of the battlefield where even a small French force could seriously delay their advance, and leaving the entire centre empty and exposed to a French counter-stroke. But the French success was not only due to a brilliant plan and the mistakes of the allies; equally important, Napoleon knew how to exploit his advantage. His troops were in the right place at the outset and could advance without confusion and without getting in each other's way, while the reserves and supports were generally where they were needed. And, in marked contrast to the allies, the French army operated efficiently with an effective chain of command, and competent officers at all levels.

Austerlitz was most unusual: generals did not normally set such traps, relying instead on exploiting the natural mistakes of their opponent – while keeping their own army in good order and avoiding mistakes of their own. In many battles neither side made such a blunder – or if made, it was not exploited – and the result depended on hard fighting, introducing the reserves at the right time and in the right place, the actions of subordinates and simply on luck. But even the conduct of a battle such as this made great demands on a general's skill and experience, and on his physical and moral stamina.

No battle was ever a foregone conclusion, for a fatal accident or mistake could ruin the best-laid plans; but equally few battles were fought on perfectly even terms. The strength and position of each army as it began the campaign usually gave one side a significant advantage. The events of the campaign might redress this imbalance, or increase it. One general might benefit greatly by being able to fight on ground of his own choosing, or even by a better appreciation of the potential of the terrain where the battle happened to be fought. The plan of one commander might be far superior to that of his opponent, either because he anticipated the enemy's intentions and countered them in advance, or because he better understood the relative capacities of each army. Either commander, or their subordinates, could make an error which would imperil the whole army. Otherwise the fighting might wax and wane during the day as each side strove for the advantage. Opportunities or crises would arise requiring quick action from the general, who at the same time had to be careful not to squander his reserves. If the battle had gone badly, he had to be ready to accept defeat and to organize and order the retreat while there was still hope of bringing off the army in good order; if it went well he had to know when to commit his last reserves and make the final effort which would rout the enemy. And even as the battle ended, he had to be considering the next move: whether it was now best to exploit his victory, or what line of retreat to adopt. It was an immense burden and in most armies it rested squarely on the shoulders of a single man, whose staff officers and subordinates were there to implement his orders, not to share any of his responsibility.

Chapter Eight
Subordinate Commanders, Staff Officers and ADCs

Armies of the Napoleonic era, as in most other times, were organized into a clearly defined hierarchy. Beneath the commanding general were several layers of senior officers, with their numbers increasing as their seniority declined, like the branches of a family tree. At the lowest level were the commanders of battalions of infantry, regiments of cavalry and batteries of artillery – the basic tactical units – each of which contained a number of regimental officers as well as the fighting soldiers and NCOs. In theory the commanding general would issue his orders to his subordinates in the first tier, who would in turn amplify and interpret these orders to their subordinates, and so on down the chain of command: thus one will could set 100,000 or more men into controlled and organized movement. In practice, complications emerged: communications were not instantaneous or certain; subordinates sometimes misunderstood or wilfully disobeyed their orders; and problems in the chain of command provided much of the friction of war which could ruin the best-laid plans.

Small armies were easier to command than large ones, and could usually have a flatter command pyramid, with fewer layers separating the general from his troops. For example, in 1812 the relatively small Anglo-Portuguese army of about 50,000 men had Wellington at the apex of the pyramid, followed by Stapleton Cotton, commanding all the allied cavalry (five brigades), and eight commanders of infantry divisions (seven Anglo-Portuguese, one Spanish) and two independent brigades of Portuguese infantry. Each of the infantry divisions was further divided into, usually, three brigades: so that only two layers of command separated Wellington from his battalion commanders. This pyramid was unusually flat for an army of this size – requiring Wellington to deal directly with no fewer than eleven subordinates – and in the following year at Vitoria, when Wellington's army was rather larger, he combined his divisions into groups of two or three with the command going to the senior divisional general, though the experiment was not completely successful. At Austerlitz, the second tier of the French command consisted of six marshals: Bernadotte, Davout, Lannes and Soult, each commanding an infantry corps, Murat at the head of the

Reserve Cavalry, Bessières commanding the Guard; and one general – Oudinot, not yet a marshal – leading an independent division of grenadiers. Each of the infantry corps was divided into divisions, brigades, regiments and battalions, so that up to four levels separated Napoleon from a *chef de battaillon*. In some later campaigns, including 1815, Napoleon added a further layer, by giving the command of two or more corps to a single officer.

At each level of command the general had a number of staff officers and aides-de-camp to assist him. This ranged from Napoleon's headquarters which, by 1809, had grown to about twenty officers answering personally to the Emperor; several hundred staff officers on Berthier's staff; a number of court officials and civilian office holders; dozens of valets, grooms, cooks and other servants; the squadron of Guard Cavalry on escort duty, and various formations associated with headquarters such as the Gendarmerie: in all many hundreds of men and horses. A marshal's staff was usually much smaller: two or three dozen officers; while the commander of a division would be lucky to have a dozen. Wellington commanded an independent, multi-national army, but was not a head of state, so it was natural that his suite – about 100 officers, including artillery and engineering staffs – should fall between that of Napoleon and a marshal. At the other end of the scale, brigades could be regarded as purely tactical not administrative units, and so might have little if any staff. One British brigadier in the Peninsula in 1813 had only a single staff officer (his 'Brigade Major') and an aide-de-camp, yet he did not live in solitary discomfort for his establishment included twelve servants, 'Four horses, Ten mules, Five sheep, Two goats, & a large Dog', and was, he thought, one of the most modest in the army![1]

Most of the work of the officers attached to the headquarters of an army was administrative or logistical: enforcing the army's discipline, handling claims for leave or promotion, arranging its marches, quarters, pay and rations, dealing with civilian authorities in the vicinity and at home, gathering intelligence and a myriad of other tasks. In battle the officers of the specialist arms – artillery, engineers and medical services – would attend to their particular duties, while other officers might be employed virtually as additional aides-de-camp.

Subordinate generals and their staff also had a quantity of administrative and logistical work to perform, which generally decreased with rank. Over time officers could do much to mould their units in ways which reflected their interests and character. Some of Napoleon's marshals had the reputation of being uninterested in administration, except as a way of enriching themselves, while others were stern disciplinarians. A. G. Macdonell, writing of the aftermath of Aspern-Essling, makes the point that 'It is characteristic of three of the Corps-Commanders that the egotistical, beauty-loving Masséna had no ambulances in his Corps; honest, incompetent Oudinot had a 50 per cent equipment; while the iron, ruthless Davout had his full 100 per cent of ambulances and his 100 per cent of doctors.'[2] Similarly in the Peninsula, it seems most appropriate that the hard-fighting, hard-disciplined Third Division was commanded by Sir

Thomas Picton. But the match was not always so good, for none of Craufurd's undistinguished successors in command of the Light Division managed to ruin that elite force – not even Erskine.

On campaign the commanders of the army's largest sub-units, whether they were divisions or corps, were responsible for organizing their march, within the orders they received from headquarters. They would sometimes fight independent battles of their own, such as Lannes at Saalfeld and Davout at Auerstädt in 1806, though these were relatively uncommon. More frequent were advance or rearguard actions or battles such as Friedland and Lützen, when the subordinate commander engaged the enemy's main army and fought for some time by himself, while the rest of the army marched to his support. In such actions the subordinate general's role was very similar to that of a general commanding a whole army: he would deploy his force, make his plans, issue his orders, inspire his men and control his reserves in much the same way, though the context of the action would be different. Even in a large set-piece battle a marshal commanding a corps of 25–30,000 men performed many of these tasks, within the overall plan laid down by the general commanding.

The commander of a division of 5–10,000 men was much closer to his troops than the commander of a corps or an army. His vision was less wide-ranging and all-encompassing, his concerns were more immediate, and his functions were different. Take Major-General James Leith, commanding the 6,700 British and Portuguese soldiers of the Fifth Division at Salamanca. For several hours before Wellington took the decision to attack, Leith's division was deployed on a gentle ridge behind and somewhat to the west of the village of Arapiles (the two Arapiles hills are to the east of the village). As the French extended their left they opened fire with artillery on the British. The range was long – a mile or more – and probably few casualties were caused, for the troops were ordered to lie down behind cover, but they found it wearing on their nerves. General Leith rode up and down the line accompanied by his staff, chatting to the officers and men, conspicuously disregarding the enemy fire. When a cannon-ball hit the ground under his horse's nose 'He took off his hat to it, and said, "I will allow *you* to pass, Sir!" The men heard him, and said, "Hurra for the General." '[3] This bravado was meant both to reassure and entertain the men – for fear would grow with boredom, and the troops had nothing to do – while Leith could observe how his regiments, one of which (1/38th) had only joined the army the previous day, were bearing the strain.

Wellington's orders for the attack (quoted above, p. 146) left relatively little to Leith's discretion, for he stipulated both the formation of the division and the time of its advance. But it was Leith who addressed his men 'with the eloquence of a Caesar', as one officer puts it, before they advanced. Other witnesses make his oratory seem less elevated: one records him saying, 'Now Boys! we'll at them'; while another says that he 'made a flying speech to each Regiment as he passed. To us he said, "As for you, 38th, I have only to say, behave as you have always done." '[4]

The worth of such speeches may be questioned. Napoleon was sceptical of the value of efforts to achieve rhetorical heights:

> It is not set speeches at the moment of battle that render soldiers brave. The veteran scarcely listens to them, and the recruit forgets them at the first discharge. If discourses and harangues are useful, it is during the campaign; to do away with unfavourable impressions, to correct false reports, to keep alive a proper spirit in the camp, and to furnish material and amusement for the bivouac.[5]

But Leith was not attempting a formal speech: just a few rough words to tighten the bonds of solidarity within his battalions and to strengthen the soldiers' confidence in him. Done well, this could be effective. Before Austerlitz, Soult rode past the regiments of Saint-Hilaire's division 'addressing each in turn with that sense of military occasion which he possessed so well. The troops now burst with eagerness and enthusiasm. "Do you remember how you beat the Russians in Switzerland?" he enquired of the 10th Light. Back came the reply "Nobody's likely to forget it today!"'[6]

Inspired by its commander's words, or ignoring them, the British division began its advance, a strong skirmishing line out in front, and then the two lines of infantry (each in two-deep line) about 100 yards apart. General Leith rode in front of the colours of the 1/38th in the very centre of the British line: 'Certain of the discipline of the troops when close to the enemy, he did not alter his station, but remained between the hostile fires.'[7] Again this had both symbolic and practical purposes. He was showing his men his confidence in their success and determination to share their fate, literally leading them by example. But he was also in the perfect position to control the pace and direction of the British advance, his vision was unimpeded by smoke or clouds of dust, so that he would be the first to see any sudden threat, or notice if the enemy were retreating, while he could watch the progress of neighbouring allied divisions and maintain a rough alignment with them. If his troops became disordered or restless, he could slow or halt the advance while order was restored. And he took upon himself the task of regulating the speed of the advance, checking the impatience which he, as much as any of his men, must have felt to get the combat over – for he understood the importance of ensuring that the troops should not be hurried, flustered and out of breath before the fighting began. His staff assisted in this, for according to Leith Hay, before the advance began 'he had despatched his aides-de-camp, Captain Belshes and Captain Dowson, to different points of the line, in order to restrain any effort at getting more rapidly forward than was consistent with the important object of its arriving in perfect order close to the enemy, and at all points making a simultaneous attack'.[8]

Andrew Leith Hay was sent off on another task: to urge the skirmishing line to drive in their French opponents and, if possible, silence the French artillery, thus clearing the way for the main advance (see above, pp. 62–3). In the course of achieving this Leith Hay's horse was shot dead, and the young man coolly waited until the main line came up, when he took a fresh horse from an orderly. The advance across a mile of open ground went smoothly, and as they approached the French position Leith and his staff, being mounted, were the first to see the French infantry just beyond the brow of the gentle ridge. They approached still closer; the French opened fire; and at nearly the same moment Leith ordered his troops to fire and charge. The attack was completely successful (see above, pp. 100–102), but not without cost. Leith and his staff were an obvious target: the general was hit in the arm by a musket shot which shattered the bone, while two of his aides, Captain Dowson and Andrew Leith Hay, were both seriously wounded.[9]

Salamanca was an unusually bloody battle for senior officers. On the allied side Le Marchant was killed, and Beresford, Cotton, Leith and Cole were wounded; while on the French, Marmont was very badly wounded, Ferey and Thomières were killed, and Clausel and Bonnet were both wounded: that is, the commander-in-chief and four of the eight commanders of infantry divisions. This was exceptional, and it is worth pointing out that only two or three of Napoleon's twenty-six marshals fell to enemy fire (Lannes, Bessières and, perhaps, Poniatowski); yet between 1807 and 1814 the marshals received twenty wounds in action between them. At a slightly lower level the losses were even more severe: over the same period thirty-two generals of division were killed or mortally wounded in action, and a further 174 were wounded. Wellington's much smaller army had ten British generals killed and fifty-five wounded; while one account states that at Leipzig the casualties included twenty-nine allied and sixty-six French generals and brigadiers. These figures, and the obvious courage displayed by men like Leith, help to explain why the rank and file of Napoleonic armies never felt the alienation from their senior officers which developed during the First World War.[10]

Leith's part in the Battle of Salamanca was ended by his wound; command of his division devolved to the next senior officer, but it seems that the division faced little further opposition – although there are few sources for this part of the battle. For a more detailed account of the role of a subordinate commander once the action was joined, we must turn to Major-General Sir Colin Halkett, commanding the 5th British infantry brigade in Alten's division at Quatre Bras. This brigade consisted of four battalions (2/30th, 33rd, 2/69th and 2/73rd) amounting to 2,360 officers and men. Arriving on the field of battle about 3.30 p.m. Halkett received an order from Sir Thomas Picton (not his own divisional commander, it should be noted, but Alten seems not to have been present, while Picton had arrived earlier and had had time to assess the state of the battle), to attack the French in the Bois de Bossu. As he prepared to advance on the wood, Halkett was approached by one of General Pack's aides-de-camp (Pack commanded a brigade in Picton's division) with the news that his brigade had nearly exhausted its ammunition and needed support. Halkett responded by detaching the 2/69th to assist Pack, placing it under Pack's orders. Advancing with his three remaining battalions, Halkett found the Brunswick Corps 'retiring rather precipitately', their duke (son of the Prussian commander at Auerstädt) having just been killed. Halkett found the officer commanding them 'and expressed my opinion as to the mode of their retrograde movement' – note how twenty years had softened the language – 'and brought them up under cover in a ditch running nearly parallel to the line of the Enemy'. However he was convinced that without the immediate support of his brigade the Brunswick troops would resume their flight, and so suspended his advance on the Bois de Bossu. One of Wellington's aides-de-camp arrived to enquire why he had halted. Halkett explained; the aide took his message back to headquarters, and returned with instructions confirming Halkett's decision and relieving him of any further obligation to pursue Picton's original orders.

While deployed there between the highway and the Bois de Bossu, Halkett and one of his aides-de-camp galloped forward to the front and observed the French preparing for a large cavalry attack. He dispatched the aide to warn the 69th and General Pack of what he had seen (although the warning did not save the 69th), and returned to prepare his other troops for the onslaught. What happened next is not entirely clear, but it seems that the Brunswick troops and the 2/30th and 2/73rd repulsed the French attack with little trouble: neither of these British battalions had more than 10 per cent casualties during the day. The 33rd were less fortunate – possibly they were more exposed to French artillery fire; in any case they broke and fled into the Bois de Bossu. Halkett rode after them as soon as possible, and later recalled that

> I had some difficulty in getting them to the order they ought to have remained in, and I took one of their Colours and advanced to the front with it, which I think had the desired effect, and soon got them into the order they ought *never* to have lost. They then appeared steady and I left them.

In the 33rd, nineteen officers and men were killed, seventy-four wounded and nine missing: 102 casualties in all, or more than one sixth of its strength.[11]

After the fighting had finished the Adjutant-General Sir Edward Barnes (one of Wellington's most senior staff officers) found Halkett and told him that his brigade was to maintain its position and provide advance posts for the army during the night. Although 'more fatigued then ever I felt', Halkett was flattered by the responsibility, and kept watch until he received instructions to withdraw and join the army on its retreat. This involved an arduous march, as the brigade was misdirected by an officer of the Quartermaster-General's staff, and obliged to cut across country through heavy ground to find the right road. Halkett had escaped from the fighting at Quatre Bras unscathed, but two days later he was wounded twice, the second time in the mouth, at Waterloo. He recovered from his wounds and remained in the army, ultimately becoming a full general (in 1841) and Governor of Chelsea Hospital, before dying in 1856 at the age of eighty-two.[12]

Halkett's experiences at Quatre Bras show a subordinate general bringing his force on to the battlefield, receiving orders from a senior officer, detaching a battalion to support a friendly brigade, checking the retreat of an allied force, giving warning of an impending enemy attack, and rallying one of his own battalions when it had been broken. Some of the details of his account may be inaccurate, for it was written many years after the battle and there are conflicting descriptions of some incidents, but it provides a good example of the range of tasks which confronted a brigade commander in action.

Occasionally subordinate commanders were forced – or inspired – or tempted – to take major tactical decisions on their own initiative. Uxbridge's decision to launch his two brigades of heavy cavalry into their charge at Waterloo was one example, although it was always understood that a cavalry commander needed the latitude to take advantage of a passing opportunity. A more extreme example occurred at Albuera where, in the face of Beresford's breakdown and refusal to give any useful orders, Major-General Lowry Cole took upon himself the responsibility to lead his Fourth Division from its position, in a dangerous counter-attack which saved the battle. He was encouraged to do so by one of Beresford's staff officers, Henry Hardinge (who ultimately rose to be commander-in-chief of the army in 1852), but if it had failed, the blame would – rightly – have fallen squarely on Cole.[13]

Normally however a subordinate general's attention was concentrated on his own section of the battlefield: on keeping his men in good order and obeying instructions from his commander. This could demand great coolness and courage, such as that shown by Robert Craufurd, calmly watching the approach of Loison's division at Busaco, ignoring the passing shots of French skirmishers, and waiting until the French had drawn close enough before giving his men the order to attack. It also required the experience and understanding of war to anticipate problems; to check the first signs of panic or disorder; to restrain the impetuosity of the soldiers; and to encourage habits of obedience without lowering the spirit of the men. Private Wheeler tells a story of how, during the Battles of the Pyrenees in 1813, his unit pursued the French too far, though without coming to any real harm. When the troops returned to their position, they

> received a lecture from Genl. Inglis for following the enemy down the hill, contrary to the sound of the field bugle. He informed us that had we remained on the hill and fired, the end would have been gained with less loss to us, for the remainder of the division were posted to gall them by cross fire. He said he could not but admire our ardour but hoped we should be more attentive in future. Courage, if not controlled by discipline was often a cause of much disaster etc. The General is a good old soul, and altho he endeavoured to look mighty angry we could see he was not so much displeased as he pretended.[14]

Conversely, the presence of senior officers could help rally a shaken unit, while their absence might complete its demoralization. 'No orders reached us, we could hear no leader's words of command, and we felt in some way abandoned on the field of battle,' writes a junior French officer about the later stages of the Battle of Leipzig. At Marengo, Napoleon personally rallied his shaken men: ' "Courage, soldiers," said he, "the reserves are coming. Stand firm!" Then he was off to the right of the army. The soldiers were shouting, "Vive Bonaparte!" ' While in the Pyrenees in July 1813 'Daddy' Hill checked some skirmishers before their precipitate retreat could lead to panic:

> At one point the light troops came running in, their faces begrimed with powder and sweat, quite close to the spot where Sir Rowland Hill and his staff were standing. I distinctly saw him turning back some men and heard his words addressing them: 'Go back my men, you must not let them up. You shall be instantly supported. You must not let them up.' Back they went cheerfully and soon disappeared among the trees and with the aid of a couple of battalion companies, that dashed from the hill at double quick, soon beat down the enemy at this point.[15]

Officers commanding large bodies of cavalry performed many of the same functions, and in much the same way, as those commanding infantry. However, the greater fluidity of cavalry tactics and the overriding importance of good order and reserves led to some differences. There was more risk in cavalry operations: more depended on precise timing and direction in a cavalry charge than in an infantry attack, and its conduct had to be managed with the greatest care. Cavalry officers cultivated an air of reckless daring and unthinking dash, with their splendid horses, gorgeous uniforms and devil-may-care manner, but in good officers this concealed either a cool, calculating brain, or – perhaps more commonly – an instinctive grasp of the ebb and flow of battle.

It was no part of the role of a senior cavalry officer to lead his men into the enemy's ranks, where he was of no more use than an ordinary private of dragoons. Riding in front of the advancing line, controlling its pace and inspiring his men by his example, was the proper place for the commander of a squadron, a regiment or at most a brigade. More senior officers were needed where they could do most good: at the head of the second line or the reserve, as Uxbridge admitted after Waterloo (see above, p. 119). Frederick the Great's cavalry commander General Zieten drew his sword only once during the Seven Years War, when he was attacked by some Austrians while making a reconnaissance on the day before the Battle of Torgau in 1760. And Marshal Murat, the pre-eminent cavalry officer of the Napoleonic Wars, once said,

> What gives me the most heartfelt satisfaction when I think of my military career is, that I have never seen a man fall killed by my hand. Doubtless it is possible that in firing a pistol-shot at enemies who attacked me, or whom I was pursuing,

I may have wounded some one, even mortally; but if so I knew nothing of it. If a man had ever fallen dead before me by my act, the picture of it would always be before me, and would pursue me to the grave.[16]

Senior officers, whether commanding infantry or cavalry, inevitably made mistakes amidst all the confusion and demands of battle. Probably the most common was to misjudge the situation facing their troops and either fail to anticipate a danger threatening them, or be overly cautious. The young Prince of Orange at Waterloo insisted that the 5th Line Battalion of the King's German Legion advance to attack French forces near La Haye Sainte, despite warnings that the French were in overwhelming strength and were supported by cavalry. Having done all he could to have the order revoked, the commander of the Hanoverian brigade, Colonel Ompteda, led his men forward. The battalion was broken with very heavy losses and he was killed. Examples of excessive caution usually had less serious consequences, and so are harder to identify, but it is generally agreed that the British cavalry could have achieved more at Vitoria, and that its brigadiers were inhibited by Wellington's anger at previous examples of their impetuosity; while Ney's flank attack at Bautzen was uncharacteristically sluggish.[17]

Such errors of judgement, while deeply unfortunate, were – up to a point – forgivable. Cowardice in the face of the enemy was not. This was rare, but not unknown, among senior officers. Captain Coignet records that at Marengo, 'A shell burst in the first company and killed seven men; a bullet killed the orderly near General Chambarlhac, who galloped off at full speed. We saw him no more all day.' At St Pierre in December 1813, Colonels Peacock and Bunbury both showed a conspicuous lack of courage, endangering their part of the line. Bunbury quietly resigned his commission, but Peacock remained with the army, misbehaved again, and was dismissed from the service in a scathing letter from the Duke of York which was circulated throughout the army. However Bunbury and Peacock were regimental, not more senior officers; and while Wellington's army contained a number of generals not noted for their ability, sense or discretion – Erskine, Slade, Long, Lightburne, Skerret and others spring to mind – there was no shortage of physical bravery.[18]

Less disgraceful, but rather more common, were occasions when generals carried their private quarrels on to the battlefield. Napoleon's marshals are famous for their feuds and rivalry, and though many of the stories about them have grown in the telling, there is no doubt this sometimes influenced their operations. This was most apparent in the Peninsula, where the logistical difficulties and the guerrillas made co-operation difficult and the Emperor was too distant to enforce it; and least evident in the presence of the enemy, where most, but not all, quarrels were forgotten. Trouble was always most likely to occur when one marshal was temporarily subordinated to another, for they regarded themselves as equals and were most unwilling to take orders from anyone but Napoleon. Such disputes were not limited to the French army.

Barclay de Tolly and Bagration found co-operation extremely difficult in 1812, while throughout the wars the Russian generals were at least as fractious as the French, with the added element of hostility between ethnic Russians and foreigners poisoning relations. Other armies faced similar problems, though to a lesser degree.

Nor would subordinate commanders always obey their orders. Sometimes this could be wholly beneficial, even if it involved stretching discretion far beyond its normal limits. At Sabugal in April 1811, Colonel Drummond, commanding the 2nd Brigade of the Light Division, received an order from General Erskine, the divisional commander, directing him not to advance or engage the enemy. But Erskine was distant from the fighting, and not a commander to inspire trust in his subordinates, while Drummond could see that if he did not intervene the 1st Brigade would be defeated. He therefore decided to ignore the order, apparently with the connivance of the staff officer who delivered it; the action was a success, and no questions were subsequently asked. In this case it is clear that Drummond acted wisely, and though it was possible that Erskine might have had good reason for his order (such as the approach of enemy troops unseen by Drummond), the risk was worth running to extricate the 1st Brigade.[19]

A second example provides rather more scope for doubt. Despite his years of experience in the Peninsula, General Picton was subordinated to Lord Dalhousie (commander of the Seventh Division) at the Battle of Vitoria. On the morning of the battle, Picton's division was in position in good time, but Dalhousie's was delayed by difficult terrain and poor arrangements. Picton waited with growing impatience as the morning slipped by and the battle began on the plain below him, and still Dalhousie did not appear, and the men of the 'Fighting Third Division' grew restless. Just before noon an aide-de-camp approached him and enquired if he had seen Dalhousie:

'No, sir! I have not seen his lordship: but have you any orders for me, sir?' – 'None', replied the aid[e]-de-camp. – 'Then pray, sir,' continued the irritated general, 'what are the orders you *do* bring?' – 'Why,' answered the officer, 'that as soon as Lord Dalhousie, with the seventh division, shall commence an attack upon that bridge,' (pointing to one on the left,) 'the fourth and sixth [*sic*: Light] are to support him.' Picton could not understand the idea of any other division fighting in his front; and, drawing himself up to his full height, he said to the astonished aid[e]-de-camp with some passion, 'You may tell Lord Wellington from me, sir, that the third division under my command shall in less than ten minutes attack the bridge and carry it, and the fourth and sixth divisions may support if they choose.' Having thus expressed his intention, he turned from the aid[e]-de-camp, and put himself at the head of his soldiers, who were quickly in motion towards the bridge; encouraging them with the bland appellation of 'Come on, ye rascals! – come on, ye fighting villains!'[20]

Picton's attack succeeded, and his conduct can be justified by the argument that Dalhousie had obviously gone astray and was delaying, not only the Seventh and Third, but also the Fourth and Light Divisions, that is, almost the whole of Wellington's centre. Yet there were great risks in divisional commanders acting independently. Adequate support could not be arranged in time, they might disrupt other plans of which they knew nothing, or get in each other's way. No general was likely to be pleased if he found part of his precious reserve entering the combat without orders, prematurely, because its commander could not resist the temptation to strike an immediate blow. It would be unfair to Picton to suggest that this criticism applies in this case; but it does explain why Wellington was disinclined to give his subordinates much discretion. Yet this too had its disadvantages: as we have seen, the British cavalry did not make the most of its advantages at Vitoria, while at the Bidassoa the commander of Wellington's horse artillery admits having left two batteries inactive when he was certain they should advance, because they had not been specifically entrusted to him and 'at times his lordship allows no troops to be moved, but in obedience to his own orders'.[21]

But these examples should not be allowed to obscure the great majority of cases where subordinate commanders exercised their normal discretion in the management of their troops, within the framework provided by the general's orders. Even the general's active interference in operational details might sometimes be welcomed. After the difficult combat of El Bodon, Major-General Charles Colville, whose brigade had borne the brunt of the fighting, wrote home praising Wellington's role in the action.

> I . . . must be ever thankful that he was at hand to direct, as he did, the general movements which his uncommon quickness and experience enables him to do with such happy effects, and by his presence authorising measures of defence and of partial offence when without such authority retreat alone would have been justified.[22]

Tempers could sometimes fray in the heat of action, but more often the pressure led to effective co-operation, especially among experienced and capable officers.

In most armies of the period staff officers played a subordinate role, helping to express and implement their general's plans, but seldom seeking to influence them. Napoleon showered Berthier with honours and rewards, and greatly valued his chief of staff's ability to expand his brief thoughts into clear instructions; but his contempt for Berthier's independent judgement is well known, and was fully justified on the few occasions – such as the first days of the campaign of 1809 – when Berthier was forced to act without Napoleon's guiding hand.

Wellington was equally master in his own house. In 1812 he thwarted an attempt by Colonel J. W. Gordon – who had been the Duke of York's military secretary, and who was an experienced intriguer – to have himself appointed chief of staff of Wellington's army. Gordon returned to London at the end of the year and was not seen again in the Peninsula. Major-General Sir George Murray, who had been Wellington's Quartermaster-General in his previous campaigns, returned, much to Wellington's delight, and no more was heard of the post of chief of staff. Murray was certainly Wellington's ablest and most trusted staff officer, but his influence on the course of operations was limited. Harry Smith gives an attractive glimpse of his working relations with Wellington when observing the French positions at Nivelle, and making plans for the British attack:

> The Duke was lying down, and began a very earnest conversation. General Alten, Kempt, Colborne, I, and other staff-officers were preparing to leave the Duke, when he says, 'Oh, lie still.' After he had conversed for some time with Sir G. Murray, Murray took out of his sabretache his writing materials, and began to write the plan of attack for the whole army. When it was finished, so clearly had he understood the Duke, I do not think he erased one word. He says, 'My Lord, is this your desire?' It was one of the most interesting scenes I have ever witnessed. As Murray read, the Duke's eye was directed with his telescope to the spot in question. He never asked Sir G. Murray one question, but the muscles of his face evinced line of the deepest thought. When Sir G. Murray had finished, the Duke smiled and said, 'Ah, Murray, this will put us in possession of the fellows' lines. Shall we be ready to-morrow?' 'I fear not, my lord, but the next day.'[23]

In the Austrian and Prussian armies, however, senior staff officers had a much greater influence. In 1805 General Mack, not Archduke Ferdinand, was the effective commander of the Austrian forces at Ulm, while General Weyrother – another staff officer – was responsible for the content as well as the form of the allied plan at Austerlitz. In 1813–15 Blücher commanded the Prussian army, but was guided in his decisions by a powerful chief of staff – first Scharnhorst and then Gneisenau. This structure was developed in response to the character and ability of the men involved. Blücher had the passion, the ability to inspire his men, the unconquerable will to victory, and the seniority needed for command, while Scharnhorst and Gneisenau had the intellect to plan a campaign, and to present Blücher with the choice of several courses of action. Neither could have succeeded without the other, nor is it likely that any of the alternative Prussian commanders – Bülow and Yorck being the most obvious – would have been more successful. But the system of, in effect, dual command persisted long after the Napoleonic Wars, finding its most famous expression in the combination of Hindenburg and Ludendorff.

The number of staff officers and their responsibilities declined sharply at lower levels of the army. Wellington's divisional commanders in the Peninsula might have only three or four staff officers, together with several aides-de-camp, to assist them in performing their duties, and these were most important in arranging marches etc. on campaign. Descending the scale even further, brigades had a single staff officer, the 'brigade-major', who was responsible for a wide variety of important if routine tasks, from organizing duty rosters to posting the pickets. In battle all these officers performed whatever tasks came to hand. As Salamanca Captain Philip Bainbrigge was assistant to the acting Quartermaster-General Colonel Delancey. Together they watched as the Fourth Division's attack faltered and the troops fell back in disorder:

> Colonel Delancey said to me 'For God's sake bring up the 6th Division as fast as possible,' then dashed in amongst the Portuguese, seized the colour of one of the regiments and endeavoured to rally them. I galloped off to the rear; as to restoring order and reforming the regiment, it required some time and the work of regimental officers.

He rode to the Sixth Division, which he found already advancing.[24]

One of the regular duties performed by the staff was to guide troops on their march and to show them what ground to occupy when the army was forming for battle. In 1815 James Shaw Kennedy – the Deputy Quartermaster-General to the Third Division – took this a step further. On the morning of Waterloo,

> the Prince of Orange, who commanded the corps, and General Baron Alten, who commanded the third division, discussed for some time how the division should be formed in order of battle. The Duke of Wellington, having joined them during the discussion, and being referred to, replied shortly, 'Form in the usual way'; and rode on. This did not solve the difficulty. . . . The discussion having continued for some time after the Duke had gone, and no determination arrived at, I asked General Alten if he would allow me to form the division; to this he at once and unqualifiedly assented; upon which I instantly left him, and proceeded with the formation.[25]

This was an unusual responsibility to entrust to such a junior officer before the fighting had even begun, but Shaw Kennedy had already proved his worth in the campaign, calmly taking over when his immediate superior was wounded at Quatre Bras. In a crisis, a junior staff officer might even carry on the work of his wounded divisional commander. For example, in the storm of Badajoz, when Major-General Colville, commanding the Fourth Division, and most of his staff were wounded or killed, Captain James, the Assistant Adjutant-General attached to the division, took over, maintaining order and bringing forward the troops, until he too was wounded.[26]

On other occasions staff officers might seize responsibility which was not really offered to them. Harry Smith was a brigade-major in the Light Division at Vitoria, and was sent to receive orders from Lord Dalhousie, who had at last appeared.

> I found his lordship and his Q.M.G., Drake, an old Rifle comrade, in deep conversation. I reported pretty quick, and asked for orders (the head of my Brigade was just getting under fire). I repeated the question, 'What orders, my Lord?' Drake became somewhat animated, and I heard His Lordship say, 'Better to take the village,' which the French held with twelve guns (I had counted by their fire), and seemed to be inclined to keep it. I roared out 'Certainly, my Lord,' and off I galloped, both calling to me to come back, but, as none are so deaf as those who won't hear, I told General Vandeleur we were immediately to take the village. There was no time to lose, and the 52nd Regiment deployed into line as if at Shorncliffe, while our Riflemen were sent out in every direction, five or six deep, keeping up a fire nothing could resist. I galloped to the officer commanding a Battalion in the 7th Division (the 82nd, I think). 'Lord Dalhousie desires you closely to follow this Brigade of the Light Division.' 'Who are you, sir?' 'Never mind that; disobey my Lord's order at your peril.' My Brigade, the 52nd in line and swarms of Riflemen, rushed at the village. . . . There never was a more impetuous onset – nothing could withstand such a burst of determination.[27]

But such anecdotes make good stories largely because they were untypical, reflecting the rare, glorious moment when a staff officer was able to act independently and influence events in his own right, rather than simply as the characterless channel through which senior officers expressed their orders.

Aides-de-camp were mostly young men – sometimes very young men – of good family who owed their appointment either to a personal connection with their general (sons and nephews were common), or to the recommendation of another general. They did anything and everything for their general from writing messages and carrying orders, to leading the dance at a ball or acting as an interpreter. Harry Smith said in jest that the only qualifications needed were the ability to ride and to eat, which was being more realistic than James's *Regimental Companion* which required 'a perfect knowledge of every military manoeuvre, an aptitude of eye in taking ground, a quick appreciation of instructions, a facility of expression, and the utmost composure of mind. He must always be thorough master of his horse, and particularly so of his temper.' But this was the *beau idéal* not the norm.[28]

On the battlefield the aide-de-camp's main role was to deliver orders and take messages. It was not always easy, amid the smoke and confusion, to find the right unit and accurately deliver the message, and it could be even harder to find the way back to the general, who might be riding from one end of the battlefield to the other. An eighteenth-century critic accused the young officers of the general's suite of being unable to resist the temptation of joining in any fighting which they passed on the way, and of incorrectly repeating their message when they arrived, having no 'conception of the confusion which can be caused by altering just a single word in the orders entrusted to them'. And while this sweeping generalization was probably unfair to many, a detailed account of Lord George Sackville's experiences at Minden shows that it was not without foundation.[29] Napoleonic officers seem to have been more professional in this respect at least, and in a task where success was taken for granted, the scarcity of complaints on this ground amounts to high praise.

The experiences of one of Marshal Ney's aides-de-camp in 1806, Victor de Saint Simon, shows some of the problems an aide might face. On the night before the Battle of Jena, Ney sent Saint Simon to Imperial Headquarters with news of his position and approach. The young man was informed by Berthier that he had just been awarded the *Légion d'honneur*, but Napoleon was much less welcoming, and sent him straight back to Ney with orders not to precipitate an action. In the darkness and confusion Saint Simon missed Ney's corps which had taken an alternative route to the plateau; he set off in pursuit, but although it was getting light there was a heavy fog, and he ran into a Prussian patrol and was seriously wounded before he broke free and finally found his way back to Ney. By then it was too late to prevent an early clash, and Saint Simon saw the French infantry repulse a Prussian cavalry charge before the pain and loss of blood from his wounds led him to lose consciousness.[30]

Other tasks were more varied. In the fighting at Waterloo, Wellington noticed 'some little confusion' in the rear of the 5th Brigade and called out for an officer on his staff to '"See what's wrong there"', while on the previous morning, Sir Alexander Gordon, Wellington's principal aide-de-camp, had been sent with half a squadron of cavalry to ride in the direction of Ligny to discover what had happened to the Prussian army.[31]

Such a use of an aide-de-camp to perform special tasks was more common in the French than in the British army. Early on 14 October 1806, when the French were advancing through dense mist at Auerstädt, Davout instructed his senior aide Colonel Burcke to reconnoitre ahead with a fighting patrol of cavalry. Burcke found a body of Prussian cavalry camped in the village of Hassenhausen and assessed their strength by the simple, if unsubtle, method of firing a few pistol shots into their midst. Having secured some prisoners in the confusion, Burcke beat his retreat and warned the leading French units that they were about to be attacked by cavalry. During the subsequent fighting General of Brigade Gauthier gave his aide-de-camp Captain Lagoublaye the command of one light and two grenadier companies of the 25th *Ligne* to capture an immobilized Prussian battery, while Davout used his Engineer Officers as additional staff, giving their chief, Colonel Touzard, the command of the 111th Regiment. In Wellington's army all these tasks, except perhaps Colonel

Burcke's, would normally have been entrusted to the relevant regimental officers.[32]

Even further removed from the British practice were the handful of senior officers whom Napoleon kept on his staff as aides-de-camp – men like Generals Rapp, Mouton and Savary – who could be given command of a division in the field, be made governor of a conquered capital, or be sent as an emissary to an enemy monarch. These men were among Napoleon's most useful and trusted subordinates, and were well rewarded with titles, estates and pensions – not to mention illicit gains from plunder, extortion and bribes. In 1805 it was Savary whom Napoleon sent on several missions to the allies in the days before Austerlitz, and who convinced them that Napoleon was nervous and reluctant to fight; while during the battle, Rapp was dispatched with four squadrons of Guard cavalry to rescue a French infantry regiment which had been overrun by Russian cavalry. Similarly, at Aspern-Essling in 1809, Napoleon sent Mouton and Rapp, with five battalions of the Young Guard, to stabilize the front after Essling had fallen. Acting on their own initiative, the two aides did more, charging into and recapturing the village; having proved successful, their disobedience was warmly praised, and Mouton was made Count Lobau.[33]

Most aides-de-camp were much younger and less experienced than these senior officers, and made their share of mistakes. These were noted down with some relish by regimental officers who naturally resented their rapid promotion, constant access to the general, and, worst of all, the supercilious air of superiority affected by some of the young men. Thus part of the blame for the false line of advance adopted by the 1st Brigade of the Light Division at Sabugal rests with Sir William Erskine's aide, who, finding the brigade halted in the fog, demanded peremptorily of its brigadier (the able and experienced Sydney Beckwith) why he did not advance. Three years later at Nivelle, William Napier was struggling to restrain the impetuosity of his men lest they become winded and disordered before they reached the French positions on the Petite Rhune. The slowness of their advance displeased the Hon. Captain Gore, aide to General Kempt, who galloped forward, waving his hat and calling on the men to charge. As a result, the impetus of the attack was spent before it reached the first French position, though the men resumed their advance and were successful, once they had regained their breath.[34]

The story of another young man, Lieutenant La Bourdonnaye, on Marshal Lannes's staff in 1809, shows this excessive enthusiasm in a more attractive light. The dandies of the army had taken to wearing extremely baggy trousers, which looked smart on horseback but were impractical on foot. La Bourdonnaye affected this style, and when Lannes ordered him to dismount and run to a bridge to deliver an order, his spurs caught in his trousers,

> he fell, and we thought he was killed. But he picked himself up nimbly, and as he started off again, he heard the marshal call out, 'Is it not absurd to go to fight with six yards of cloth about your legs?' La Bourdonnaye wishing, in his first battle

under Lannes's eyes, to show his zeal, drew his sword, hacked and tore his trousers off at mid-thigh, and being thus released, set off running bare-kneed. Although we were under fire, the marshal and the staff laughed at the new-fashioned costume till they cried; and when La Bourdonnaye came back, he was complimented on his ready ingenuity.[35]

A more serious, if hardly less high-spirited, account of the experiences of an aide-de-camp in action is provided by the recollections of Captain Charles Synge at Salamanca, where he was aide to Lieutenant-Colonel Pack, who commanded an independent brigade of Portuguese infantry. Synge was at headquarters when Wellington took the decision to attack and he

> was tempted to remain longer than I intended just to see what the Duke would do, and had galloped towards our advance (now becoming our right [i.e. Paken-ham's division]), when I met the Prince of Orange coming from it. He too was galloping, but halloed out as he passed, 'Oh, Synge, it is to be a fight after all. Pakenham is to begin on the right. Hurrah!' This made me pull up. I felt I was out of bounds and turned to retrace my steps to my own General. Anybody else would have blown me up for leaving him, but he always spoiled me, and I am ashamed to say I often presumed on his forbearance to go larking when our own Corps was inactive.

Pack's brigade was facing the Greater Arapile, which was strongly occupied by the French. His orders were discretionary: to attack it if he saw any need or opportunity, but not otherwise. He therefore decided to deploy his brigade as if to attack the hill, and then wait on events. In advance of his main line he formed four companies of grenadiers who were to act as the storming party, and who were to be supported by the fire of the Caçador battalion. Thus formed the brigade lay down and waited until Pack received a message from General Cole asking him to attack the French in order to relieve the pressure on his Fourth Division. The order for the advance was given, and Synge begged for and received the command of half the forlorn hope – two parties of about fifty grenadiers each who were to lead the way in front of the storming party. As they advanced through standing rye they came under heavy fire, and a number of the grenadiers fell. Pack rode up 'and said in a whisper "Synge! I think those fellows won't carry it for you." I said, "Oh! yes, they will, we are over the worst of it." I meant the ground.' Up the slope they went in the face of the French artillery which was struggling to depress the muzzles of its guns sufficiently to fire on them. The slope was so steep and rough that Synge had difficulty keeping on horseback even though his horse – like that of most aides-de-camp – was exceptionally good. Just below the summit the attack finally faltered and stopped as the men took cover behind a bank or natural wall. Enemy infantry was only a few yards away.

I was addressing some few words of encouragement, as well as the breathless state of anxiety I was in permitted, (my poor old Ronald [his horse] with great difficulty keeping his position on the steep), and two or three of the storming party were trying to scramble up the scarp, when the whole line opposed to us fired, knocked me over and literally cut to pieces the few that had climbed the 'wall'. My thigh was broken, and in falling, having no hold of the saddle, I could not in any manner save myself. Ronald made a couple of springs down the hill while I was falling, and this, together with the mangled bodies of those who fell back off the scarp on the head of Hill's column, which in the confusion of loading was unable to see what was happening above, caused a sensation of panic which was complete.

The French line followed up their volley by charging up to the edge of the scarp, down which they leapt when they saw our confusion.

Sir Niel Campbell's Grenadiers, the left column and all, went! – the disaster was complete. I had fallen to the ground on the near side of my horse, it being the left thigh that was broken, and was in great agony owing to a sort of instinctive effort to use the broken limb in which the marrow also seemed to be breaking.

He lay on the slopes of the hill for the rest of the battle. At first he was convinced that he was dying, and wished that a stray bullet would end his suffering. But as the hours passed and he did not lose consciousness, hope revived, and the thought of the stray bullet turned to dread. As evening fell and the battle drew to its close, Pack's brigade advanced again, meeting little opposition, and the general found his aide:

At last he stopped his horse, looked for a second, and then said, 'My dear Synge, is that you?' I said, 'Yes, General, here I am.' The dear fellow put his hand across his eyes and as soon as he could speak asked me to tell him the worst at once, what my wounds were. I told him. He then said a word of comfort, sent for a surgeon, and went on with his men.

The surgeon dressed the wound and Synge was carried back to Salamanca, a journey which caused as much pain as all that had gone before, and there began the long road to recovery.[36]

Staff officers and aides-de-camp may have been the glittering peacocks of the army, always getting the best food and the best quarters, and never the boring tedious jobs out of sight and out of mind, but they were used hard in battle and paid for their prominence with heavy casualties.

Chapter Nine
Regimental Officers

Regimental officers played a crucial role both in preparing their unit for battle and in leading it in combat. The commanding officer in particular did more than anyone else to determine the character of his regiment and set its standard of efficiency. An enthusiastic, knowledgeable colonel, blessed with a pleasant manner, could ensure that his subordinates did not neglect their work without arousing resentment, and make the men proud of their regiment without fussing over details or inflicting unnecessary punishments. Conversely, an ill-tempered martinet could make life a misery for officers and soldiers alike; while the excessive good humour of a lazy, indulgent commanding officer might equally quickly destroy his regiment's discipline and cohesion. As one British subaltern of wide experience concluded in his reminiscences:

> the great secret, in a good marching, good fighting, or loyal regiment, one not given to the habit of deserting, is being *well commanded*; because the finest body of men may be ruined, the efforts of the bravest regiment paralysed, and the best disposed corps become marauders and deserters, from having an inefficient man at their head.[1]

One of a commanding officer's main tasks at home, or in cantonments, or even on the march, was to supervise his officers and maintain harmony among them, while making sure that they understood their trade and paid proper attention to their men. Officers in the best regiments, renowned for their *esprit de corps* and welded together by years of shared privations and common danger, may well have been a band of brothers pulling contentedly together; but such regiments were rare. More common were units where the officers were divided into two or more antagonistic factions, or were united by shared hostility to the policies of a newly appointed commanding officer. In 1814 George Napier was given command of the 71st Highland Light Infantry – a previously excellent regiment which had been worn down by many campaigns culminating in heavy losses, including the gallant Colonel Cadogan, at Vitoria; and then, in six months, thoroughly disorganized and demoralized by the egregious Colonel Peacock (see above, p. 165). To restore discipline Napier had, much against his inclination, to adopt a severe approach to his officers and men, which made him very unpopular and led to a spate of anonymous threatening letters. This was an unusually, though not uniquely, bad example; but in many other regiments there were quarrels which led to duels, forced resignations or long-running feuds.[2]

The long war saw a great improvement in the quality and professionalism of officers in all European forces, although by about 1812 this had passed its peak in some of the Continental armies. British officers in the early 1790s did not gain a reputation for assiduity or understanding their business. But thanks to the Duke of York, and perhaps also to the growth of the militia and Volunteers which made military knowledge respectable, even fashionable, they improved immensely between 1795 and 1807. The amount of training given to new officers still varied widely from regiment to regiment according to the colonel's whim, but blatant ignorance and disdain for basic regulations and manoeuvres was dying out, and more regiments were seeking to emulate the extremely high standard set by the 43rd Light Infantry:

> When an officer entered this corps it was an invariable custom to send him to drill with a squad, composed of peasants from the plough tail, or other raw recruits, first learning the facings, marching, and companies evolutions. That being completed, the officer put on cross belts and pouch, and learned the firelock exercise; then again he marched with the same: and when it was considered that the whole was perfect, with, and without arms, they began to skirmish in extended files, and last of all learned the duties of the sentry, and to fire ball cartridge at a target. The officer after all this was not considered clear of the adjutant, until he could put a company through the evolutions by word of command, which he had already practised in the ranks. It generally took him six months . . . at four times a day (an hour at each period) to perfect him in all he had to learn. . . . Subalterns inspected squads on parade: the company was then formed and given over to the captain, who, with the rest of the officers, never quitted their company to lounge about, so long as the soldiers continued under arms. The corps paraded twice a week in heavy marching order, and the mess was equally well conducted, in a system of style and economy happily blended.[3]

Such training was necessary, for an ignorant officer could endanger the whole unit. Thomas Morris tells how his company was sent forward to skirmish at Quatre Bras under an officer of the old school, a captain who had been thirty years in the service but never before in action, and who was incapable of conducting his troops even through their ordinary evolutions on the parade ground without help from the sergeant. Threatened by French cavalry he was at his wits' end, and the company was only saved when the adjutant rode to their rescue and took command. It is impossible to tell how common were such incidents. They are seldom mentioned in memoirs, but this may reflect discretion, a reluctance to speak ill of the dead, or a fear of provoking controversy and a libel case, as much as any lack of material. One British officer complains with feeling, though in general terms, of inexperienced colleagues who repeatedly ordered their men to fire too soon, and it seems reasonable to assume that such mistakes were not infrequent.[4]

No system, of course, could weed out all the incompetent or cowardly officers, and no amount of training could substitute for experience in action, but some steps could be taken. A practice recorded in one British cavalry regiment, and probably much more widespread, was leaving one or more unreliable officers in the rear to guard the baggage, where, if they could do no good, they were at least unlikely to imperil the regiment. Similarly a French officer recalls a colleague who 'had never been on the fighting line; the sight of a sword made him pale, and he confessed it frankly'. Yet he was not punished, and the regiment made what use it could of him, leaving him behind at the depot to train generations of recruits.[5]

The soldiers in the ranks watched their officers closely and drew their own conclusions. According to Edward Costello, the British troops in the Peninsula 'divided the officers into two classes; the "come on" and the "go on"'; and he quotes the irrepressible Tom Plunket once reproaching an officer: 'The words "go on" don't befit a leader, Sir.' Another veteran of the 95th, Rifleman Harris, elaborates the point, and adds some unfashionable conclusions:

> The officers, too, are commented upon and closely observed. The men are very proud of those who are brave in the field, and kind and considerate to the soldiers under them. An act of kindness done by an officer has often during the battle been the cause of his life being saved. Nay, whatever folks may say upon the matter, I know from experience, that in *our* army the men like best to be officered by gentlemen, men whose education has rendered them more kind in manners than your coarse officer, sprung from obscure origin, and whose style is brutal and overbearing.[6]

It followed that the death of a popular officer, especially early in the action, might have a great effect, demoralizing those who were already disheartened, but angering those who were confident. As Pakenham's division closed on the French at Salamanca, Major Murphy was shot dead while leading the 88th, and his bleeding body, caught by one foot in a stirrup, was dragged across the front of the regiment by his frightened horse. The troops, already excited by their long advance and impatient at the French fire, were exasperated by the sight and, according to one of their officers, demanded to be let loose to avenge Murphy. On the other hand, when the unpopular Major Champion de Crespigny was killed in July 1813, 'joy was seen on every countenance and,' wrote Private Green, 'I verily thought we should have had three cheers, for several of our men began to cry "Hip! Hip!" which was always the signal for cheering. He was a cruel man to us, and his death was considered a happy release.'[7]

Such a reaction suggests that not all the officers who fell did so to enemy fire. There must have been examples in the Napoleonic, as in every other, period of soldiers taking advantage of the confusion of action to dispose of an unpopular officer, but recorded instances are extremely rare. It has been suggested, though not proved, that Colonel Cameron of the 92nd Highlanders was shot at Quatre Bras by a discontented soldier of his own regiment whom he had had flogged a few days before. Ill-disciplined armies in the early stages of the French Revolution and the Spanish uprising sometimes lynched their generals, but not in action, and so this falls into a different category. So does the wounding of Stapleton Cotton in the gathering dark on the evening of Salamanca, when the general failed to respond to the challenge of a Portuguese sentry. There is no Napoleonic equivalent for the story – which has perhaps been improved in the telling – of the unpopular major in the 15th Foot at Blenheim, who turned to address his regiment before the battle, apologized for his past behaviour, and asked that if he had to fall, it should be by the enemy's fire. A voice is said to have called out from the ranks, 'March on, sir; the enemy is before you, and we have something else to do than to think of you now.' At the close of the battle the major turned to his troops and raised his hat to call for a cheer, only to be shot dead by one of his men.[8]

Relations between officers and men varied widely even within a single army. This did not simply reflect the quality of the regiment, but also different philosophies. The ethos of the Light Division stressed a humane approach, with officers expected not only to set their men a good example, but to take a personal interest in them as individuals. This admirable system worked well in an elite force, though it may be doubted if it could have been applied to the whole army in the early nineteenth century. The alternative approach is described by William Grattan, a subaltern in the 88th, which was an excellent regiment in battle, though one with a reputation for plundering and harsh punishments off the field: 'the officers never tormented themselves or their men with too much fuss. We approached their quarters as seldom as we possibly could – I mean as seldom as was necessary – and thereby kept up that distance between officers and privates so essential to discipline.' Yet Grattan's own memoir shows a good knowledge of the men under his command, and the shared discomforts and dangers of campaigning – where regimental officers fared little better than their men, bivouacking in the open, going short of food, and marching long distances in all weathers – overcame the formal gulf and bred a strong camaraderie.[9]

At the human level, the quirks and quiddities of individuals often triumphed over theories, social barriers and official regulations. George Bell, an ensign in the 34th, marched back to Lisbon with no other company than his soldier servant Tom Tandy, and his account of the march puts more abstract descriptions into perspective:

We had a ride on the donkey, and carried the gun turn about. I was commanding officer and Tom as respectful as on parade, while sober. The first night on our new line of march he got right jolly on wine. He had no money nor credit, but a winning way at the wine-house, and a singular way when he lost his balance. I found him in heavy marching order, firelock in hand, when I thought him in bed for the night. 'Ho, Tom,' I said, 'where are you going?' 'Back to the regiment,' he said. 'I go no further: no service on this road.' I gave him a punch that floored him right into his little den, where he lay as quiet as a turtle until I took away his gun, knapsack, and ammunition, then locked him up a close prisoner till morning, when he turned out quite fresh and as penitent as priests, who'll never do it again until the next time! And so Tom worried me all the way, but only at night, when I usually locked him up.[10]

While the number of officers varied considerably between units, and between armies, a rough average was one officer to every twenty or thirty soldiers in an infantry battalion. They were rather more numerous in the cavalry and artillery – about one to fifteen or twenty men, probably reflecting the fact that these arms generally acted in smaller bodies. Bonnet's French infantry division at Salamanca had 238 officers and 6,283 men – or one officer to every 26.4 men – divided into twelve battalions, each having about twenty officers and 524 men (in fact it would have been slightly fewer, for some officers and a few men would have comprised the regimental headquarters). This was typical of Marmont's infantry, but the officer:man ratio in his cavalry was 1:19, and in his artillery 1:17. There were proportionately more officers in Wellington's army: one for every twenty men in the infantry, one to nineteen in the artillery, and one to fifteen in the cavalry. The figures for Waterloo were much the same, with both armies having about one officer to twenty-two men. Interestingly, the best contingents in Wellington's army, the British and King's German Legion, had the most officers proportionately (1:20 and 1:19 respectively), while in the Brunswick contingent the ratio was as low as one officer to thirty-two men. Yet there was no automatic correlation between the number of officers and the quality of the unit, for the ratio in Napoleon's Imperial Guard (1:28) was considerably lower than in the rest of his army.

The establishment strength of a British battalion of infantry was normally one lieutenant-colonel, two majors, ten captains, and twenty subalterns (lieutenants and ensigns), forty or more sergeants, and 1,000 rank and file (i.e. corporals and ordinary soldiers). However there seems to have been wide variation even in these theoretical totals, while the number of men actually serving in a battalion in the field was usually much lower. In practice, a battalion with 500 rank and file might have only half a dozen officers of the rank of captain or above, so that some companies would be commanded by lieutenants. Similarly the number of non-commissioned officers with the regiment would be far below the establishment total, though they would maintain, and even increase, as a proportion of the unit's strength.[11]

The non-commissioned officers, and particularly the sergeants, did a great deal of the administrative and other routine work, playing a large part in training, drill and supervising the men's daily lives. They were crucial to the domestic economy and morale of a regiment, whether in quarters, on campaign or in battle, yet they received little reward. Wellington pressed the British government to increase their pay, but this encountered opposition from both the hard-pressed Treasury and from the Duke of York.[12] Promotion to the commissioned ranks was rare, and not always successful: not all gallant sergeants could leap the social gulf, and many officers – and men too – resented their elevation. Even in the French army, social mobility declined sharply after the early years of the Revolutionary War, and the 'baton-in-the-knapsack' remained largely an illusion for the poor boys conscripted into Napoleon's regiments.

But it was not only the few officers promoted from the ranks who might find their first months in the regiment difficult: many new officers were subject to a severe trial of teasing, practical jokes and other pranks which tested their spirit and patience before they were accepted by their new comrades. There is some evidence that this was most severe in the best regiments; certainly it was so in the 95th Rifles, as Kincaid freely admits:

> I don't know how it was, nor do I know whether we differed from other regiments in the same respect, but our first and most uncharitable aim was to discover the weak points of every fresh arrival, and to attack him through them. If he had redeeming qualities, he, of course, came out scathless, but, if not, he was dealt with most unmercifully. Poor Tommy [Dangerfield] had none such – he was weak on all sides, and therefore went to the wall.[13]

Edward Costello, also of the 95th, tells the story of how another new officer finally stopped his tormentors, by quietly letting it be known that he kept a clean pair of pistols, and was ready to meet any of them in a duel at any time they chose. In the Royal Dragoons too, some veteran officers gave 'Johnny Newcomes' a torrid reception, expecting them to empty their pockets to pay for lavish dinners, and sometimes getting them into more serious trouble. This worse-than-schoolboy bullying reflects little credit on those involved, yet it was not wholly senseless. Officers in an active regiment like the 95th had learnt to trust and depend on each other in action. A newcomer, probably filling the shoes of a dead or wounded comrade, was an unknown quantity who had to be tested, while his assumption that he was good enough to join them was, unconsciously, resented. And sometimes this resentment and suspicion were fully justified. In 1812 a self-assured new officer called Avarne joined the Royal Dragoons. Before long, he had heard so much talk of 'stabbing, wounding and killing' that he came down with severe diarrhoea and begged to be sent to the rear. Here an experienced officer, his junior, saw 'yellow fever in Mr Avarne's eyes', and played upon his feelings until Avarne resigned from the regiment –

thus assisting the junior officer's promotion by one step. With better handling Mr Avarne might have made a good officer; or he might have remained in the regiment until his nerve broke in front of the enemy, where his failure might have thrown the whole unit into confusion. It was a rough, crude sorting process which must have cost the regiments many potentially good officers, without eliminating all the fools and cowards, but it probably helped build cohesion, confidence and mutual reliance among those who passed through the initiation.[14]

Life as a regimental officer, even once accepted by comrades, was not unalloyed bliss, as John Aitchison's reflections make clear:

> Were any misfortune to deprive my worthy parent of the means of supporting me . . . how could I live? Not by my pay for that is barely sufficient for my clothes! . . . Do not imagine from this that I absolutely hate my profession – by no means – the profession of arms always has been and ever will be respectable – I rejoice in contributing in any way my assistance to add to the renown of my country, and I glory in having acted in deeds which have immortalized my regiment [the 3rd Foot Guards] and have enhanced the character of the army – but how dearly purchased! – at two and twenty I find myself unequal to extraordinary exertion, and I am compelled to live as *cautiously* abstemious as a ruined *debauchee* and what is worse, I am left in doubt whether I shall ever be restored to my former health, but I am galled most at *the want of independence* which I can never gain.[15]

However, Aitchison was suffering from malaria at the time, and had just written to discourage his brother from joining the army, so he was inclined to take the gloomy view. John Kincaid's rather sentimental, but equally sincere, retrospective view provides a corrective:

> No officer during that time had one fraction to rub against another; and when I add that our paunches were nearly as empty as our pockets, it will appear almost a libel upon common-sense to say that we enjoyed it; yet so it was – our very privations were a subject of pride and boast to us, and there still continued to be an *esprit de corps* – a buoyancy of feeling animating all, which nothing could quell; we were alike ready for the field or for frolic, and when not engaged in one, went headlong into the other.
>
> Ah me! when I call to mind that our chief support in those days of trial was the anticipated delight in recounting those tales in after years, to wondering and admiring groups around our domestic hearths, in merry England; and when I find that so many of these after years have already passed, and that the folks who people these present years, care no more about these dear-bought tales of former ones than if they were spinning-wheel stories of some 'auld wife ayont the fire'; I say it is not only enough to make me inflict them with a book, as I have done, but it makes me wish that I had it all over to do again; and I think it would be very

odd if I would not do exactly as I have done, for I knew no happier times, and they were their own reward![16]

*

When a battalion of infantry formed in line for battle, the commanding officer, mounted on horseback, normally took his station a few yards in front of the very centre of the unit. Behind him, in the line, where the two centre companies joined, stood two ensigns each carrying one of the battalion's flags, supported and defended by four sergeants. The commanders of the companies normally stood in the front rank on the right-hand side of their companies, with a sergeant occupying the rear rank behind them. The remaining subalterns and sergeants formed behind the line where they could keep the troops in their ranks and maintain order. The major, or majors, and the adjutant were mounted, and took position behind the subalterns and towards the centre of the unit. Behind the line in the centre were the bandsmen, surgeon and other ancillary figures, at least on parade – in action their position was sometimes altered according to the terrain and other local circumstances.

It is not clear if there was much variation in the position of the other officers and NCOs, for surviving memoirs, diaries and letters generally take such details for granted. However we do know that at Salamanca, Colonel Wallace ordered the officers of the 88th to place themselves in front of the centre of their companies, to maintain better control of their men in a long advance under fire, which was likely to be noisy and distracting; so that in this, as in other respects, the drill regulations were not invariably followed, although Grattan describes it as 'a rare occurrence'.[17]

The commanding officer in action had many and varied tasks to perform, depending largely on whether his battalion was integrated into a larger formation, or acting more independently. Thus the commanders of the battalions in Leith's or Pakenham's attack at Salamanca had little scope for tactical initiative, at least during the initial advance. Their task was to set their men an obvious, immediate example of courage and coolness; to make sure their troops remained in good order and held their place in the line; and, especially in the battalions on either flank, to keep watch for any unexpected enemy threat. Later, after the initial attack, they may have had more room for independent action.

Where a battalion was not acting as part of a larger body, its commander might have to decide on its formation, ordering it into square at the sight of enemy cavalry, or to lie down to minimize losses from enemy artillery. He could decide to send out the battalion's light company to skirmish, or recall it if it was in danger. He controlled, or endeavoured to control, the battalion's fire, trying to restrain the men until the enemy reached effective range. Above all he endeavoured not only to preserve order in the regiment, but to anticipate and forestall anything which might threaten its cohesion, whether enemy forces, rough ground or even the flight of friendly forces.

The surviving exhortations from commanding officers to their men repeatedly stress the same few points. 'Now, my young tinkers, stand firm! While you remain in your present position, old Harry himself can't touch you; but if *one* of you give way, *he* will have every mother's son of you, as sure as you are born!' 'I tell you again they cannot hurt us if you are steady, if you get out of time, you will be knocked down.' 'Be steady, my boys, reserve your fire till they are within ten paces, and they will never penetrate you.' Three different officers at three different battles, with the same message which must have been repeated hundreds of times on battlefields all over Europe throughout the period.[18]

At Sabugal in 1811 Colonel Beckwith's 'manner of command . . . was nothing more than a familiar sort of conversation with the soldier'. Compelled to fall back he called out, 'Now, my lads, we'll just go back a little if you please,' and when his riflemen began to run, he quickly shouted an admonishment, 'No, no, I don't mean that – we are in no hurry – we'll just walk quietly back, and you can give them a shot as you go along.' This was enough to steady good troops who trusted their commander, and whose underlying confidence was very high. Beckwith ignored a slight wound which left his forehead streaming with blood, and maintained his calm, soothing manner. Having reached a new position he called out, 'Now my men, this will do – let us show them our teeth again!', and the riflemen turned and continued the fight.[19]

Captain Parquin's commanding officer, Major de Vérigny, was almost as good at keeping his men steady in action. At Fuentes de Oñoro, when the regiment came under heavy artillery fire, he

> rode slowly among the men, talking to them quietly as was his usual custom at moments of danger.
>
> 'Parquin,' he said, pointing to the chasseur who was under fire for the first time and whose pale face betrayed the apprehension he felt, 'Parquin, I can see by this fellow's face that he is going to make good use of his sabre when we charge.'
>
> The chasseur, who immediately recovered his determination at these words, brandished his sabre and declared: 'You may count on that, sir.'[20]

The more junior officers played similar roles, though with less responsibility for taking decisions. They conveyed their commander's orders to their men, and supervised the troops' performance. Neither they nor the sergeants – at least in line regiments – carried muskets, so they were free to concentrate their efforts on maintaining order, closing the ranks when casualties made gaps, and correcting any mistake in drill before it could cause serious problems.

Many writers contrast the differing styles of British and French officers:

> How different the duty of the French officers from ours. They, stimulating the men by their example, the men vociferating, each chaffing each until they appear in a fury, shouting, to the points of our bayonets. After the first huzza the British

officers, restraining their men, still as death. 'Steady, lads, steady,' is all you hear, and that in an undertone.[21]

And yet there are many first-hand accounts of British officers seeking to encourage, not restrain, their men's enthusiasm, leading them forward in an impetuous charge.

So long as the troops remained in good order and were enthusiastic, the officer's task was relatively simple, but when the men began to hesitate and grow uncertain, the need for leadership became greater. Charles Napier, describing his part in command of the 50th at Coruña, writes:

> After passing the 42nd we came to the wall, which was breast high and my line checked, but several officers, Stanhope one, leaped over, calling on the men to follow. At first about a hundred did at a low part, no more, and therefore, leaping back, I took a halberd and holding it horizontally pushed many over the low part; and again getting over myself . . . all got over, yet it required the example of officers and the bravest men to get all over.

Though he claims to have remained cool, Napier admits that 'the check at the wall had excited me and made me swear horribly'.[22]

At Talavera, the light company of the Fusiliers fell back to the regiment in some disorder, and the whole regiment, mostly made up of raw soldiers, coming under heavy fire and shaken by the sight of their comrades hurrying back, staggered and might have broken. But their colonel, Sir William Myers, leapt from his horse, grabbed one of the colours, and rallied the regiment.[23] Three years later at Salamanca the regiment (part of Cole's division) was again under pressure. Its initial attack had succeeded, but left the British in some disorder, and the French were making a counter-attack:

> They [the French] then advanced up the hill in the most beautiful order without firing a shot except a few individuals in the rear of the column. When about 30 paces distant our men began to waver, being still firing & not properly formed. The Ensigns advanced two paces in front & planted the colours on the edge of the hill & Officers stept out to encourage the men to meet them. They stopt [?] with an apparent determination to stand firm, the enemy continued to advance at a steady pace & when quite close the Fuziliers gave way.[24]

Once broken, it became the duty of the officers to take the first available opportunity to rally their men, halting their flight as soon as they were free from immediate danger, and calling on their men to re-form their ranks. This was as difficult and demanding a task as any officer faced, for they themselves were despondent and sick at heart at having been worsted, and the men, having broken the bonds of discipline and obedience, might be surly and even dangerous. Rallying a unit tested both the courage of the officers and the moral authority they had gained over their men, but in the end it was only possible if the men themselves were willing to return to the ranks. Officers could employ psychological pressure and provide an inspiring example, but they could not force their men to fight.

Theoretically, officers and NCOs were entitled to cut down any man who turned to run, for his flight might start a panic which could jeopardize the safety of the whole unit. But there is little or no evidence of this occurring in practice – in part, perhaps, because most officers were armed only with swords, and sergeants with halberds, while their men were armed with muskets and bayonets. Nor does it seem that Napoleonic officers threatened their men to make them advance, as happened in the First World War; though they might push and jostle their men forward as Charles Napier describes doing at Coruña. One case which went further than this was at Martinique in 1794 when Captain Faulkner, RN commanded a naval battery on shore. He quarrelled with an artillery officer and while angry struck a seaman with his sword, accidentally killing him. The upshot is interesting, for it suggests that such conduct was generally regarded as unacceptable. Faulkner was recalled to his ship in disgrace, while the seamen in the battery went on strike, demanding that he be court-martialled. Far from being treated as mutineers, they were coaxed back to work and Faulkner was tried – though acquitted. It is worth adding that he was a popular captain of his ship, and fell in action soon afterwards.[25]

In action, the perspective of most regimental officers was very limited, not extending 'much beyond the range of what was likely to affect himself and the few soldiers immediately about him'.[26] Only very rarely did a junior officer get a chance to display tactical initiative in a way which changed the course of an action. One such incident occurred at Sabugal, when the British 43rd were advancing to support the 52nd amid showers of rain. Lieutenant Hopkins, commanding the company on the extreme right of the line, saw through the rain a French force turning the British flank. Colonel Beckwith, commanding the brigade, and Major Patrickson, commanding the battalion, were too far to the left to be consulted in time, so Hopkins approached Captain Duffy, the nearest superior officer, who commanded the neighbouring company, and asked his permission to take his, Hopkins's, company to oppose the French threat. Duffy replied that he could not take upon himself the responsibility for detaching a company from the regiment without orders. But Hopkins realized that there was no time to be lost, and, throwing caution to the winds, he led his company to a little knoll some distance to the right. Some men of Duffy's company, presumably without orders, followed Hopkins, so that he had a total force of more than 100 men. This was enough to check the French advance, and Beckwith soon rode up, approved the dispositions Hopkins had made, and praised his independent judgement. The action was far from over, but thanks to Hopkins's boldness one of the most dangerous moments of the day had passed safely. Indeed Beckwith later told William Napier that

Hopkins was 'one of the finest soldiers he ever beheld; and that so far as a man commanding one company could decide a battle, Hopkins decided the battle of Sabugal'.[27]

Such opportunities arose seldom, but some junior officers were still required to exercise their intelligence. When a light infantry company was detached to skirmish in front of its battalion – or even further afield – its commander might have to act on his own initiative. Similarly the commander of a reserve squadron of cavalry might have to decide whether or not to throw his unit into a mêlée. At Eylau, Captain Kirmann, in Charles Parquin's regiment, saw that a group of cossacks was threatening the flank of the regiment (which was engaged frontally at the time), and forestalled the danger by deploying his squadron to face them. And much of the success of the famous charge of the heavy dragoons of the King's German Legion at Garcia Hernandez was due to the quick wits of Captains von der Decken and von Reitzenstein, who recognized and exploited a fleeting opportunity.[28]

There was some debate as to whether officers were also expected to exercise their strength and skill by taking a personal part in the fighting, except in self-defence. One eighteenth-century English authority declared flatly that 'no officer is supposed to fight himself, any more than to defend his head; his business is to see the men fight and do well; that's sufficient'. This view, rather less dogmatically held, seems to have been the prevailing wisdom in the Napoleonic period, and no attempt was made to regularly equip officers in the British or foreign armies with muskets, despite the views of those who, like Edward Costello, argued that it would significantly increase a battalion's firepower. Nonetheless some officers could not resist setting their men an example in this, as in other respects. Lieutenant Maclean borrowed a musket and fired several shots while attacking La Petite Rhune at Nivelle, although, significantly, a sergeant reloaded the weapon for him (see above, p. 21). Lieutenant Strode of the 95th always carried a rifle in action, using it with skill. And at Busaco, Captain John Jones of the 52nd broke from the British line, rushed upon the leading French officer, cut him down with his sword and 'immediately cut off the medal with which the major was decorated, and appropriated it to himself'. Such active souvenir hunting was hardly setting his men an example of discipline or restraint, though it seems that contemporaries felt that the incident reflected credit on the 'fiery Welshman'.[29]

Whatever his lack of discretion and good taste, Jones undoubtedly displayed great courage, and this, in theory at least, was the *sine qua non* of an officer on active service. Most, after the ordeal of their first combat, do not seem to have found it difficult to maintain at least the minimum standard, while there are innumerable tales of conspicuous gallantry and reckless bravery. For the few at the other end of the scale, there were a variety of sanctions, ranging from the fairly light-hearted banter provoked by a minor misdemeanour, to more serious punishments. A French officer in d'Erlon's corps at Waterloo describes the conduct of a fellow officer, a rather thin and very tall captain, upwards of six feet four inches in height. He had served in Spain but had failed to bring back a great reputation for courage, fond as he was of rattling his R's in conversation. While our column under a heavy fire of canister shot was painfully toiling up the slope occupied by the enemy, our gallant friend, probably through inadvertence, kept edging closer and closer to the rear rank of the company in front of us, and doubtless considering it unfair to present a higher target to the enemy than his neighbours, he tried hard to conceal his head behind the shoulders of the man before him; with this object he bent his body nearly double in a most unsoldierlike attitude. Nor was this all, for soon perceiving that his position was becoming unpleasant, he turned sharply round, facing his company and stepped backwards balancing his sword as we do on parade to mark the cadence and correct the dressing, but in doing so in order not to lose the friendly shelter in his front he leant backwards in a still more ungraceful attitude than his previous one. He may at any rate boast of having afforded us a hearty laugh in a very serious moment.[30]

By his conduct this officer would have destroyed his reputation and standing in the regiment, and would be the butt of endless jibes and comments, but no official notice was likely to be taken of his behaviour, although he might be passed over for promotion or selected for more than his share of tiresome chores.

Less amusing, and much more common, was the conduct of disheartened officers who made slight wounds the pretext of going to the rear, while others sometimes did so without even this poor excuse. Such behaviour may often have been passed over, officially at least, but at times it led to serious consequences. In 1748 the captains and lieutenants of a company of the regiment of Médoc dealt directly with one of their number. They dragged him in front of the regiment, pulled off his coat and tore it up, broke his sword, beat him with a stick and chased him away.[31]

After Waterloo the officers of the Royal Dragoons held an unofficial inquiry into the conduct of Lieutenant Bridges, whose behaviour in the battle, and on at least one previous occasion, had been more than suspect. Bridges had not bivouacked with the regiment on the evening of Waterloo, nor had the surgeon treated him for a wound. Hope that he had been honourably killed was dispelled by accounts that he 'had been seen going to the rear at a famous pace', and it was soon ascertained that he had comfortably ensconced himself in a safe position far behind the battle line. Summoned to defend himself,

Bridges stuttered and stammered his excuses which became increasingly ridiculous. First, he said, that 'his saddle had turned'. Then that 'his horse had run away and landed him in the Prussian camp.' To all this the assembled officers listened, we are told, 'with patience'. But clearly the truth was not in him, and he was given the option of resigning from the regiment or being put under arrest to be tried by court martial. Naturally he opted for the former but, according to the [unofficial regimental] *Journal*, got away with it in the eyes of the world, carrying off his resignation with a high hand. 'He let it be known that he was sick of the old Royals, and that the Hussars would be more to his taste, and when he returned home strutted about Town as if he was the most meritorious officer imaginable, complaining bitterly of the treatment he had received at the hands of the regiment on which account he had refused a Waterloo medal. Indeed, with such effrontery did he utter his impudent language that in the neighbourhood of his father's seat in Hampshire he remained a gallant, meritorious and very much ill-used young officer.'[32]

On this same occasion the commander of the Royals also compelled the resignation of a far better officer, Ralph Heathcote (whose letters have been published as *Ralph Heathcote. Letters of a Young Diplomatist and Soldier during the Time of Napoleon*), whose behaviour, while open to question, was probably quite innocent. But if in this case the regiment behaved with undue severity, it had previously displayed excessive leniency towards a number of officers whose conduct was a disgrace, but who went out of their way to cultivate the good will of Colonel Clifton. The Royals was not a happy regiment in this period, with divisions running deep in the officers' mess, but it was probably not unusual in being more inclined to turn a blind eye to the misconduct of an officer than to take action; and, if action were taken, to prefer private pressure to a public scandal. As a result, only two British officers were cashiered for cowardice during the whole of the Peninsular War.[33]

Such tolerance was unlikely to extend to officers of other regiments, at least in the heat of battle. Captain Dyneley describes how, when Pack's brigade broke at Salamanca, he caught a fleeing Portuguese officer, and tried to shame him into doing his duty. 'I stopped him short and made all the men at the guns hiss and abuse him, then gave him over to the 40th regiment, who hooted him from right to left; but the fellow did not care, he saved his head which was his object.' But this was unusual, for most officers cared deeply for their honour, reputation or self-esteem, and young officers in particular could feel humiliated by defeat, even if in fact they had no grounds to reproach themselves. At Austerlitz a captured Russian artillery officer was brought before Napoleon: 'he struggled, wept, and twisted his hands in despair, crying out, "I've lost my battery! I've been shamed in front of the whole world! I want to die!" Napoleon spoke consolingly to him, "Be calm, young man! There is no disgrace in being beaten by the French." '[34]

While some officers improperly absented themselves from battle, others went to great lengths to be with their unit even when they had every excuse and opportunity to stay away. George Hennell had been detached before Vitoria, but the prospect of heavy fighting made him hasten to rejoin. Such was 'the high sense of honour' in his regiment that he knew that his fellow officers would have teased him if he had been absent; but in his own mind this was not his principal motive: 'It was likely to be a general engagement and, supposing it the last we should have, I did not chuse to be absent.' The pressure of public opinion was strong, however, and a cavalry officer who missed Waterloo due to a combination of a riding accident and a severe attack of boils was not a happy man:

> I would give a great deal had I seen and been in the engagement of the 18th, but accidents will happen to all people at different times. My consolation is that every officer and man knew that I was unable to do any duty whatever at the time the regiment marched, for I suppose you are aware what some ill-natured people might say.

But public opinion cannot account for the conduct of John Montagu, a young ensign in the 52nd who was ordered to escort a party of invalids from Brussels further to the rear. After a day's march they encountered a small detachment of their own regiment commanded by an ensign junior to Montagu. The young man seized his chance, handed over command of the invalids, and hurried back to the regiment in time for the battle.[35]

While courageous and praiseworthy, such conduct is not really surprising. A battle was the culmination of the campaign, the focus for the whole army's activity, and although it would be both dangerous and unpleasant, it was understandable that a young officer should wish to take part with his comrades. An old soldier who had been in many previous actions might take a more relaxed attitude, though most would feel some regret at missing an important action – especially a victory. Thus Charles Colville, who commanded the British troops at Hal on the day of Waterloo, wrote home,

> I am not such a fire eater as to think it necessary to say that I have fretted myself at having been unavoidably absent from it, but at the same time am aware that I should have felt a proud satisfaction in being able to inform you of my having shared in the efforts of a day which must be recorded as perhaps the most important in modern history.[36]

A much stronger sense of disappointment was likely to be felt by an officer – or a soldier – who was unavoidably absent from his unit, and so missed the experience which his comrades shared, binding them closer together and, partly at least, excluding him.

Officers lost heavily in action. According to an unpublished return in the War Office papers, which may not be authoritative but which appears plausible, 621 British officers were killed in action in Wellington's campaigns between 1808 and 1815, and a further 3,186 were wounded. And Martinien's list of officers in the French army who were killed and wounded between 1805 and 1815 includes some 60,000 entries.[37] Moreover it seems clear that officers usually suffered casualties at a disproportionately heavy rate compared to their men. Accurate figures for strength and losses, especially for rank and file, are often hard to obtain, particularly for the battles in central Europe. There are good figures however for many, though not all, the major actions in the Peninsula. Taking Barrosa, Fuentes, Albuera and Vitoria as a sample, we find that French officers lost disproportionately at each, and that if the figures for the four battles are combined, officers amounted to 3.4 per cent of the total force, but 4.9 per cent of the casualties. This means that a French officer in these battles was, on average, 44 per cent more likely to be wounded or killed than one of his men.[38]

The same result applies to other armies. In eleven of fifteen Prussian brigades fighting at Ligny and Waterloo, the officers suffered more than their fair share of casualties, with the average overall being 25 per cent more than the men (i.e. if the rank and file sustained 10 per cent casualties, the officers sustained 12.5 per cent on average; if the rank and file lost 20 per cent, the officers lost 25 per cent, and so on).[39] Philip Haythornthwaite's analysis of British casualties in six Peninsular battles confirms the phenomenon. In five, Busaco, Barrosa, Fuentes, Salamanca and Nivelle, the officers lost disproportionately heavily, and while the margin fluctuated greatly, Haythornthwaite concludes that in general 'officers were probably about one fifth more likely to be hit than other ranks'. The exception was Albuera where officers and men alike suffered extraordinarily heavy losses of around 40 per cent. This suggests, though it does not prove, that once casualties became very heavy, the disproportionate loss of officers diminished and ultimately disapperared. (French officers at Albuera lost more heavily than their men, but the excess was less than in the other battles sampled – about half the average.) It might also be thought that where a unit was not closely engaged, and suffered only from stray shots and long-range artillery fire, the disproportion would be much less. But this is not borne out by a check of the twenty-two British units which at Salamanca lost twenty or fewer casualties. Between them these units lost thirteen officers and 173 men, the officers amounting to 7 per cent of the casualties, while they had only comprised 5 per cent of the combined strength of these units.[40]

At Waterloo, 22 per cent of Wellington's rank and file were casualties, compared to 29 per cent of his officers. In the British contingent the figures were 30 per cent and 34 per cent respectively. Significantly, the only allied contingent where the officers did not sustain casualties at a greater rate than their men was the Dutch-Belgian, whose disappointing performance may have been due to a lack of leadership and commitment from its officers. Finally, the return in the War Office papers already mentioned shows that officers amounted to 6.55 per cent of total British casualties in Wellington's campaigns, or one for every 15.3 other ranks, a rate considerably greater than their presence in the army (5–5.5 per cent, one for eighteen or twenty soldiers) would imply.[41]

These figures require some explanation, especially as the normal position of many of a unit's officers, behind the front ranks, should have afforded them some protection. Three factors seem to have been involved, but it is impossible to determine their relative importance. First, it is probable that men were much more likely than officers to slip away to the rear, whether on the pretext of a slight wound, helping a wounded comrade, or some other excuse. This meant that the number of men actually exposed to enemy fire was somewhat lower than that shown in the 'morning state', and consequently the proportion of officers to men was rather higher. This would affect poor troops more than good ones, unless the officers were also bad. Second, the enemy might concentrate their fire on a unit's officers. The colours in the centre of an infantry battalion, with the commander riding in front, was a natural target. Skirmishers might also direct their fire on enemy officers, whether to disrupt their cohesion or, as Colonel Landmann observed, for less laudable motives (see above, pp. 66–7). It was not until 1813 that British officers discarded their distinctive cocked hats, which made them immediately identifiable at a considerable distance, and adopted a shako similar in profile to that of their men. In the same year Marshal Soult – shamelessly exaggerating – complained that the British riflemen

> are specially ordered to pick off the officers. When senior officers go to the front, either to make observations or to encourage their troops, they are almost always hit. We lose so many officers that after two consecutive actions the battalion is almost destitute of them. In our casualty lists the proportion is often one officer to eight men. I have seen units where there were only two or three officers left, though not one sixth of the rank and file were *hors de combat*.[42]

The third factor which almost certainly contributed to the excessive losses of officers was their willingness to expose themselves at moments of greatest danger in order to encourage their men. This is supported by any number of anecdotes of friends and foes alike, but again, it is impossible to measure.

Not only did officers have more casualties than their men, it appears that, in the French army at least, a significantly higher proportion of their casualties were killed rather than wounded. Thus at Talavera, 17 per cent of French officer casualties were killed, compared to 10.5 per cent of other ranks. At Busaco, in II and VI Corps, the figures were 23.5 per cent and 19.9 per cent, and in the Battles of the Pyrenees, according to Soult's unreliable returns, the discrepancy was even greater: 27 per cent compared to 13 per cent. Similar results were produced at Barrosa, Sabugal, Fuentes and (on Soult's corrupt figures) Albuera, but not, strangely, at Vitoria. However, this discrepancy does not appear in British casualty statistics, where the proportion of officers killed generally reflects quite closely that of the rank and file, both for specific actions and for Wellington's campaigns as a whole.[43]

The principal reason for this is the great under-representation of officers among the missing. When this is taken into account the problem usually, though not always, disappears, or is reduced to insignificance. There were two causes of such under-representation. Officers were more reluctant to surrender, and so fought on beyond the point of prudence and were killed, where their men, yielding to superior force, were taken prisoner. And greater efforts would be made to identify the bodies of officers who had been killed in action, ensuring that they would have been entered in the return as dead, while some of the soldiers who fell with them would be listed as missing.

Other factors may also have contributed slightly to this higher mortality rate. Officers might continue in action with a slight wound – and so risk being killed – when a soldier would go to the rear. The accuracy of allied riflemen may have resulted in a greater mortality among officers, though this could hardly have contributed much to the overall result. Officers may have been reluctant to report themselves as wounded for fear of distressing friends and family at home, while their death could hardly be concealed. And some soldiers who disappeared from the ranks early in the day may have been recorded as wounded, when it was only their courage that was impaired.

All these results apply to whole armies, where infantry formed the great majority of the troops engaged and would swamp any peculiarities in the casualty figures for other arms. In particular it seems plausible that cavalry officers, being better mounted and often better horsemen, might suffer fewer casualties in a charge and mêlée, than their men. But the evidence shows that on most occasions cavalry officers, like their infantry counterparts, suffered disproportionately heavy casualties. It may be that this disproportion was lower or even non-existent in extended charges such as Le Marchant's at Salamanca, or when a regiment was ruined, such as the 23rd Light Dragoons at Talavera, but the figures are too small or uncertain for firm conclusions to be drawn. For example, Le Marchant's brigade recorded the loss of only four officer casualties at Salamanca, so that a single bullet could increase the figure by 25 per cent. In any case, relatively few cavalry casualties normally occurred in hand-to-hand fighting, where the hypothetical advantage of officers would be most relevant.[44]

Although officers suffered disproportionately heavy casualties in battle, this did not mean that their presence in the army gradually declined over the course of a long campaign or war. Wounded officers received far better treatment than their men, and so were more likely to recover, and to do so more quickly. More importantly, the great majority of losses were not due to enemy action, but to sickness and exhaustion (see above, Chapter 1 pp. 7–9). Officers suffered significantly less than their men from these scourges, and again were better treated when they were ill. So, although it appears paradoxical, officers were both more likely to fall gloriously in action, *and* more likely to survive the war than their men.[45]

Chapter Ten
Morale and Cohesion

The aim of a battle in the Napoleonic period was not to annihilate the enemy, but to send his men reeling to the rear in a complete rout. This was achieved by undermining the intangible bonds of morale and cohesion which kept men in the ranks, obedient to their officers, and believing that if they continued to fight they would triumph. Inflicting casualties was the most obvious, and perhaps the most important, way of sapping the enemy's resolve; but it was not the only way, and it was not uncommon for a victorious army to suffer more casualties up to the point where the battle was decided than its opponent, only for the balance to be reversed in the immediate pursuit.

Battle involved mental as well as physical attrition, wearing away at individual and collective determination as well as at the number of men in the ranks. 'A fit of passion is no trial of a man's courage,' wrote one British officer,

> but a whole day's battle really is. If, after 3 or 4 hours fatigue & witnessing the destructive effects of cannon & musketry, you are ordered to charge an enemy you will discover what quantity of that necessary ingredient you possess. There are few but feel something more than usual on going into battle. The first is, no doubt, the worst, but do not imagine that after the second or third all feeling is lost. Old soldiers know well what a ball can do & many feel more than they express.[1]

The strength of a unit consisted not only in the number of muskets or sabres it could put into the line, but also in its mental toughness, which decided its ability to endure the strains of battle. At the heart of this toughness lay confidence – not the foolish confidence of a mob of volunteers who had never seen a shot fired in action, and who would run at the first sight of the enemy, but confidence founded on the experience of victory. Unbroken success in action might lead to arrogance, but it would instil a faith in victory which could sometimes overcome enormous odds. The British Light Division is a pre-eminent example. Constantly in action, always performing with credit, the men soon developed a confidence in themselves and their officers (if not always their divisional commanders) which made defeat seem almost inconceivable. This spirit carried them through difficult actions at the Coa and Sabugal without being shaken, and led them to believe themselves – with good reason – the pick of the army.

Napoleon's Imperial Guard, the most famous elite force of the period, was rather different. In the early years it was recruited from distinguished veterans, and though in time conscripts were included – the 'Young Guard' – the core units of the Old Guard remained exclusive. But until 1813–15 the Guard saw relatively little fighting – much to the disgust of the rest of the army. It was Napoleon's ultimate reserve, but save in those last years, he seldom needed to draw upon it, although its artillery and cavalry were used more frequently. Instead, the Guard acted as a model for the rest of the army, a focus for emulation and envy. Good soldiers were taken from their line regiments, spent a few years in the Guard, and were then often given commissions in line regiments. Similarly, officers might spend some time in the Guard before being promoted back into the line, supposedly with their skills honed and their ambition excited. Whether it worked so well in practice is open to doubt. The Guard was widely resented in the rest of the army, and commanders felt that by creaming off their best men it weakened the quality of the remainder. But it is impossible to balance such intangible, uncertain costs against the definite value which Napoleon gained from having such a devoted, loyal *corps d'élite* to fall back on in any emergency. Certainly he thought there was a substantial net gain, as the great expansion of the Guard shows.

Experience of success in the field was the best foundation of confidence and good morale. In its absence – and all soldiers began as inexperienced recruits – the next best thing was intensive training, but this was rare in any army in the Napoleonic period. It is no coincidence that the British regiments in the Light Division had been exceptionally well trained before the Peninsular War broke out, or that the army with which Napoleon performed his great campaigns of 1805–7 was the best trained that he ever commanded. But without experience even the best training produced a brittle unit, liable to collapse into panic if things went wrong. Conversely, experience had to include a reasonable amount of success to be useful. Soldiers who fought in a succession of defeats could have no confidence in victory, and probably included a very high proportion of those who had learnt the wisdom of making an early departure from the battle-field. And yet Soult's ragged army, which had suffered six major and many minor defeats over the previous ten months, fought well at Toulouse in April 1814.

Studies of soldiers in twentieth-century wars suggest that their effectiveness in combat steadily rose with experience until it reached a plateau, and after some time – depending partly on the circumstances and nature of the fighting – it then diminished as 'combat fatigue' or 'burnout' set in.[2] There is little evidence of this phenomenon in the Napoleonic period, though it is possible that the decline of the French army after 1807 was partly caused by weariness and exhaustion, especially among the NCOs and officers. However, there are other explanations for the French decline – notably the accumulated losses since 1805 and the war in Spain – which may be sufficient without invoking combat fatigue. The British Light Division probably saw more fierce combat over the six years of the Peninsular War than any French or allied unit in the era, but its zest, confidence and dash were undiminished – indeed they were greater than ever – in the final year of the war. The most probable reason for the absence of combat fatigue was that even for the Light Division, action, while bloody, was relatively rare. For example, in 1812, after the horrors of the storming of Ciudad Rodrigo and Badajoz, it was little engaged at Salamanca, and did not take part in the siege of Burgos, while the long campaign was followed by five months of relaxed life in cantonments, allowing minds as well as bodies to recover from their exertions. There was also a constant flow of fresh officers and men joining the units to replace both casualties and officers who had resigned or transferred to other regiments. For, of course, any officer in the British army who felt battle weary could resign his commission and leave the army, or transfer to a regiment in a less onerous situation, though there was naturally great reluctance to do so.

Officers and men alike felt pride in the achievement of their unit, which in turn spurred them on to further exertions. On the morning after the storm and sack of Ciudad Rodrigo, the 95th Rifles marched out of the town, dirty and begrimed by the fighting, many still half-drunk or with hangovers, laden with loot and dressed in all manner of ridiculous purloined finery, one even with a monkey on his shoulder. As this ragged group left the town they passed the Fifth Division who formed up on the left of the road, presented arms, and cheered them. Compared to such heartfelt tributes, some attempts to arouse regimental pride seem forced. At Walcheren in 1809 the eccentric Colonel Mainwaring made a long speech to his men on the fiftieth anniversary of the Battle of Minden, where the regiment had distinguished itself. Yet Private Wheeler seems to have been impressed, and as the regiment was full of new recruits who were about to see action for the first time, Mainwaring's words may have had some benefit. More immediately relevant was Soult's reminder to the 10th *Léger*, on the morning of Austerlitz, of their previous victory over the Russians in Switzerland, six years before (quoted above, p. 160).[3]

In the French army soldiers who distinguished themselves in action were awarded special decorated arms, or later the *Légion d'honneur*, and granted privileges and extra pay. They became figures of pride and emulation for new recruits, so that many years later Charles Parquin could remember in detail the story of all but one of those who had received the honour in his regiment at the time he joined it.[4] Some foreign armies, though not the British, had a similar, if usually more limited system of honours; and even without any formal rewards, the achievements of veterans with a reputation for courage, ability or character would be impressed on new recruits, making them feel proud, if a little unworthy, of belonging to such distinguished company.

The most potent symbol of regimental pride was the colours, or in the French their famous regimental eagle. The colours were often the focus of ferocious fighting in a mêlée: their defence was essential to a regiment's honour and their capture was regarded as a great achievement. Many tales of extraordinary gallantry collect around the colours; some seem to have grown in the telling, but there is no doubt of the genuine feeling of a letter home written two days after Albuera by G. Crompton, 'A miserable L[ieutenan]t of the unfortunate 66th Regt', as he signed himself.

> We fought them till we were hardly a Regiment. The Commanding Officer was shot dead, and the two Officers carrying the Colours close by my side received their mortal wounds. In this shattered state our Brigade moved forward to charge. Madness alone would dictate such a thing, and at that critical period Cavalry appeared in our rear. It was then that our men began to waver, and for the first time (and God knows I hope the last) I saw the backs of English soldiers turned upon [the] French . . .
>
> Oh, what a day was that. The worst of the story I have not related. Our Colours were taken. I told you before the 2 Ensigns were shot under them; 2 Sergeants shared the same fate. A Lieutenant seized a Musket to defend them, and he was shot to the heart; what could be done against Cavalry? General Stewart, who marched us wildly to this desperate attack without any support, praised rather than censured our conduct, but I should think the malicious World will take hold of it with scandal in their mouths.[5]

Prominently displayed in the centre of the regiment, the colours made an obvious target for enemy fire and casualties in their vicinity could be very heavy even without hand-to-hand fighting. When Sergeant Lawrence was ordered to the colours at Waterloo, it 'was a job I did not at all like. . . . There had been before me that day fourteen sergeants already killed and wounded while in charge of the colours, with officers in proportion and the staff and colours were almost cut to pieces.' And William Milne reported from Barrosa:

> As I commanded the left centre company & consequently stood next to the colours, I could scarcely turn my head round, without seeing someone fall. I lost about thirty five men in my Company, killed & wounded, out of fifty or sixty that were present. I saw there three or four Officers & four Sergeants fall in the course of a quarter of an hour.[6]

Handling the colours was awkward and uncomfortable, as well as dangerous and honourable. Even in perfect conditions the flags were heavy and unwieldy, while strong winds or rain could make them almost impossible to manage. Both hands were generally needed to control the flag, so that it was almost impossible for an officer to use his sword effectively with one hand while holding on to the flag with the other, and in a wood the ensign might be more concerned with the trees than with the enemy. Yet for all this, the colours were a powerful symbol of regimental pride and unity, and in regiments of line infantry at least their presence in the field was due to practical value, not mere sentiment.

Light infantry and cavalry regiments however sometimes left their colours safely at home rather than risk them in battle, where their defence would have impeded the unit's normal style of fighting. At Waterloo, when the strength of the British 5th Brigade fell to only 800 men, the colours were sent to the rear. Some must have felt this to be an ominous sign, but others were relieved that the flags were safe. Colonel Mainwaring is said to have been so concerned about the colours of the 51st at Fuentes de Oñoro that he ordered them burnt just as the action began! A cloud of mystery surrounds this story, which only appears at second or third hand, but something happened, for Mainwaring was sent home in virtual disgrace soon after, and in the following year an inspecting officer reported that 'The Regiment has no Colours in the Country'. Hardly less strange is the story of the 2/69th which lost its colours at Quatre Bras, and tried to conceal the fact, getting the regimental tailors to make a new set. After such examples of extreme veneration it is refreshing to find Charles Napier – of all men – admitting that when his regiment came under heavy fire at Coruña, 'The colours also were lowered, because they were a mark for the enemy's great guns: this was by the advice of old John Montgomery, a brave soldier who had risen from the ranks.'[7]

Obviously not all units were of equal quality, and while a *corps d'élite* might be concentrated in reserve, the best solution for an army of very uneven quality was to distribute the inferior units through the force. The presence of the good troops would then steady and encourage the others in an implied reversal of Gresham's Law (that bad currency drives out the good). It also meant that if a poor unit did break, the panic would be less likely to spread far: confident veterans would not be unduly perturbed by the flight of raw troops for whom they probably felt some contempt. In the Peninsula, Wellington distributed his Portuguese troops throughout his army, usually adding one Portuguese brigade to two British in a division; he firmly resisted attempts to concentrate them in a single force, arguing that without a leavening of British veterans their performance would be doubtful. He faced similar problems in the Netherlands in 1815, especially with the Dutch–Belgian contingent, but after some discussion he was able to achieve the same solution. In this case, British and King's German Legion troops made up less than half the army, and this raises the question of whether there came a point when it was better not to distribute a small force of good troops among a much larger body of bad ones. After all, a single good battalion is unlikely to inspire a whole division of poor troops to fight well – instead it is likely to be swept away in their rout. Spanish commanders often faced this dilemma. At Saguntum in October 1811 Blake concentrated his best troops on the plain, and kept his less experienced and reliable units on one flank, where the ground was rough and they outnumbered their opponents by about four to one. In the abstract this seems a sensible arrangement designed to get the best value from a very mixed army, but the result was unfortunate, for while the good troops on the plain fought well, the other wing was put to flight despite its numbers, and the battle was a disaster for the Spanish cause.[8]

Confidence, experience and training were the principal factors determining the effectiveness of units in battle. Discipline was also very important in instilling an unhesitating obedience to orders and a ready proficiency at drill which could prove vital. A well-trained unit with a high standard of discipline – which does not necessarily mean a ready resort to harsh punishments – would enter battle with more confidence than one in which discipline was lax. The men would hold their fire longer and be more ready to follow their officers into danger, while the officers would feel greater confidence in their men.

Modern theories sometimes pass from these basic elements to other indicators of good morale which seem less applicable to the Napoleonic period. 'Smartness' or pride in a uniform is sometimes mentioned, but Kincaid for one would disagree: 'Smoothing irons were not the fashion of the times, and, if a fresh well-dressed aide-de-camp did occasionally come from England, we used to stare at him with about as much respect as Hotspur did at his "waiting gentlewomen".' While according to Grattan, Wellington never looked to see if a soldier's trousers were black, blue or grey, and did not care how his officers dressed: 'The consequence was, that scarcely any two officers were dressed alike! Some with grey braided coats, others with brown; some again liked blue; while many from choice, or perhaps necessity, stuck to the "old red rag".' Nor was this view confined to the officers, for Sergeant Anton writes, 'The man in patched clothes and a piece of untanned hide about his feet, when he looked around him, saw others in some respects as ill-appointed as himself; and he almost felt a pride in despising any new-comer with dangling plumes, plaited or crimped frills, white gloves, and handsome shoes – all good-for-nothing frippery to the hardy, toil-worn soldier, the man of flint, powder, and steel, as he thought himself.'[9]

Other writers suggest that morale is likely to crumble without regular pay, reasonable food, adequate shelter and, though its effects are recognized as more uncertain, periodic leave home and reliable mail to and from family and friends. All this is a world away from the lot of a Napoleonic soldier. Until 1813 Wellington's army was not even issued with tents, and so slept under the stars in all weathers except when in cantonments. Food was often scarce, and seldom such as would tempt even the least refined modern appetite – hard ship's biscuit and crude hunks of tough, freshly slaughtered cattle, with only a large iron kettle to boil it in. Pay was derisively low, very irregular, and usually months in arrears. Leave was unheard of, and though soldiers' letters seem to have been efficiently transmitted, only a small proportion of the rank and file took much advantage of the service. None of this caused much discontent, for it did not offend the soldiers' expectations, nor was it so very much worse than what many of them had experienced in civilian life. There was certainly grumbling if the army outmarched its rations, and soldiers would risk a flogging by helping themselves to anything they could find, but this did nothing to dampen their fighting spirit. Indeed on the evening before Vitoria, Major Roberts of the 51st encouraged his men by telling them that if they had no bread that night, they would have plenty on the following evening after they had beaten the French and captured their supplies.[10]

Similarly, patriotism or ideological commitment are often invoked, and many politicians in the early years of the French Revolution and in the Spanish uprising argued that a free people wielding arms in defence of their liberty would always triumph over the forces of oppression, and poured scorn on professional armies who fought for a cause they did not believe in. It made fine rhetoric, but the newly raised patriot volunteers ran away just the same, often crying treason and even murdering their elected officers. But if enthusiasm was no substitute for regular training and discipline, it could sometimes be an important factor in inspiring men to volunteer, or at least to accept conscription. It probably consoled some men for the privations of campaigning, and kept others in the ranks after a defeat, although such feelings were hard to sustain. In some countries, notably Spain and Russia, the struggle against Napoleon was encouraged by the belief that the French were the enemies of religion, and perhaps even that their leader was the Antichrist. Whether this ever counted for as much as the experience of the casual brutality of French occupation may be doubted, but it was useful in regions where the French had never penetrated. Even in the ranks of Wellington's army, where professional pride is more obvious than any dislike of the French, there are occasional glimpses of patriotic feeling, as in an 1813 letter from Private William Windsor – a far less accomplished writer than Wheeler – to his wife: 'My dear, I hope these few lines will not trouble you, for I long to see the day when I hope to fire 60 rounds of ball cartridge in defence of my king and country, religion and laws, against our most inveterate enemy, who wants to bring all nations under his feet.'[11]

Such sentiments probably influenced only a small minority of Wellington's – or any other – army, though, of course, we can never be sure. At a less elevated level, soldiers were notorious for their love of strong drink, but again its role in battle is very uncertain. One British commissariat officer writes, 'I can positively assert that during the time I was with the troops, both in the Peninsula and Waterloo, no spirits were issued previous to any action, but only in the evening when all was over.' Other accounts cast some doubt on this, and those soldiers and officers who had a private supply would be likely to take a swig or two as the battle began. There are quite a few references to French soldiers being given a liberal issue of alcohol before going into battle. On the morning of Austerlitz, for example, Saint-Hilaire's and Vandamme's infantry are supposed to have received 'triple rations (almost half a pint) of the gut-busting military brandy'. While a French commissary told his British counterpart 'that during the action casks of brandy were brought on to the ground, the heads knocked out, and the men about to attack were allowed to help themselves'. But it is difficult to fully credit these stories. Such doses might well have made the soldiers 'fighting drunk', but they must also have affected their ability to perform complicated evolutions, and the equally complicated steps required to load, fire and reload their muskets. It would seem that either the stories have grown in the telling, or that the presence of danger effectively sobered the men.[12]

The best soldiers were not always the most admirable men in other respects. Indeed it is probably only a Victorian conceit to expect to find virtue and extraordinary bravery intimately linked. As well as being one of the best regiments in the army, the British 88th were a pack of plundering rogues, while Edward Costello of the 95th admits, 'I cannot brag of our fellows being the honestest branch of the British army.' Captain Kincaid of the same regiment tells us that, 'I have often heard it disputed whether the most daring deeds are done by men of good or bad repute, but I never felt inclined to give either a preference over the other, for I have seen the most desperate things done by both.' He goes on to support his opinion with numerous examples. The men who so thoroughly sacked and pillaged Ciudad Rodrigo, Badajoz and San Sebastian were certainly inflamed by the horrors they had been through in storming those fortresses. But many in the storming parties were volunteers, and while some stepped forward from daring and a desire to distinguish themselves, others had at least one eye to the orgy that followed.[13]

However, the strongest bond which held a unit together in action was not drink or patriotism, or even training and discipline, important though they were, but group loyalty, the commitment of soldiers to each other, and their pride. Cut off from their families and civil society, leading a life that was unusually harsh and often dangerous, soldiers depended on each other for encouragement, companionship and even survival. Their regiment was often their only home for many years, which is one reason why ill or injured soldiers might be reluctant to leave it for hospital. When Private Wheeler – who was more lucky than most – was seriously wounded in the foot, he reflected on the possibility of being sent to recuperate in England.

> As much as I desire to see my dear native land, my home and all my dear relations, old playmates and neighbours, I would much rather rejoin my Regiment again and take my chance with it. Then, when this long protracted war is over, if fortune should favour me I should have the proud satisfaction of landing on my native shores with many a brave and gallant comrade, with whom I have braved the dangers of many a hard fought battle. This is the first time of my being absent from my Regiment since I entered into it and I hope it will not be long before I should hear the sound of its soul stirring bugles again.[14]

Such feelings were particularly important in action when the men encouraged each other. One British veteran recalls: 'In our first charge I felt my mind waver; a breathless sensation came over me. The silence was appalling. I looked alongst the line. It was enough to assure me. The steady determined scowl of my companions assured my heart and gave me determination.' In other armies the soldiers talked a good deal in the ranks, encouraging each other and breaking down the disheartening sense of isolation which is a common product of fear, even when men are in close formation. And just as this social support helped men perform well, it deterred them from performing badly. Sergeant Anton reflected that

A man may drop behind in the field but this is a dreadful risk to his reputation, and even attended with immediate personal danger, while within the range of shot and shells; and woe to the man that does it, whether through fatigue, sudden sickness, or fear – let him seek death, and welcome it from the hand of a foe, rather than give room for any surmise respecting his courage; for when others are boasting of what they have seen, suffered, or performed, he must remain in silent mortification.[15]

Other accounts agree that soldiers often inflicted their own rough and ready punishments on comrades who had let the unit down in action. In the French army a man might receive fifty blows with an old shoe from his own mess-mates, though a new recruit was much more likely to be punished than a veteran braggart, who was quick with his fists or his sword, despite being notorious for his absences in battle. Similarly, a man who left the troop in order to plunder at Waterloo was reported to Captain Tomkinson by the men, and booted by them when he returned the following morning. Such punishments even extended beyond the unit. An unwounded corporal of the Guards who slipped away from Hougoumont and spread rumours that it had fallen to the French had the misfortune to fall in with the 95th. They could see that his report was false, and gave him 'a good booting, telling him in future to beware how he spread such incorrect, dispiriting reports' – though they may have expressed it rather more pungently. On the other hand, some men evidently established a customary right to cowardice, accepting the contempt that went with it. Thus on the morning of Waterloo, before the regiment was engaged, a man in Tomkinson's troop got off his horse and ran to the rear. 'He was an old soldier, yet not the wisest, and had been shoemaker to the troop for many years. The men after the day was over did not resent his leaving them, knowing the kind of man and his weakness.' And apparently Tomkinson shared their toleration.[16]

In general, officers seem to have been most reluctant to take official action in cases of this kind. George Napier, writing many years later, advocated a humane approach:

As to the *skulker*, if he is an officer, never have any mercy on him. Should he be a private soldier, reason with him, and endeavour to make him sensible of the shame and folly of his conduct before you attempt harsher means. Always bear in mind the difference between your situation as an officer and his as a private.

You have every stimulus for exertion – honours, rank, fame, comfort, and often pecuniary emolument; what has the soldier? nothing but the consciousness of having performed his duty, and that universal feeling among British soldiers, the glory of having upheld his country's character for bravery! But these are no substantial benefits, and of course he cannot be expected to have the same energy as his officer; for which reason that officer should never permit himself to hurt the feelings of a private by swearing at him or using harsh expressions. Try every method before you resort to punishment – let that be the last; but when it is absolutely necessary, let it be inflicted with solemnity, and, as far as possible (if one may use the expression), with feeling.

Such impeccably Victorian liberal sentiments seem a long way from the confused reality of the battlefield, which is probably better represented by the behaviour of Captain Brotherton who, seeing a sergeant hiding behind a tree while his men were exposed to enemy fire, 'rode up to him, and licked him as long as I could stand over him, with the flat of my sabre, and ordered him out of the field'.[17]

According to Michael Glover, 'In all the squalid tales of crime in the General Orders of the Peninsular army there is no court martial on a charge of cowardice against a man in the ranks.' Officers knew well that their units contained a number of 'nervous' men, but preferred to keep the matter private rather than bring discredit on the regiment. Hearing a man grumbling loudly in the ranks, Brotherton 'thought it advisable to make an example of the man at the moment, instead of bringing him to trial afterwards'. He therefore posted him as a vedette in an exposed position under heavy fire some distance in front of the regiment – which won the general approval of the men in the ranks. Rather to Brotherton's chagrin, however, the grumbler survived unhurt, although many others in the unit were killed or wounded.[18]

Wherever possible, officers liked to implicate their men in the punishment of such offenders, thus strengthening the bonds within the unit rather than creating a divide between authority and its victims. In late 1812 a soldier was caught deserting from the 95th Rifles. He should have been tried by a general court-martial and shot, but Major Cameron, commanding the battalion, disliked the discredit this would bring, and instead tried him by a regimental court-martial which sentenced him to 'only' 400 lashes. When the battalion was formed to watch the flogging, Cameron declared that if the men would stand surety for the soldier's future good conduct he would be pardoned. A stony silence ensued. When the man, Stratton, had received the first twenty-five lashes, Cameron again asked, 'Will you not be answerable, men, for Stratton's conduct? Well, then, if his own company will be answerable for his good behaviour I shall forgive him.' Again, silence and another twenty-five lashes. Then the major said,

'Now, Sir, if only one man in the regiment will speak in your behalf, I shall take you down.' Still silent, while the third bugler commenced: when the prisoner had received about sixteen lashes, a voice from the square called out, 'Forgive him, Sir!' – 'Stop, bugler stop!' said the Major; 'who was the man that spoke?' 'I did, Sir!' was the answer. 'Step into the square'; when a man of the prisoner's own company came forward. 'Oh! is it you, Robinson?' said Major Cameron; 'I thought as much; as little-good-for-nothing a fellow as himself; but take him down.'

That done, the major praised the regiment's 'moral worth' because 'not a man would speak in that fellow's behalf, except the man who did, whom you know as well as I do'.[19]

It is an ugly story, but it testifies powerfully – as it was no doubt meant to – to the importance of retaining the respect of one's peers. Stratton's crime however was desertion, not cowardice; desertion not in action, but on campaign. Quite a few British soldiers were tried, and usually shot, for desertion; but none, apparently, for cowardice. After Talavera, the Spaniards court-martialled a number of their men who had run away so disgracefully on the evening before the battle. Twenty-seven of these men were taken out on to the battlefield and shot on the morning after the battle – an action which British soldiers viewed with disapprobation verging on horror, and even Wellington, never famous for his clemency, is said to have appealed for their lives. Evidently the British army then believed that while an occasional, or even habitual, lack of courage was disgraceful, it should not be a capital offence.[20]

Despite all the bonds and social sanctions, many men left their unit during the battle using a variety of excuses. Some of them returned, others really got lost and even fought with other units, but most took advantage of the opportunity and made their way to the rear. The commonest pretext was to assist a wounded comrade from the fighting line to a dressing station. The official attitude to this varied. Napoleon tried to prohibit it at both Austerlitz and Wagram: 'Let no one leave the ranks on the excuse of carrying away the wounded. Let everybody be convinced that we must beat these hirelings of England . . .' and 'The wounded who cannot move themselves, will stay on the field. In the name of honour it is forbidden to quit the battlefield to help casualties to the rear.' Although Suchet claims that this order was scrupulously obeyed in his division at Austerlitz, such prohibitions were usually ineffective, and other commanders preferred to try to limit and control the practice. Marshal Ney instructed his corps, 'The most rigorous orders shall be given that no wounded soldier shall be carried by his comrades further than the first hospital. Two men shall suffice for a fracture, and one for a slight wound.' While in October 1813 Wellington issued a General Order which stressed that it was only permissible on the orders of the company commander, and that the number of men involved should be kept to a minimum. Bandsmen and other supernumeraries were meant to assist in this task, but they are seldom referred to, and probably only dealt with the first casualties.[21]

The men were, of course, meant to return to their unit once they had left their wounded comrade at a dressing station. Some may have done so, but it remained a large drain on a unit's strength. Captain Tomkinson prided himself on the fact that on the evening of Waterloo his troop had 'less than one man away assisting each wounded'. This has important implications, for it means that each non-lethal casualty suffered might cost a unit, on average, two men: the wounded man himself, and another helping him to the rear. Colonel Mainwaring made this explicit, instructing his men to fire low: 'you will then hit them in the legs and there will be three gone, for two will pick him up and run away with him'.[22]

Poor troops undoubtedly suffered more from this cause than good ones, for their discipline was lax and their men were eager to take advantage of any excuse to leave the front line. The absurd extreme of this was observed by Captain Mercer approaching Quatre Bras where many of the Belgian wounded had 'six, eight, ten and even more, attendants'. At the opposite end of the scale an officer in the 43rd Light Infantry writes that at Salamanca 'their spirit was so great, that I had the greatest trouble to get any man in the midst of the fight to fall out and assist the wounded; the reply was always, "No sir, I would rather go on with the company."' In the 95th Rifles in 1811 a man who had spent an action assisting the wounded to the rear was shunned by his comrades, while as the war went on 'no good soldier would venture, under so frivolous a pretence, so to expose himself to the indignation of his comrades, excepting for any very extreme cases'. Finally there is a story of the 23rd Fusiliers at Waterloo, which may be a little too neat to be perfectly true. Sir Henry Ellis, the commanding officer, ordered that 'no man should fall out of the ranks to assist anyone wounded, whether officer or soldier, and that the order comprised himself as others'. After such an invitation to fate, it was hardly surprising that Ellis was badly wounded. He 'quietly left the square alone, and was seen to fall from his horse soon after. Such was the discipline of the regiment, that his orders were strictly obeyed, and he was left where he fell', and there he died.[23]

Such devotion to duty was uncommon, and it is clear that in most units many of the less badly wounded were assisted to the rear, with the number of attendants and the likelihood of their return reflecting the morale of the unit. This means that good troops would suffer a much smaller diminution of their strength than poor troops, from the same number of casualties; and that the discipline and morale of the unit receiving a volley had almost as great an influence on its effectiveness as the morale and discipline of the troops firing. Naturally this effect compounded, so that a good unit exchanging fire with a poor one benefited both from its greater coolness in firing, and from the greater impact the casualties it inflicted had on its target.

There were many other excuses which soldiers used to leave the ranks in action. According to Ney, one common dodge was to claim that a musket was broken or hopelessly fouled, and needed to be replaced. Ney ordered that his officers and NCOs pay strict attention to this, and replace any genuinely unfit weapons with those taken from the killed or wounded, and not allow men to use it as a reason for leaving the ranks.[24]

Nervous infantry were inclined to fire off all their ammunition at an absurdly long range and then hurry to the rear, believing that they had a perfect excuse. This was normally a symptom of inexperience. A few such men in a steady unit might be controlled by their neighbours or a sergeant, but if a whole unit was this raw and ill-disciplined, there was little that could be done except hope that they would benefit from having been in battle and perform better next time.

When a unit was advancing, men would also feign death or wounds, falling to the ground and hoping that the battalion (it was obviously more suitable for infantry than cavalry) would pass on, leaving them behind. When advancing up the Greater Arapile at Salamanca, Charles Synge saw that

> several of my little party fell, at first I supposed killed, for the enemy opened their guns as soon as they saw what we were about; but one man near my horse fell in such a manner that it struck me it was sham, and as he lay on his face I gave him rather a sharp prod with my sword – there was no time for any other appeal to his 'honour' – on which he turned up perfectly unhurt! What became of him afterwards I know not; I had other matters to think of.

It is impossible even to guess at the scale of this problem. Presumably it too would be worst with poor troops and those under very heavy fire, but Ardant du Picq's claim that more than half of Macdonald's 22,000-strong 'column' at Wagram 'played the dummy in order not to go on to the end' appears equally unsubstantiated and implausible.[25]

Cavalry were not immune to such disorders. One particularly unpleasant trick was to deliberately wound your own horse just before contact, thus providing an apparently honourable reason for falling out. The dangers were that the startled horse might panic, throw you, or even gallop forwards into the enemy; or else, as in one case, that the enemy might break without contact, leaving the ruse exposed and your horse-loving officer enraged.[26]

Far more honourable, but still a potentially large drain on a unit's strength, was the need to escort prisoners to the rear. In cavalry regiments this was usually the task of the farriers, who were not expected to charge with the unit, but were meant to look after the wounded, and perhaps also collect spare horses. As they were unsupervised, it is not surprising that they gained a reputation for being avid looters. No large body of prisoners could be entrusted to them (pity any that were!), and at Waterloo a whole squadron of the Inniskilling dragoons (and possibly detachments from other regiments) was employed to escort the thousands of prisoners from d'Erlon's corps to Brussels.[27]

One last occasion for men leaving the ranks must be mentioned, though it seldom appears in polite memoirs. 'I felt an urgent call to relieve nature,' writes Captain Coignet, but it was strictly against orders to move a step towards the rear. There was no alternative but to go forward in advance of the line, which I did; and, having put down my musket, I began operations with my behind to the enemy. All at once a cannon-ball came along, ricochetted within a yard of me, and threw a hail of earth and stones all over my back. Luckily for me I still had my pack on, or I should have perished.[28]

Captain Sillery of the Royal Artillery suffered from diarrhoea at the Battle of Talavera. When his battery came under fire he was attacked by a renewed bout of his complaint and, turning to a fellow officer, he said,

'I shall not go to the rear, it may be said that I was afraid.' He then deliberately walked a hundred yards in front of the brigade, and disembarrassing himself of part of his clothes, yielded to the irresistible necessity of the case; after readjusting his dress, and calmly putting on his sword and sash, he returned leisurely to his post. The transaction excited a great deal of mirth, notwithstanding the heat of the action.[29]

Bad as this is, the full unpleasantness of such an ailment at such a time could only be felt by a man on horseback, as is made clear by a young French aide-de-camp at Borodino:

At Dorogobuzh I had again been smitten with the diarrhoea which had afflicted me so badly at Smolensk, and in the course of this day I went through the worst sort of agony one can imagine, because I did not want either to quit my post or dismount. I dare not describe just how I managed to dispose of what was tormenting me, but in the process I lost two handkerchiefs which I threw as discreetly as I could into the trench of the fortifications we passed. This was a serious loss in a country devoid of washerwomen. . . .[30]

Despite such heroic expedients, soldiers were usually allowed to retire a discreet distance to the rear in order to relieve themselves – as Sillery's words, and even Coignet's account, imply. But how did men in close-packed squares cope?

Men who left their ranks on any one of these grounds might do so from genuine need, or from fear, or from exhaustion; but they might also do so in order to plunder the fallen. For it was not only camp followers and local peasants who wandered the battlefield robbing the dead and wounded, even stripping them of their clothes. More will be said about this in Chapter 13, but it needs to be mentioned here as a further drain on a unit's effective strength. For plundering began long before the fighting had ended. When Pack's brigade was broken at Salamanca, Dyneley saw that the French 'had a party without arms in their rear for the purpose of stripping and plundering our wounded, which I saw them do; for they had the poor fellows naked before they had been down two minutes'. The historian of the 52nd Light Infantry writes of 'The man Lewis, of the 52nd, who although a sad plunderer was a gallant soldier . . . generally contrived to have an attack of rheumatism soon after getting into action, and thus got out of sight of his officers, for the purpose of filling his haversack'. And an officer in Picton's division at Waterloo wrote that in the immediate aftermath of the repulse of d'Erlon's attack,

> I saw (the truth must be told) a greater number of our soldiers busy rifling the pockets of the dead, and perhaps the wounded, than I could have wished to have seen; with some exertion we got them in. Those of our own regiment the Colonel beat with the flat of his sword as long as he had breath to do so. The fellows knew they deserved it; but they observed, some one else would soon be doing the same, and why not they as well as others?[31]

The cumulative effect of all these drains on a unit's strength is impossible to measure, for almost all the men thus lost to a unit in action had found their way back by the time the returns were filled in. A battalion which entered battle with 600 officers and men, and lost 100 (dead and wounded), would not have 500 men left in the ranks at the close of the action, but there is no way of guessing whether its likely final strength was 450, 400 or only 300. Better units lost fewer men from these causes than poor ones, as did units in armies which appeared to be winning the battle, for despondent men were naturally more inclined to slip away. According to one contemporaneous account of Marengo, by four o'clock in the afternoon there were not 6,000 French infantry left in good order in the main line. 'A third of the army was actually put *hors de combat*', another third had left their units on the pretext of carrying wounded men to the rear, while 'Hunger, thirst, and fatigue, had imperiously forced a great number of officers to withdraw also.' And a senior British officer believed that by the 'Crisis' of Waterloo, there were scarcely 25,000 effective troops left in Wellington's line. These estimates cannot pretend to be precisely accurate, and may be exaggerated for rhetorical effect. They can neither be proven nor disproven, for there was no means by which either contemporaries or we can measure the magnitude of the problem.[32]

Individuals misbehaving led to a steady erosion of the strength and cohesion of a unit, but sometimes the whole unit's morale collapsed suddenly, and it either broke and ran or refused to obey orders. This could occur in a wide variety of circumstances, some of which reflected no discredit on troops who were simply being asked to do too much. Late in the hard-fought Battle of St Pierre (13 December 1813, part of the Battles of the Nive) Gruardet's brigade of Darmagnac's division refused to advance when ordered to make an obviously hopeless attack. And in July 1794, at the end of an arduous campaign in the Caribbean, even Sir Charles Grey's elite force of light infantry had lost their will to fight and refused to make any fresh attacks. Grey was never the most patient of men, but he did not blame them, and their disobedience went unpunished.[33]

Much to his chagrin, William Napier found that not even the men of his beloved 43rd were always to be relied upon, especially when they were under cover and their officers were not all of one mind. His account of the incident at Cazal Noval (14 March 1811) is so full of interest that it is worth quoting at length:

> I arrived [with two companies] just in time to save Captain Dobbs, 52nd, and two men who were cut off from their regiment. The French were gathering fast about us, we could scarcely retreat, and Dobbs agreed with me that boldness would be our best chance; so we called upon the men to follow, and, jumping over a wall which had given us cover, charged the enemy with a shout which sent the nearest back. But then occurred the most painful event that ever happened to me.
>
> Only the two men of the 52nd followed us, and we four arrived unsupported at a second wall, close to a considerable body of French, who rallied and began to close upon us. Their fire was very violent, but the wall gave cover. I was, however, stung by the backwardness of my men, and told Dobbs I would save him or lose my life by bringing up the two companies; he entreated me not, saying I could not make two paces from the wall and live. Yet I did go back to the first wall, escaped the fire, and, reproaching the men, gave them the word again, and returned to Dobbs, who was now upon the point of being taken; but again I returned alone! The soldiers had indeed crossed the wall in their front, but kept edging away to the right to avoid the heavy fire. Being now maddened by this second failure, I made another attempt, but I had not made ten paces when a shot struck my spine, and the enemy very ungenerously continued to fire at me when I was down. I escaped death by dragging myself by my hands – for my lower extremities were paralysed – towards a small heap of stones which was in the midst of the field, and thus covering my head and shoulders. Not less than twenty shots struck this heap. However, Captain Lloyd and my own company, and some of the 52nd, came up at that moment, and the French were driven away.
>
> The excuses for the soldiers were – 1st That I had not made allowance for their exertions in climbing from the ravine up the hill-side with their heavy packs, and they were very much blown. 2nd Their own captains had not been with them for a long time, and they were commanded by two lieutenants, remarkable for their harsh, vulgar, tyrannical dispositions, and very dull bad officers withal; and one of them exhibited on this occasion such miserable cowardice as would be incredible if I had not witnessed it. I am sure he ordered the men not to advance, and I saw him leading them the second time to the right. This man was lying down with his face on the ground; I called to him, reproached him, bade him remember his uniform; nothing would stir him; until losing all patience I threw a large stone at his head. This made him get up, but when he got over the wall he was wild, his eyes staring and his hands spread out. He was a duellist, and had wounded one of the officers some time before. I would have broke him, but

before I recovered my wound sufficiently to join, he had received a cannon-shot in the leg, and died at the old, desolate, melancholy mill below Sabugal. Everything combined to render death appalling, yet he showed no weakness. Such is human nature, and so hard it is to form correct opinions of character![34]

Although Napier was able to resume his active military career, the bullet stayed lodged in his spine for the rest of his life, giving him great pain. But what is most striking about his account is his eagerness to explain and excuse the misbehaviour of his troops (though not their officers), and the prevailing tone of hurt rather than anger.

Such incidents were probably more common than one would expect from reading memoirs which are often discreetly silent about events that reflected poorly on the regiment. However, some behaviour was impossible to conceal or excuse. Perhaps the most notorious, if not the worst, case of this kind was the conduct of the Duke of Cumberland's Hussars at Waterloo. This was an inexperienced regiment, made up of wealthy volunteers who were wholly unprepared for a battle of the severity of Waterloo. By about five o'clock they had had enough. Either on the day, or earlier in the campaign, they had lost one officer and seventeen men killed, and thirty-three men wounded – about 10 per cent of their strength. Lord Uxbridge, seeing them moving to the rear, apparently *en masse* and in fairly good order, sent his aide-de-camp Captain Seymour to halt them. 'On delivering the order to the Colonel,' Seymour wrote,

> he told me that he had no confidence in his men, that they were Volunteers, and the horses their own property. All this time the Regiment continued moving to the rear, in spite of my repeating the order to halt, and asking the second in command to save the character of the Regiment by taking command and fronting them. I was unsuccessful, and in the exigence of the moment I laid hold of the bridle of the Colonel's horse, and remarked what I thought of his conduct; but all to no purpose.
>
> I then returned to Lord Anglesey [i.e. Uxbridge], and reported what had passed. I was again ordered to deliver the message to the Commanding Officer of the Regiment, that if they would not resume their position in the Line, that he was to form them across the high road *out* of fire. They did not even obey this order, but went, as was reported, altogether to the rear.

Conduct such as this could not be overlooked, and the colonel was court-martialled and cashiered, while the regiment was broken up and distributed through the army where they were made to perform demeaning jobs such as escorting forage details. According to Captain Mercer, who encountered some a fortnight after the battle, the young gentlemen were 'irate at this degradation. . . . They are all amazingly sulky and snappish.'[35]

The Cumberland Hussars were most unfortunate: a completely raw unit, they had been thrown into one of the most severe battles of the age, and after some hours of anxious waiting, enlivened only by the losses of men due to artillery fire, their nerve had collapsed. Not that this excuses their misconduct, which was blatant and without redeeming features, but if – like many other units – they had been introduced to the experience of battle more gradually, they might have gained confidence and in time become good soldiers. Much the same can be said for many of the Netherlands units which also went to the rear in disorder at Waterloo. Some of these were only militia; others, though regulars with many old soldiers, were newly formed units, lacking cohesion, *esprit de corps*, and confidence between officers and men.

The fate of the Prussian 25th Line Regiment at Ligny shows how such underlying weaknesses could be exacerbated by experience in action. The core of this regiment was the Lutzow Volunteer Corps, which had taken part in the campaigns of 1813–14, although not in the forefront of the fighting. With peace it had been incorporated into the regular army, though many of the officers and soldiers had returned to civilian life. At the end of May 1815 it received a draft of about 1,000 recruits, and a further 330 arrived on 13 June, bringing the strength of the regiment to 82 officers and 2,337 men, so that over half the force was newly joined. These recruits were trained soldiers, but they had formerly served in the French army; their homes had been part of Prussia for only a few months, so they felt loyalty neither to the country, nor to the regiment.

At Ligny the regiment formed part of Tippelskirchen's brigade in Pirch's corps. It is not clear precisely what happened, but it seems that it took part in a successful counter-attack on the village of Wagnelée, then pressed on towards St Amand and Ligny. It came under heavy fire from French skirmishers concealed in the high corn, about 150 paces away. The 1st and 2nd battalions attempted to deploy into line, but were considerably disordered and, from inexperience, the left wing of the first battalion overlapped with the right wing of the second, causing great confusion. All 'might yet have turned out well', writes a Prussian officer who was present, 'but at this terrible moment an enemy battalion came from the left at full charge and hurled itself upon us and swept everything before it in the wildest flight'. The two battalions were thoroughly broken and most of the new recruits never rallied, though the officers and some of the experienced men – and the Fusilier battalion – continued in the action.

The regiment was punished for its misbehaviour. On 18 June, as Pirch's corps advanced towards Waterloo, it was left at the heights of St Lambert to act as a link with Thielemann's corps at Wavre. Christian Nagel, the officer already quoted, fretted at the slight: 'This vexed us bitterly, for we were burning to fight; but many regiments met the same fate.' Worse was to follow. The brigadier ordered that Blücher's proclamation thanking the army for its success in the campaign not be read to the 1st and 2nd battalions. This incensed Nagel, who wrote an angry letter of protest, but to no avail. In October the Fusilier battalion received its colours and many decorations, but again the other two battalions were ignored. It was not until early 1816 that the authorities relented and granted flags to these battalions – having made their point that such misconduct would be followed by disgrace.

The 25th Line had been unfortunate as well as culpable. Thrown into heavy fighting it had become disordered, and was taken by surprise by the French fire. Yet its losses were not extraordinarily heavy – even Nagel claims only twenty officers and about 600 men killed and wounded, and the Fusilier battalion probably suffered a disproportionate share of these. It does not seem to have been in action for very long before it broke, nor to have been under heavy artillery fire before advancing on Wagnelée. It broke because it was a relatively poor unit without great discipline or cohesion; because its psychological equilibrium had been shaken when it suddenly came under fire, and was further upset by the confusion caused by a faulty deployment; and because it was threatened with immediate physical contact – the French battalion charging it in the flank – which it was in no state to repel. In such circumstances most regiments would break, but good troops would rally in the rear and return to the fight.[36]

The threat of contact was a great test of a unit's resolve and frequently precipitated a rout, as could any threat to the flank or rear. Surprise greatly magnified the effect of fear, so that if previously unnoticed enemy troops suddenly opened fire or charged, a unit was much more likely to break than if it had mentally and physically prepared to meet them. The cohesion of a unit could be undermined by the losses it had already suffered during the battle – or even earlier in the campaign – and by the strain of remaining idle under fire. Its confidence would naturally be greatly hurt if it had been broken in earlier fighting, or if the battle or campaign seemed to be going badly. The death of a popular general or the flight of friendly troops – especially good infantry – would have a generally lowering effect on morale, while the defeat of an elite force like the Imperial Guard might precipitate the flight of the whole army. Poor troops were naturally more likely to be discouraged by such sights, while morale generally grew more brittle as the day's fighting wore on.

Units held back in reserve had to endure hours of nerve-racking inactivity, not knowing when or if they were going to be sent into action, trying to guess the course of the battle from what little they could see, and from whether the firing sounded louder or more distant. Reinforcements hurrying to reach the battlefield met a stream of wounded – and others – heading in the other direction, and their comments were not always encouraging:

'Do not go so fast, do not hurry,' they say, 'to be killed, it is not necessary to run so quickly.'
'The enemy is ten times more numerous than we.'
'They've cut off my leg, they'll cut off something else of yours.'
'You look like living corpses.'
'Hello, look at that one, does he not seem dead?'

'He is; yesterday he forgot to get buried; he remembers it today,' etc.

In vain are they told to be silent; an arm in a sling, a gash across the face guarantee impunity, give the right of insolence, and the jeremiads continue so long as they find someone to listen to them.[37]

Once on the battlefield, troops' spirits would rise when they began to advance. The prospect of coming into action was frightening, but most wanted to get it over with rather than remain in suspense. It was very important that troops, especially infantry, retained their good order, dressing and alignment, but not at the cost of frequent halts which destroyed the momentum of their advance. S. L. A. Marshall, writing about a much later war, said that, 'Once halted, even if there has been no damage, the line never moves as strongly or as willingly again. After three or four such fruitless delays, men become morally spent rather than physically rested. All impetus is lost and the attack might better be called off.' And Clausewitz agreed that 'The soldier who is advancing becomes insensible even to danger, the one who is standing still loses his presence of mind.'[38]

Countering such pressures were the natural strength and cohesion of the unit, faith in the army's generals and confidence in victory. More specifically soldiers would be encouraged by the presence of a particularly respected or loved senior officer, and even more so by a Napoleon, a Wellington, or a Blücher. Previous successes, on the day or earlier in the campaign, would heighten their confidence, as would observing the success of friendly troops nearby. Close support from artillery often brought psychological advantages out of all proportion to its material effect, and this was one of the principal arguments for the retention of battalion guns. Similarly, the arrival of fresh troops from reserve – or even better, reinforcements which had not been with the army at the beginning of the battle, such as Desaix's divisions at Marengo – was a great fillip to morale.

Nonetheless, as the battle went on, units in the firing line gradually lost their cohesion and became increasingly vulnerable to any sudden shock. In a long battle of attrition, order would gradually dissolve until the whole unit might virtually dissipate of its own accord. A Swiss-French infantry officer describes how, at Leipzig,

> Our companies were becoming more and more disorganised, and very soon the battalions, being crowded together, presented nothing more than unformed heaps, which still fired a few shots and whose officers no longer had any influence unless they stayed there in person and physically held the soldiers back. This could not last very long. . . . The men broke and fled.[39]

Few memoirs or soldiers' letters describe in any detail what occurred when a unit broke: it all happened in a few confused moments, which soldiers were not particularly eager to recall. But it seems likely that a sudden shock – whether the

casualties from an enemy volley, or the sight of enemy troops charging forward
– would lead to a large number of men turning and pushing their way past their
officers and sergeants (supposing that they were still resolute), and that their
panic would quickly spread throughout the unit. Sometimes a call would ring
out to retreat or fall back, as if it was an official order; on others it might be the
cry which was always likely to signal a rout: '*sauve qui peut*', or 'save yourself'.
Not that all the men would be equally affected, but once the unit was broken,
the bravest man could do no good by remaining behind. One British soldier
recalls that when his regiment charged the French, the latter 'did not fancy such
close quarters, and the moment our rush began they went to the right-about.
The principal portion broke and fled, though some brave fellows occasionally
faced about and gave us an irregular fire.'[40]

George Bell gives a spirited account which conveys something of the experience, if not the details, of such a flight and its aftermath:

> We 34th for the last hour had been amusing ourselves in comparative safety,
> picking off our friends in the distance, when a very large column came down
> upon us to stop our play. There was but one escape for us now – to run away, or
> to be riddled to death with French lead. The officer commanding, a brave man,
> saw how useless it was to contend against such a multitude, gave the word to
> retire at the double, and away we went down hill at a tearing pace. I never ran so
> fast in my life! Here the French had another advantage, rather a cowardly one.
> They kept firing after us for pastime. Every now and then some poor fellow was
> hit and tumbled over, and many a one carried weight over the course, i.e. a bullet
> or two in the back of his knapsack.
>
> We were now broken and dispersed. Our bugles sounded, few heard them –
> some too far away! The old corps was severely handled. We hoisted a flag at the
> bottom of the hill, Freeman blew his well-known blast, and all that heard the
> sound rallied here.[41]

As they ran, many of the men would throw away their muskets, ammunition
pouches, and even their packs. The longer the flight lasted the more dispersed
the unit became, and the more difficult to rally. Officers and men alike would be
ready, almost eager, to believe that the whole battle was lost, so that the disgrace
of their flight would be forgotten in the wider defeat.

It was important to rally broken troops as quickly as possible, but futile to
attempt to do so while they were still within range of the enemy. According to
Marbot, 'Generals and colonels should get as quickly as possible to the head of
the flying mass, then face about, and by their presence and their words arrest the
movement of retreat, and re-form the battalions.' And Marshal Macdonald
recommended sending 'some detachments of cavalry out of range', because 'the
fugitives would naturally stop on reaching them'. Broken troops were also likely
to head for cover, particularly villages or woods, and once there an attempt
might be made to rally them.[42]

Whether the attempt to re-form the unit would succeed depended less on how much the unit had suffered than on its underlying quality. For even though it took more to break good troops, they were still more likely to rally. The general state of the action was also very important: if it was early in the day and only a couple of units had been broken, perhaps by a cavalry charge, they were likely to rally behind their supports and return to the fray. But as the battle went on resilience lessened, reserves were committed, and panic was more likely to spread. When the enemy was advancing vigorously it was usually impossible to collect broken troops to make a fresh stand, though they might re-form if they came across a friendly body which could give them a respite from pursuit.

Above all it needed time and a sense of security for the men to catch their breath and the officers to reimpose their authority. The colours were often the focal point around which the unit could be rallied, both physically and psychologically. Sergeants would take up their position as markers and gradually the men would fall – or be pushed – into place. Cavalry seem to have been readier to rally, just as they were more prone to breaking, while artillery had the shame of losing their guns as an incentive to keep together.

Not all the men of a broken unit would rally: some would have lost touch with their comrades accidentally, others deliberately in order to go to the rear or begin plundering. The extent of this loss would depend on the length and circumstances of the flight, the experience and discipline of the troops, whether they were fresh or had already been worn down by a day's fighting, and on numerous other factors. The experience of having been broken might weaken the unit's cohesion for the rest of the battle and even beyond. Again the extent of the impact depended on the circumstances and on the type of troops involved: experienced cavalry were quite used to breaking, rallying and charging again, and thought little of it; while a good infantry unit might go through a number of campaigns without ever being thoroughly disordered and broken.

Those who did make their way to the rear would discover a scene of far greater confusion, fear and disorder than they had left in the front. Here were thousands of wounded, frightened and discouraged men, mixed with camp followers, commissaries and other non-combatants, all devoid of discipline or any common purpose other than to get away. For several miles they were not safe as enemy round-shot, shells and even musket balls continued to fall amongst them – indeed some observers thought that the fire was much heavier behind the allied line at Waterloo than in it.[43] Wild rumours spread quickly among the fugitives, usually of defeat, which could precipitate a stampede as men became convinced that the enemy was on their heels. Kincaid, as usual, paints the picture vividly:

The rear of a battle is generally a queer place – the day is won and lost there a dozen times, unknown to the actual combatants – fellows who have never seen an enemy in the field, are there to be seen flourishing their drawn swords, and 'cutting such fantastic tricks before high heaven, as make angels weep,' while

others are flying as if pursued by legions of demons; and, in short, while everything is going on in front with the order and precision of a field-day, in rear
everything is confusion worse confounded.

Kincaid goes on to describe how a wounded fellow officer dragged himself to
the rear at Vitoria, 'in the hope that, among the passing thousands, some good
Samaritan might be found with compassion enough to bind up his wound, and
convey him to a place of shelter'. At length he saw a staff-surgeon whom he
knew amongst the throng of fugitives and called out to him, feeling sure of
relief. But the surgeon, after a few words of empty comfort, clapped spurs to his
horse and was soon out of sight. Next came a volunteer, who always seemed to
get separated from the regiment when it went into action, and, by his own
account, performed prodigies of valour with some other regiment and left them
at the close of day, modestly withholding his name. On this occasion however,
the gallant volunteer was well to the rear, and far from rallying a shaken
regiment, was leading a string of loose horses which he had collected and
presumably intended to sell to the Commissary-General. He too expressed
concern at seeing Kincaid's friend wounded, but rather than offering to help,
asked him to hold the horses while he collected some more! And this was in the
rear of a good army, in a victorious battle.[44]

At Aspern-Essling, when the bridges broke, a huge crowd, 10,000 or 15,000
strong, collected at the bridgehead waiting to cross to the safety of Lobau. The
rear of the allied army at Waterloo was even worse: 'The road [to Brussels] was
in several places completely blocked up. A great part of the baggage of the army
as well as numbers of waggons laden with provisions and forage had been
overthrown and the contents strewed all over the road, and even private carriages were upset and plundered.' Unwounded men rode or walked along, often
firing their muskets or carbines into the air and threatening anyone who tried to
stop them.

> The road was thronged with Belgian fugitives in whole companies, both horse
> and foot, intermingled with numerous wounded officers and soldiers giving sad
> and desponding accounts of the progress of the action, together with numerous
> prisoners of all ranks and sorts, forming a melancholy exhibition of the usual
> occurrences in the rear of a general action.

Nor were the unwounded officers limited to the Belgians, for Sir Robert Hill
encountered an acquaintance among those fleeing and expressed a hope that he
was not badly hurt. 'He observed an awkwardness on the part of the officer, who
at length replied, "I am not wounded, Sir Robert, but I have had several very
narrow escapes."'[45]

The confusion in the rear of Waterloo was probably much greater than in
most battles, because of the intensity of the fighting and the mixed nature of
Wellington's army, but it was only a foretaste of the much greater confusion

that might engulf the whole army if it were defeated and broken. The foundation of any army is not weapons, tactics and uniforms, important though they are, but the morale and cohesion which keep men in the ranks, full of purpose and struggling for victory – the very antithesis of the chaos, selfishness and fear that predominate in the rear.

Chapter Eleven
Attitudes and Feelings

At the very heart of war lies death. Deliberate killing distinguishes battle from almost all other human activities, and although the object of military operations was to break the enemy's will to resist, rather than to annihilate his forces, there was no avoiding the fact that many men would lose their lives in the process. Soldiers, far more than most people, had to confront their own mortality, often at a very young age. They had to endure the death of friends and comrades, and sometimes, if they were officers, the loss of men under their command who might have lived if they, the officer, had acted differently. And they had to discover how they felt about killing the enemy.

Few men ever forgot their baptism of fire, and for most it marked a vital transition in their life. Before it, young officers in particular were oppressed with anxiety: would fear overcome them? would they disgrace themselves? Fear of failure and of the unknown combined with the fear of shot and shell. George Wood admits what many must have felt:

> It was now that I could have dispensed with the honours of a military life; and had it been as honourable to have gone to the rear as to the front, I should certainly have preferred the former, and that in double quick time; for whatever heroes may say, yet to me I must confess it caused a little imperceptible tremor . . . stifling this sensation, I soon found that spirit which I imbibed from my ancestors take possession of my heart, and which, thank God! never forsook me in the hour of danger.[1]

Moyle Sherer agrees:

> My bosom beat quick, very quick; it was possible, that the few minutes of my existence were already numbered. Such a thought, however, though it will, it must, arise, in the first awful moment of expectation, to the mind of him who has never been engaged, is not either dangerous or despicable, and will rather strengthen than stagger the resolution of a manly heart.[2]

In this crisis a veteran might often help to reassure the young man. Thomas Brotherton was only sixteen when he first came under fire, carrying one of the colours of the Coldstream Guards in Egypt in 1801.

> The sergeant behind me . . . said in a respectful but half-joking way, 'How do you feel, sir?' to which I replied, 'Pretty well, but this is not very pleasant!' for the men were falling fast. The sergeant, who was a seasoned veteran, liked the reply, for he seemed to take me under his special protection and care ever after. . . . Probably, had I pretended to feel quite at my ease and to despise the danger altogether, the shrewd old sergeant would have put me down as a 'humbug'.[3]

Colin Campbell, the future Lord Clyde, was even younger at his first action, at Vimeiro. His company was in the rear of the battalion, which was deployed in open column of companies, when it came under artillery fire. His captain, an experienced officer, took him by the hand and led him to the front of the regiment, where they walked up and down for some minutes, in full view of the enemy guns, until the young man's nerves had steadied. Many years later Campbell said that this 'was the greatest kindness that could have been shown me at such a time, and through life I have felt grateful for it'.[4]

With the ordeal of their first action behind them, soldiers could begin to come to terms with the nature of their trade. Not that fear ever disappeared completely. Charles Napier admits that at one point during the Battle of Coruña, where he led his men with extravagant bravery, he 'felt very cowardly and anxious', feelings much increased by his being extremely short-sighted and without his spectacles. Edward Costello describes an incident early in 1814 where he and four fellow riflemen had to leave secure cover behind a stone wall and retreat across an open field under heavy fire. They did so one at a time, and Costello admits that he 'funked dreadfully'; yet he was a man who had volunteered for the storming parties at both Ciudad Rodrigo and Badajoz.[5]

But though fear could thus strike at the bravest and most experienced soldiers, for most men, most of the time, it sank into the background, especially once the action had begun. They developed, or at least affected, an air of philosophical detachment from their fate. Captain Bréaut des Marlots reflected, 'It's a lottery. Even if you get out of this, you'll have to die some day. Do you prefer to live dishonoured or die with honour?' Nor were such feelings confined to educated officers, as the letter of a barely literate soldier in the King's Dragoon Guards, written in May 1815, shows: 'We are onley 15 miles from Mr Boney Part Harmey wish we expect to have a rap at him exerry day. . . . There is no dout of us beting the confounded rascal – it ma cost me my life and a meaney more that will onley be the forting of war – my life I set not store by at all.' A few young officers, particularly the German volunteers of 1813, were carried away by romantic ideas about war and by their idealistic patriotism. One of them wrote, 'Seldom have I experienced the goodness of living more keenly, felt more sweetly chained by the bonds of the present; but at the same time how easy, how pleasant a death that would unite one with those noble souls.' But such sentiments were always confined to a few, and usually did not survive much experience of the prosaic realities of campaigning.[6]

Other soldiers combined a cavalier disregard for danger with a passion for the excitement of battle and a dedicated pursuit of honour and glory. Dining with friends in April 1809 General Lasalle spoke, perhaps with some bravado, but his life well matched his words:

> 'I've lived a full life,' Lasalle argued. 'What's the point of living? To earn a reputation, get ahead, make your fortune? Well, I'm a general of division at 33, and last year the Emperor gave me an income of 50,000 francs.'
>
> 'Then you must live to enjoy it,' Roeder replied.
>
> 'Not at all,' said Lasalle. 'To have achieved it, that's satisfaction enough. I love battles, being in the noise, the smoke, the movement; so long as you've made your name, and you know your wife and children won't want for anything, that's all that matters. For myself, I'm ready to die tomorrow.'

Yet according to Kincaid, even the hardened veteran officers of the Light Division flinched at the idea of making a will.[7]

This avowed disregard of death – whether real, feigned, or some mixture of the two, as the pose gradually became real – must have helped men face the dangers of battle bravely, and encouraged their fellows. Yet it could be put to a sore trial by a presentiment of death. On the morning of 6 July 1809, the second day of the Battle of Wagram, Lasalle was morose and showed none of his usual good spirits. When Napoleon passed with his suite, Lasalle handed a secretary a document which proved to be a petition in favour of his children. At the very end of the day, when the battle was won and the fighting almost over, he was shot dead. Such presentiments are often recounted in memoirs and almost invariably they appear to have been justified. Perhaps the oddest was the anxiety of Harry Smith's Spanish wife, Juana, before the Battle of Nivelle, where she was convinced that either her husband or his horse would be killed; and indeed the horse did not survive the day. The point, of course, is that such stories have no impact if the fear is not justified. That lover of good anecdotes, Captain Kincaid, admits as much: 'On the subject of presentiments of death in going into battle, I have known as many instances of falsification as verification. To the latter the popular feeling naturally clings as the more interesting of the two; but I am inclined to think that the other would preponderate if the account could be justly rendered.' There is another point underlying these stories: such presentiments were widely respected by soldiers and evidently brought no discredit even when they were disproved. Thus they may have provided a safety-valve for the feelings of officers who were otherwise expected to be cheerful as well as courageous in the face of danger.[8]

A battle brought the risk not only of being killed in action, but also of being horribly wounded, and either permanently maimed or dying after weeks of suffering. Compared to this, or to an inglorious death from typhus or dysentery in an army hospital, a 'clean' death in battle seemed less terrible. A French officer writes of the end of his divisional commander, killed at Salamanca: 'Here Ferey met the form of death which the soldier prefers to all others, he was slain outright by a roundshot.' Many mortally wounded officers displayed the utmost fortitude and courage in their last hours. Sir John Moore bore his wound without complaint and was full of concern for the future of his staff and the safety of the whole army. And when Colonel Cadogan, the excellent commander of the 71st Highland Light Infantry, was hit at Vitoria, he refused to be moved to the rear, but lay, propped against two knapsacks, watching the progress of the battle, until he could see no more.[9]

Some men turned to religion to help them through the stress of battle. Neither the British nor the French army displayed much outward sign of religious feeling; indeed, Napoleon's forces retained some of the violent anti-clericalism of the Revolutionary armies. Russian forces, however, were encouraged by processions of monks carrying a sacred icon or relic through their ranks before a battle; and a young British officer serving with the Portuguese records his surprise at seeing the whole regiment fall to its knees for a short prayer before commencing its advance. British soldiers, by contrast, received little spiritual support, and most were probably like Costello, who offered his first prayer for years when he was wounded at Badajoz. But others found more real comfort from their religion. An enthusiastic Methodist in the Guards, Sergeant John Stevenson, consoled himself with the thought that the Lord could save them in any crisis, and that, even if the worst happened, it was better to be with Christ in Heaven than on earth; while Christopher Ludlam of the 59th stated that after his conversion he no longer feared going into battle because 'sudden death would be sudden glory'. Such faith was rare, however. More typical was the young Frederick Mainwaring (he was only fourteen or fifteen), who steadied himself in his baptism of fire by 'breathing a short prayer to heaven . . . [such as] we are told never ascend in vain'. And when Private John Marshall, serving in the 10th Hussars at Waterloo, was about to charge:

> I am not ashamed to say, that well knowing what we were going to do, I offered up a prayer to the Almighty, that for the sake of my children and the partner of my bosom, he would protect me, and give me strength and courage to overcome all that opposed me, and with a firm mind I went, leaving all that was dear to me to the mercy of that Great Ruler, who has so often in the midst of peril and danger protected me.[10]

Religion could also provide some consolation for the loss of those who died under an officer's command. For example, Major-General Robinson, who commanded a brigade in Picton's division at Vitoria, reflected that, 'I have lost some

Officers of great value but they died in the execution of their duty, and I hope will be rewarded elsewhere.' In this case the battle had gone well, and while the losses were regrettable, they were a natural consequence of war. But when things went wrong, and the deaths were either unnecessary or due to error, they were felt much more keenly. At one point at Coruña, Charles Napier was isolated with a small group of men far in advance of the regiment, under heavy fire. Two of the party were killed by stray shots fired by their own comrades well to the rear. 'This misery shook us all a good deal,' Napier recalls, 'and made me so wild as to cry and stamp with rage.' And in October 1813 Charles Colville was annoyed when Colonel Douglas, commanding the Portuguese brigade in Colville's division, pushed a demonstration too far, and sustained about 150 casualties. 'Demonstration, difficult as it is to make in front of an enemy in force without bringing on fire, is an object too indefinite to admit of one's being satisfied to lose men upon it.' Wellington agreed, writing to Colville,

> I am concerned to be obliged to disapprove of his [Douglas's] conduct. He has just lost 150 men for nothing, and in disobedience to your orders. . . .
> . . . it is unworthy of one of his reputation to get his Brigade into scrapes for the sake of the little gloriole of driving in a few pickets, knowing as he must do that it is not intended he should engage in a serious affair. . . .

And yet, the Portuguese had behaved well in the action and probably inflicted as many casualties as they had received. But this, in the eyes of both Wellington and Colville, was not enough to justify their deaths in an action which had no wider military purpose.[11]

In general, soldiers did not grieve long over their fallen comrades. Rifleman Harris recalls one incident: 'Within about half an hour after this I . . . had as completely forgotten him as if he had died a hundred years back. The sight of so much bloodshed around will not suffer the mind to dwell long on any particular casualty, even though it happen to one's dearest friend.' Rocca agrees:

> The frequency of danger made us regard death as one of the most common occurrences of life. We grieved for our comrades when wounded, but if they were dead, we showed an indifference about them often even ironical. When the soldiers in passing recognized a companion numbered with the slain, they would say, 'He is now above want, he will abuse his horse no more, his drinking days are done,' or words to that purpose; which manifested in them a stoical disregard of existence. It was the only funeral oration spoken over the warriors that had fallen.

And, according to George Bell, British officers were scarcely more sentimental:

> I lost two of my messmates for whom I was very sorry, particularly for the joyful, rosy-faced lad Phillips. But there was no real grief for any one beyond a week or

two – all a shadow that passed away. Their effects were sold by auction. We bought their clothes and wore them, and they were sold again perhaps in a month, being once more part of the kit of deceased officers killed in action.

This view is confirmed by the report that, when the Royal Dragoons passed through the Spanish village where Major Jervoise of the regiment had died the previous year, several officers visited his grave, but far from behaving with respect, they 'cut indecent jokes, laughing and jeering at the memory of a man whose heart was good and whose soul was brave'.[12]

But if this was the general attitude, there were exceptions. The 42nd Highlanders lost heavily in the campaign in Egypt in 1801, especially in the Battle of Alexandria. On the morning after the battle Lord Dalhousie was distressed to see 'most of them, officers as well as men, crying like children' in their encampment. While sometimes the death of a particular friend or comrade would strike home and defeat any attempt at indifference or nonchalance. Thus in April 1812 William Napier wrote home to his wife,

[Lieutenant-Colonel Charles] Macleod is dead, and I am grovelling in misery and wretchedness – my temples ache with the painful images that are passing before me. He was the best and will be the last of my friends, for I cannot endure the torture that I feel again, and where can I find another like him? . . . I had buoyed myself up with the hope of meeting him, and now I must weep over his grave.

In the following year Napier was again reduced almost to despair by the death of a young lieutenant, Edward Freer, who had been in his company for four years, and whom Napier had come to regard as a younger brother. Nor did Napier forget the young man, for when he came to write his great *History* many years later, it included a glowing obituary of Freer:

low in rank for he was but a lieutenant, rich in honour for he bore many scars, . . . young of days – he was only nineteen, and had seen more combats and sieges than he could count years. So slight in person and of such surpassing and delicate beauty that the Spaniards often thought him a girl disguised in man's clothing, he was yet so vigorous, so active, so brave, that the most daring and experienced veterans watched his looks on the field of battle, and, implicitly following where he led, would like children obey his slightest sign in the most difficult situations. His education was incomplete, yet were his natural powers so happy that the keenest and best-furnished intellects shrunk from an encounter of wit; and every thought and aspiration was proud and noble, indicating future greatness if destiny so willed it. Such was Edward Freer of the forty-third . . . and the sternest soldiers wept even in the middle of the fight when they saw him fall.[13]

*

Attitudes to the enemy varied enormously during the Napoleonic Wars, with the Peninsula seeing both the chivalrous and good-humoured fighting between the British and the French, and the pitiless, horrible war of atrocity and counter-atrocity between the French and the guerrillas. The character of each of these conflicts was set very early on, but their terms escalated, as courtesy was met with greater courtesy, barbarity with greater barbarity. Yet Britain and France were traditional enemies, divided by religion, whose governments each blamed the other for the long war; while Spain and France had long been allies, and despite the Revolution had much in common. But the Anglo-French war in the Peninsula was fought by professionals, on territory belonging to neither; while the Spanish resistance mobilized all classes of society, and was sustained both by the outrages committed by the French, and by anger at their presence on Spanish soil.

Napoleon's campaigns in central Europe never quite attained the gentlemanly manners of the Anglo-French war in the Peninsula, but until the invasion of Russia, they remained essentially professional. The campaigns of 1812–14, however, were marked by gross brutality approaching, if not equalling, the horrors of the Spanish war. Whether it was Russian peasants and cossacks murdering French stragglers, Prussians avenging themselves for years of humiliation and occupation, or Burgundians rising against the depredations of half-starved allied soldiers, the populace joined in the war and greatly magnified its misfortunes.

Some professional soldiers encouraged this development. Scharnhorst, Gneisenau and other Prussian 'patriots' had planned a 'people's war', modelled on Spain, between 1809 and 1811. Indeed in 1809 the Austrians and Major Schill both attempted to incite uprisings in Germany, though their calls fell flat outside the Tyrol. In 1814, and particularly in 1815, Blücher and his army deliberately behaved with great severity and ill-discipline in their advance through France. Nor had the French much right to complain. They had been the first to let the genie out of the bottle in the 1790s, and though their armies had since grown more professional, their passage was always marked by widespread looting, rape and plunder. In Spain they had begun the war with treachery and deception, and as early as the Dos de Mayo had begun the cycle of excessive retaliation. Their subsequent attempt to establish an enlightened and humane regime – not even his greatest enemies ever pretended that Joseph Bonaparte was an ogre – was thus corrupted from the outset. While in the face of popular resistance, compounded by tales of French officers and soldiers killed by horrible tortures, they quickly resorted to mass executions and a fruitless attempt to overawe the population.

Such barbarities were least evident where regular armies opposed each other on campaign and in battle. Not that the French and Spanish armies ever treated each other with the same respect as did the British and French, but many of the constraints of regular warfare continued to be accepted on both sides. As for the British, they commonly, though not invariably, regarded the French as admirable and worthy opponents, almost comrades in arms, who shared with them the discomforts of the countryside and a dislike of the population. There are many stories of fraternization between outposts, and even of men cheerfully mingling on neutral ground during a lull in the middle of a battle: for example, when both sides collected their wounded and drew water from the Portina brook during a pause in the fighting at Talavera. At Santarem in 1811, when Wellington was trying to starve Masséna out of Portugal, British outposts shared their rations with their hungry French counterparts. Late in 1813 Harry Smith and a French officer discussed where they should post their sentries for the night, and the Frenchman obligingly withdrew his some distance when Smith expressed a fear that they were too close and might create an alarm in the dark when they were relieved. Other officers and men sometimes exchanged provisions, and on one occasion an officer doing the rounds at night found both British and French sentries at their posts, but the remainder of both pickets taking shelter in a ruined house between the lines, amicably sharing the contents of its cellar! Wellington would not have approved of quite this degree of fraternization, but he always encouraged a policy of 'live and let live' between sentries, believing that the 'killing of a poor fellow of a vedette or carrying off a post could not influence a battle', or do any good. And he always maintained the courtesies with his French opponents, arranging for the exchange of captured officers, sending or asking for news of those who were badly wounded, and many other such matters.[14]

Some British officers were beginning to view war as a rough game in which a gentleman might be killed, but in which he should never cheat or act dishonourably. Such a view was still in its infancy, almost a century from its apogee in the age of Kipling and Newbolt; but when George Napier, writing his recollections for his children, had described the fraternization between the outposts, he commented:

> You see by this that there is never any personal animosity between soldiers opposed to each other in war, but I daresay it strikes you as very odd that men should shake hands with each other, drink and eat together, laugh and joke, and then in a few minutes use every exertion of mind and body to destroy one another. But so it is, and I hope it will always be the case. I should hate to fight out of personal malice or revenge, but have no objection to fight for '*fun and glory*'.[15]

Such views were not confined to the British. Even French and Spanish officers could develop a superficial camaraderie on rare occasions. Rocca tells the story of a Spanish officer who brought a message to the French garrison at Ronda under a flag of truce. The French commander invited the Spaniard to dine in the mess while he considered his answer, and Rocca was told to look after the visitor.

The Spanish officer did not at first depart from that sobriety which characterizes his countrymen. But when we drank his health, he returned the compliment, and, emulating our example, he now studied to keep up with us. We were only comrades at supper, but we were brothers at the dessert. We vowed an ever-lasting friendship; and, among other proofs of esteem, we promised to fell each other in single combat the very first time we should again meet.[16]

In battle, soldiers expected their opponents to abide by certain unwritten rules of the game, while particularly chivalrous conduct was widely discussed and admired. At El Bodon, in 1811, a French cavalry officer 'had raised his sword to cut [Lt.-Col.] Felton Hervey down, when perceiving his antagonist has only one arm [he had lost the other at Oporto, two years before], he instantly stopped, brought down his sword before Hervey in the usual salute and rode past'. The previous year, at Busaco, a young man, perhaps an officer, belonging to the King's German Legion went forward among the French wounded, giving them the drink they craved, and trying to make them comfortable. When he first appeared, the French skirmishers, fearing that he meant harm, redoubled their fire, but as soon as they saw what he was doing, the firing ceased and was replaced by loud cheering.[17]

Equally, both armies might unite in condemning conduct which fell below the accepted standard. A French vedette rode to within sixty yards of a British dragoon, also on sentry duty, on the morning of Fuentes de Oñoro, and chal-lenged him to single combat. The watching infantry expected the dragoon to accept the challenge, or at worst simply to refuse it; instead he unslung his carbine and fired at the Frenchman. The shot missed, as did two or three more, before the Frenchman, having proved his gallantry, turned and rode back. The British infantry cheered him loudly, 'while we hissed our own dragoon, who, it was afterwards stated, for the credit of the gallant regiment he belonged to, was a recruit'. At Waterloo, when a French hussar callously shot dead a British cavalryman who was struggling to disentangle himself from his fallen horse, there was an indignant 'groan of execration' from the ranks of the British cavalry who were looking on, 'and an exclamation of "No quarter to them!"'[18]

There was some disagreement over the morality of picking off enemy officers and soldiers when the firers were in safety. Brotherton, who as a cavalry officer was more likely to be a target than the beneficiary of such fire, was strongly opposed to it. When he saw a German officer, armed with a rifle, shooting at French officers and soldiers during a lull in the fighting 'I remonstrated with him on his barbarous conduct, and shamed him out of it, but not before he had hit several poor fellows who were actually employed in burying their dead. The remembrance of such conduct makes my blood curdle in my veins even at this time!' On another occasion Brotherton argued forcefully with a Portuguese monk, the leader of a party of guerrillas, who was firing at a French column from some inaccessible rocks. In both these cases it was the complete safety of the firer which aroused Brotherton's ire and disgust; though he admits that he was unable to convince the cleric that it was wrong to kill Frenchmen who could not, at that moment, retaliate, whatever they had previously done, but perfectly all right to do so when your own life was also in jeopardy.[19]

Riflemen, however, naturally took another view of the question, although few of them would have approved of firing on troops burying their dead or retrieving their wounded. Edward Costello tells without hesitation a story which in some ways seems even worse. According to this tale, during the retreat to Coruña, Major-General Sir Edward Paget rode up to the Rifles and offered his purse to any man who would shoot the gallant French general who was leading the pursuit. Tom Plunket immediately ran 100 yards back towards the advancing French, threw himself on the ground, took careful aim and killed General Colbert, returning to the regiment and receiving his reward amidst the cheers of his comrades. Sir William Cope, writing his history of the Rifle Brigade half a century later, could not believe that Paget would have bribed a soldier 'to slay a chivalrous and brave enemy', though he might, without discredit, have rewarded Plunket for his good shot after the event. It is true that Costello was not with the regiment at the time, and may well have been mistaken in the details of the story; but still it is significant that a veteran of the campaigns in the Peninsula saw nothing discreditable in the tale.[20]

A much less distasteful incident occurred in the fighting at Sabugal. The British were being hard pressed, and the French were led on with great gallantry by an officer on a grey horse. 'Old Beckwith, in a voice like thunder, roared out to the Riflemen, "Shoot that fellow, will you?" In a moment he and his horse were knocked over, and Sydney exclaimed, "Alas! you were a *noble fellow.*"' Not even the most squeamish officer was likely to object to this, for both sides were equally in danger, and there was a compelling and immediate military need for rendering the Frenchman *hors de combat*.[21]

Such admiration mixed with regret at the death of an enemy was surprisingly common, and not limited to officers. Moyle Sherer overheard two British soldiers commenting on the fall of a prominent French officer,

> 'I was sorry to see him drop, poor fellow,' said one.
> 'Ah!' said another, 'He came so close there was no missing him; I did for him!'
> 'Did you!' rejoined the first speaker; 'By God, I could not have pulled a trigger at him. No; damn me, I like fair fighting and hot fighting; but I could not single out such a man in cold blood.'[22]

Most infantry, packed closely in their ranks and firing at large blocks of the enemy, never knew if their shots took effect, let alone saw an identifiable individual fall as a result of their actions. But skirmishers, and particularly riflemen, with their accurate weapons, open order and fire-at-will, could not avoid realizing what they had done. Edward Costello was already an experienced soldier when, in a skirmish in the spring of 1811, he saw a single French soldier remain at his post, firing, when his comrades fell back.

> I had got within fifty yards when I fired. In an instant I was beside him, the shot had entered his head, and he had fallen in the act of loading, the fusil tightly grasped in his left hand, while his right clutched the ramrod. A few quick turns of the eye as it rolled its dying glances on mine turned my whole blood within me, and I reproached myself as his destroyer. An indescribable uneasiness came over me, I felt almost like a criminal. I knelt to give him a little wine from a small calabash, which hung at my side, and was wiping the foam from his lips, when a heavy groan drew my attention aside, and turning round my head I beheld, stretched near him and close to the wall, another wounded Frenchman, a sergeant. 'Hélas,' exclaimed the wounded man, the big tears suddenly gushing down his sun-burnt countenance, as he pointed with his finger to my victim, 'vous avez tué mon pauvre frère' (you have killed my poor brother), and indeed such was the melancholy fact.
>
> The sergeant, a stout heavy man, had fallen, his thigh broken by a shot. The younger brother, unable to carry him off the field, had remained, apparently with the intention of perishing by his side.
>
> We halted for the night on an adjacent hill, about a mile in advance. . . . I took advantage of the few moments leisure our position afforded to return to the French sergeant. But I found him and his brother both as naked as they were born, perforated with innumerable wounds, no doubt administered by the Portuguese. I turned back to the camp, but in a very poor humour with myself.[23]

Others felt a similar revulsion even when they had acted purely in self-defence. Sir John Moore told George Napier that in the fighting at the fort of Calvie in Corsica he had been confronted by a French grenadier about to bayonet him, and had run the Frenchman through with his sword and killed him. Napier continues, 'thank God, I was lucky enough never to use my sword in the same way as Sir John Moore was forced to use his (and he told me he should never forget the horrid sensation it gave him when drawing the sword out of the man's body, and that it was always a painful recollection to him)'. And yet both Moore and Napier were dedicated soldiers, famous for their conspicuous gallantry in action, leading from the front and receiving many wounds.[24]

In the mêlée at Sahagun, Alexander Gordon of the 15th Hussars was about to cut down a fleeing French officer when he thought he recognized the face and uniform of Lieutenant Hancox of his own regiment.

> The shock I felt from the idea that I had been on the point of destroying a brother officer instead of an enemy deprived me of all inclination to use my sword except in defence of my own life; and the hostility I had cherished against the French only a few minutes before was converted into pity for them. When I met Hancox

after the action, I found that he wore an oilskin cover on his cap, and was not the person I had followed, who I conclude, was an officer of the *grenadiers à cheval* or *compagnie d'élite*, which is attached to each regiment of dragoons in the French service, and doubtless was much astonished at my sudden appearance and abrupt departure. For my own part, I shall always consider it a most fortunate circumstance that I was thus deceived, since I have escaped the feeling of remorse to which I should have been exposed had I taken that man's life.[25]

In the French army, however, or at least in some cavalry regiments in it, a young officer was expected to prove his courage by engaging in single combat with the enemy soon after joining his unit. The ungallant reaction of a British dragoon has already been described, and Captain Brotherton, without resorting to a carbine, equally disliked such affairs:

> it has been my lot to be engaged in several single combats in the field, during the Peninsular War, yet they were never of my own seeking, but that I was provoked to them by the braggadocio manner of the French officers; for I hold it to be very bad taste and feeling to engage *designedly* in these single combats, which in a *melee* are unavoidable. War would indeed be more horrible than it is if such individual hostilities were encouraged, which were only suited to a barbarous age. For the sake of example, an officer cannot well decline a challenge to single combat offered in the bullying manner with which the officer commanding a French regiment of dragoons bore himself towards me on one occasion.

In that encounter, the Frenchman, though a strong man on a powerful horse, did not wait to cross swords, but turned and ran, arousing hisses from both sides. In another such duel, Brotherton encountered a very young French officer who displayed more courage, and the two fought between the opposing lines of skirmishers, who stood by and watched quietly. Brotherton was wounded in the hand and one of his bridles cut, but at the same moment he delivered a thrust to the Frenchman's body which terminated the fight, both officers riding back to their units. 'I thought I had but slightly wounded him,' Brotherton recalls,

> but I found, on inquiry the next day, when sent on a flag of truce, that the thrust had proved mortal, having entered the pit of his stomach. I felt deeply on this occasion and was much annoyed, as I had admired the chivalrous and noble bearing of this young officer. He was a mere youth, who, I suppose, thought it necessary to make this display as a first essay, as French officers usually do on their first appearance in the field, and indeed, I believe it is expected of them by their comrades. I shall never forget his good-humoured, fine countenance during the whole time we were engaged in this single combat, talking cheerfully and politely to me, as if we were exchanging civilities instead of sabre cuts.[26]

Such single combats were probably not very common, for although they make good stories, they are not often mentioned in memoirs, and they sit awkwardly with the general fraternization between the outposts. The initiative almost always came from the French, for the British in general seem to have shared Brotherton's disapproval. One young British officer who was caught up in the excitement of battle, wanted to challenge his French counterpart but was firmly snubbed by his commander, who told him that 'his presence with the company was more important'. But as this occurred actually during a battle, such a response is not surprising.[27]

Not all soldiers felt any concern at the death of their enemies. Charles Cocks was an unusually intelligent and professional officer, yet he shows no compunction in writing home after one mêlée, 'I was only personally engaged once with a Chasseur and had the fortune to kill him the first blow. . . . This affair was pleasing, as it is the first time we have had anything to say to the lancers.' An officer in the 18th Hussars at Waterloo – who had been promoted from the ranks – described how his men had cut their way through a body of French infantry which made little or no resistance, and then turned around 'and had the same fun coming back'. Private Wheeler was equally unconcerned when he described how, at Waterloo, he and two comrades watched a reconnoitring French officer approach them where they were hidden, before they shot him and plundered his body. On an earlier occasion Wheeler says he was 'over joyed' to kill a Frenchman; though there he had more reason, for he had been wounded and the French soldier had plundered him: by killing the Frenchman Wheeler was able to have his revenge, recover his own property, and gain possession of whatever was in the other's pack and haversack. Such incidents were not uncommon in the skirmishing line, and several of the stories quoted in Chapter 4 testify to a similar, light-hearted, disregard for the enemy's life. Indeed at one time the 95th Rifles developed a conceit that each and every rifleman could and ought to kill a Frenchman in action.[28]

Given the frequency with which the Rifles did battle, and the accuracy of their weapon, they may have gone some way towards approaching this goal, but in this they were unusual, for relatively few soldiers ever killed an enemy. As killing and death are so closely associated with war, this statement appears paradoxical, and needs to be explained. First there is the fundamental point that the number of soldiers who killed was less than the number of those who were killed, or who died from their wounds; for some soldiers certainly killed more than one enemy in their career, but none could die more than once. Next comes the fact that the great majority of soldiers in the Napoleonic Wars were not killed in action: many survived, and most of those who died (two thirds or more) succumbed to disease and exhaustion rather than enemy action. From this it seems likely that fewer than one in four soldiers ever killed an enemy, and most of these deaths would have been the result of unaimed musketry, or of artillery fire, where no individual would recognize his part in any particular death. These figures may still seem odd, but they fall into place when we recall that in a typical battle of the period, fewer than 6 per cent of those present were killed, and that those present were only part of their whole army.[29]

Soldiers at the time naturally did not make such calculations. Most of those who had been seriously engaged in several major actions (and many, of course, never were, if only because they died of disease before they could see much service) probably assumed that they had killed one or more enemy with the shots they had fired. In any case they could not allow such considerations, or any feeling of pity for the enemy, to greatly influence their conduct in action. For most men, their guiding principle had to be that which Major O'Hare of the 95th explained to some newly joined riflemen:

> 'Do you see those men on the plain?' asked the Major, as he pointed to the French camp. On several of the men answering 'Ees, Zur!' Major O'Hare, with a dry laugh, continued, 'Well then, those are the French, and our enemies. You must kill those fellows, and not allow them to kill you. You must learn and do as these old birds here do,' pointing to us, 'and get cover where you can. Recollect, recruits, you come here to kill, and not be killed. Bear this in mind: if you don't kill the French they'll kill you.' – 'Ees, Zur!' said they again.
>
> The Major's logic, although it elicited roars of laughter from the old soldiers, I believe had more effect with the recruits than if Demosthenes had risen for the purpose.[30]

Such sentiments, combined with loyalty to the regiment and pride in professional expertise, probably amounted to the whole of the philosophy of many soldiers and some officers. Others, particularly in the French army, were enraptured by the love of glory and the romance of the Napoleonic adventure. Eugène de Beauharnais, one of the most honourable and reasonable of Napoleon's inner circle, had campaigned with his stepfather since 1796, and commanded an army of his own in 1809, but it was not until after the disaster in Russia that he would write, 'I don't look for glory now. The price is too high.' For some it was never too high. General Marulaz was an adventurer, a *beau sabreur*, and a rival of Lasalle; for him and many like him,

> warfare was a fine way of life, untrammelled by gloomy reflections about starving peasants, ruined crops and burning villages. For them warfare meant the taste of wine drunk from the bottle, the smell of greased leather and horsesweat, the sound of jingling columns crossing the Rhine and the Danube.
>
> Above all it meant the excitement of the battlefield; light cavalry deploying at the gallop, long lines of trotting cuirassiers: *sabres au clair, casques en tête, crinières au vent*. Cannon-smoke, trumpet calls, thudding hooves and flying artillery: and in the distance, mounted on a superb charger, a mere detail of the conflict yet somehow towering over all, the figure of a man wearing a colonel's undress uniform of the Guard Chasseurs; bare-headed, inscrutable, raising his shabby cocked hat in answer to the swell of cheering and the salute of waving swords.[31]

British officers were less susceptible, but by no means immune, to this appeal. Charles Colville described the Battle of Nivelle in a letter to his brother-in-law, the Reverend Roger Frankland:

> The day was one of the luckiest that ever came out of the heaven. The whole army moved forward from their respective points almost at the same moment at daybreak, and from the mountains behind, where many must have been beholders of the whole line of operations in one coup d'oeil, it must have been the grandest sight possible.
>
> Success was so general and everything went on so swimmingly, that I think it was altogether the most animating and (shall I say it to a parson?) agreeable day of the kind I was ever engaged in: the loss not being in any comparison to the difficulties overcome, and the killed bearing a small proportion to the wounded; in my British brigade being only 50 out of 400.[32]

Even a surgeon described another encounter as

> altogether as shewy a little piece of fighting as I ever witnessed. The brilliant musketry along the side, and from the crest of the hill – the cheering of our men as they mounted – the continued advance of numerous bugles – the roar of our Artillery reverberating in long echoes from one side to another of the deep ravine at the bottom – all was very fine and grand.[33]

Napoleonic soldiers well understood the realities of war, which they experienced from day to day. Few believed that it was 'sweet and fitting to die for their country', though most held that there were worse fates than death in battle. Many of those who have been quoted in this chapter had been wounded, often more than once, and had endured operations without antiseptics or anaesthetics. For some, the attraction of war and the pursuit of glory never palled. They were not unusual: many people of diverse societies and religions, from different continents over many centuries, have felt the same appeal, and it remains a thread – although not the dominant thread – in our culture today.

Part IV
The End of the Day

Chapter Twelve
Victory or Defeat?

Napoleonic battles consisted of a number of smaller combats which added up to a more or less coherent whole. Thus at Waterloo the fight for Hougoumont was almost completely independent of the great French cavalry charges, the struggle for Placenoit, the fall of La Haye Sainte and the final French attack. Each of these combats was decided by its local circumstances: the number and quality of the troops on each side, their tactics and morale, the advantages conferred by terrain, by a score of lesser factors, and by luck. Each might be extended or protracted by the introduction of fresh troops, as the commanders drew on their reserves to exploit a success or reinforce a threatened sector. And the result of each combat contributed to the emerging shape of the battle as a whole.

If one army was consistently successful in these phases or episodes of a battle it would soon gain both a moral and a tactical ascendancy. It would hold its positions if they were under attack, or drive the enemy from theirs if it was advancing. By breaking enemy units it would compel the opposing general to throw his reserves into the battle prematurely, and it would develop a momentum which was likely to carry it to victory. The troops would be exhilarated by their success and their confidence would be enhanced, while the enemy would become despondent and demoralized, so that one success would prepare the way for another.

But in many battles the trend of individual combats did not greatly favour either army, with local successes in one part of the field being offset in another, or overturned by reinforcements. The cumulative effect of combats in this type of battle was to batter and exhaust both armies, absorbing their reserves and reducing their cohesion, so that they became vulnerable to a final decisive attack. A Prussian officer describes the appearance of his men late in the day at Ligny:

> The light of the long June day was beginning to fail. . . . The men looked terribly worn out after the fighting. In the great heat, gunpowder smoke, sweat and mud had mixed into a thick crust of dirt, so that their faces looked almost like those of

mulattos, and one could hardly distinguish the green collars and facings on their tunics. Everybody had discarded his stock; grubby shirts or hairy brown chests stuck out from their open tunics; and many who had been unwilling to leave the ranks on account of a slight would wore a bandage they had put on themselves. In a number of cases blood was soaking through.

As a result of fighting in the villages for hours on end, and of frequently crawling through hedges, the men's tunics and trousers had got torn, so that they hung in rags and their bare skin showed through.[1]

Clausewitz observed a similar degeneration in the armies at Borodino:

the action gradually reflected the weariness and exhaustion of the armies. The masses of infantry had melted away so drastically that perhaps less than one-third of the original number was still in action: the rest of the troops were dead, wounded, engaged in carrying away the casualties or rallying in the rear. Everywhere there were wide gaps. The mighty artillery . . . now spoke only by sporadic shots, and even these did not seem to ring out in the old strong and thunderous style, but sounded languid and muffled.[2]

While in *On War* he generalizes that

men who have been engaged for a long continuance of time are more or less like burnt-out cinders; their ammunition is consumed; they have melted away to a certain extent; physical and moral energies are exhausted, perhaps their courage is broken as well. Such a force, irrespective of the diminution in its number, if viewed as an organic whole, is very different from what it was before the combat.[3]

It was for such moments that Napoleon husbanded his Imperial Guard. At Ligny, the Guard and Milhaud's cuirassiers attacked the exhausted Prussian centre in the gathering gloom of evening. Blücher had virtually no reserves left in hand; his fighting troops were physically and morally spent, unable to summon up the will to check the advance of the most famous elite troops in Europe. With their centre broken, and the cohesion of their entire army threatened, the Prussians had no choice but to accept defeat and to withdraw.

At Borodino, Napoleon, famously, refused to commit the Guard, and the Russian army, although it had had the worst of the fighting, remained unbroken at the end of the day. The decision cost Napoleon what was probably his last, slender chance of breaking the Russian resolve of continuing the war to the bitter end.

At Waterloo, the perfect moment for the Guard to attack came with the fall of La Haye Sainte, when the centre of Wellington's line was battered and crumbling. But Napoleon was preoccupied by the Prussian threat to his flank and rear, and an hour passed before the Guard began its advance. By then, Wellington had reconstructed his line, moved his last reserves into place, and brought into the centre two brigades of light cavalry from the extreme left where, thanks to the Prussians, they were no longer needed. The Guard's attack was supported by the exhausted remnants of the rest of the French army which made feeble attacks all along the line. But the Guard was broken, Wellington signalled a general advance, and the French army dissolved into a confused mass of fleeing men. As this example shows, the final attack, even if made with a fresh elite force, still had to be conducted with skill and timing if it was to succeed, and at the end of a long, fierce battle the line between victory and defeat could be very fine.

Not all major engagements were this close or saw this level of attrition. Some battles, such as Austerlitz, Friedland and Salamanca, were won and lost by tactical brilliance on one side and blunders on the other. These battles were not without hard fighting, and even some local successes for the defeated army – for example the breaking of Pack and Cole at Salamanca – but from the outset, one army was severely compromised and fighting at such a disadvantage that recovery was always most unlikely.

The antithesis of such victories were those battles where each army fought the other to a standstill, without either being able to produce a final decisive attack. Borodino, Eylau and Albuera were notable examples: battles famous for their savage fighting, heavy casualties and lack of tactical finesse. At the end of such a battle neither general could be sure whether he had won or lost, and both would feel that their army could not sustain another day's fighting.

Then there were battles where one army was hopelessly outmatched by the other. At its most extreme such an action might be completely one-sided. There were a number of these actions involving Spanish troops in the Peninsular War. At Gamonal (10 November 1808) the Conde de Belvedere, with 10,000 mostly raw troops, attempted to halt the French advance, not realizing that it consisted of 70,000 veterans under Napoleon. In the end only the advanced guard – 25,000 men commanded by Soult – were needed to utterly rout and disperse Belvedere's army. Napoleon, showing his customary style with statistics, admitted a loss of only fifteen killed and fifty wounded, and put the Spanish loss at 3,000 casualties and 3,000 prisoners. Sir Charles Oman gives a more sober, but scarcely less remarkable set of figures: no more than 200 French casualties, compared to 2,500 Spanish killed and wounded, with a further 900 taken prisoner.[4]

Gamonal was perhaps the most extreme, but by no means the only example, of such a one-sided contest. Ucles and Alba de Tormes were almost equally striking, and while some Spanish infantry fought well at Ocaña and the Gebora – even driving back the first French attack at Ocaña – the result of these battles was never really in doubt. There were other engagements, not involving the Spanish, where the defeated army, though showing some spirit, was plainly outnumbered, outclassed, and out-generalled; Jena and Vitoria being the most famous examples. Some individual combats in such battles might be hard-fought, but in the battle as a whole the victors had an overwhelming predominance. This often reflected a superiority in both numbers and quality, with no compensating advantages from the terrain or generalship – indeed, to fight at all at such a disadvantage usually implied that the victorious commander had already established his ascendancy during the campaign.

Finally there were battles where the object of the successful army fell short of breaking the enemy. Some of Wellington's defensive battles fall into this class, most obviously Busaco, but also Talavera and Fuentes de Oñoro. Here his tactical object was limited to maintaining his position and repulsing the enemy's attacks. He did not trust his army to attempt to follow up the French discomfiture and convert their rebuff into a rout. There were good reasons for this restraint. At Busaco, the ridge was so steep and rough that it would have made his downhill advance in a counter-attack almost as difficult and dangerous as the French found their attacks. Masséna still had his cavalry, artillery and one corps of infantry untouched, nor were the two broken corps so thoroughly discomposed that they would have fled at the sight of an allied advance; while Wellington's Portuguese were completely raw, and even his British troops were not as competent, confident and experienced as they became. He also hoped that simply halting the French in that desolate region would be enough; and that lack of supplies would soon force Masséna to fall back to the Spanish frontier. Similar arguments apply to Fuentes: the French army was far from broken at the end of the battle; its powerful cavalry would have rendered any allied advance perilous; while merely repulsing the French was enough to achieve Wellington's immediate strategic objective: the recapture of Almeida. Fear of the opposing cavalry may also have played some part at Talavera, though the main reason here for the decision not to make any attempt to follow up the victory was clearly that the British army was exhausted by the severity of the fighting, which had left one man in four a casualty.

Such victories could produce great strategic benefits. Masséna's army lost many more – some 15,000 men – during the winter of 1810–11 in Portugal than were killed in any battle in the Peninsular War; and this followed and was substantially caused by the rebuff, without even a battle, which he suffered at Torres Vedras. But it is true that a purely defensive battle was much less likely to yield obvious and immediate results than one in which the fight was taken to the enemy. Troops who were allowed to withdraw at will, collect themselves, catch their breath and rally without harassment, would only flee in panic and disperse if they were very bad indeed. The most glamorous and decisive battles always involved a measure of attack – if only the limited general advance which Wellington signalled at Waterloo. But a good general was not seduced by the glamour; he concentrated on the broader picture, balanced risks and costs against possible gains, and acted accordingly – just as Wellington did throughout his career.

None of these engagements was determined solely, or even primarily, by the relative number of casualties in each army. No one during the course of a battle knew how heavily their own army, let alone that of the enemy, was suffering;

nor was anyone in the mood for calculations of this kind. During the course of the fight casualties were often fairly equal: the ultimate victors might even lose more heavily, only to redress the balance once they had established their ascendancy. Frederick the Great's army suffered more casualties than the armies of his opponents in all his victories except Rossbach and Leuthen; while according to Clausewitz:

> it is known by experience, that the losses in physical forces in the course of a battle seldom present a great difference between victor and vanquished respectively, often none at all, sometimes even one bearing an inverse relation to the result, and that the most decisive losses on the side of the vanquished only commence with the retreat, that is, those which the conqueror does not share with him. The weak remains of battalions already in disorder are cut down by cavalry, exhausted men strew the ground, disabled guns and broken caissons are abandoned, others in the bad state of the roads cannot be removed quickly enough, and are captured by the enemy's troops, during the night numbers lose their way, and fall defenceless into the enemy's hands, and thus the victory mostly gains bodily substance after it is already decided.[5]

One caveat which needs to be made here is that Wellington's defensive victories all showed a marked balance of casualties in favour of the allies (1,252 allied, compared to over 4,100 French at Busaco, for example), even though they contained no pursuit other than immediate following up of defeated French columns. But Wellington was always exceptionally economical of his men's lives in battle.[6]

What mattered in deciding a battle, as in the individual combats of which it was composed, was not the body count, but the destruction of the enemy army's cohesion and will to fight. The infliction of casualties, and the underlying quality of the troops were, of course, major factors in determining which side broke first; but even in battles of attrition they were not the only factors. This was why the great tactical strokes were so important: they did not make the enemy easier to kill, but they disrupted his army, shook his confidence, broke the cohesion of some of his units, and forced him to deploy his reserves.

The need thoroughly to disrupt the enemy's army in order to thoroughly defeat it explains why the object in many battles was to break through the enemy's main line. In Napoleon's favourite *manoeuvre sur les derrières* an attack on the enemy's flank absorbed his reserves and forced him to improvise a new line, but the final, decisive attack occurred at the junction between the old and new lines. If an army's main line was broken, and this could not be checked or contained by the reserves, the army would be split in two, making coherent control impossible, and even a unified retreat very difficult – the two parts of the army were more likely to fall back in divergent directions. It also provided a powerful symbol of defeat: enemy troops penetrated to the heart of the army's position and could not be expelled. The critical fighting of the day often occurred at this point: Soult's advance on to the Pratzen plateau at Austerlitz; the French failure to follow up rapidly the fall of La Haye Sainte at Waterloo; and the repulse of Sebastiani and Lapisse at Talavera are only a few of the examples which could be cited.

At some point during the battle – unless it was a stalemate – the defeated commander would realize that the day was lost. By this stage he would already have lost control over much, and sometimes over all, his army; but his task now became to do what he could to salvage all that he could from the wreckage. Yet it was important that he had the mental toughness and resolution not to despair too soon. Marengo had appeared a lost battle before Desaix's return gave the French a second chance, while Napoleon might well have conceded defeat after Eylau. The general had to judge, often in failing light, if his army was capable of continuing the fight that afternoon or evening, or on the following day, and whether persistence might see the enemy falter. Clausewitz writes that 'Lost ground and want of fresh reserves, are . . . usually the principal causes which determine a retreat'. But if a battle was closely contested, other things could come into play, including the general's pride making him reluctant to admit defeat, and the wider strategic context of the battle – for example whether, by retreating, he would collect reinforcements or, alternatively, expose a valuable base of operations. Sometimes the decision was complicated by politics: after Borodino, Kutusov did all he could to avoid the responsibility for ordering a retreat, wishing to escape the blame and knowing that he was already deeply unpopular with the Emperor Alexander.[7]

Once the decision to retreat had been taken, the next issue was to choose the line of retreat. Often an army had been driven from its natural line of retreat during the battle and might have only one road open to it, as happened to the French at Vitoria. Or it might have been broken into several fragments which retreated in diverging directions. The allied army at Austerlitz was so broken that different parts fled north-east, south-east, south, and even west – this last direction taking them into the original positions of the French army, where they were rounded up and captured after some further fighting. If the army was in better order than this, its commander could give thought to the strategic situation, and choose the most advantageous line of retreat. The most famous example of this was the Prussian retreat due north from Ligny to Wavre, which kept them in touch with Wellington's army, rather than east or north-east towards their bases.

Organizing the retreat of a defeated army was one of the most difficult tasks a general could face, and much inevitably had to be left to the good sense and initiative of subordinate commanders and regimental officers. Everyone was tired and despondent; it was often growing dark, and the chaos which always existed in the rear of the army was threatening to spread throughout the whole force. Colonel von Reiche, the chief of staff of Zieten's corps, describes his part in helping to calm and direct the Prussian retreat from Ligny:

Although it was almost dark I could still see my map clearly enough to realise that Tilly was not marked on it. Thinking it likely that a number of other officers would have the same map, and that uncertainty and confusion could easily result, I proposed that instead of Tilly another town lying further back but on the same line of march should be named as the assembly point – somewhere which we could assume would be shown on every other map. I remarked that even if two withdrawal points were detailed, they were both in the same direction, so there would be no fear of confusion. Gneisenau agreed. On his map I found that Wavre was just such a place.

How far my suggestion contributed to the fact that the retreat extended as far as Wavre I must leave open.

Next I stationed the staff officer I had with me, Lieutenant von Reisewitz, at the point on the Roman road where the track now to be taken branched off, and instructed him to direct any troops who arrived to follow it. The detachments which had already taken the Roman road or the Namur road could not, of course, be recalled. In itself this was a bad thing, yet it had the advantage that the enemy would be deceived as to the line of our withdrawal.

. . . As the troops directed on to the road were all split up, General Gneisenau ordered me to collect them and form them up. Anyone who has ever been given such a task, in similar circumstances, will know the endless difficulties one has to contend with in order to carry it out. I tried to deal with the problem by first halting the head of the throng and letting the rest of the men fall in on this. When, after a great deal of trouble, I had managed to get one group halted and was trying to stop the men who were going past in the meantime, the group broke up again; and this went on for a while until I succeeded in attracting a few officers and non-commissioned officers to assist me. Particularly helpful in this business was my hat with its white plume, because in the dark people mistook me for a general, an error I was glad to put up with.

When I had disentangled the skein to the point where the men stood grouped under regiments and formed up in ranks and files, they marched off in good order. Feeling worn out, I lay down under a tree, holding onto the bridle of my poor horse, which had had nothing to eat or drink all day and all night. I could scarcely have credited such an animal with so much endurance, but it seems to have been one of those occasions, with him as with human beings, when one is so keyed up that one can stand unbelievable strains.[8]

A more junior Prussian officer, the gunner Lieutenant von Reuter (whose earlier experiences were quoted in Chapter 3), also played his part in the retreat, helping to form a rearguard in the centre, where the French had broken the Prussian line.

It was now about eight o'clock p.m., and the growing darkness was increased by heavy storm clouds which began to settle down all around us. My battery, in order to avoid capture, had, of course, to conform to this general movement [of retreat]. I now noticed that there was an excellent artillery position about 1,500 paces behind the village of Brye, close to where the Roman road intersects the road to Quatre Bras. . . . I made for this point with all haste, so that I might there place my guns and cover with their fire the retreat of my comrades of the other arms. A hollow road leading to Sombreffe delayed my progress some minutes. At length I got over this obstacle and attained my goal; but just as I was going to give the word, 'Action rear,' Von Pirch's (II) infantry brigade began to debouch from Brye. The general saw in an instant what he took for a selfish and cowardly movement of retreat on my part, dashed his spurs into his horse, and galloped up to me nearly beside himself with passion, and shouting out, 'My God! Everything is going to the devil!' 'Truly, sir,' said I, 'matters are not looking very rosy, but the 12-pounder battery, No. 6, has simply come here to get into a position from whence it thinks it may be able to check the enemy's advance.' 'That, then, is very brave conduct on your part,' answered the general, at once mollified; 'cling to the position at all hazards, it is of the greatest importance. I will collect a few troops to form an escort to your guns.' While this short, but animated, discussion had been going on his brigade had come up close to where we were. He formed it up to cover us, and sent everyone who was mounted to collect all retreating troops in the neighbourhood for the same purpose, while, as they came up, he called out to them, 'Soldiers, there stand your guns, are you not Prussians!'

During the time that a sort of rear-guard was thus formed, the battery had opened fire on the enemy's cavalry, which was coming up rather cautiously, and had forced them to fall back again. Later on, a 6-pounder field battery and half a horse artillery battery came up and joined us. The fight then became stationary, and as the darkness came on, fighting gradually ceased on both sides.[9]

Even Christian Nagel, whose regiment had fared so badly in the fighting (see above, pp. 211–12), insists that morale remained good: 'We were defeated, we knew that; but far from looking upon ourselves as beaten, all of us were filled with a steadfast spirit, full of unshaken confidence in ourselves and the coming day, and we spoke a good deal with each other.'[10] These accounts probably contain a good measure of self-justification and exaggeration, but there is no doubt that the bulk of the Prussian army did withdraw in good order, despite the severity of the fighting at Ligny, and that the retreat was well managed. A large body of fugitives – perhaps 8,000 or 10,000 men – fled eastwards, away from the main army. These were mostly recruits from Prussia's new provinces, like those who had so diluted and weakened Nagel's regiment, so their loss probably did the army little real harm.

In other battles the retreat of the defeated army was affected by a variety of local circumstances. At Aspern-Essling, Friedland and Leipzig, the retreat was complicated by a major river close to the rear and problems with the bridges. The French managed this best at Aspern-Essling, where the fighting had not gone too badly against them, but at Leipzig, where they had been thoroughly beaten, the bridge was blown up prematurely, leaving many thousands of French troops, some still in good order, on the far bank, unable to make their escape. At Salamanca, Clausel was able to buy time for the flight of his broken divisions by deploying Ferey's division in a strong position as a rearguard. In the process Ferey's men lost heavily, and though they commenced their retreat, when the time came, in fairly good order, they soon dissolved into the general rout; but presumably their sacrifice was worth it, for otherwise Wellington might have taken thousands more prisoners, and pressed the retreating army much more closely.

Two contrasting examples from Austerlitz show the importance of the leadership provided by subordinate commanders. The force under the Austrian General Kienmayer and the Russian General Dokhturov, part of the most southerly allied column, made a skilful fighting retreat from Tellnitz, falling back in good order over the frozen Satschan Pond towards Neudorf. They lost some of their artillery, equipment and prisoners and suffered casualties from French fire, but they remained a respectable force. The much larger allied force under General Buxhöwden was less fortunate. Partly this was a matter of luck – it was under more pressure from the French, and its line of retreat was more difficult – but it was also due to bad management. An attempt to cross a rickety bridge over the Littawa failed when the bridge collapsed under the weight of guns and caissons, leaving most of the troops on the north bank, though their commander had already crossed. Some of the Russians made their way across the frozen pond, a few were drowned when the ice broke, and many were captured by the French. One of Alexander's ministers, Prince Czartoryski, encountered Buxhöwden at the end of the day: 'The poor general had lost his hat, and his uniform was in disarray. As soon as he caught sight of me he cried out, "I've been abandoned! I've been sacrificed!"' His troops might have said the same, with much more reason.[11]

The French did not effectively pursue the broken allied army after Austerlitz. Most French troops camped on or just beyond the battlefield; Bagration's corps disengaged itself from its battle with Lannes and retreated without harassment across the face of Bernadotte's I Corps. Murat received no orders from Napoleon to launch a pursuit, or even to observe the line which the allies were taking. As a result the French completely lost contact with the broken army, and for some hours on the following day believed that it was heading in a wholly different direction from its main line of retreat. Almost exactly the same thing happened, with much more serious consequences, after Ligny, when the French not only failed to pursue the Prussians on the night of 16 June – which was understandable – but wasted many hours on the morning of the 17th.

In fact, sustained pursuits were extremely rare, the two best examples being after Jena and Waterloo. Several reasons can be suggested for this: the victorious army was often, though not always, exhausted by the battle; dark was falling, and in the confusion the risk of 'friendly fire' and other accidents increased sharply. The triumphant general was often worn out by the stress and strain of the day, and was unable or unwilling to summon the mental energy needed to organize fresh movements. After Austerlitz, Napoleon rode slowly over the battlefield with Berthier, Soult and the staff, giving some help to the wounded they encountered. They then crowded into a small post house which the Russians had used as a dressing station, dried their clothes by the fire, and had some food. Napoleon began to compose a proclamation to the army, but was too weary to finish even this relatively simple and gratifying task. Nor was organizing a pursuit easy, for the general would not know where many of his units were, nor how much they had suffered, and would only be receiving the first – often confused and inaccurate – reports of the enemy's retreat.[12]

Yet an effective pursuit was the best possible way of converting a retreat into a rout. Troops would not rally if they felt threatened, while even those who began the retreat in good order were likely to panic if they were harassed and harried in their march. This was above all the forte of light cavalry, who could easily outpace men on foot and take advantage of any disorder. A few regiments of hussars could collect thousands of prisoners and spread fear and dismay through the countryside; while by giving the enemy no time to rally they might ensure the almost complete dispersal of his army.

In the absence of an effective pursuit, several other factors helped to determine the severity of a defeat. One was, of course, the nature of the battle. After a very hard-fought action in which casualties were high, many units were broken and the cohesion of the whole army was shaken, it might dissolve completely under the stress of a retreat. Yet this did not always happen, as the Russians after Eylau and Borodino, the Austrians after Wagram, and the French after Albuera, show – for in all these cases the defeated army withdrew in fairly good order. This was much more difficult if its line had been ruptured, as at Austerlitz and Salamanca, though Ligny shows that it could be done.

The underlying spirit of the troops was as important as the events of the battle and the existence of pursuit. This spirit was not quite the same as the quality of the soldiers. Tactical precision and knowledge of drill were at a discount in the confusion of a retreat, and determination and experience had become more significant than confidence. At Alba de Tormes in 1809 an inexperienced Spanish army suffered what should have been a fairly slight defeat; but the shock of battle acting on poor troops, compounded by a night march, led to the almost complete dissolution of the army. By contrast, Blücher's army of 1813–15 was repeatedly beaten, but never really broken. It was protected in its early defeats by the weakness of Napoleon's cavalry, but it soon developed a dogged spirit and trust in its commander which lost battles could not shake. The Prussian infantry of these years were not nearly such good soldiers as Wellington's Peninsular veterans, yet it may be doubted if the latter could have sustained their morale so well in the face of adversity. For them, defeat in battle was unheard of and would have shaken their confidence to the core, while the Prussians had experienced it before, and knew that it was not the end of the world, nor even of the war.

The experience of retreat varied widely. Despite his injuries, Blücher remained cheerful after Ligny: 'We have taken a few knocks and shall have to hammer out the dents!' His mood may have been helped by the bottle of champagne he had drunk, but it was widespread in the army. 'Shortly after midnight,' Christian Nagel writes, 'we decamped; it appeared the enemy was approaching. At the village of Tilly we encountered troops around invigorating fires, near which we also encamped. That did us good; soon I lay fast asleep. Towards daybreak everything was again in movement and after covering several miles, all the troops bivouacked near the town of Wavre, where Blücher had his main headquarters.' While Lieutenant Reuter writes that

> During the course of the night this rear-guard . . . continued its retreat unmo-
> lested by the enemy, crossed the Dyle on the 17th at Wavre, and there we again
> found our baggage. During the retreat I had the good fortune to be able to horse
> three guns of Meyer's battery which I found on the road unable to get along,
> and drew them off with me. Yet Captain Meyer, annoyed at still having to leave
> three of his guns behind, was extremely rude to me because I could help him no
> further.[13]

Blücher was hardened to war and his defeat at Ligny did not deprive him of hope, but for the Emperor Alexander, Austerlitz was a crushing disappointment. He was observed riding across the battlefield, attended only by his surgeon and groom. After a while he dismounted, covered his face with a cloth, and burst into tears. Major Toll rode up and tried to offer some consolation; Alexander pulled himself together, silently embraced Toll and rode forward. They found Kutusov at the village of Hodiegitz, which was full of wounded soldiers and confusion. After a brief conference Alexander hurried on, through the darkness and rain, for another seven miles. Here he collapsed on a pile of straw in a peasant's hut and was helped to sleep by exhaustion, a dose of camomile and opium, and some wine.[14]

For ordinary soldiers a rout was a terrifying as well as a miserable experience. A French officer describes the scene after Salamanca:

> a shapeless mass of soldiery was rolling down the road like a torrent – infantry,
> cavalry, artillery, waggons, carts, baggage-mules, the reserve park of the artillery
> drawn by oxen, were all mixed up. The men, shouting, swearing, running, were
> out of all order, each one looking after himself alone – a complete stampede. The
> panic was inexplicable to one who, coming from the extreme rear, knew that
> there was no pursuit by the enemy to justify the terror shown. I had to stand off
> far from the road, for if I had got near it, I should have been swept off by the
> torrent in spite of myself.[15]

And a Prussian prisoner caught up in the rout after Waterloo writes,

The things I witnessed exceeded anything I had expected, and were beyond belief. Had I not actually seen it all, I should have considered it impossible for a disciplined army – an army such as the French was – to melt away to such an extent. Not only the main road, as far as one could see in either direction, but also every road and footpath was covered with soldiers of every rank, of every arm of the service, in the most complete and utter confusion. Generals, officers, wounded men – and these included some who had just had limbs amputated: everybody walked or rode in disorder. The entire army had disintegrated. There was no longer anyone to give orders, or anyone to obey. Each man appeared bent on nothing but saving his own skin. Like a turbulent forest stream this chaotic mass surged around the waggon in which I was sitting with several companions in misfortune. . . .

. . . very occasionally someone would shout to us: '*Sauvez-vous!* We are lost! Thank God we shall have peace at long last! We shall be going home!' Several times the cry came up from the rear 'He's coming! The enemy's coming! *Sauve qui peut!*' and then everyone ran in desperate haste. Some threw down their weapons, others their knapsacks, and they took refuge in the corn or behind hedges, until the reassuring shout of: 'No, no, it's all right! They're our own men!' calmed the panic.

A single cavalry regiment could have taken many thousands of prisoners here, because there was no question of offering resistance or of sticking together. Along this road I saw no guns at all, though near Beaumont a solitary cannon lay abandoned. Even in Beaumont there were no longer any regular authorities, as they had all fled.[16]

Even the most senior officers could get caught up in the confusion, and be torn between the desire to save themselves and a sense of responsibility towards their men. Marshal Macdonald recalls his experiences after Leipzig:

I escaped . . . with a firm resolve not to fall alive into the hands of the enemy, preferring to shoot or drown myself. Dragged along, as I have said, by the crowd, I crossed two little arms of the Elster, the first on a little bridge, holding on to the hand-rail, for my feet did not touch the boards (I was lifted up, and ten times over was nearly upset); the other upon a horse, lent me by a quartermaster, whose name I am sorry to have forgotten, though I have since rendered him a service.

I found myself in an open field, still surrounded by the crowd; I wandered about, it still followed me, convinced that I must know a way out, though I could find none marked on my map. There was still the main arm of the river to cross. Lauriston, who had been with me before we crossed the streams, was separated from me.

Some of Prince Poniatowski's aides-de-camp came and told me he was drowned; I still thought he was behind me. . . .

. . . one of my aides-de-camp, Beurnonville, seized my bridle and said:

'Monsieur le Maréchal, we cannot help that; the important thing is to save you.'

Thereupon he hurried me away at a gallop to free me from the unhappy crowd that still surrounded me, and told me that Colonel Marion, who commanded the engineers in my army corps, had succeeded in crossing to the other side. He had had two trees cut down and thrown across the river, joining them with doors, shutters, and planks. We hastened thither, but the place was blocked by troops. I was told that Marshals Augereau and Victor had crossed this frail structure on horseback, notwithstanding all the representations that were made to them; that as the extremities were not fastened, the two trees had slipped apart, the flooring had given way. There remained nothing but the two trunks, and no one dared cross them.

It was my only chance; I made up my mind and risked it. I got off my horse with great difficulty, owing to the crowd, and there I was, one foot on either trunk, and the abyss below me. A high wind was blowing. I was wearing a large cloak with loose sleeves, and, fearing lest someone should lay hold of it, I got rid of it. I had already made three-quarters of my way across, when some men determined to follow me; their unsteady feet caused the trunks to shake, and I fell into the water. I could fortunately touch the bottom, but the bank was steep, the soil loose and greasy; I vainly struggled to reach the shore. Some of the enemy's skirmishers came up, I know not whence. They fired at me point-blank, and missed me, and some of our men, who happened to be near, drove them off and helped me out.

I was wet from head to foot, besides being in a violent perspiration from my efforts, and out of breath. The Duke of Ragusa [Marshal Marmont], who had got across early in the day, seeing me on the other bank, gave me a horse; I wanted dry clothes more, but they were not to be had.

One of my grooms, named Naudet, who had charge of my pocket-book, not daring to come across, confided it to a soldier, who undressed and swam with it. I had no money to give him. Marshal Marmont lent me his purse, and I gave it to the man. He accompanied us, naked as he was, for three leagues, and I was still dripping. . . .

. . . On the other side of the Elster the firing continued; it suddenly ceased. Our unhappy troops were crowded together on the river-bank; whole companies plunged into the water and were carried away; cries of despair rose on all sides. The men perceived me. Despite the noise and tumult, I distinctly heard these words:

'Monsieur le Maréchal, save your men! save your children!'

I could do nothing for them! Overcome by rage, indignation, fury, I wept![17]

Chapter Thirteen
After the Fighting

On the evening after a battle, as the defeated army fled through the night in fear and confusion, the victors usually camped on or near the battlefield, exhausted, emotionally drained, but elated by their success and filled with relief. One British officer wrote on the day after Waterloo, 'I am so hoarse from hurraing all yesterday, that I can scarcely articulate. I have been four days without washing face or hands, but am in hourly expectation of my lavender water, etc. I am very tired.' Most wants were rather less sophisticated than lavender water, and one rifleman's account shows how he and his comrades savoured the taste of another victory:

> As soon as our fires were lighted, the men, who had been under arms from three o'clock in the morning until eleven at night, and consequently had not tasted food for the whole of the day, began to fill their hungry maws from the luxuries of the French camp. Roast fowls, hams, mutton, etc., were in abundance, and at midnight the wine and brandy went round in horn tots which we generally carried about us. The men mostly lay stretched on the ground, their feet towards the fires, and elbows resting on their knapsacks; as soon as the grog began to rouse up their spirits from the effects of the day's fatigue each one commenced enquiries about absent comrades, for riflemen in action, being always extended, seldom know who falls until the affray is over.[1]

Such talk was not limited to skirmishers. On the day before Waterloo, the British Life Guards had been in the thick of the small combat at Genappe. That night a number of them, together with some of their officers, crowded into a house to keep out of the rain. Their surgeon was among them, and he noticed that the soldiers, despite the presence of their officers, soon 'talked freely and fully over the business of Genappe among each other, and related many anecdotes of great exploits, heroic stands, and indeed even comical occurrences in the heat of battle, which passed away a weary night in a situation in which no one could sleep'.[2]

On the night after Salamanca the British Sixth Division, which had taken a prominent role in the fighting and suffered heavy casualties, was on the point of collapsing with exhaustion when ordered to halt and camp. Nonetheless the men 'sat up through the night talking over the action, each recalling to his comrade events that had happened'. According to Kincaid,

> There is nothing in this life half so enviable as the feelings of a soldier after a victory. Previous to a battle, there is a certain sort of something that pervades the mind which is not easily defined; it is neither akin to joy or fear, and, probably, *anxiety* may be nearer to it than any other word in the dictionary; but, when the battle is over, and crowned with victory, he finds himself elevated for a while into the regions of absolute bliss![3]

This was not always the case. Few on the British side felt any jubilation on the morning after Waterloo: such feelings were deadened by exhaustion, the savagery of the battle, and the extent of the losses, so that even Wellington, hardened by war and clear-sighted as always, admitted to being quite broken down, and having 'no feeling for the advantages we have acquired'. After a successful skirmish in front of Salamanca in 1813 – the first fighting of the year's campaign – Sir Augustus Frazer found himself sickened by war:

> In the evening there was an illumination I am told; but I was tired and went to bed, though not without some sorrowful ideas at the sight I had witnessed. There was not even the false emotion of honour where there was no danger, and to slaughter flying enemies, though duty requires it, is nevertheless shocking. I spoke to many of the wounded: none uttered a complaint.[4]

Such unhappiness was naturally more common after a defeat, and the feelings of Captain Hodenberg of the Heavy Dragoons of the King's German Legion on the night following their unsuccessful combat at Venta del Pozo must have been experienced by other officers and men on many such occasions:

> A more unhappy night than that after the combat I have never spent. Every nerve had been strained during the day: I had fought as hard as any other of my brother officers, and exerted every faculty of mind to keep up the spirits of the men. A total relaxation, mental as well as bodily, was the consequence, which, impressed with our severe misfortunes, produced in me the deepest melancholy. I had, besides lost all my baggage, servants, and horses, and had literally nothing left, save the clothes that I wore and the horse that I rode. To this was added the total want of food for the last twenty-four hours, and a miserable cold night under the ruins of a house, without even a fire to keep us from shivering.[5]

On the following morning active operations would resume, though with a difference, as the result of the battle had affected the relative strength and confidence of the armies. According to Kincaid, the day after an inconclusive victory such as Fuentes 'is always one of intense interest. The movements on each side are most jealously watched, and each side is most diligently occupied in strengthening such points as the fight of the preceding day had proved to be most vulnerable.' A more decisive victory produced another, perhaps surprising result, which Kincaid also records with characteristic jauntiness:

> I do not know how it is, but I have always had a mortal objection to be killed the day after a victory. In the actions preceding a battle, or in the battle itself, it never gave me much uneasiness, as being all in the way of business; but, after surviving the great day, I always felt as if I had a right to live to tell the story; and I, therefore, did not find the ensuing three days' fighting half so pleasant as they would otherwise have been.

Edward Costello felt much the same, and with a rather more substantial reason, for he had acquired a great sum of money in the plundering after Vitoria. On the following day: 'About twelve o'clock we marched in pursuit of the enemy through the town of Salvatierra, many of our men gibing me for my wealth, saying, among other agreeable things, that if I fell they would take care of my knapsack for me. To tell the truth, I was not over-anxious to go much to the front, as I began to look on my life as of some value.'[6]

The plundering after Vitoria was quite extraordinary; unlike that following any other battle in Europe in the period, for the French army had been escorting convoys carrying the produce of five years' systematic looting, and all this was abandoned as they fled. Wellington hoped that some at least of this booty would be secured officially and be used to pay off part of the army's arrears, but for once he was shown to be hopelessly naive. Soldiers who had endured years of privation had no hesitation in making the most of the windfall, and if the resulting distribution was grossly inequitable, so were most aspects of their lives, not least the distribution of wounds and death on the battlefield. Costello probably did as well as any private soldier, for he took possession of 'a small but exceedingly heavy portmanteau' which proved to contain silver and gold to the value of about £1,000. This chest was too heavy to carry, and in getting assistance from a sergeant and two men of the 10th Hussars he nearly lost the whole, once they realized the value of the load. But Costello was not to be done out of 'the only prize I had made after years of hardship and suffering' – especially by men from a regiment which had just joined the army – and he seized his rifle and successfully intimidated the three hussars, loaded his treasure on a mule and made his way back to the regiment without further adventure. Here he was faced with a dilemma, for there was nowhere for him to deposit his loot in safety. In the end he entrusted £300 to the quartermaster, several sums to other officers and distributed the remainder of the silver, perhaps £100, among the men of his own squad: 'very little of the latter, however, I ever received back. But after all money, as may be imagined, was of very little use during some of the hardships we afterwards endured . . . I frequently offered a doubloon for a single glass of rum, and was not always able to obtain it.'[7]

Costello was prudent in the management of his windfall, but lucky to be allowed to keep it. No regimental commander seems to have been so foolish as to attempt to strip his men of their plunder – which would surely have risked a mutiny – but several ensured that the treasure was shared equally throughout the regiment. Thus Colonel Hervey realized that while most of the 14th Light Dragoons had kept in the ranks, done their duty, and gained little or nothing, the farriers were gorged with loot. This he appropriated and divided among the whole regiment, 'to the joy and glee of the whole corps, who were justly entitled to it'.[8]

Another senior officer, Sir James Kempt, apprehended a soldier plundering one of the French wagons, and was going to send him to the rear as a prisoner, when the man begged to be allowed to go his way with his loot, telling Kempt that the remaining boxes in the wagon were all filled with gold. At this Kempt let him go and secured the wagon with a substantial guard for the benefit of his whole brigade. Unfortunately, morning revealed that the boxes contained nothing but hammers, nails and horseshoes![9]

Over the next day or two a giant impromptu market was held where the allied soldiers sold off the loot which they could neither consume nor carry away. No one seems to have questioned their title to the goods, and neither the local Spanish civilian population, nor the officers of the army, showed any hesitation in buying. Fine horses, mules, carriages, clothes, assorted trinkets and other bric-à-brac were all sold ridiculously cheaply, for a quick sale was imperative. Soon the army resumed its march, pursuing Joseph's army past Pamplona, penetrating into the Pyrenees, where it would spend most of the next eight months experiencing much fighting and great hardship. The memory of those extravagant, bacchanalian, never to be repeated hours after Vitoria may have sustained many who, unlike Costello, gained nothing lasting and tangible from the victory.

Vitoria was unique, but plundering on a lesser scale was common after all battles of the period. Nor was it only camp followers, stragglers, farriers and local peasants who collected what they could find after – or even during – the battle. Soldiers from all units took part, and Rifleman Harris has no hesitation in admitting that after Vimeiro, 'I strolled about the field in order to see if there was anything to be found worth picking up amongst the dead.' He found a silver fork, probably dropped by an earlier looter, but would not touch some rich gold and silver crosses in a dying French soldier's pack. 'He looked the picture of a sacrilegious thief, dying hopelessly, and overtaken by Divine wrath. . . . I felt fearful of incurring the wrath of Heaven for the like offence, so left him, and passed on.' He found the body of an officer of the 50th Regiment, quite dead and already plundered, but whose shoes were better than Harris's, and so the corpse was robbed of its footwear. A French soldier – either one of the wounded or a fellow looter – fired at him, and Harris fired back, killing the Frenchman.

Not surprisingly, Harris shows no compunction over this, though he admits that it was a relief to be sure that the man he had shot was indeed French, not British. Such 'after-hours' murders must have been common, though they would have added comparatively little to the day's casualties.[10]

Harris was not unusual in appropriating the equipment and possessions of comrades who had fallen, and such incidents range from the outrageous to the distasteful, to the perfectly inoffensive. There could be no objection to a soldier with a fouled musket using that of a wounded or dead comrade; while a dead officer's kit was routinely auctioned off to his fellow officers, the proceeds going to his family. When a freshly joined soldier on Wheeler's left was killed, Wheeler quickly took possession of his new kit, reflecting that 'Exchange is no robbery.' Equally practical but much less acceptable was Sergeant Cooper's conduct after Toulouse: 'Having had several of my accoutrements stolen, I went among the dead to select such as I wanted. One of the 42nd, or Highland Watch, had a belt that suited me. Though he was not quite dead I stripped him of it.' After this, one is almost pleased to read that Rifleman Orr, caught when trying to sell a ring which had belonged to Captain Daniel Cadoux of his regiment, was sentenced to 500 lashes. Dead men's shoes are bad enough, but adding to the pain of a dying man by rolling him about in order to steal his belt or ring is beyond the pale.[11]

According to Kincaid, a horse was the only thing that an officer could regard as a legitimate prize – though even this was in flagrant contravention of several General Orders, which stipulated that all captured horses, mules and bullocks should be offered for sale to the Commissary General. Although he did not mention it, Kincaid would certainly not have objected to the acquisition of food and other supplies – indeed advancing troops often benefited from the culinary preparations of those forced to retreat. Yet he would not have approved of the transfer of money, watches and other such valuables from a prisoner to an officer, though ordinary soldiers would certainly despoil prisoners of all these and more. Probably not all officers were so scrupulous, but Kincaid does seem to represent the general British view. Colonel Landmann went even further, when at Vimeiro he took the money belts of two captured French officers into safe custody, his name and reputation in the army serving as guarantee of their return, as soon as the prisoners could be sure of retaining them.[12]

Surprisingly, military decorations seem to have been regarded more equivo-cally, as legitimate, or almost legitimate, trophies. We have already seen how Captain Jones of the 52nd cut down a French officer and appropriated his medal at Busaco (see above, p. 186). Captain Verner took a French officer prisoner at Waterloo, and protected him from soldiers who were going to pillage him. 'The officer had an order on his breast, which I felt anxious to obtain, but I did not like to take it, as I thought it might hurt his feelings, altho' I felt confident he would not be permitted to retain it.' Sir Augustus Frazer had similar scruples. He had attended to General Sarrut, who had been badly wounded and captured at Vitoria, and on the following day wrote home, 'General Sarrut is dead. Poor man!! I wish now I had taken his decoration of the Legion of Honour, but though I saw it, the general thanked me so warmly, and squeezed my hand with such earnestness, that I felt it would have been ungenerous to have taken the prize.' But Captain Kelly of the Life Guards, who killed a French officer on the day before Waterloo, did not hesitate to cut off his epaulettes as a souvenir.[13]

Prisoners were generally resigned to losing their valuables – although not while they were under the protection of an officer of Frazer's rank. Such losses mattered comparatively little, if they survived and were not physically ill-treated. Surrendering in the heat of battle has always been dangerous and uncertain; and whatever high-minded laws of war may say, in practice it has always been a privilege, not a right. During the storm of Ciudad Rodrigo, Kincaid saw a considerable body of enemy soldiers who had thrown down their arms and were endeavouring to surrender, calling out that they were only 'Pauvres Italianos'. However for some reason the British troops had 'imbibed a horrible antipathy to the Italians, and every appeal they made in that name was invariably answered with, – "You're Italians, are you? then d—n you, here's a shot for you"; and the action instantly followed the word.'[14]

A sense of reciprocity was a key element in creating the willingness to take prisoners, and the good humour that generally pervaded battles between the British and French served both sides well in this respect. Troops were always wild after carrying a fortress by storm, and enemy soldiers – whether of Italian, French or any other nationality – were in great jeopardy in the hours following the fall of Ciudad Rodrigo, Badajoz or San Sebastian. On the other hand, troops who capitulated by a negotiated convention were usually safe – although Dupont's army was illegally detained and treated very badly after Bailen.

In a number of cases the ire of British troops was aroused by a perception that the French had not fought fairly, and the word would pass through the ranks of a regiment, either before or during a battle, to take no prisoners. We have already seen that this was the reaction among some British cavalry to the shooting of one of their number when he was trapped under his fallen horse at Waterloo (see above, p. 225). On the retreat to Torres Vedras in 1810, Charles Cocks wrote home: 'We charged the enemy with a few of our rearguard, in the river, and nearly took the colonel of the French dragoons. I hope we shall come across that regiment again; they refused quarter to one of our hussars and we mean to pay them.' Cocks evidently had his wish, for three days later, after another skirmish, he noted in his journal:

When they have the worst of it the French cavalry have a way which must not be allowed. They cry for pardon but still keep galloping to the rear, or perhaps throw themselves on the ground, and it is impossible to get the prisoners off when you are certain of being attacked yourself by a superior force. We were obliged to cut down or shoot several who did this.

And in Egypt in 1801, the 42nd Highlanders refused quarter after one of their men had been killed while burying a French corpse.[15]

In many battles the cry went up that enemy skirmishers were pretending to be dead or wounded, waiting till the advancing troops had passed them, and then firing into their rear. This seems rather fanciful – some skirmishers probably did take such refuge, but why then draw attention to themselves by firing? – and such fire may often have really been stray shots from friendly troops; but in the heat of the moment the cry was believed, and many wounded men were bayoneted to death on this pretext.[16]

Knowing all this, an officer or soldier who was compelled to attempt to surrender on a battlefield had good grounds for apprehension, but sometimes there was little choice. Captain Dyneley was forced to make the attempt after his detachment of guns was overrun in the petty disaster of Majadahonda, and despite some travails he lived to describe the experience in a long, lively letter to his mother and sisters. The Portuguese cavalry had broken, and Dyneley and his gunners were fleeing to the rear:

At this time I was galloping about a dozen yards in rear of the last gun, and had continued about a quarter of a mile further when, whether my horse made a trip, or whether one of the cowardly scoundrels [the Portuguese dragoons] in crossing upset him, I know not, but certain it is that we came head over heels together, and away he went leaving me upon the ground. I was hurt a little by the fall and had one of my shoes nearly torn off my foot. How I escaped being ridden over I know not, for the dust was so great that it was impossible to see a yard before one; however, as soon as I had got upon my feet and had run about 50 yards, I found the enemy had got in upon one of our right guns, and I saw them cut the drivers from their horses. I thought I had no business there and so ran on and came upon the second right gun which the French had been at; the three drivers were lying dead by their horses' side. I then returned, when I discovered the gun I had left was not in the hands of the enemy but had been upset, and our poor fellows, my friend Bombardier Morgan at their head, had dismounted to right it. I went towards them, but before I had gone many yards, I heard a terrible shriek of '*Avanti, Avanti ah traditor inglese,*' I looked behind me and discovered about four squadrons not more than 50 yards in my rear. The officer commanding them rode and made a cut at me but I made my bow and escaped. As soon as he could pull up his horse he came at me again. When I saw this I sang out '*Ufficiale inglese prigioniere,*' he then came up brandishing his sword over my head, saying '*Mi dia la sua spada, Mi dia la sua spada,*' all I had to say on this subject was '*si, si, si*'. As soon as he had taken it from me, he opened the pocket of the sabretasche in which were a few old morning states, my tourniquet, and a letter from Moseley, telling me of the death of Mr Hawkes, and troubling me for £16 12s. 4d. This the fellow seemed very much pleased with (if you ever saw one of Hawkes' bills you will remember they are very fine) and he gave me in charge to a dragoon and rode off, thinking, I suppose, he had at least made a lord prisoner.

As soon as the officer was gone, my guard, with the assistance of two others, set to plunder me. When these fellows first came up they made a cut or two at me but missed, and then brought up with '*deme sua denaro*'. I put my hands into my pockets and brought out 12 dollars, which I divided between them. They then said '*moire*' (more), I said I had no more, upon which they felt outside my pockets, and pulled my cravat about and off, then they sat still and left me alone. I went to the gun and was trying to unhook one of the leading horses in order to make my escape to the right, as they had gone to the left, but I was detected in the act by three Polish lancers, who came galloping down upon me; the instant they arrived they put their lances to my chest and demanded my money. I said I had none, they told me to give it them directly or they would put me to death, I again said I had none, they asked me if I had a watch, I said 'yes'. At this moment two fresh fellows arrived, and the whole five from their horses made a dash at me for my time-piece, one of them put his hand into my pantaloon pocket in which was the silver pencil-case Charles gave me, my pocket comb and lip-salve box Dora gave me. The fellow having grasped his booty, could not get his hand out again, and he more than once lifted me off my feet; at last he extricated himself by tearing my pocket entirely out. Finding they had not got my watch, they returned and succeeded in getting it, and made off with it, previously agreeing to share it amongst the five. They had no sooner left me than two other fellows came up with '*deme sua denaro*'. I told them that I had given it all up and turned my pockets out to show them. They said I had more. I said 'no', upon which they commenced thrashing me across the shoulders with the flat of their swords; when they found they could get nothing, one of them said '*deme sua vestita*' (my jacket). I said I was an English officer and had no other; they appeared a little ashamed and rode off.

A staff officer then rode up and asked me what country I came from? 'England,' says I, 'signor', which seemed to please him mightily, and he took me off to a General officer who was near at the time, who addressed me in English – at least, it was nearer our language than any other. He asked me what cavalry we had in the field, I said 8,000; he told me I had told a lie and desired I would speak the truth. I said that Lord Wellington had that number with him, but that perhaps he had not at that moment more than 3,000 in the field, (though I knew his Lordship had not more than the latter number altogether with this part of the army). The General then rode away shaking his fingers at me and saying I was a bad one.

I was then given in charge to one of his orderlies to be marched to the rear. He had not taken me above 100 yards before he desired me to give up my spurs, a very favourite pair Bertie Cator gave me many years ago at Malta; by the time I had got them off, up came all the poor fellows belonging to our guns, some of them most dreadfully mangled. Though we were all sorry to find ourselves in such a situation, yet we were naturally happy to be together. At this moment a General rode across near me, and I called to him to allow his surgeon to dress my wounded, which he instantly consented to do and I got them bound up as comfortably as I could expect; one poor fellow, a corporal, had nine wounds. I had him dressed first and laid aside, and was attending to another, when the corporal called to me to say he was dying and that a Frenchman was stripping him. I looked round and there the fellow was pulling his boots off; he paid no attention to what I said, and I suppose if I had said much more he would soon have had mine off.

Well, having got the worst of them dressed we marched off to a village (I do not remember the name) about two leagues from the field. On the road there I got most completely knocked up and made Bombardier Morgan give me his arm; however, I soon found I could go but little further and the sentry behind me kept constantly hitting me with the butt-end of his musket with '*allons! allons! coquin*,' I thought then how Richard Hill [his brother-in-law] would have laughed if he could have seen Master Tom kicked along in that way. At last a dragoon took compassion on me and lugged me along by one hand while Morgan kept the other side up. On our march, I told Morgan in confidence, I intended to make my escape the very first opportunity and that I would take him with me, for which purpose he had better act as my servant; he was delighted with the idea and said he would come into any plan I wished.[17]

After many further hardships and some surprising encounters – including one with the English wife of a Dutch general in the French army, who carried 'an old Twining's tea-canister' with her – Dyneley and Morgan did manage to make their escape, and were back with the army only a week after they had been captured.

Other accounts tell much the same story, except that relatively few prisoners managed to escape. Charles Napier was captured at Coruña after being seriously wounded. One French, or rather Italian, soldier made a determined effort to kill him after he had surrendered, and was only thwarted by the interference of a French drummer. Even so, he might not have survived that night if it had not been for the care of an Irish soldier who had also been taken prisoner. Thereafter Napier was treated extremely well, and was released a couple of months later by Marshal Ney, together with twenty-five badly wounded British soldiers.[18]

Captain Brotherton was captured in December 1813 when he became isolated in a mêlée. He received three wounds, and would have suffered more if he had not been wearing a stout leather cuirass which he had had made after being wounded in the previous year. His greatest difficulty in surrendering was that he had twisted his silk sword knot round and round his wrist before charging, and so found it almost impossible to give up his sword. He seems to have been rather better treated than Napier or Dyneley and a French surgeon, finding a money bag round his neck, tried to conceal it, but Brotherton insisted that it be given to the soldiers who had captured him, 'whose lawful prize it was'. By this time a regular system of exchanging captured officers between the two armies was well established, so Brotherton's captivity should have been brief – Wellington tried to organize an exchange the next day – but for some reason the French refused to release him, and he was detained for several months.[19]

If unable to escape and not exchanged, British and French prisoners could expect long years of captivity in harsh prison camps or the hulks. French officers in Britain were often given great freedom in return for their parole or pledge of honour not to escape, a trust which was sometimes abused. The conditions for the ordinary prisoners, especially those detained in the hulks, were deplorable; though little or no worse than those endured by criminals. Their greatest trial was the length of their captivity, for while Napoleon's wars with the Continental Powers were generally concluded within a few months or years, and prisoners on both sides were released, the Anglo-French war dragged on continuously from 1803 to 1814. There were some negotiations in 1810 for a wholesale exchange of prisoners (including Spanish, Portuguese and those of other allies on both sides), but, although the terms proposed strongly favoured France, Napoleon would not agree, and the talks came to nothing.[20]

In general, Britain and France treated each other's prisoners fairly well. Once their surrender had been accepted and they had been pillaged of their valuables, most prisoners were not further maltreated, and the wounded were looked after with as much care as circumstances allowed. Standards always fell when an army was defeated and forced to retreat: soldiers were more hostile to their captives, less able or willing to help them, and long marches with few supplies were often necessary. The suffering of Captain Dyneley and his men was exacerbated by these conditions. After Waterloo, however, things were very much worse, partly, perhaps, because of the merciless Prussian pursuit, and partly for other reasons. British prisoners were given few supplies, were cruelly ill-treated, and, when they could no longer keep up with the French columns, some were shot in cold blood.[21]

Such behaviour was not unusual in some parts of the war, especially in Spain and Russia. In 1813 a British officer wrote in all seriousness that the guerrilla leader Mina was said to be 'very merciful and never kills Prisoners unless they are badly wounded'. Even when most of Spain had been liberated and the guerrillas had been incorporated into the regular army, the same 'mercy' prevailed. 'The Garrison of Saragossa marched past here and the Officers said four Men had been shot that Morning. They consult the Surgeon if a Prisoner knocks up, who at once passes Sentence as we do on a Glandered Horse.' The army was not in retreat, no enemy forces were in pursuit, and there was no necessity for such conduct, but the Spaniards had much to revenge. As early as January 1809, Rocca records that prisoners taken at the Battle of Ucles, who were too weak to keep up with the column, were shot; and the French justified this as retaliation for some of their men whom the Spaniards had hanged.[22]

In Russia, in 1812, while many prisoners were casually shot in this way, others were executed in a more organized fashion:

Yesterday such a transport of 400 prisoners passed us, escorted by Italians of the Second Regiment, who have carried out these military executions. The Commandant at Dorogobuz allowed thirty prisoners to be shot while we were there, because being ill they could go no further. That the Russians would be justified in taking reprisals upon the prisoners they take from us appears to have struck nobody.[23]

In fact, the Russians had already begun to retaliate in kind for the violence the French had brought to their country, and as Napoleon's forces retreated, immense numbers of prisoners fell into their hands. One Russian officer recorded their fate with dismay in his diary: 'these poor people can scarcely drag themselves along; they are escorted by cossacks who kill them with lances the moment they no longer have the power to walk'. 'All this disorder is accompanied by cossacks constantly slogging prisoners with a knout and calling out: "Allo, marcher, Camerade!"' 'I saw a French prisoner sold to peasants for twenty rubles; they baptized him with boiling tar and impaled him alive on a piece of pointed iron.'[24]

Such refinements of cruelty were generally the work of irregulars and outraged civilians, rather than professional soldiers, and had little or no place on the battlefield. There are however a number of reports – though not involving the British, or the French fighting them – of professional officers issuing explicit orders to their troops to take no prisoners. At Ligny, Lieutenant-General François Roguet of the Imperial Guard is reported to have told his grenadiers 'that the first man to bring me a Prussian prisoner will be shot'; while Thiébault unblushingly records in his memoirs that at Austerlitz he ordered his men not to take any prisoners or leave any wounded enemy behind them, and that this order was strictly followed until the last hour of the battle. Fortunately it seems likely that such statements are exaggerated. At Austerlitz, the French took no fewer than 11,500 allied soldiers prisoner, while the defeated allies managed to secure 573 French captives. And though the casualty figures for the battles in central and eastern Europe are not generally detailed or reliable, they do not indicate any wholesale killing of the wounded.[25]

In the evening, after the fighting had stopped, the battlefield would be covered with wreckage. A battle with 100,000 combatants – which was by no means particularly large – might easily produce 10–12,000 casualties. Of these 1,500 or 2,000 would be killed outright or die on the field of their wounds, but this left 9–10,000 maimed and bleeding men scattered over a few square miles. In addition to the men there would probably be several thousand horses, some dead, some horribly wounded, others uncontrollably wild. Wandering over the battlefield would be a curious mixture of straggling soldiers looking for their unit, others intent on plunder, camp followers, soldiers' wives and local peasants intent on good or evil – or often a mixture of both. The cries of the wounded, the smell of blood, vomit and burnt flesh, and the thousand chance horrors of a face without a head, or a head without a face: there was no serenity, dignity or glory in the scene.

Some of the wounded had already been helped to dressing stations in the rear, some had made their own way back, and others remained on the field: there seems to be no way of telling which was the most common. All suffered dreadfully from the pain of their wounds, and from thirst caused by loss of blood. The experiences of Captain Barralier at Salamanca combine so many of the perils endured by the wounded that they are worth quoting at length. He had transferred from the 71st Highland Light Infantry into the Portuguese service, and joined his new regiment – the 23rd – just six days before the battle, and was wounded early in the action.

At this moment I received gun-shot wound which passed through both my thighs and scrotum. I fell to the ground. A sergeant and some men of my company remained by me for a moment, and I handed my sword to the sergeant, requesting him to give it to Colonel Stubbs, in order that it might be forwarded to my father. Then I sank back, not giving the least sign of life, I was abandoned and plundered, and the men reported me to Colonel Stubbs as dead. It might have been about four o'clock in the afternoon, when I somewhat recovered my senses, and found myself lying exposed to the fire of the 23rd Welch Fusiliers and the French. I was struck while in that position by a musket ball, which pierced my cap and grazed my forehead. Placing my hand on the part struck, no blood appeared of any consequence. Perceiving a hollow near me, I attempted to remove to it, but was unable from loss of blood and stiffness of my limbs, in this melancholy state I had to remain for nearly two hours, exposed to the fire of both friend and foe. A French cavalry regiment now passed me, and some of the horses actually leaped over me, but I received no injury. Soon after a French Infantry [battalion] in close column of companies passed; a French soldier placed his bayonet on my breast; I made the distress sign of a mason, and fortunately was instantly saved by a French officer, who pushed the bayonet away. Thus was my life most miraculously preserved. Half an hour after the French repassed, but in disorder, and I shortly saw the red coats approaching. I now felt sure of obtaining assistance. The regiment halted close by me, and I called out to the officers, that I was an officer of the 71st Highland Light Infantry, and begged to be removed from the field. It was the 23rd Welch Fusiliers, and several of the officers came up to me. They returned to the regiment, and a few minutes after a field officer and four or five other officers stood beside me. I told them who I was, and entreated to be removed, but I had the mortification of seeing the field officer face about, and call out 'Forward'. The officers and men called out shame, but the regiment moved to the front. Thus was I, a Captain in the same division as the Welch Fusiliers, left as a dog to perish for want of aid, by a man who could have had no feelings for a fellow creature. This was Brevet Lieutenant-Colonel Offley, who, I afterwards heard, very shortly met with his death.[26] My feelings now overcame me, and I know not how long I remained insensible. When I rallied, the action was still raging, but at some distance. I now observed a straggler passing at a few paces from me, and I beckoned to him, and on his coming up, asked him to remain by me. But the fellow thought I was a dying man, and expected plunder. He cocked his musket, and was in the act of dispatching me, notwithstanding that I kept telling him I was a Captain in his brigade (the straggler belonged to the 7th Caçadores). Instant death was before me, but Providence at that moment sent me aid. A British soldier of the 74th Regiment came up, and cried out, 'Is it you Mr Barralier?' My reply was, 'Yes my lad, shoot that villain.' He raised his musket, and I was instantly relieved from an assassin. The soldier of the 74th Regiment removed his knapsack, and placed it under my head, and covering me with his great coat and blanket, gave me water – all the poor fellow had. I begged him to remain by me; his reply was, 'Sir, my regiment is in action, and I must try and join.' But having assured him that he would not be punished for remaining with me, and that I would take all the responsibility, he did remain. This soldier had left England for Portugal in the same transport as myself, and was servant to Ensign Hamilton of the 74th Regiment. I kept calling for water, and as there was none at hand, he left me to go and procure some.

Again I was left alone on a bloody field, and nothing but dead men around me. My reflections were anything but pleasant, but having already been providentially saved in two instances, I thought that if I was once removed from the field, I might survive. Little did I know the condition I was then in!

Night was now drawing in fast, and my late deliverer was not making his appearance. The time he had been absent seemed very long, and I began to fear that he might have lost his way, when a sergeant of the 60th Regiment came near me, and I beckoned to him. He came up to me, gave me water and some wine, arranged my covering, and did all he could to aid me in my forlorn condition. I entreated him to remain by me, but his reply was, 'I would willingly do so, but my regiment is now in action, and I must join.' All my solicitations were unavailing, and he was about to leave me, when despair caused me to hold out my hand to him. He took it, and at once he seemed electrified. After a few moments he exclaimed, 'I will stay by you, and try to save you; I cannot leave you.' My heart was now in my mouth, I was for some moments unable to speak. Again the German gave me water, and then said, 'There is a regiment close at hand, and I will go and acquaint the commanding officer how you are situated.' He left me, and my hopes now revived; and very shortly after I heard voices approaching, and a man cried out, 'Who are you?' My reply was 71st. 'A lie, by God! What is your name?' 'Barralier.' 'What are you doing here?' 'I am in the Portuguese service.' 'You must not remain here,' and the officer turned away. Shortly after he returned, accompanied by several officers, and they had me placed in a blanket. Ensign Stopford and eight men were ordered to take me to the first place they could obtain medical aid. Ensign Stopford of the 68th Regiment often stopped the men to see if I was still alive, and at one period he placed his hand on my forehead as I had not answered to his kind inquiries, and exclaimed, 'he is dead.' The pressure of his hand aroused me and I faintly said, 'No, sir, I am not dead.' The march was continued, and in the dead of night Ensign Stopford had me laid on blankets in a peasant's hut, at about three miles from Salamanca: he then left me, after he had procured me medical aid. Thus was I providentially saved, and removed from a gory field. . . .

After Ensign Stopford left me, an assistant-surgeon of the German Legion first dressed my wounds, I asked him if I could recover: after some hesitation, he said I might, if well attended to. In a miserable hut I was now left, surrounded on all sides by wounded and dying men of all nations, some calling out 'water;' others, 'agua' and 'de l'eau'. In fact such was the incessant calling and noise made by the wounded of the several nations, that although I was suffering severely, I had to call out to them in their different languages, that if they did not desist I would have them removed – that I was a captain, and that as much care was taken of them as of me. This had the desired effect.

Barralier says that thanks to the good care and skill of Staff-Surgeon Macgregor he ultimately made a partial recovery; and he lived to publish his account in 1851, almost forty years after he had been wounded.[27]

Despite the groans of those around him, Barralier was fortunate to spend the night of the battle under cover, having had his wounds dressed. Many of the wounded remained on the field overnight at the mercy of plunderers or those seeking revenge, like the Spanish soldier in the 95th who regularly slaughtered wounded Frenchmen until his comrades forced him to desist. Even if they survived the night, not all the wounded were always collected on the following day. Three days after Waterloo, Sir Augustus Frazer visited the battlefield with a party of stray gunners and collected several wagon-loads of the wounded, and these were not the last. For many more days wounded men continued to be found in the woods or concealed by the standing corn or by corpses, yet still miraculously alive. The carnage at Waterloo was exceptionally severe, but four days after the much less serious fighting at the Bidassoa, Harry Smith found a wounded French soldier. The man lost both his legs but recovered, and was repatriated to France in good spirits.[28]

Throughout the battle and for days afterwards the surgeons worked constantly, treating the wounded as best they could without effective anaesthetics or antiseptics.[29] They had to work quickly, often crudely, extricating musket balls or shell fragments, and amputating limbs. Sometimes they came under fire, or might have to fly in order to avoid being overrun by the enemy; and sometimes they were operating in extreme heat, as in Egypt or southern Spain, or in intense cold, as at Eylau. They were, of course, grossly under-staffed, and after hours of work their simple instruments grew blunt and their arms tired, protracting the agony for their patients.

Most of the wounded bore their suffering with extraordinary fortitude:

I must confess that I did not bear the amputation of my arm as well as I ought to have done [George Napier recalls], for I made noise enough when the knife cut through my skin and flesh. It is no joke I assure you, but still it was a shame to say a word, as it is of no use. . . . Staff Surgeon Guthrie cut it off. However, for want of light, and from the number of amputations he had already performed, and other circumstances, his instruments were blunted, so it was a long time before the thing was finished, at least twenty minutes, and the pain was great. I then thanked him for his kindness, having sworn at him like a trooper while he was at it, to his great amusement, and I proceeded to find some place to lie down and rest, and after wandering and stumbling about the suburbs for upwards of an hour, I saw a light in a house, and on entering found it full of soldiers, and a good fire blazing in the kitchen.[30]

Captain François, who was wounded at Borodino, was equally stoic:

The doctor comes over to me and examines my wound. Thrusting his little finger into the hole made by the musket-ball, he seizes his lancet, makes the usual cross on each hole, and puts his probe right through my leg between its two bones. 'Lucky wound, this,' he says, pulling out some splinters. Then he gives me first aid and tells me to go to the army's ambulance at Kolotskoië.[31]

The evacuation of the wounded to hospitals well to the rear was slow and painful. Water transport was probably the best, but was seldom available; more common were rough country carts over terrible roads, or having to walk. Early in the war in Spain, a French doctor received a convoy of eighty wagon-loads of wounded:

None had left the waggons for five days, their straw was fouled, some lay on mattresses covered with pus and excrement. They were covered with rags and pieces of carpet. We got them out as best we could and as many wished to relieve themselves, we had to hold them suspended for the purpose. These manoeuvres took a good two hours in a frightful stench.[32]

And when they arrived at a hospital, it was sometimes little improvement:

The courtyard is poisoned by the substances emptied into an open ditch, which overflows. Corpses are piled at the foot of the stairs leading to the main rooms, where they empty themselves, spreading a frightful odour. The stench is general in the wards, each mattress having harboured ten or twelve patients without ever having been washed. The meat ration has been cut by half in order to enrich the director and the bursar. The chief provisioner, one Rose de Hagueneau, a fraudulent bankrupt, joined in order to re-establish his affairs. The Emperor knows that such a situation is nearly universal: he swears, raves and the evil continues.[33]

Typhus and dysentery, even more than the effect of wounds, surgery and gangrene, were the greatest threats under such conditions, and large hospitals exacerbated the problem. In the Peninsula, Sir James McGrigor had great success by reducing the role of general hospitals and treating more patients in small regimental hospitals. But a large battle produced so many casualties that it overwhelmed all the medical resources of an army, and the wounded had to be brought together in nearby towns and villages, simply to provide them with food and shelter. According to one account, a quarter of the casualties taken to the main hospital at Brünn after Austerlitz died within a month, mostly of typhus; but the smaller, better hospital of the Imperial Guard, which was far from the other hospitals, had many fewer deaths.[34]

The best and most detailed figures are for Waterloo, and they present a much less distressing picture. Of the 130 men of the King's Dragoon Guards wounded at Waterloo, sixty had rejoined the regiment by late October, a little more than four months after the battle. This is too small a sample to be taken as representative, but it is supported by a return dated 13 April 1816 which details the fate of the 7,687 British and King's German Legion soldiers who had been wounded during the operations of 16–18 June 1815. Only 856 of these (11 per cent) had died, and a further 854 remained in hospital. Surprisingly few – 236 (3 per cent) – had suffered amputations; presumably this only includes those who survived. Almost two-thirds of the wounded, 5,068 men, had rejoined their regiments. Of the remainder, 506 were discharged, and 167 had been transferred to garrison battalions. On the basis of the these figures, well over 80 per cent of the wounded would recover, most of them well enough to continue active service in the army. The total number of dead, including those who fell on the day, was only one and a half times the number originally reported as killed in the action.[35]

These figures may need to be qualified, as many circumstances were particularly favourable. The British were the victorious army, and the battle was neither preceded nor followed by extended operations. It took place in rich country with a large city less than twenty miles away, which was able to provide extensive hospitals, nursing and care for the wounded; while attempts to control infectious disease seem to have been remarkably successful. All this gave British soldiers a better than normal chance of recovering, though this had to offset the very high level of casualties which overwhelmed the preparations that had been made. But a study of British casualties over the whole war – from 1793 to 1815 – shows that these figures are not grossly distorted. Only 12.5 per cent of British non-commissioned officers and men who were listed as wounded subsequently died of their wounds, while the better care given to officers ensured that only 8.3 per cent of them died. The figure may have been higher in other armies – although until quite late in the Peninsular War the British medical service did not have a particularly high reputation – but there is no reason to believe that it was radically different, except when infectious diseases took hold, or, as in the retreat from Moscow, other influences were the real cause of higher mortality.[36]

The influx of large numbers of wounded could have a more harmful effect on the local population than either the devastation and plundering which armies brought with them, or the actual destruction to property caused by a battle. But while some civilians responded by robbing and murdering the wounded, others were humane. At Lützen dozens of young men and women made repeated trips on to the battlefield to collect the wounded and carry them into the town; while after Waterloo, the inhabitants of Brussels went to extraordinary lengths to care for the wounded.[37] But the greatest battle of the age was fought on the outskirts of Leipzig, and its consequences were most unhappy, if a rather highly coloured account, written a month after the fighting, is to be believed:

> By this five days' conflict our city was transformed into one vast hospital, 56 edifices being devoted to that purpose alone. The number of sick and wounded amounted to 36,000. Of these a large proportion died, but their places were soon supplied by the many wounded who had been left in the adjacent villages. Crowded to excess, what could be the consequence but contagious diseases? especially as there was such a scarcity of the necessaries of life – and unfortunately a most destructive nervous fever is at this moment making great ravages among us, so that from 150 to 180 deaths commonly occur in one week, in a city whose ordinary proportion was between 30 and 40. In the military hospitals there die at least 300 in a day, and frequently from 5 to 600. By this extraordinary mortality the numbers there have been reduced to from 14 to 16,000. Consider too the state of the circumjacent villages, to the distance of 10 miles round, all completely stripped; in scarcely any of them is there left a single horse, cow, hog, fowl, or corn of any kind, either hay or implements of agriculture. All the dwelling-houses have been burned or demolished, and all the wood-work about them carried off for fuel by the troops in bivouac. The roofs have shared the same fate; the shells of the houses were converted into forts and loop-holes made in the walls, as every village was individually defended and stormed. Not a door or window is anywhere to be seen, as those might be removed with the greatest ease, and, together with the roofs, were all consumed. Winter is now at hand, and its rigours begin already to be felt. These poor creatures are thus prevented, not only by the season, from rebuilding their habitations, but also by the absolute want of means; they have no prospect before them but to die of hunger, for all Saxony, together with the adjacent countries, has suffered too severely to be able to afford any relief to their miseries.[38]

The dead were as likely to cause disease as the wounded, but there were no resources for anything better than crude mass graves for all but a favoured few. A visitor to Waterloo after the battle describes the scene: 'The general burying was truly horrible; large square holes were dug about six feet deep, and thirty or forty fine young fellows, stripped to their skins, were thrown into each, pell mell, and then covered over in so slovenly a manner that sometimes a hand or a foot peeped through the earth.'[39]

The passage of a few weeks or a couple of months did not improve matters, and when an army passed over an old battlefield later in the campaign, it could be an unnerving sight. At Sabugal Kincaid found 'that the dead had been nearly all torn from their graves, and devoured by wolves'. Another British officer was dismayed to find many of the dead still unburied on the field of Salamanca weeks after the battle; vultures and, worse still, pigs were feasting on the corpses of men and horses; many of the bodies had been collected, covered with branches and burnt, but ineffectually, and as a consequence 'the air had become very offensive, and the whole scene was extremely revolting'. The sight of Borodino, nearly two months after the battle, helped to demoralize Napoleon's army as it began its long retreat. A 'multitude of dead bodies, which deprived of burial [for] fifty-two days, scarcely retained the human form. . . . The whole plain was entirely covered with them. None of the bodies were more than half buried. In one place were to be seen garments still red with blood, the bones gnawed by dogs and birds of prey: in another were broken arms, drums, helmets and swords.'[40]

Epilogue

In July 1815 Wellington's victorious army camped on the outskirts of Paris. The Reverend Edward Cockayne Frith, chaplain of the Fifth Division, held Divine Service on the following Sunday and preached to the officers and men of his division.

> The beautiful manner in which he dwelt on the battle, and the sad and sudden loss of friends and comrades, drew tears from many; and when he wound up with the sad pangs it would cause at home, to the widows and orphans, the parents and friends of those that had fallen, concluding with the text, 'Go to your tents and rejoice, and return thanks to the Lord for the mercies he has granted you,' there was hardly a dry eye in the whole division.[1]

After a generation of almost continuous warfare, peace had at last come to Europe, and the soldiers were going home.

The transition from war to peace was not easy. Many of the returning veterans would find their native districts devastated by the passage of armies, with villages pillaged and burnt, livestock slaughtered or driven away, and their families raped or murdered; for the long war had crossed and recrossed Europe from Riga to Cadiz. The experiences of the veterans, and the problems which faced their societies, are large subjects worthy of study in their own right. All that can be attempted here is to trace the fortunes of a few British veterans who, returning to a relatively prosperous society which had largely escaped the direct ravages of war, nonetheless faced problems which hint at the range of difficulties that confronted old soldiers across Europe.

None of the veterans were as young or as innocent as they had been when they had joined the army; some were debilitated by their exertions or by disease, while others would suffer for the rest of their lives from the effects of malaria, rheumatism or wounds. A number of officers and men had continued to serve – and serve well – despite injuries one would have thought would have incapacitated them. Edward Costello lost his trigger finger at Quatre Bras, but remained in the army until discharged in the reductions of the following year. Private John Cowley of the 48th Regiment was wounded in the back by a shell-splinter at Badajoz, in the right leg and face at Salamanca, shot in the side at Vitoria, lost his right forefinger near Pamplona, and was wounded in the neck at Toulouse! George Napier, Colonel Felton Hervey and General Edward Paget all continued to serve with distinction despite losing an arm, while Lieutenant-Colonel Richard Collins, who lost a leg at Albuera, returned to the Peninsula with an artificial leg and commanded a brigade in the Seventh Division until he died in 1813. Kincaid records the effect of constant exposure to enemy fire on the surviving officers of the 95th:

> At the close of the war, when we returned to England, if our battalion did not show symptoms of its being a well-shot corps, it is very odd: nor was it to be wondered at if the camp-colours were not covered with that precision, nor the salute given with the grace usually expected from a reviewed body, when I furnish the following account of the officers commanding companies on the day of inspection, viz: –
>
> Beckwith with a cork-leg – Pemberton and Manners with a shot each in the knee, making them as stiff as the other's tree one – Loftus Gray with a gash in the lip, and minus a portion of one heel, which made him march to the tune of dot and go one – Smith with a shot in the ankle – Eeles minus a thumb – Johnston, in addition to other shot holes, a stiff elbow, which deprived him of the power of disturbing his friends as a scratcher of Scotch reels upon the violin – Percival with a shot through his lungs. Hope with a grape-shot lacerated leg – and George Simmons with his riddled body held together by a pair of stays. . . .[2]

And this was the most active regiment in the British army! But the most poignant story of all must be that of Captain John MacCulloch, also of the 95th, who lost the use of one arm at Foz de Arouce in 1811, and returned to serve at Waterloo, where he lost his good arm. Remarkably, this was not enough to spoil his taste for military life, and when his wound had healed he presented himself to Wellington with the statement 'Here I am, my lord; I have no longer an arm left to wield for my country, but I still wish to be allowed to serve it as best I can.' Wellington granted his request, and MacCulloch was promoted to major in a veteran battalion before dying in 1818.[3]

When the veterans first hobbled home they generally received a warm welcome. Lieutenant George Wood had served in the 2nd battalion of detachments at Talavera, and returned home soon afterwards:

> Quitting this rocky harbour [the Scilly islands], we arrived at Gosport, where we landed, as may easily be conceived, in a most motley and tattered condition. Our coats were patched over with different coloured cloth, for which purpose we had even cut off our skirts. My own coat was mended with the breeches of a dead Frenchman, which I found on the field – the only trophy I yet had to boast of

having retained from the spoils of the enemy. In this state we marched for Salisbury, when we were invited to dine with the Mayor and Corporation of that town. It so happened that I sate [*sic*] next to a major of the local militia, whose splendid uniform and sparkling epaulettes, contrasted with my thread-worn patched jacket and mud-like looking shoulder-knot, once so brilliant on these parades, afforded a fertile source of amusement for the jocose part of the company. However the jest was rather in my favour, – a circumstance which caused some mortification to my bedizened neighbour.[4]

While Richard Henegan of the Field Train writes that

On landing at Portsmouth, we experienced the proud gratification of feeling, by our reception, how great was the interest manifested in England for the army of the Peninsula. Every little act of courtesy and kindness was proffered almost enthusiastically, and the very name of 'a Peninsular officer', seemed a talisman, by which privileges were granted, and restrictions withdrawn.

Even the customs officers turned a blind eye to a box of contraband cigars in Henegan's portmanteau, though a brother officer, Colonel Birch of the Engineers, who preferred the open, honest, manly path, free from any pretence or dissimulation, naturally lost his.[5]

These officers were returning home during the course of the war. After Waterloo, popular patriotism rose to a crescendo with illuminations, pageants, dinners and public celebrations of all kinds, but then it quickly faded. Long before the Army of Occupation left France in 1818 the war had become yesterday's news, and even a 'Waterloo hero' had lost the lustre of novelty. Little provision was made for the veterans who were discharged from the army, and not all homecomings proved prosperous. The anonymous memoirist of the 71st Highland Light Infantry spent his years in the army regretting his impulsive enlistment. At last, having served at Waterloo, he received his discharge in the autumn of 1815:

I left my comrades with regret, but the service with joy. I came down to the coast to embark, with light steps and a joyful heart, singing 'When wild war's deadly blast was blawn'. I was as poor as poor could be; but I had hope before me, and pleasing dreams of home. I had saved nothing this campaign; and the money I had before was all gone. Government found me the means of getting to Edinburgh. Hope and joy were my companion until I entered the Firth. I was on deck; the morning began to dawn; the shores of Lothian began to rise out of the mist. 'There is the land of the cakes,' said the captain. A sigh escaped me; recollections crowded upon me, painful recollections. I went below to conceal my feelings and never came up until the vessel was in the harbour. I ran from her and hid myself in a public house. All the time I had been away was forgot. I felt as if I had been in Leith the day before. I was so foolish as to think I would be known and laughed at. In about half an hour I reasoned myself out of my foolish notions; but I could not bring myself to go up the Walk to Edinburgh. I went by the Easter Road. Everything was strange to me, so many alterations had taken place; yet I was afraid to look any person in the face lest he should recognize me. I was suffering as keenly, at this moment, as when I went away. I felt my face burning with shame. At length I reached the door of the last house I had been in before leaving Edinburgh. I had not the power to knock; happy was it for me that I did not. A young girl came into the stair. I asked if Mrs ——— lived there. 'No,' she said, 'she flitted long ago.' 'Where does she live?' 'I do not know.' Where to go I knew not. I came down stairs and recognized a sign which had been in the same place before I went away. In I went, and inquired. The landlord knew me. 'Tom,' said he, 'Are you come back safe? Poor fellow! Give me your hand.' 'Does my mother live?' 'Yes, yes; come in, and I will send for her, not to let the surprise be too great.' Away he went. I could not remain, but followed him and, the next minute, I was in the arms of my mother.

But after the welcome home came disillusionment. Although he was well educated, the veteran soldier could not find steady work, even labouring. After finishing his memoirs in 1818 he talked of emigrating to South America or Spain where he had served, but was last seen working on the roads and wishing that he was a soldier again.[6]

It was a story which was to be repeated hundreds if not thousands of times in different ways. Edward Costello tells how Tom Plunket, the crack shot who killed General Colbert on the retreat to Coruña, was finally wounded at Waterloo and invalided to England. He passed a medical board at Chelsea Hospital, but was so disgusted at being awarded a pension of only sixpence a day in recognition of his wound and long service that he 'expressed himself to the Lords Commissioners in a way that induced them to strike him off the list altogether'. After being reduced to absolute penury he re-enlisted in the army, this time in a line regiment. Here he was soon encountered by his old commanding officer Sir Sydney Beckwith, who arranged first his immediate promotion to corporal and soon after his discharge on a pension of a shilling a day. On this he could just about live, for his wife also received a pension of the same amount in recompense for injuries sustained when an ammunition wagon exploded at Quatre Bras. However, as Costello observes, 'nothing more unsettles a man than the ever-changing chequered course of a soldier's life', and Plunket gave up his pension under a scheme to encourage the settlement of Canada, in exchange for a grant of land and a lump sum equal to four years' pension. But 'Tom was not a man to rusticate on the other side of the Atlantic amid privations' and within a year he was back in England and penniless. Costello saw him some years later 'in Burton Crescent, most picturesquely habited, and selling matches. . . . I asked him how he got on, when with one of his usual cheerful smiles he informed me, that the match-selling business kept him on his legs.' Years later he died suddenly in Colchester, still desperately poor. He and his wife had eked out a living tramping the country separately selling needles and tape, but happened to be together when he suddenly collapsed and died. Several retired officers in the town began a collection and raised £20 for the widow, while a colonel's wife paid for Plunket's funeral and 'a handsome tombstone to perpetuate his memory'.[7]

Costello's own subsequent career was rather more fortunate, though not without periods of great poverty, despite his Vitoria loot. After Waterloo he served for a time in the Army of Occupation in France and fell in love with, and secretly married, a local girl, Augustine Loude, against her father's wishes. When he was discharged from the army he was given a pension of sixpence a day, which was not enough to support a wife and newborn child, and he could get no work. Facing starvation, Costello appealed to Wellington's brother, Dr Gerald Wellesley, the rector of Chelsea, who gave him £5 which just sufficed for the little family to return to France. Augustine's father proved inexorable and the couple parted, both ultimately to marry again. In 1834 the First Carlist War broke out in Spain, and Costello soon returned to the Peninsula in the British Legion, rising to the rank of captain but disliking the experience – things were not so well managed as in the Light Division. He was again wounded, left Spain, and, in March 1838, was appointed a Yeoman Warder of the Tower of London. He served there for more than thirty years, wrote his memoirs with the aid of a lawyer named Meller, and died in July 1869 at the age of eighty.[8]

By no means all old soldiers found civilian life so hard, though tales of poverty predominate in surviving memoirs – partly, perhaps, because it was both piquant and an incentive to writing. A few soldiers had risen from the ranks to become officers, others based careers on connections made in the army, while many more prospered in ways quite unrelated to their years of military service. Thomas Morris, for example, ends his memoirs with the characteristic statement that, on leaving the army, 'I . . . returned home to London, and soon, unassisted attained a respectable position in civil society.' Not all officers forgot their men. Thomas Brotherton, by then a lieutenant-colonel and former aide-de-camp to the King, often went to see Sergeant Stuckey – the sergeant who had helped him through his baptism of fire in Egypt in 1801 – at Chelsea Hospital, until the sergeant died, at the age of eighty-four, in about 1840.[9] Many others led quiet lives not much better and not much worse than if there had been no war. Certainly a career in the ranks of the British, or probably any other, army of the period, despite the extraordinary success of a few French soldiers, was not the high road to wealth, social advancement, or even a modest level of security. But prosperity is not the only object in life, and many young men joined the army quite eagerly in search of a life of adventure beyond the oppressive confines of their local community, and not all regretted their folly.

Officers naturally received better treatment than the men. In the British army regimental officers for whom there was no current military employment were entitled to draw 'half-pay' so long as they did not accept other employment which would prevent them returning to the army in the event of war. 'Half-pay' did not, in fact, amount to half the pay the officer had received on active duty; it related to a century-old scale of payment which had received little modification, so that in extreme cases it was less than one quarter of an officer's full pay. In theory it was a retainer fee, but no age limits or medical standards were enforced, and the officers could resign without penalty if ever called upon to do their duty. This made it, in effect, a pension, and in the early 1800s some ensigns and lieutenants were still drawing their half-pay when well into their eighties or even older – the legacy of some months' or years' service in an almost forgotten war more than half a century before. But even as a pension half-pay was not very generous: in 1801 a captain received £87 8s. 6d. per annum – barely enough to live on with any shred of respectability – and, of course, junior officers received even less.[10]

Life was a dreary struggle for most of these men if they were wholly dependent on their half-pay, while if they were married with children, real poverty could only be avoided by extremely skilful management. In the years after Waterloo many retired to the Continent where living was cheaper, while others sought a prosperous new life in the colonies – and occasionally found it. The range of occupations open to a retired officer was extremely limited, and service in the army was poor preparation for most of them. Officers were usually too old to take to medicine or the law, while commerce was generally as unacceptable to them as they were unsuited to it. Government positions were few and eagerly sought, though Britain's overseas possessions, from Heligoland to Corfu, St Helena to South Australia, provided employment for many officers in the decades ahead; while others, with official permission, took employment in the service of foreign countries from Egypt to Chile. Others, particularly when there was a living in the gift of the family, took holy orders and their greater experience of the world may have made them better clergymen. Finally, a surprising number, encouraged by the success of Napier's *History* and the interest it generated, wrote their memoirs. This would not have made their fortune, but let us hope that they enjoyed the mental exercise, the reliving of past triumphs, the renewal of old acquaintances, and the excitement and éclat – at least within their local circle – of publication.

Many officers, of course, had private means to supplement their half-pay, while others were independently wealthy or had become so during the war. There were senior officers, from Wellington downwards, who had made their reputation in the war, and who flourished afterwards, either leading an active public life, as Wellington did, or enjoying the life of a prosperous country gentleman. Other younger men, such as Colin Campbell, the future Lord Clyde, began their career in the struggle against Napoleon, and went on to make their fame in future wars. Indeed Peninsular and Waterloo veterans were to dominate the senior ranks of the British army for the next half-century, their experience not always proving an unambiguous blessing.

But although the provision for junior officers was inadequate, and that for ordinary soldiers was miserly, the total cost of pensions and half-pay was a heavy burden on the British Treasury not only in the depressed years immediately after the war, but for decades afterwards. The number of army pensions rose from barely 20,000 in 1792 to more than 61,000 in 1819, and because old soldiers could apply at any time, and many did not do so until they could not provide for themselves, it continued to increase for years. In 1828 there were 85,000 pensions being paid – almost as many as there were soldiers then serving – while new pensions were still being granted to Peninsular and Waterloo veterans as late as the 1870s. Even at an average of only a shilling a day, this was a substantial expense, while the cost of the half-pay officers was even greater. After the war Parliament insisted on the immediate abolition of income tax against the government's wishes, while receipts from other taxes were falling due to the post-war depression. In this context there was simply no capacity to increase significantly total spending on pensions and half-pay, even if the ministers had been inclined to do so. Not that the government seems to have had any such desire, while the opposition Whigs and radicals were constantly calling for further large reductions in government expenditure, and moved to reduce soldiers' pensions when they came to power in the 1830s. But if the total funds were limited, they might have been distributed differently, and few modern readers will applaud the justice of a system by which the Duke of Wellington received a Parliamentary grant of £200,000 following Waterloo – having already received large sums during the Peninsular War – while a sergeant received only 1s. 6d. a day if he had been blinded or lost a limb in action.[11]

Most contemporaries, however, took economic and social inequalities for granted, and there was far more ill-feeling at the time over the question of medals than over pensions and financial awards. The British army had no regular system of issuing medals or other awards for outstanding conduct, although some regiments did so. The only medals issued by the army as a whole were limited to senior officers to commemorate a particular victory and were normally granted to all officers of sufficient standing who had been present on the day – usually only those who had commanded a battalion or similar unit. After Waterloo, however, Wellington suggested that something be done for the whole army, and in 1816 every British soldier who had taken the field on the 16, 17 or 18 June 1815 was given a 'Waterloo Medal', and was credited with two years' additional service.

This immediately caused trouble on two fronts: a rumour swept through the ranks that the soldiers' medals were to be made of brass, while those of the officers were to be gold. This nearly caused a mutiny, but was easily checked when Wellington intervened and assured the troops that all the medals would be silver. Less easily assuaged was the resentment of the numerous Peninsular veterans who had not been at Waterloo, but who felt that they had endured far more over the years and were now seeing their achievement implicitly belittled. One soldier of the 95th who missed Waterloo through illness was so incensed by the sight of young soldiers flaunting the distinction that he used to assault them and throw away their badge. Repeated offences of this kind led to his imprisonment, but there was much sympathy for him among the veterans of the Light Division, and when he was released they sent him back to the regiment in a coach and four, bedecked with ribbons, and with all the pomp and ceremony of a conquering hero.[12] Officers felt the point just as keenly, as George Wood made clear in his memoir published in 1825:

> this part of the Peninsular War [the Battles of the Pyrenees] . . . I think, was certainly the most arduous and enterprising duty that British troops ever performed: I do not by any means except the last campaign in Flanders; for that, with the exception of the three days' conflict, I regard as a mere party of pleasure in comparison with the affairs of the Pyrenees and the disastrous retreats of the Peninsula. The troops in Flanders were never without the Commissariat at hand, plenty of all kinds of necessaries, a general run of good weather, with the exception of two or three days, and a fine country to pass through. . . .
>
> God forbid that I should be thought to mention the glorious field of Waterloo with envy! I am too well aware of the laurels gained by the heroes who fought there, to depreciate their merit in the least; on the contrary, I revere them: but to those officers who have fought in Spain, and who have also shared in the magnanimous victory of La Belle Alliance, I submit my ideas with confidence. They will surely admit, that the troops in the Peninsula behaved with as much bravery as those who had fought at Waterloo; and that the important service rendered their nation by the troops in the Spanish conflict, was not inferior.
>
> Oh! that I had had the good fortune to have been at the renowned battle of Waterloo, instead of the various actions, retreats advances – advances and retreats again! how easily should I have gained a medal, honour, and fame! . . .
>
> . . . It is not the intrinsic value of these baubles that makes the soldier so covetous of them; for were only a part of the brass cannon that has been captured in the different actions melted down and converted to this use, it would be as dear to the breast it hung on as the purest gold: nor is it for the gaiety of the variegated ribbon dangling at the button-hole that the veteran desires it; but for the heartfelt satisfaction he would feel when retired to his peaceful abode, where he could still keep the spark of martial glory alight, by showing this badge of emulation and distinction to his children, his family, and friends, – a badge which would entitle him to say, 'Merit, like this, my boys, has supported your King, your Constitution, your laws, and your freedom; gain but these, and you will for ever secure them.'

Evidently the old slight remained sore, but it was not finally corrected until 1848 when the silver General Service Medal was issued to some 30,000 claimants of all ranks who had taken part in any of the principal victories of the war of 1793–1814, with clasps signifying each of the major actions at which the soldier had been present.[13]

Like George Wood, most veterans looked back on the war with pride, tinged with regret for their lost youth. Very few expressed any moral qualms about what they had done, while even those who had found religion – and who often included long agonized accounts of their conversion in their memoirs – were more likely to repent their drunkenness, their profanities and the casual brutalities incidental to a soldier's life, than their part in battle. This was natural enough, for society as a whole had little doubt as to the moral justification of the war, and pacifism remained the preserve of a tiny minority. Nor do the surviving recollections show much sign of lasting psychological damage. The soldier's life might unsettle a man and make him resist a return to a routine of steady drudgery, but few seem to have found it difficult to live with the memory of what they had been through, even if it included such horrors as the storming of Badajoz.

Most soldiers recalled their service with relish. Many had enjoyed it at the time – despite the danger and the privations – and they enjoyed it even more in retrospect – especially the danger and the privations. Forgotten were the long months of tedium in uncomfortable winter quarters, the forced companionship of incompatible comrades, the frustration caused by slow mails, lack of money or army regulations; forgotten too was the gnawing uncertainty about the future; all this was swept aside, while memory retained the vivid impression of frosty mornings, stony beds and scanty provisions, of good fellowship and of moments of intense excitement, danger and exhilaration. In part this was simple nostalgia, but only in part. War is certainly not all glory, but it is not all hell either.

Notes

Abbreviations
JSAHR   *Journal of the Society for Army Historical Research*
Martinien   Martinien, A. *Tableaux par corps et par batailles des Officiers Tués et Blessés pendant les Guerres de l'Empire (1805–1815)* (Paris, Éditions Militaires Européennes, n.d.)
USJ   *United Service Journal* – also called, at different times, the *United Service Magazine*, and *Colburn's United Service Journal*

CHAPTER ONE: THE EVE OF BATTLE

1. *Memoirs of Baron Lejeune*, 2 vols (London, Longmans, Green, 1897), vol. 1, p. 127. The account of the torchlight procession is based on *ibid.*, pp. 27–8, *Memoirs of Baron de Marbot* (London, Longmans, Green, 1892), vol. 1, p. 197, and Count Philippe de Segur, *An Aide-de-Camp of Napoleon* (London, Hutchinson, 1895), p. 245 – sources which frequently contradict each other. See also Christopher Duffy, *Austerlitz 1805* (London, Seeley, Service & Co., 1977), p. 90, and p. 173 where he discusses these and other sources for the incident.

2. Captain von Linsingen quoted in Christopher Duffy, *Borodino and the War of 1812* (London, Seeley, Service & Co., 1972), p. 90.

3. Soldier [Anon.], *A Soldier of the Seventy-First* edited by Christopher Hibbert (London, Leo Cooper, 1975; first published 1819), p. 23.

4. Jean-Baptiste Barrès, *Memoirs of a Napoleonic Officer* edited by Maurice Barrès (New York, Dial Press, 1925), pp. 55–73; this portion of Barrès's memoirs was written at the time and gives a more honest view of the life of a soldier than the rest, which was rewritten many years later.

5. Edward Costello, *The Peninsular and Waterloo Campaigns* edited by Antony Brett-James (London, Longman, 1967), p. 150.

6. Capt. Sir John Kincaid, *Adventures in the Rifle Brigade and Random Shots from a Rifleman* (Glasgow, Richard Drew, 1981), p. 81. In fact, Wellington's army outnumbered the French.

7. *A Hawk at War. The Peninsular Reminiscences of General Sir Thomas Brotherton CB* edited by Bryan Perrett (Chippenham, Picton, 1986), p. 13.

8. Gleig quoted in Philip J. Haythornthwaite, *The Armies of Wellington* (London, Arms & Armour, 1994), p. 204.

9. 'Next to a battle lost, the greatest misery is a battle gained.' *Oxford Dictionary of*

Quotations 3rd edition citing the Diary of Frances Lady Shelley. At times the misery was about equal, when the battle was nearly drawn, but after a really decisive victory such as Salamanca or Waterloo, the plight of the vanquished was incomparably worse than that of the victor.

10. Gunther E. Rothenberg, *The Art of Warfare in the Age of Napoleon* (London, Batsford, 1977), p. 61.

11. Statistics for Austerlitz are far from perfect, with estimates of the French army varying considerably. The figures used are based largely on Duffy, *Austerlitz*, p. 157 (see also p. 87), with the Guard from A. Martinien, *Tableaux par corps et par batailles des Officiers Tués et Blessés pendant les Guerres de l'Empire (1805–1815)* (Paris, Editions Militaires Européennes, n.d.). (Henceforth cited simply as Martinien.)

12. Salamanca figures: Sir Charles Oman, *A History of the Peninsular War*, 7 vols (New York, AMS Press, 1980; first published Oxford, Clarendon, 1902–30), vol. 5, pp. 598–9; Albuera figures, *ibid.*, vol. 4, pp. 631–2; in both cases the Portuguese and Spanish troops present had proportionally fewer losses than the British and German.

13. Figures from Scott Bowden, *Armies at Waterloo* (Arlington, Empire Games, 1983), p. 325 (for strength and overall losses) and Capt. William Siborne, *The Waterloo Campaign 1815*, 5th edition (Westminster, Constable, 1900; first published 1844), p. 564 (for proportion killed); however it should be noted that the two give different totals.

14. Sir Charles Oman, 'French Losses in the Waterloo Campaign', *English Historical Review*, vol. 19, Oct. 1904, pp. 681–93, and vol. 21, Jan. 1906, pp. 132–5; 1904, p. 684 (for d'Erlon) and 1906, p. 134 (for the Guard). There are no accurate figures for French rank and file losses at Waterloo; however they would probably not have been quite so heavy as casualties among the officers.

15. W. B. Hodge, 'On the Mortality arising from Military Operations', *Quarterly Journal of the Statistical Society*, vol. 19, Sept. 1856, p. 267.

16. Henry Lachouque and Anne S. K. Brown, *The Anatomy of Glory* (London, Arms & Armour, 1978), p. 51 for Imperial Guard; the other figures, which are mostly very rough, from David Chandler, *The Campaigns of Napoleon* (New York, Macmillan, 1974), pp. 334–5. There is a strange dearth of information on the strength of the French army as a whole, rather than Napoleon's field force.

17. Total force in the Peninsula from WO 17/2470 General Return – excluding sergeants and trumpeters the figure for the rank and file is 57,326, but these figures should not be regarded as precise, and are used here only to give a general indication. Strength of the army as a whole from Sir John Fortescue, *The County Lieutenancies and the Army 1803–1814* (London, Macmillan, 1909), p. 293.

18. Col. H. C. B. Rogers, *Napoleon's Army* (London, Ian Allan, 1974), p. 109; Richard Riehn, *1812. Napoleon's Russian Campaign* (New York, Wiley, 1991), p. 395. In the context of 1812 any estimate of the number 'who died from their wounds' can only be very rough, while the figures make no allowance for sick and wounded men who were successfully evacuated before the retreat began. I have seen no estimate of their number, but it may have been quite large – perhaps another one in twelve – in which case only about half of those who followed Napoleon into Russia, say 300,000 men, perished from disease, privation and exposure.

19. Hodge, 'On the Mortality . . . Military Operations', pp. 233, 237, 264–5, 267. I have adjusted some of these figures, where Hodge gives only rank and file, to allow for officers, sergeants, etc.

CHAPTER TWO: BATTLES AND BATTLEFIELDS

1. Sir Harry Smith, *The Autobiography of Sir Harry Smith, 1787–1819* edited by G. C. Moore Smith (London, John Murray, 1910), p. 134. For an explana-

tion of the difficulties of firing downhill, see Brent Nosworthy, *Battle Tactics of Napoleon and his Enemies* (London, Constable, 1995), pp. 78–9, 208.

2. Quoted in Antony Brett-James, *Europe Against Napoleon* (London, Macmillan, 1970), p. 178.
3. Quoted *ibid.*, pp. 178–9.
4. Erckmann-Chatrian, *Waterloo* (New York, Scribner's, 1869), pp. 242–5. Though this is fiction, Erckmann and Chatrian drew on many first-hand accounts of the fighting and their story, though highly coloured, is less vainglorious than many memoirs.
5. William Grattan, *Adventures in the Connaught Rangers* edited by Charles Oman (London, Edward Arnold, 1902), pp. 71–2.
6. Lt. William Swabey, *Diary of Campaigns in the Peninsula for the Years 1811, 1812 and 1813* edited by Col. F. A. Whinyates (London, Trotman, 1984), p. 109 notes these in his entry for 20 June 1812.
7. Dorsey Gardner, *Quatre Bras, Ligny and Waterloo: a Narrative and a Criticism* (London, Kegan Paul, Trench & Co., 1882), p. 207n.
8. Rothenberg, *Art of Warfare in the Age of Napoleon*, p. 218.
9. Marshal Ney, *Military Studies* translated by G. H. Caunter (London, Bull & Churton, 1833), pp. 109–10. Charles Esdaile suggests that 'hoes' is probably a mistranslation for some other tool.
10. Letter of Lt. Maclean dated 12 Dec. 1813 quoted in Sir Richard Levinge, *Historical Records of the 43rd Light Infantry* (London, Clowes, 1868), pp. 196–7. It is interesting to compare this contemporary first-hand account with Napier's own in his *History of the War in the Peninsula and South of France*, 6 vols, (London, Boone, 1853; first published 1828–40), vol. 5, pp. 368–9.
11. Duffy, *Borodino*, pp. 124–8; quote from von Meerheim is *ibid.*, p. 126.
12. Anton in W. H. Fitchett (ed.), *Wellington's Men. Some Soldier Autobiographies* (London, George Bell & Sons, 1900), p. 291.
13. Rovera quoted in *Memoirs of Sir Lowry*

Cole edited by Maud Lowry Cole and Stephen Gwynn (London, Macmillan, 1934), pp. 46–7.
14. Anton in Fitchett, *Wellington's Men*, p. 302. See below, pp. 184, 208–9 for two examples of good troops proving reluctant to leave the cover of a wall and continue their advance.
15. Kincaid, *Adventures in the Rifle Brigade*, p. 169; Gen. Cavalié Mercer, *Journal of the Waterloo Campaign* (London, Peter Davies, 1969), p. 169; letter of Sir Hussey Vivian in *Waterloo Letters* edited by Maj.-Gen. H. T. Siborne (London, Cassell, 1891), p. 149.
16. Even so, Wellington is said to have commented on a painting of Waterloo by Sir William Allan, ' "Good – very good – not too much smoke." ' Elizabeth Longford, *Wellington. The Years of the Sword* (London, Weidenfeld & Nicolson, 1969), caption to plate 47, p. 393.
17. *Recollections of Rifleman Harris* edited by Christopher Hibbert (Hamden,Connecticut, Archon, 1970), pp. 26–7.
18. Nadezhda Durova, *The Cavalry Maiden. Journals of a Female Russian Officer in the Napoleonic Wars* (London, Paladin, 1990), p. 143; William Verner, *Reminiscences of William Verner (1782–1871) 7th Hussars* (London, Society for Army Historical Research special publication no. 8, 1965), pp. 44–5; letter from Lt. Charles Booth, 9 Nov. 1810, in Levinge, *Historical Records of the 43rd Light Infantry*, p. 137; Rifleman William Green, *Where My Duty Calls Me* edited by John and Dorothea Teague (West Wickham, Synjon Books, 1975), p. 19.

CHAPTER THREE: ARTILLERY

1. Marshal Marmont, *The Spirit of Military Institutions* (Westport, Connecticut, Greenwood, 1974; first published 1864), p. 75; Philip Haythornthwaite, *Weapons and Equipment of the Napoleonic Wars* (Poole, Dorset, Blandford Press, 1979), p. 91.
2. Patrick Griffith, *French Artillery* (London, Almark, 1976), p. 10.

3. Gay de Vernon quoted in Rothenberg, *Art of Warfare in the Age of Napoleon*, p. 74.
4. Harry Smith, *Autobiography*, pp. 99–100. See also Sgt W. Lawrence, *The Autobiography of Sergeant William Lawrence* edited by George Nugent Bankes (London, Sampson Low, Marston, Searle & Rivington, 1886), p. 102. Lawrence was hit in the chest by an almost spent cannon-ball and hurt, although not seriously injured.
5. Wellington to Liverpool, 12 March 1812, *The Dispatches of Field Marshal the Duke of Wellington . . .* compiled by Col. Gurwood, 8 vols (London, Parker, Furnivall & Parker, 1844) (henceforth cited as *Wellington Dispatches*), vol. 5, pp. 543–5; Lt.-Col. A. Dickson to Maj.-Gen. Macleod, 6 June 1813, PRO WO 55/1196, p. 12 on the substitution of musket for carbine balls; Maj.-Gen. B. P. Hughes, *Firepower. Weapons Effectiveness on the Battlefield, 1630–1850* (London, Arms & Armour, 1974), p. 38.
6. Ammunition proportions from Hughes, *Firepower*, p. 36. Both Hughes and Haythornthwaite, *Weapons and Equipment of the Napoleonic Wars* give excellent accounts of the technical aspects of the subject.
7. Cairnes to Maj.-Gen. W. Cuppage, RA, 25 July 1813, *The Dickson Manuscripts* edited by Maj. John H. Leslie, 5 vols (Cambridge, Trotman, 1987–91; first published 1908), vol. 5, pp. 1016–17; Cairnes quotes Wellington's dispatch correctly but leaves out the additional phrase that 'the army is particularly indebted to that corps'. Despite this it is plain that the artillery felt – not for the first or last time – that Wellington's praise was inadequate.
8. Swabey, *Diary*, 26 March 1812, p. 81, and 12 June 1813, p. 195; David G. Chandler, *Dictionary of the Napoleonic Wars* (London, Arms & Armour, 1979), pp. 252–3 (for Lodi); Christopher Duffy, *The Military Experience in the Age of Reason* (London, Routledge & Kegan Paul, 1987), p. 235 (for Frederick the Great).

9. Charles Parquin, *Napoleon's Army* translated and edited by B. T. Jones (London, Longman, 1969), p. 101; Commandant J. Colin, *The Transformations of War* (Westport, Connecticut, Greenwood, 1977; first published 1912), p. 27; see below p. 42 for more on ammunition consumption. At Wagram, the grand battery consisted of 112 guns occupying a front of more than 2,000 yards, or about eighteen yards per gun; James R. Arnold, *Napoleon Conquers Austria. The 1809 Campaign for Vienna* (London, Arms & Armour, 1995), p. 151.
10. Dickson to Maj.-Gen. J. Macleod, RA, 28 Nov. 1813, *Dickson Manuscripts*, vol. 5, p. 1120.
11. Dyneley to John Dyneley, 25 July 1812, and to Capt. J. K. Douglas, RA, 5 Aug. 1812, *Letters Written by Lieut.-General Thomas Dyneley . . .* (London, Trotman, 1984), pp. 32–6.
12. Swabey, *Diary*, 17 Nov. 1812, p. 157.
13. Dyneley to his sister Dora, 23 Nov. 1812, Dyneley, *Letters*, pp. 57–8. See also Oman, *History of the Peninsular War*, vol. 6, pp. 148–50 and Fortescue, *A History of the British Army*, 13 vols in 20 (London, Macmillan, 1899–1930), vol. 8, pp. 618–19. Captain Macdonald was invalided back to England, but recovered from his wound and was reappointed to the troop in 1816.
14. Adye quoted in Haythornthwaite, *Weapons and Equipment of the Napoleonic Wars*, pp. 165–6.
15. Baron de Jomini, *The Art of War* translated by Capt. G. H. Mendell and Lt. W. P. Craighill (Westport, Connecticut, Greenwood, 1971), p. 317.
16. Reuter quoted in Capt. E. S. May (ed.), 'A Prussian Gunner's Adventures in 1815', *USJ*, Oct. 1891, pp. 45–6; this passage is also quoted in Antony Brett-James, *The Hundred Days* (London, Macmillan, 1964), pp. 76–7.
17. Capt. W. H. R. Simpson (ed.), 'Extracts from the Memoir of Baron Alexander de Senarmont . . .', *Minutes of the Proceedings of the Royal Artillery Institution*, vol. 1, 1858, pp. 337–9; Maj. A. F. Becke, 'Friedland, 1807', *Journal of the*

Royal Artillery*, vol. 44, 1917, pp. 90–2. Griffith, *French Artillery*, pp. 41–2 gives French losses as sixty-six casualties compared to Becke's figure of fifty-six.

18. Adye quoted in Haythornthwaite, *Weapons and Equipment of the Napoleonic Wars*, p. 166.

19. Mercer, *Journal of the Waterloo Campaign*, pp. 164–5.

20. Swabey, *Diary*, 21 June 1813, p. 201.

21. Gen. Carl von Clausewitz, *On War*, 3 vols (London, Routledge & Kegan Paul, 1949), vol. 3, p. 195. For these figures to be accurate the battalion must have been unusually strong, and the battery crowded together.

22. B. P. Hughes, *Open Fire: Artillery Tactics from Marlborough to Wellington* (Chichester, Antony Bird, 1983), p. 20 (60 to 120 per hour); Haythornthwaite, *Weapons and Equipment of the Napoleonic Wars*, p. 67.

23. Rogers, *Napoleon's Army*, p. 84 (for Boulart); Rothenberg, *Art of Warfare in the Age of Napoleon*, p. 144 (for ammunition consumed at Wagram and Borodino); Sir Richard D. Henegan, *Seven Years' Campaigning*, 2 vols (London, Henry Colburn, 1846), vol. 1, p. 345n (for Vitoria); Capt. Francis Duncan, *History of the Royal Regiment of Artillery*, 2 vols (London, John Murray, 1872), vol. 2, p. 438 (for Waterloo). These figures for ammunition consumption are probably not completely accurate – that for Borodino looks rather high even given the nature of the battle – but they produce quite credible averages of between 70 and 155 rounds per gun per day (the latter being for Borodino). (Another source gives a more plausible figure of 60,000 artillery rounds fired by the French at Borodino – or just over 100 per gun. Michael and Diana Josselson, *The Commander. A Life of Barclay de Tolly* (Oxford University Press, 1980, p. 138.) These are supported by other sources: for example, Dyneley's battery fired an average of eight-two rounds per gun at Salamanca (Dyneley, *Letters*, p. 82). Mercer (*Journal of the Waterloo Campaign*, p. 185) claims to have fired nearly 700 rounds

per gun – which is obviously a slip of the pen for the total fired by the battery, which gives a plausible average of 116 rounds per gun. Thus it seems reasonable to accept these figures of ammunition consumption as generally, if not precisely, accurate.

24. Modern authorities: Hughes, *Firepower*, p. 38; Haythornthwaite, *Weapons and Equipment of the Napoleonic Wars*, p. 64. Kutaisov paraphrased in Duffy, *Borodino*, p. 46; Col. Landmann, *Recollections of My Military Life*, 2 vols (London, Hurst & Blackett, 1854), vol. 2, pp. 208–9; Müller paraphrased in Hughes, *Firepower*, p. 41; Capt. William Webber, *With the Guns in the Peninsula* edited by Richard Henry Wollocombe (London, Greenhill, 1991), p. 112.

25. Quoted in Hughes, *Firepower*, p. 26.

26. *Ibid.*, pp. 36–7 quoting Müller.

27. Nosworthy, *Battle Tactics*, pp. 365–6 says that experienced officers did not recommend using canister at ranges over 400 or 500 metres.

28. Hughes, *Firepower*, p. 65, see also *ibid.*, pp. 59–64.

29. Adye quoted in Haythornthwaite, *Weapons and Equipment of the Napoleonic Wars*, p. 166.

30. Dickson to Maj.-Gen. J. Macleod, RA, 7 Nov. 1813, *Dickson Manuscripts*, vol. 5, p. 1099; Wilson quoted in Rogers, *Napoleon's Army*, p. 80. In some armies the drivers were not even soldiers at all: for example, the Spanish army until 1812.

31. Quoted in Duffy, *Borodino*, p. 87.

32. Wellington to Mulgrave, Paris, 21 Dec. 1815, *Supplementary Despatches, Correspondence and Memoranda of . . . the Duke of Wellington* edited by his son the Duke of Wellington, 15 vols (London, John Murray, 1858–72) (henceforth cited as *Wellington's Supplementary Despatches*), vol. 14, pp. 618–20. For a good discussion of this issue, which defends the reputation of the artillery, see Lt.-Col. Henry W. L. Hime, *History of the Royal Regiment of Artillery 1815–53* (London, Longmans, Green & Co., 1908), pp. 125–40. However, while it is relatively easy to show that Wellington's

complaints were exaggerated, it is impossible to prove that they were groundless.

33. Duncan, *History of the Royal Regiment of Artillery*, vol. 2, pp. 430–3. On Siborne's figures the disproportion is even greater, with the British artillery in total sustaining 303 casualties from a total strength of 2,967 officers and men, or 10.2 per cent: Capt. W. Siborne, *History of the War in France and Belgium in 1815 . . .*, 3rd edition (London, Boone, 1848), pp. 560, 564. See also 'A Waterloo Letter: the Royal Artillery and its Casualties' edited by Maj. P. E. Abbott, *JSAHR*, vol. 42, Sept. 1964, pp. 113–20. This is most interesting, but again it concentrates almost entirely on the horse artillery.

34. Bowden, *Armies at Waterloo*, p. 134; Martinien; Oman, 'French Losses in the Waterloo Campaign', p. 690; the figure of 287 does not allow for losses earlier in the campaign, but Martinien shows these to have been slight, and they would not significantly influence the result.

35. Peninsular figures from statistical tables in Oman, *History of the Peninsular War*; Austerlitz from Martinien.

36. Duffy, *Military Experience in the Age of Reason*, p. 245.

37. The arithmetic is as follows: for 100 wounded add 25 killed: 13 of the wounded according to the Invalides figures are due to the artillery; allow another 13 of the 25 killed, giving a total of 26 out of 125 or 20.8 per cent.

38. George W. Adams, *Doctors in Blue. The Medical History of the Union Army in the Civil War* (New York, Schuman, 1952), p. 113. I am grateful to John Koontz of Boulder, Colorado, who sent me this information in 1984.

39. George Hennell, *A Gentleman Volunteer. The Letters of George Hennell from the Peninsular War, 1812–13* edited by Michael Glover (London, Heinemann, 1979), pp. 91–2; Revd William Leeke, *The History of Lord Seaton's Regiment at the Battle of Waterloo*, 2 vols (London, Hatchard, 1866), vol. 1, p. 32; Capt. Coignet, *The Notebooks of Captain Coignet* (London, Peter Davies, 1928), p. 143.

40. Verner, *Reminiscences*, pp. 43–4.

41. Lt.-Gen. Sir W. Napier, *Life and Opinions of General Sir Charles James Napier*, 4 vols (London, John Murray, 1857), vol. 1, p. 96.

42. Quoted in Richard Holmes, *Firing Line* (London, Cape, 1985), p. 159.

43. Landmann, *Recollections of My Military Life*, vol. 2, pp. 203–5.

44. François in Antony Brett-James, *1812* (London, Macmillan, 1966), p. 127; Capt. George Wood, *The Subaltern Officer* (Cambridge, Trotman, 1986; first published 1825), pp. 57–8.

45. George Jeffrey, *Tactics and Grand Tactics of the Napoleonic Wars* edited by Ned Zuparko (Brockton, Massachusetts, Courier, 1982), p. 151.

CHAPTER FOUR: LIGHT INFANTRY

1. John A. Lynn, *The Bayonets of the Republic. Motivation and Tactics in the Army of Revolutionary France, 1791–94* (Urbana and Chicago, University of Illinois Press, 1984), pp. 261–77.

2. Quoted in Gunther E. Rothenberg, *Napoleon's Great Adversaries. The Archduke Charles and the Austrian Army* (London, Batsford, 1982), p. 184. Austria had, of course, lost her traditional source of light infantry when Napoleon annexed Croatia (part of the Illyrian Provinces) in 1809.

3. Peter Paret, *Yorck and the Era of Prussian Reform 1807–1815* (Princeton University Press, 1966) esp. Chapters 4 and 5 and p. 209. Paret's account pays great attention to the role of light infantry, regarding it as central to the efforts to reform the Prussian army. See also Dennis E. Showalter, 'Manifestation of Reform: The Rearmament of the Prussian Infantry, 1806–1813', *Journal of Modern History*, vol. 44 no. 4, Sept. 1972, pp. 364–80, esp. p. 374 which acts as a useful corrective to Paret's enthusiasm.

4. Capt. T. H. Cooper, *A Practical Guide for the Light Infantry Officer . . .* (London, Muller, 1970; first published 1806), p. xv.

5. Kincaid, *Adventures in the Rifle Brigade*, p. 8.

6. Quoted in Ardant du Picq, *Battle Studies* (New York, Macmillan, 1921), pp. 157–8.

7. Siborne, *Waterloo Letters*, p. 301.

8. Paddy Griffith, *Forward Into Battle. Fighting Tactics from Waterloo to the Near Future*, 2nd edition (Swindon, Crowood Press, 1990), pp. 39–40.

9. Quoted in Kincaid, *Adventures in the Rifle Brigade*, p. 143.

10. David Gates, *The British Light Infantry Arm c. 1790–1815* (London, Batsford, 1987), pp. 79–84. See also Paret, *Yorck and the Era of Prussian Reform*, pp. 271–3, and Showalter, 'Manifestation of Reform', pp. 374–5.

11. Leach quoted in Antony Brett-James's introduction to Costello, *The Peninsular and Waterloo Campaigns*, pp. xvii–xviii.

12. Quoted in Paret, *Yorck and the Era of Prussian Reform*, p. 106.

13. Quoted *ibid.*, p. 161.

14. *Ibid.*, p. 169n.

15. Gates, *British Light Infantry Arm*, pp. 91, 96–7.

16. Quoted in Paret, *Yorck and the Era of Prussian Reform*, p. 186.

17. *Ibid.*, pp. 151–2, 187 and plan opposite p. 105. Paret seems to forget this when writing, 'Between 1812 and 1815 the Prussian line infantry frequently fought with one-third or more of its men deployed as skirmishers' (p. 97). As a consequence he consistently overrates the importance of skirmishing in battle, and attributes solely to political motives the comments of officers who, with the experience of the war, questioned the claims made for light infantry by the reformers before 1812. See also Peter Hofschröer, *Prussian Light Infantry 1792–1815* (London, Osprey 'Men-at-Arms', 1984), pp. 12–15.

18. 'Light Infantry Movements' by 'C.J.T.S.' in *USJ*, 1829, Pt 2, p. 601.

19. Paret, *Yorck and the Era of Prussian Reform*, p. 173. These distances were very similar to those set out in the Austrian regulations of 1807: Rothenberg, *Napoleon's Great Adversaries*, p. 111.

20. Oman, *History of the Peninsular War*, vol. 4, pp. 328–9 gives an excellent account of the incident.

21. Cooper, *Practical Guide for the Light Infantry Officer*, p. 10. S. J. Park and G. F. Nafziger, *The British Military: Its System and Organization, 1803–1815* (Cambridge, Ontario, Rafm, 1983), p. 36 state confidently that skirmishers 'always had their bayonets unfixed', but give no source.

22. Kincaid, *Adventures in the Rifle Brigade*, pp. 8–9.

23. Oman, *History of the Peninsular War*, vol. 5, p. 422.

24. *Ibid.*, pp. 597, 599.

25. Hennell, *A Gentleman Volunteer*, p. 144.

26. *Ibid.*, pp. 144–6.

27. Journal of Lt. Edward Macarthur, B.L. Add. Ms. 44,022, ff.10–11.

28. Moyle Sherer, *Recollections of the Peninsula* (Staplehurst, Spellmount, 1996; first published 1824), p. 238.

29. Oman *History of the Peninsular War*, vol. 6, p. 758.

30. 'The Diary of Captain Neil Douglas, 79th Foot, 1809 to 1810' edited by Antony Brett-James, *JSAHR*, vol. 41, June 1963, pp. 104–5. Douglas's company thus sustained 45 per cent casualties in this brief incident. Oman, *A History of the Peninsular War*, vol. 3, p. 550 gives the total loss of the 79th in the battle as seven men killed, one officer and forty-one men wounded, one officer and six men missing.

31. Quoted in Michael Glover, *Wellington's Peninsular Victories* (London, Batsford, 1963), pp. 41–2: no source given.

32. Manuscript letter by Leach quoted in Col. Willoughby Verner, *History & Campaigns of the Rifle Brigade* (London, John Bale, Sons & Danielsson, 1919), vol. 2, p. 148. This account of Busaco is based on *ibid.*, pp. 144–8, Oman, *History of the Peninsular War*, vol. 3, pp. 378–81, 546, 551, 553, Lt.-Col. G. L. Chambers, *Bussaco* (Felling, Worley, 1994; first published 1910), pp. 89–99, and Donald D. Horward, *The Battle of Bussaco: Massena vs. Wellington* (Tallahassee, Florida State University Press, 1965), pp. 114–17, 173. The attempt by

Hughes (*Firepower*, p. 150) to distribute
French losses lacks credibility, especially as he makes no allowance whatever
for the losses inflicted by the allied skirmishers. As indicated, the primary
sources for the skirmishing in this part
of the battle are disappointing, but it is
very hard to find primary sources for
any action which describe skirmishing
in detail, and in particular the use of
supports in battle, rather than in theory.
This is all the more puzzling given the
wealth of primary source material relating to the Light Division.
33. Siborne, *Waterloo Letters*, p. 327.
34. Sir Andrew Leith Hay, *A Narrative of
the Peninsular War*, 3rd edition (London, John Hearne, 1839), p. 258.
35. *Letters and Journals of Field-Marshal Sir
William Maynard Gomm, G.C.B.* edited
by Francis Culling Carr-Gomm
(London, John Murray, 1881), p. 278;
Leith Hay, *Narrative of the Peninsular
War*, pp. 258–9.
36. Lt.-Col. Neil Bannatyne *History of
the Thirtieth Regiment* . . . (Liverpool,
Littlebury Bros, 1923) pp. 278–81.
Bannatyne was writing after Oman
and Fortescue and takes account of
their work. He makes a case which
other sources do not refute, although
it makes this part of the battle harder to
understand. But then, every battle, if
studied closely, is full of contradictions,
ambiguities and uncertainties.
37. Lynn, *Bayonets of the Republic*, p. 268.
38. Oman, *History of the Peninsular War*,
vol. 2, pp. 523–4 citing the *Military
Journal* of Leslie of Balquhain.
39. Quoted in Haythornthwaite, *Armies of
Wellington*, p. 96. For another such
example of a private duel see Sgt
William Lawrence, *Autobiography*, pp.
44–5.
40. Mercer, *Journal of the Waterloo Campaign*, pp. 173–4.
41. Capt. T. A. Mackenzie *et al.*, *Historical
Records of the 79th Queen's Own Cameron
Highlanders* (London, Hamilton,
Adams; Devonport, A. H. Swiss, 1887),
pp. 55–6.
42. *Ibid.*, pp. 55–6. Officers are slightly
over-represented among the casualties,

but no more so than normal: for more
on this question see below pp. 189–92.
43. Landmann, *Recollections of My Military, Life*, vol. 2, pp. 219–22.

CHAPTER FIVE: INFANTRY COMBAT

1. Figures from Oman, *History of the Peninsular War*, vol. 5, pp. 596–8, 601–3.
2. *Ibid.*, vol. 5, p. 462.
3. St Cyr quoted in Theodore A. Dodge,
Napoleon, 4 vols (Boston and New
York, Houghton, Mifflin, 1904), vol. 2,
p. 182; Marmont, *The Spirit of Military
Institutions*, p. 49.
4. Quoted in Michael Glover, *Wellington's
Army in the Peninsula, 1808–1814*
(Newton Abbot, David & Charles,
1977), p. 55.
5. Ardant du Picq, *Battle Studies*, pp. 143–
5, also pp. 52–4.
6. See Lynn, *Bayonets of the Republic*,
pp. 250–1 where he quotes examples
from the Battle of Jemappes of the
manoeuvre working well and of it
coming to grief when the enemy was a
little too close.
7. Frederick Myatt, *The Soldier's Trade.
British Military Developments, 1660–
1914* (London, Book Club edition,
1974), pp. 95–6.
8. [Lt. William Grattan], 'Reminiscences
of a Subaltern', Pt 4, *USJ*, no. 29, April
1831, p. 181.
9. *Ibid.*, pp. 181–2.
10. Piers Mackesy, *British Victory in
Egypt, 1801. The End of Napoleon's
Conquest* (London, Routledge, 1995), p.
37.
11. *The Private Journal of F. Seymour
Larpent* . . . edited by Sir George
Larpent, 2nd edition, 2 vols (London, Richard Bentley, 1853), vol. 1,
p. 104.
12. Paddy Griffith, *Military Thought in
the French Army, 1815–51* (Manchester
University Press, 1989), p. 122.
13. Friedrich von Ammon and Dr Theodor
Herold, *Soldier of Freedom. The Life of
Dr Christian Nagel, 1787–1827* (Cleve,
1829; translation San Francisco, 1968),
p. 63; Erckmann-Chatrian, *Waterloo*, p.

226; Bugeaud quoted in Chandler, *Campaigns of Napoleon*, p. 348.

14. Napier quoted in Jay Luvaas, *The Education of an Army. British Military Thought, 1815–1940* (University of Chicago Press, 1964), p. 24; see also J. A. Houlding, *Fit for Service. The Training of the British Army, 1715–1795* (Oxford, Clarendon, 1981), p. 295.

15. Prussian tests in Paret, *Yorck and the Era of Prussian Reform*, pp. 271–3; see also Showalter, 'Manifestation of Reform', *passim*; Griffith, *Forward Into Battle*, p. 29; Hughes, *Firepower*, pp. 10–11; Glover, *Wellington's Army*, p. 48, and Chandler, *Campaigns of Napoleon*, pp. 341–2.

16. 'Memorandum on Firing and Drill' by Mackenzie, n.d., Historical Manuscripts Commission, *Supplementary Report on the Manuscripts of Robert Graham Esq. of Fintry* edited by C. T. Atkinson (London, HMSO, 1942) (henceforth cited as *HMC Graham of Fintry*), p. 62.

17. Quoted in Paret, *Yorck and the Era of Prussian Reform*, p. 158n.

18. *Ibid.*, p. 273; Hughes, *Firepower*, p. 27. Earlier tests had produced much lower results, see Houlding, *Fit for Service*, pp. 262–3.

19. Both quoted in Holmes, *Firing Line*, pp. 172–3. The point is confirmed by Duffy, *Military Experience in the Age of Reason*, pp. 212–13, who states that the rare instances of troops maintaining fire by command were almost all in units in 'their first experience of combat after an intensive period of peacetime training'. See also Houlding, *Fit for Service*, pp. 350–2.

20. Lynn, *Bayonets of the Republic*, p. 246; Nosworthy, *Battle Tactics*, pp. 193, 208, agrees that complicated systems of fire drill usually collapsed in action.

21. Quoted in Mackesy, *British Victory in Egypt*, p. 91; see also n. 19 above.

22. Hughes, *Firepower*, p. 59.

23. Coignet, *Notebooks of Captain Coignet*, p. 76.

24. Quoted in Duffy, *Military Experience in the Age of Reason*, pp. 202–3.

25. Richard Glover, *Peninsular Preparation. The Reform of the British Army, 1795–*

1809 (Cambridge University Press, 1963), pp. 112–13; Paret, *Yorck and the Era of Prussian Reform*, pp. 13–14 for Frederick the Great.

26. Napier, *Life of Charles Napier*, vol. 1, pp. 97–8; Ney, *Military Studies*, p. 99.

27. Anon., 'The 29th at Roliça', *USJ*, 1830, pp. 746–7.

28. Major Patterson quoted in Griffith, *Forward Into Battle*, pp. 26–7.

29. 'Captain Synge's Experiences at Salamanca' edited by F. St L. Tottenham, *The Nineteenth Century*, July 1912, p. 59. Synge was Pack's aide-de-camp and this article prints some of his recollections.

30. Maj.-Gen. Stutterheim, *A Detailed Account of the Battle of Austerlitz* (Cambridge, Trotman, 1985; first published 1807), pp. 101, 104–5.

31. Griffith, *Forward Into Battle*, p. 39.

32. Hennell, *A Gentleman Volunteer*, p. 136; Clausewitz, *On War*, vol. 3, p. 204.

33. Costello, *The Peninsular and Waterloo Campaigns*, p. 125.

34. Henegan, *Seven Years' Campaigning*, vol. 1, pp. 344n–46n. He assumes that *all* the infantry in Wellington's army used their *entire* initial stock of ammunition, as well as half that issued from the reserve train. But many units were only lightly engaged – ten British and a number of Portuguese battalions suffered fewer than ten casualties each – and would have fired little if at all. This must lead him to overestimate the amount of ammunition consumed. On the other hand he divides the resulting figure by total French losses (which he significantly overstates), completely discounting the casualties inflicted by the allied artillery and cavalry. It may be that these mistakes roughly cancel themselves out, for his final result – that 459 rounds were fired for each casualty inflicted – is not wildly implausible.

35. Saalfeld figures from Marshal Foch, *The Principles of War* (London, Chapman & Hall, 1918), p. 322; Prussian losses at Saalfeld from Chandler, *Dictionary*, p. 387. Authorities' estimates: Griffith, *Forward Into Battle*, p. 28; Nosworthy, *Battle Tactics*, pp. 204–5; Hughes, *Firepower*, p. 27; Jeffrey, *Tac-*

tics and Grand Tactics of the Napoleonic Wars*, p. 6; Duffy, *Military Experience in the Age of Reason*, p. 209. For an example of contemporary comment see *HMC Graham of Fintry*, pp. 60–1. By contrast the 1.4 million musket rounds said to have been fired by the French at Borodino seems implausibly low: Josselson, *The Commander*, p. 138.

36. Henegan, *Seven Years' Campaigning*, vol. 1, p. 345n; Siborne, *Waterloo Letters*, p. 399.

37. Sgt John S. Cooper, *Rough Notes of Seven Campaigns* . . . (Staplehurst, Spellmount, 1996; first published 1869), p. 95.

38. *A Soldier of the Seventy-First*, p. 88 and p. 61.

39. H. Ross-Lewin, *With the 32nd in the Peninsula* . . . (Dublin, Hodges 1904), p. 184.

40. Lemonnier-Delafose quoted in Oman, *History of the Peninsular War*, vol. 5, p. 464.

41. Lemonnier-Delafose, *ibid*., p. 465.

42. *Ibid*., pp. 597–9 (allied losses), 470 (Ferey's losses). My own calculations based on Martinien and the figures in Oman suggest that this may be an overestimate of the French losses, and that a figure of about 1,000 casualties is more probable, but there can be no certainty on the point.

43. John R. Elting, *Swords Around a Throne. Napoleon's Grande Armée* (London, Weidenfeld & Nicolson, 1988), p. 481.

44. Maj.-Gen. John Mitchell quoted in Nosworthy, *Battle Tactics*, p. 209.

45. Duffy, *Military Experience in the Age of Reason*, p. 245 (for the Invalides figures); Chandler, *Campaigns of Napoleon*, p. 344 (for Larrey).

46. Stuart's dispatch of 6 July 1806, printed in the 'Appendix to the Chronicle', p. 592 of the *Annual Register* for 1806.

47. Lt.-Col. Joseph Anderson, *Recollections of a Peninsular Veteran* (London, Edward Arnold, 1913), pp. 14–15; original emphasis.

48. 'The Life of James FitzGibbon a Veteran of 1812' quoted in Dyneley, *Letters*, p. 10n.

49. Dyneley, *Letters*, p. 10.

50. Captain Wachholz quoted in Oman, *History of the Peninsular War*, vol. 6, p. 618. It is worth noting that another eyewitness account quoted by Oman (p. 619n) – that of Captain Tovey himself– does not really support Wachholz's description of bayonet fencing, so that even this instance remains open to question.

51. Anon., 'Operations of the Fifth or Picton's Division in the Campaign of Waterloo', *USJ*, vol. 13, no. 151, June 1841, pp. 179–80.

52. Lt.-Col. Gough to his wife, quoted in R. S. Rait, *The Life and Campaigns of Hugh, first Viscount Gough, Field Marshal*, 2 vols (London, Constable, 1903), vol. 1, p. 53.

53. Baron Thiébault, *The Memoirs of Baron Thiébault*, 2 vols (London, Smith, Elder & Co., 1896), vol. 2, pp. 159–65; Duffy, *Austerlitz*, pp. 115–20 provides context and information about Austrian forces; Jean A. Lochet, 'Some Comments and Considerations on French Tactics, Part VII', *Empires, Eagles and Lions*, no. 72, June 1983, pp. 21–34, esp. p. 30 gives some useful information about the proportion of veterans in Thiébault's brigade. See also Stutterheim, *Detailed Account of the Battle of Austerlitz*, pp. 102–6 for an account of these events from an Austrian perspective.

54. George Napier, *Passages in the Early Military Life of General Sir George T. Napier* (London, John Murray, 1884), pp. 141–2; artillery casualty figures from Oman, *History of the Peninsular War*, vol. 3, p. 551.

55. Manuscript journal and letter of Leach of the 95th, quoted by Verner, *History of the Rifle Brigade*, vol. 2, pp. 144n, 148.

56. George Napier, *Passages in the Early Military Life*, pp. 142–4; William Napier, *History of the War in the Peninsula* . . ., vol. 3, pp. 26–7.

57. Letter from Lt. Charles Booth, 9 Nov. 1810, in Levinge, *Historical Records of the 43rd Light Infantry*, pp. 136–7.

58. Casualty figures from Horward, *Bussaco*, pp. 172–5. As well as the primary sources cited above see *ibid*., pp. 114–22, Oman, *History of the Peninsular War*, vol. 3, pp. 397–83; Fortescue,

History of the British Army, vol. 7, pp. 523–5; Chambers, *Bussaco*, pp. 89–99; Verner, *History of the Rifle Brigade*, vol. 2, pp. 144–50 and, for some interesting background about the Légion du Midi and the Hanoverian Legion, Elting, *Swords Around a Throne*, pp. 368–70, 711 n35. Jean Jacques Pelet, *The French Campaign in Portugal 1810–1811* edited and translated by Donald D. Horward (Minneapolis, University of Minnesota Press, 1973), pp. 178–9 gives a brief and not very helpful account from a French perspective.

59. Ensign John Aitchison, *An Ensign in the Peninsular War. The Letters of John Aitchison* edited by W. F. K. Thompson (London, Michael Joseph, 1981), p. 57 – letter of 14 Sept. 1809.

60. Col. George Paton *et al.*, *Historical Records of the 24th Regiment . . .* (London, Simpkin, Marshall, 1892), p. 105.

61. Aitchison, *Ensign in the Peninsular War*, pp. 56, 58 – letters of 31 July and 14 Sept. 1809.

62. General Chambray quoted in Griffith, *Forward Into Battle*, p. 36. Griffith points out that this account forms the basis of Bugeaud's much-quoted description of encounters between French columns and British lines – Bugeaud himself seeing little service against the British.

63. This implies that the second wave of French battalions was held remarkably far behind the first; alternatively they may have been caught up in the rout of the first wave, but quickly rallied when the British attack lost impetus. Neither explanation is entirely satisfactory.

64. Julia V. Page (ed.), *Intelligence Officer in the Peninsula. Letters and Diaries of Major the Hon. Edward Charles Cocks 1786–1812* (New York, Hippocrene, 1986), pp. 39–40 – letter of 11 Sept. 1809.

65. [Capt. Peter Hawker], *Journal of a Regimental Officer during the Recent Campaign in Portugal and Spain . . .* (London, Trotman, 1981; first published London, Johnson, 1810), p. 102n; Page, *Intelligence Officer*, p. 36 – letter of 30 July 1809.

66. There is a problem here, with more than enough allied troops facing Sebastiani and not enough facing Lapisse. The only alternative I can suggest is that one or two of Mackenzie's battalions were actually facing Lapisse, though this contradicts all the authorities. Lapisse's division was slightly weaker (approximately 6,800 men compared to 8,100 in Sebastiani's) but they sustained almost exactly the same level of casualties: 25.8 per cent and 26.9 per cent respectively.

67. Oman, *History of the Peninsular War*, vol. 2, pp. 540–3. Oman quotes Colonel Desprez that the cavalry were Spanish, but says that there were no Spanish cavalry in this part of the field. However Cocks (Page, *Intelligence Officer*, pp. 39–40) shows that the British Light Dragoons were much further north suporting the KGL infantry – a point supported by Unger's map, reproduced in Hughes, *Firepower*, pp. 140–1. This charge *may* have been connected with the successful charge of the *Regimentio del Rey* against Leval's division (see Oman, pp. 535–6), as the battalion charged was closest to Leval's troops. Cocks praises the Spanish cavalry: it 'charged and took two pieces of cannon, two generals and many prisoners' though a few weeks later, after further quarrels between the allies, he belittled their achievement (Page, *Intelligence Officer*, pp. 36, 39).

68. Strength and casualty figures from Oman, *History of the Peninsular War*, vol. 3, pp. 645–53 and 541; comment about Mackenzie from Page, *Intelligence Officer*, p. 37. Lapisse was not killed outright as Oman says, but died on 30 July: see Martinien, p. 13. This whole account of Talavera is based on Oman, vol. 3, pp. 538–43 supplemented by Aitchison, *Ensign in the Peninsular War* and Page (both published after Oman). Beamish, Napier (who, of course, was not at Talavera) and Fortescue add little.

69. Wellington to Bathurst, 22 June 1813, *Wellington's Dispatches*, vol. 6, pp. 539–43; C. T. Atkinson (ed.), 'A Peninsular Brigadier. Letters of Major-General Sir

F. P. Robinson, K.C.B. . . .', *JSAHR*, vol. 34, no. 140, Dec. 1956, p. 161 explains the circumstances, but see also Fortescue, *History of the British Army*, vol. 9, p. 181; Harry Smith, *Autobiography*, p. 42.

70. Jomini, *Art of War*, p. 298.

71. Leith Hay, *A Narrative of the Peninsular War*, pp. 258–60.

72. Casualty figures from Oman, *History of the Peninsular War*, vol. 5, pp. 597–8. Oman (p. 470) estimates Maucune's losses at 2,000 casualties, though my own calculations suggest that this may be rather too high. Many of the casualties would have been inflicted by the British cavalry.

73. Quoted in Rothenberg, *Napoleon's Great Adversaries*, pp. 183–4.

74. Anon., 'A French Infantry Officer's Account of Waterloo', Pt 2, *USJ*, Jan. 1879, p. 67.

CHAPTER SIX: CAVALRY COMBAT

1. Scotty Bowden and Charlie Tarbox, *Armies on the Danube, 1809* (Arlington, Empire Games, 1980), pp. 140–54; Bowden, *Armies at Waterloo*, pp. 228–73; Oman, *A History of the Peninsular War*, vol. 5, pp. 595, 598.

2. Mercer, *Journal of the Waterloo Campaign*, p. 189n; Elting, *Swords Around a Throne*, pp. 230, 233–4; David Johnson, *Napoleon's Cavalry and its Leaders* (London, Batsford, 1978), pp. 16, 95–7.

3. Marmont, *Spirit of Military Institutions*, p. 59; Capt. L. E. Nolan, *Cavalry: its History and Tactics* (London, Bosworth, 1853), pp. 69–70.

4. Marbot, *Memoirs*, vol. 1, p. 379.

5. Jomini, *Art of War*, p. 308; Duffy, *Austerlitz*, p. 146.

6. Elting, *Swords Around a Throne*, p. 241 ('in every land'); A. J. de Rocca, 'Memoirs of the War in Spain', *Constable's Miscellany*, vol. 28, *Memorials of the Late War*, vol. 2 (Edinburgh, Constable, 1828) (hereafter cited as *Memoirs of the War in Spain*), p. 72 ('plunderers, wasters').

7. Figures based on those in Bowden and Tarbox, *Armies on the Danube*, pp. 140–54.

8. *Ibid.*, pp. 162–8; Bowden, *Armies at Waterloo*, p. 151.

9. A. E. Clark-Kennedy, *Attack the Colour! The Royal Dragoons in the Peninsula and at Waterloo* (London, Research Publishing, 1975), p. 79 quoting the regimental journal on the light cavalry sabre; Haythornthwaite, *Armies of Wellington*, p. 103 quoting an anonymous 'Officer of Dragoons' writing in the *United Service Journal* for 1831 on the heavy cavalry's weapon.

10. Parquin, *Napoleon's Army*, p. 143; other authorities: Glover, *Wellington's Army*, p. 48; the Marquess of Anglesey, *A History of the British Cavalry 1816 to 1919* (London, Leo Cooper, 1973), vol. 1, p. 97; Michael Mann, *And They Rode On. The King's Dragoon Guards at Waterloo* (Salisbury, Michael Russell, 1984), p. 5.

11. Johnson, *Napoleon's Cavalry and its Leaders*, p. 16; see also p. 96. Yet another modern authority has described it as 'one of the two finest cavalry swords ever made': R. Scurfield, 'The Weapons of Wellington's Army', *JSAHR*, vol. 36, Dec. 1958, p. 149.

12. Leith Hay, *Narrative of the Peninsular War*, p. 243; Haythornthwaite, *Armies of Wellington*, p. 139 (for the soldier with sixteen wounds).

13. Regulations quoted in Clark-Kennedy, *Attack the Colour*, p. 22; Mercer, *Journal of the Waterloo Campaign*, pp. 152–3; Siborne, *Waterloo Letters*, p. 74 (Royal Dragoons at Waterloo).

14. Anton in Fitchett, *Wellington's Men*, p. 293; Swabey, *Diary*, 15 July 1812, p. 114; Marbot, *Memoirs*, vol. 2, p. 381.

15. Prussian account quoted in Duffy, *Military Experience in the Age of Reason*, p. 228; Elting, *Swords Around a Throne*, pp. 241–3; Smithies quoted in Rogers, *Napoleon's Army*, p. 52; Dyneley, *Letters*, p. 46.

16. Lynn, *Bayonets of the Republic*, pp. 216 and 194.

17. Quoted in Georges Blond, *La Grande Armée* translated by Marshall May

(London, Arms & Armour, 1995), p. 124.

18. Landmann, *Recollections of My Military Life*, vol. 2, p. 202; Durova, *The Cavalry Maiden*, pp. 91–2.

19. On 14th Light Dragoons: Antony Brett-James, *Life in Wellington's Army* (London, Allen & Unwin, 1972), p. 180; on Napoleon's problems: Johnson, *Napoleon's Cavalry and its Leaders*, p. 97.

20. Brotherton, *A Hawk at War*, pp. 64–5.

21. Oman, *A History of the Peninsular War*, vol. 6, p. 759.

22. F. N. Maude, 'Cavalry' in *Encyclopedia Britannica*, 11th edition, 1910, vol. 5, p. 566; Seidlitz quoted in Anglesey, *History of British Cavalry*, vol. 1, p. 98.

23. Nolan, *Cavalry*, pp. 68–9; Marmont, *Spirit of Military Institutions*, p. 64; Napoleon quoted in Elting, *Swords Around a Throne*, pp. 539–40; Jomini, *Art of War*, p. 307; Ardant du Picq, *Battle Studies*, p. 188.

24. Ardant du Picq, *Battle Studies*, p. 187; Johnson, *Napoleon's Cavalry and its Leaders*, Chapter 4 *passim*. However, Kellermann was renowned for the speed and impetuosity of his charges.

25. Ardant du Picq, *Battle Studies*, pp. 188–9; Nolan, *Cavalry*, pp. 205–6 (Sohr).

26. Quoted in Napier, *History of the War in the Peninsula*, vol. 3, p. 369.

27. William Bragge, *Peninsular Portrait 1811–1814. The Letters of Captain William Bragge Third (King's Own) Dragoons* edited by S. A. C. Cassels (Oxford University Press, 1963), pp. 63–4. I have deleted the editor's explanatory interpolations from this passage.

28. Lt. Norcliffe Norcliffe to his father, 10 Aug. 1812, 'A Family Regiment in the Peninsular War' by Maj.-Gen. J. C. Dalton, *The Cavalry Journal*, vol. 18, no. 68, April 1928, pp. 285–7; this letter had previously been published in *The Cavalry Journal*, Oct. 1912.

29. Rocca, *Memoirs of the War in Spain*, p. 77.

30. Both quotes from Brett-James, *1812*, pp. 124–5.

31. Lt.-Col. Tomkinson, *The Diary of a Cavalry Officer in the Peninsular War and Waterloo Campaign, 1809–15* edited

by his son James Tomkinson (London, Swan Sonnenschein & Co., 1895), pp. 135, 136n. Yet at Villagarcia in 1812 Tomkinson himself refused a direct order from his commanding officer to halt and rally his men, so intoxicating was the sight of the enemy flying before him. *Ibid.*, p. 153.

32. Siborne, *Waterloo Letters*, p. 77; Tomkinson, *Diary*, p. 304. Nolan, *Cavalry*, p. 214 argues that colourful and distinctive uniforms, with obvious variation between regiments, would assist rapid rallying.

33. 'Eques', 'British Cavalry', *Royal Military Chronicle*, vol. 2, Oct. 1811, pp. 489–91.

34. Siborne, *Waterloo Letters*, p. 9.

35. They lost 381 killed, 578 wounded and 288 missing, making a total of 1,247 casualties from an initial strength of under 2,785 or 45 per cent. Bowden, *Armies at Waterloo*, p. 269. This was for the whole of the battle and includes many casualties suffered after the charge, but many unwounded men, not listed as casualties, would have been absent escorting prisoners, helping wounded comrades to the rear, or taking advantage of the confusion to slip away. According to one witness, by the end of the day the two brigades together amounted to only a single squadron. Siborne, *Waterloo Letters*, p. 40.

36. Siborne, *Waterloo Letters*, pp. 9–10.

37. R. B. Long to C. B. Long, 16 June 1812, *Peninsular Cavalry General (1811–13) The Correspondence of Lieutenant-General Robert Ballard Long* edited by T. H. McGuffie (London, Harrap, 1951), p. 196. There are good accounts of both Campo Mayor and Maguilla in Oman, *History of the Peninsular War*, vol. 4, pp. 258–65 and vol. 5, pp. 522–4; see also Long, *Peninsular Cavalry General*, pp. 70–81 on Campo Mayor.

38. Clark-Kennedy, *Attack the Colour*, p. 61 quoting the unofficial, contemporary journal of the Royal Dragoons.

39. Wellington to Lord John Russell, 31 July 1826, quoted in Sir Charles Oman, *Wellington's Army 1809–1814* (London, Edward Arnold, 1913), p.

104; Rocca, *Memoirs of the War in Spain*, pp. 76–7.

40. Wellington, 'Instructions to the General Officers commanding Brigades of Cavalry in the Army of Occupation', Cambrai 1816, *Wellington's Dispatches*, vol. 8, pp. 337–8; original emphasis. It is interesting to compare Wellington's views with those of Jomini. They are in broad agreement on most points, especially the importance of retaining a reserve. Jomini, however, argued that the second line should normally be in column, and favoured the use of chequered lines. Jomini, *Art of War*, pp. 310–11.

41. Nolan, *Cavalry*, p. 219.

42. D. Le Marchant, *Memoir of the late Major-General Le Marchant* (London, 1841), pp. 290–1.

43. Austrian regulations: Rothenberg, *Napoleon's Great Adversaries*, p. 113; Sahagun: Capt. Alexander Gordon, *A Cavalry Officer in the Corunna Campaign 1808–9. The Journal of Captain Gordon of the 15th Hussars* (Felling, Worley, 1990; first published 1913), p. 102, see also the Marquess of Anglesey, *One Leg. The Life and Letters of Henry William Paget, First Marquess of Anglesey, K.G., 1768–1854* (London, Cape, 1961), pp. 78–81; Eylau: Parquin, *Napoleon's Army*, p. 53; eighteenth-century opinion: Duffy, *Military Experience in the Age of Reason*, pp. 222–3. For other examples of French reliance on carbine fire see Anglesey, *One Leg*, p. 84, Tomkinson, *Diary*, pp. 5–6, Paul B. Austin, *1812. The March on Moscow* (London, Greenhill, 1993), p. 293.

44. D'Urban to J. Wilson, quoted in Oman, *Wellington's Army*, p. 235.

45. Rocca, *Memoirs of the War in Spain*, p. 81.

46. Verner, *Reminiscences*, p. 45.

47. Tomkinson, *Diary*, 3 May 1811, p. 101; Marmont, *Spirit of Military Institutions*, p. 56; Nolan, *Cavalry*, p. 234.

48. Mercer, *Journal of the Waterloo Campaign*, p. 167; R. Blakeney, *A Boy in the Peninsular War* (London, John Murray, 1899), p. 197; Siborne, *Waterloo Letters*, p. 50.

49. C. T. Atkinson, 'A Waterloo Journal' [Sergeant Johnston, Scots Greys], *JSAHR*, vol. 38, 1960, p. 40.

50. Tomkinson, *Diary*, p. 51.

51. Francis Hall, 'Recollections in Portugal and Spain during 1811 and 1812', *Journal of the Royal United Service Institution*, vol. 56, Nov. 1912, pp. 1540–1.

52. Fuentes: Oman, *A History of the Peninsular War*, vol. 4, pp. 618, 622, 624; Austerlitz: Duffy, *Austerlitz*, p. 138, and Martinien; Maguilla: Tomkinson, *Diary*, p. 173 and Oman, *op. cit.*, vol. 5, pp. 523–4; Sahagun: Fortescue, *History of the British Army*, vol. 6, pp. 336–7, Gordon, *A Cavalry Officer in the Corunna Campaign*, p. 115n, Anglesey, *One Leg*, p. 81. There is remarkable variation in the figures for Sahagun, with scarcely two sources agreeing on any particular.

53. Duffy, *Austerlitz*, p. 124; Oman, *A History of the Peninsular War*, vol. 6, pp. 74–5.

54. Oman, 'A Dragoon of the Legion', *Blackwoods' Magazine*, vol. 193, March 1913, p. 301 – quoting the letters of Capt. Carl von Hodenberg of the 1st Heavy Dragoons of the King's German Legion.

55. Nolan, *Cavalry*, p. 225.

56. Brotherton, *A Hawk at War*, pp. 41–2; original emphasis. For more on this incident see a letter from Lt.-Col. Badcock in the *USJ*, no. 42, May 1832, pp. 97–8.

57. Nolan, *Cavalry*, pp. 247–8.

58. Quoted in Duffy, *Austerlitz*, pp. 124–6.

59. Oman, *A History of the Peninsular War*, vol. 4, p. 327.

60. Thomas Morris, *The Napoleonic Wars* edited by John Selby (London, Longman, 1967), p. 77.

61. F. M. Richardson, *Fighting Spirit* (London, Leo Cooper, 1978), p. 52.

62. Col. G. Gawler, *The Essentials of Good Skirmishing*, 2nd edition (London, Parker, Furnivall & Parker, 1852), p. 26. For an example of this feeling in action see John Green, *The Vicissitudes of a Soldier's Life* (Louth, privately printed, 1827), p. 91.

63. Katzbach: Marbot, *Memoirs*, vol. 2, p. 381; Waterloo: Capt. Gronow, *The Reminiscences and Recollections of Cap-*

tain Gronow (Frome, Surtees Society, 1984), pp. 71–2, Morris, *The Napoleonic Wars*, p. 79; Parquin, *Napoleon's Army*, p. 102; Duffy, *Austerlitz*, pp. 135–6; alternating fire: Morris, *op. cit.*, p. 77.

64. Unnamed officer quoted in Gardner, *Quatre Bras, Ligny and Waterloo*, p. 284; Gronow, *Reminiscences and Recollections*, p. 190.

65. J. B., 'Formation of a Solid Square', *Royal Military Chronicle*, vol. 3, no. 16, p. 275; Major Lindsay: Siborne, *Waterloo Letters*, pp. 337–8; four-deep line: John Koontz, 'Reasons for Studying Napoleonic Drill Regulations', *Empires, Eagles and Lions*, no. 74, Sept. 1983, p. 6.

66. Oman, *A History of the Peninsular War*, vol. 4, p. 391.

67. A. Z. 'The Heavy Cavalry at Salamanca', *USJ*, Nov. 1833, p. 354; original emphasis.

68. For example, the 1st Royals at Quatre Bras: see Siborne, *Waterloo Letters*, pp. 373–4.

69. Segur, *An Aide-de-Camp of Napoleon*, pp. 391–2.

70. Kellermann's account quoted in Marmont, *Spirit of Military Institutions*, p. 161; see also 'General Kellermann's Charge of Cavalry at Marengo', *USJ*, vol. 3, 1831, Pt 3, p. 220, and Johnson, *Napoleon's Cavalry and its Leaders*, pp. 27–8.

71. Oman, *A History of the Peninsular War*, vol. 4, pp. 382–5, 631.

72. Siborne, *Waterloo Letters*, pp. 61, 75, 71.

73. Quoted in H. C. Wylly, *History of the 1st & 2nd Battalions, The Sherwood Foresters, 1740–1914*, 2 vols (Frome, for the regiment, 1929), vol. 1, p. 225. It should be noted, however, that it is difficult to reconcile Brown's account with other versions of what happened to the regiment in the battle.

74. Leeke, *History of Lord Seaton's Regiment at the Battle of Waterloo*, vol. 1, p. 13; for a cavalryman unsuccessfully trying to get his horse to trample a wounded man on the ground see the Journal of William Brooke of the 2/48th in Oman, *Studies in the Napoleonic Wars* (London, Methuen, 1929), p. 178.

75. A.Z., 'The Heavy Cavalry at Salamanca', p. 353.

CHAPTER SEVEN: THE ROLE OF THE GENERAL

1. Anglesey, *One Leg*, p. 133.

2. James Marshall-Cornwall, *Marshal Massena* (Oxford University Press, 1965), p. 204; the full text, in French, is in Oman, *History of the Peninsular War*, vol. 3, p. 549; the deletions are not lengthy or particularly important. I have restored the paragraphing as in Oman.

3. General Wimpfen, 'Plan of Attack upon the French Army on its March between Es[s]ling and Aspern towards Hirschstadten', Gerarsdorf, 21 May 1809, in W. Müller, *Relation of the Operations and Battles of the Austrian and French Armies in the Year 1809* (Cambridge, Trotman, 1986; first published London, Goddard, 1810), pp. 22–4.

4. Quoted in Duffy, *Austerlitz*, p. 95.

5. Grattan, *Adventures in the Connaught Rangers*, pp. 241–2; cf. Oman, *History of the Peninsular War*, vol. 5, pp. 434–6.

6. Le Marchant, *Memoir of the Late Major-General Le Marchant*, pp. 288–9; but cf. Viscountess Combermere and Capt. W. W. Knollys, *Memoirs and Correspondence of Field Marshall Viscount Combermere* [Sir Stapleton Cotton], 2 vols (London, Hurst & Blackett, 1866), vol. 1, p. 274 which gives a different impression.

7. Leith Hay, *Narrative of the Peninsular War*, p. 257.

8. William Wheeler, *The Letters of Private Wheeler 1809–1828* edited by Capt. B. H. Liddell Hart (London, Michael Joseph, 1951), pp. 87–8. See also Levinge, *Historical Records of the 43rd*, pp. 167–8 and Leith Hay, *Narrative of the Peninsular War*, p. 259 for other such glimpses.

9. On Wagram: Arnold, *Napoleon Conquers Austria*, p. 128; on Ligny: *Notebooks of Captain Coignet*, p. 276; on Eylau: Johnson, *Napoleon's Cavalry and its Leaders*, p. 53.

10. Marbot, *Memoirs*, vol. 1, pp. 423–4;

Harry Smith, *Autobiography*, p. 121; description of Napoleon quoted in Arnold, *Napoleon Conquers Austria*, p. 147.

11. These two notes are both reproduced and transcribed in *The Battle of Waterloo* edited by John Langdon Davies, Jackdaw folder no. 18 (New York, Grossman, 1968).

12. Lt.-Gen. Sir Hussey Vivian, 'Reply to Major Gawler on his "Crisis of Waterloo"', *USJ*, July 1833, pp. 310–23, and Oct. 1833, pp. 145–9.

13. Socrates quoted in Gen. Sir Archibald Wavell, *Generals and Generalship. The Lees Knowles Lectures delivered at Trinity College, Cambridge in 1939* (Harmondsworth, Penguin, 1941), p. 14.

14. Lt.-Col. C. O. Head, *The Art of Generalship* (Aldershot, Gale & Polden, n.d. [1930s]), pp. 62–3.

15. Quoted in Josselson, *The Commander*, p. 177.

16. Review of 26th *Léger* and grumbling: Arnold, *Napoleon Conquers Austria*, pp. 16, 24; reaction to Napoleon's wound: Parquin, *Napoleon's Army*, p. 88.

17. Oman, *History of the Peninsular War*, vol. 6, p. 662.

18. Quoted in Longford, *Wellington*, p. 490.

19. Oman, *History of the Peninsular War*, vol. 6, pp. 488–522.

20. Maj. Roverea's journal quoted in *Memoirs of Sir Lowry Cole*, pp. 72–3; Fortescue, *History of the British Army*, vol. 8, pp. 202–3, 210–11; Samuel E. Vichness, 'Marshal of Portugal: The Military Career of William Carr Beresford 1785–1814', unpublished PhD thesis submitted to Florida State University, 1976, pp. 424, 432–7.

21. Sir Henry Bunbury, *Narratives of Some Passages in the Great War with France (1799–1810)* (London, Peter Davies, 1927), p. 165.

CHAPTER EIGHT: SUBORDINATE COMMANDERS, STAFF OFFICERS AND ADCS

1. Atkinson (ed.), 'A Peninsular Brigadier', p. 163.

2. A. G. Macdonell, *Napoleon and His Marshals* (London, Macmillan, 1934),

p. 193. As usual, Macdonell makes a sound point memorable by a witty flourish which strays from literal exactitude.

3. 'The Staff at Salamanca' extract from the unpublished Autobiography of Sir Philip Bainbrigge, *USJ*, Jan. 1878, pp. 72–3.

4. Gomm, *Letters and Journals*, p. 278 (Caesar); Bainbrigge, 'The Staff at Salamanca', pp. 72–3 ('Now boys!'); Ensign Freer's diary in J. P. Jones, *History of the South Staffordshire Regiment (1705–1923)* (Wolverhampton, Whitehead, n.d. [1923]), p. 37 (the 38th).

5. Napoleon's maxims quoted in Wavell, *Generals and Generalship*, p. 42.

6. Pétiet quoted in Duffy, *Austerlitz*, p. 106.

7. [Andrew Leith Hay], *Memoirs of the late Lieutenant-General Sir James Leith* (Barbados, privately printed, 1817), p. 99.

8. Leith Hay, *Narrative of the Peninsular War*, p. 258.

9. Gomm, *Letters and Journals*, p. 278; Leith Hay, *Narrative of the Peninsular War*, p. 261.

10. French figures from Martinien; British from a paper in WO 79/50 (unpaginated, but brief) which evidently includes 1815, and may not be completely accurate. Leipzig figures from Rothenberg *Art of Warfare in the Age of Napoleon*, p. 82 – the French figure is supported by (or derived from?) Martinien.

11. Two letters from Halkett in Siborne, *Waterloo Letters*, pp. 321–4, original emphasis; *ibid.*, pp. 334–7 (letter from Lt. Pattison, 33rd Regiment); strength and casualty figures from Bowden, *Armies at Waterloo*, p. 234 and Siborne, *History of the War in France and Belgium in 1815 . . .*, p. 555. See also Brig. B. W. Webb-Carter, 'A Line Regiment at Waterloo', *JSAHR*, vol. 43, no. 174, June 1965, pp. 61–2. Thomas Morris, *The Napoleonic Wars*, p. 68 states that the 73rd were also broken, but this is not confirmed by other accounts or by its losses (four killed, forty-eight wounded and no missing, for the whole battle).

12. Siborne, *Waterloo Letters*, pp. 323–4; *Dictionary of National Biography*.

13. *Memoirs of Sir Lowry Cole*, pp. 72–8; Oman, *History of the Peninsular War*, vol. 4, pp. 389–90.

14. *Letters of Private Wheeler*, pp. 122–3.

15. Capt. Rieu quoted in Brett-James, *Europe Against Napoleon*, p. 144 (Leipzig); *Notebooks of Captain Coignet*, p. 77 (Marengo). Cadell's *History of the 28th Regiment* (a first-hand account) quoted in Brig.-Gen. F. C. Beatson, *With Wellington in the Pyrenees* (London, Tom Donovan, 1993; first published 1914), p. 212; another account of this incident can be found in Walter Henry, *Surgeon Henry's Trifles. Events of a Military Life* edited by Pat Hayward (London, Chatto & Windus, 1970), p. 81.

16. Quoted in A. Hilliard Atteridge, *Marshal Murat* (London, Nelson, n.d. *c.* 1912), pp. 375–6; on Zieten: Duffy, *Military Experience in the Age of Reason*, p. 230; on the general point, see also Chandler, *Campaigns of Napoleon*, pp. 355–6, 546–7.

17. Baron Ompteda, *A Hanoverian-English Officer A Hundred Years Ago. Memoirs of Baron Ompteda* translated by John Hill (London, Grevel, 1892), pp. 310–12; Oman, *History of the Peninsular War*, vol. 6, p. 440.

18. *Notebooks of Captain Coignet*, p. 74; on Chambarlhac see also Chandler, *Dictionary*. On Peacock and Bunbury see Oman, *History of the Peninsular War*, vol. 7, pp. 270–1; *The General Orders of Field Marshal the Duke of Wellington . . .* edited by Lt.-Col. Gurwood (London, Clowes, 1837), pp. 69–70; and C. M. H. Millar, 'The Dismissal of Colonel Duncan Macdonald of the 57th Regiment', *JSAHR*, vol. 60, no. 242, Summer 1982, pp. 71–7. The incapacity of the officers named is well known, and Wellington's famous letter commenting on Erskine and Lightburne (to Torrens, 29 Aug. 1810) is printed with their names (which were deleted in earlier editions) in Antony Brett-James (ed.), *Wellington at War, 1794–1815* (London, Macmillan, 1961), pp. 198–9.

19. Oman, *History of the Peninsular War*, vol. 4, p. 194 and n.

20. H. B. Robinson, *Memoirs of Lieutenant-General Sir Thomas Picton . . .*, 2nd edition, 2 vols, (London, Bentley, 1836), vol. 2, pp. 209–10. The Sixth Division was not at Vitoria, but the Light Division was part of the allied centre.

21. *Letters of Colonel Sir Augustus Simon Frazer, K. C. B. . . .* edited by Maj.-Gen. Edward Sabine (London, Longman, 1859), p. 291.

22. Quoted in John Colville, *The Portrait of a General* (Salisbury, Michael Russell, 1980), p. 71. Both the fact that this was a private letter to family at home, and the content of his other letters, encourage one to accept that this praise was perfectly sincere.

23. Harry Smith, *Autobiography*, pp. 142–3; S. G. P. Ward, *Wellington's Headquarters* (Oxford University Press, 1957), pp. 139–52 gives an excellent account of Wellington's relations with Murray, which should be supplemented by his admirable article 'General Sir George Murray', *JSAHR*, vol. 58, no. 236, pp. 191–208; see also Glover, *Wellington's Army*, p. 138.

24. Bainbrigge, 'The Staff at Salamanca', p. 74; Ward, *Wellington's Headquarters*, pp. 36–8 (on brigade-majors).

25. Sir James Shaw Kennedy, *Notes on the Battle of Waterloo* (London, John Murray, 1865), pp. 98–9.

26. Colville, *Portrait of a General*, p. 97 (quoting a letter from Colville).

27. Harry Smith, *Autobiography*, pp. 97–8.

28. James quoted in Geoffrey Dutton and David Elder, *Colonel William Light – Founder of a City* (Melbourne University Press, 1991), p. 59; Harry Smith, *Autobiography*, p. 35.

29. Criticism quoted in Duffy, *Military Experience in the Age of Reason*, p. 177; on Minden, see Piers Mackesy, *The Coward of Minden. The Affair of Lord George Sackville* (London, Allen Lane, 1979), pp. 98–9, 125–6.

30. Charles Esdaile, 'A Visit to Jena and Auerstadt', *Age of Napoleon*, no. 16, p. 19 drawing on Saint Simon's unpublished memoirs.

31. Siborne, *Waterloo Letters*, pp. 154 (Gordon) and 339 ('what's wrong') – in

this case it was a staff officer not an aide-de-camp who executed the order, showing how they performed much the same role in battle.

32. Details of Davout's operations from Rogers, *Napoleon's Army*, pp. 139–41.

33. Duffy, *Austerlitz*, pp. 76–9, 137–9; *Memoirs of General Count Rapp written by himself* (Cambridge, Trotman, 1985; first published London, Colburn, 1823), pp. 61, 137–8; Arnold, *Napoleon Conquers Austria*, pp. 74–5.

34. Oman, *History of the Peninsular War*, vol. 4, p. 191 (Sabugal); H. A. Bruce, *Life of General Sir William Napier*, 2 vols (London, John Murray, 1864), vol. 1, p. 131 (Nivelle).

35. Marbot, *Memoirs*, vol. 1, p. 394.

36. 'Captain Synge's Experiences at Salamanca', pp. 57–63.

CHAPTER NINE: REGIMENTAL OFFICERS

1. [Grattan], 'Reminiscences of a Subaltern', p. 180.

2. George Napier, *Passages in the Early Military Life . . .*, pp. 264–7; for other examples see Clark-Kennedy, *Attack the Colour*, passim, and Haythornthwaite, *Armies of Wellington*, p. 36.

3. Captain Cooke quoted in Gates, *British Light Infantry Arm*, p. 123; see also Glover, *Wellington's Army*, pp. 41–2; Wood, *Subaltern Officer*, pp. 5–6 and Houlding, *Fit for Service*, p. 367n who says that in 1758 officers in the 43rd – then too an excellent regiment – were trained in a similar way.

4. Morris, *The Napoleonic Wars*, p. 68; Maj. Patterson quoted in Griffith, *Forward Into Battle*, pp. 26–7; see above, p. 79.

5. Clark-Kennedy, *Attack the Colour*, pp. 37, 43; Captain Elzéar Blaze, *Recollections of an Officer of Napoleon's Army* (New York, Sturgis & Walton, 1911), p. 126.

6. Costello, *The Peninsular and Waterloo Campaigns*, p. 82; *Recollections of Rifleman Harris*, p. 28.

7. Murphy: Grattan, *Adventures in the Connaught Rangers*, p. 246; Private

Green quoted in Glover, *Wellington's Army*, p. 73.

8. Holmes, *Firing Line*, pp. 330–1. Holmes gives no source for the suspicion that Colonel Cameron's death was not due to enemy fire, and it is not mentioned in Gardyne, *The Life of a Regiment. The History of the Gordon Highlanders* (Edinburgh, Douglas, 1901), vol. 1, pp. 431–7 or in the *Dictionary of National Biography* (Cameron, John, 1771–1815), though this may be due to a natural reluctance to touch on the subject. For two examples of British soldiers killing one of their officers see Larpent, *Private Journal*, vol. 1, pp. 98–9, 113–14; but these did not occur in action and the culprits were immediately arrested and subsequently executed.

9. Grattan, *Adventures in the Connaught Rangers*, p. 129.

10. Maj.-Gen. Sir George Bell, *Soldier's Glory being 'Rough Notes of an Old Soldier'* edited by Brian Stuart (London, G. Bell & Sons, 1956), pp. 39–40.

11. Park and Nafziger, *The British Military*, pp. 25–9, 37–8 discusses the problems surrounding establishment figures, showing that any simple generalization is likely to have many exceptions.

12. Wellington to Liverpool, 10 June 1812, *Wellington's Dispatches*, vol. 5, pp. 704–6; Bathurst to Wellington, 6 Aug. and 10 Sept. 1812, *Wellington's Supplementary Despatches*, vol. 7, pp. 374–5, 417–18.

13. Kincaid, *Adventures in the Rifle Brigade*, p. 265.

14. Costello, *The Peninsular and Waterloo Campaigns*, p. 72; Clark-Kennedy, *Attack the Colour*, p. 75, and p. 64 (Mr Avarne).

15. Aitchison's diary for 26 May 1811 in *An Ensign in the Peninsular War*, p. 11; cf. p. 58.

16. Kincaid, *Adventures in the Rifle Brigade*, p. 271.

17. Grattan, *Adventures in the Connaught Rangers*, p. 244; Lt.-Col. H. F. N. Jourdain and Edward Fraser, *The Connaught Rangers* (London, Royal United Service Institution, 1924), vol. 1, pp. 97–8.

18. F. S. Tidy, 3/14th at Waterloo, quoted in Haythornthwaite, *Armies of Wellington*, pp. 97–8 ('tinkers'); Col. Mainwaring to 51st at Fuentes d'Oñoro, *Letters of Private Wheeler*, p. 56 ('tell you again'); and Col. Brown at Barrosa, Henegan, *Seven Years' Campaigning*, vol. 1, p. 210.

19. Kincaid, *Adventures in the Rifle Brigade*, pp. 237–8. Kincaid's account is so lively and vivid that one is inclined to doubt its accuracy. Certainly the words quoted may not be precisely those Beckwith used, but there is ample corroboration of the essence of Kincaid's story in other accounts of the action. See Verner, *History and Campaigns of the Rifle Brigade*, vol. 2, pp. 252–8, and Wellington to Liverpool, 9 April 1811, *Wellington's Dispatches*, vol. 4, pp. 733–5, which contains the unusually emphatic praise that 'It was impossible for any officer to conduct himself with more ability and gallantry than Col. Beckwith.'

20. Parquin, *Napoleon's Army*, pp. 134–5.

21. *A Soldier of the Seventy-First*, p. 60.

22. Napier, *Life of Charles Napier* vol. 1, p. 98.

23. Cooper, *Rough Notes*, p. 22.

24. Copy of an unpublished letter dated 27 July 1812 from an officer engaged in the Battle of Salamanca, National Army Museum Ms 6807-333.

25. Michael Duffy, *Soldiers, Sugar and Seapower. The British Expeditions to the West Indies and the War against Revolutionary France* (Oxford, Clarendon, 1987), pp. 83–4.

26. Siborne, *Waterloo Letters*, p. 325.

27. Hopkins's own account, and a letter from Napier to Col. Gurwood repeating Beckwith's remark, are both printed in Levinge, *Historical Records of the 43rd*, pp. 146–50.

28. Parquin, *Napoleon's Army*, p. 53; Maj. N. L. Beamish, *History of the King's German Legion*, 2 vols (London, T. & W. Boone, 1832–7), vol. 2, pp. 82–5.

29. Eighteenth-century view quoted in Duffy, *Military Experience in the Age of Reason*, p. 220; Costello, *Peninsular and Waterloo Campaigns*, pp. 55–6 (Lt. Strode) and 56n (Costello's opinion);

W. S. Moorsom, *Historical Record of the Fifty-Second Regiment . . . 1775–1858* (London, Richard Bentley, 1860), p. 124 (Capt. Jones).

30. Anon., 'French Infantry Officer's Account of Waterloo', p. 460.

31. Duffy, *Military Experience in the Age of Reason*, p. 76.

32. Clark-Kennedy, *Attack the Colour*, pp. 63, 115–16, 120–1.

33. Oman, *Wellington's Army*, p. 238.

34. Dyneley, *Letters*, p. 56; Segur quoted in Duffy, *Austerlitz*, p. 140.

35. Hennell, *Gentleman Volunteer*, p. 102; letter of Lt. John Hibbert quoted in Mann, *And They Rode On*, p. 82; Moorsom, *Historical Record of the Fifty-Second*, p. 264.

36. Colville, *Portrait of a General*, p. 200.

37. WO 79/50 'Return of the Numbers of killed and wounded under the command of Lord . . . Wellington . . .' (unfoliated, but brief). These figures include the King's German Legion and other foreign units in the British service, but may not include British officers serving in the Portuguese army, or losses in the Coruña campaign. The figures given for 1812 in the annual breakdown are wrong, duplicating those for 1814, but this error (presumably a copying mistake by a clerk), is not carried into the figures for the total loss.

Martinien gives the figure of 60,000 in the 'avertissement' in the front of the volume, and a sampling of the pages makes it appear plausible. Some individuals would, of course, appear more than once, being entered each time they were wounded.

38. Based on figures in Oman, *History of the Peninsular War*, vol. 4, pp. 613–14, 628–30, 634–5 and vol. 6, pp. 754–6, 761–2.

39. I owe these figures to John Koontz of Boulder, Colorado, who sent them to me in a private letter dated 18 Jan. 1984; so far as I know, they have not previously been published.

40. Haythornthwaite, *Armies of Wellington*, p. 28; Salamanca figures based on Oman, *History of the Peninsular War*, vol. 5, pp. 595–8.

41. Waterloo figures based on Bowden,

Armies at Waterloo, pp. 272, 325. Due to problems with some returns aggregating losses for the whole campaign, these figures are not precisely accurate, but this does not affect the point being made here. WO 79/50 'Return of the Numbers killed and wounded . . .' (see n. 37 above).

42. Soult quoted in Oman, *Studies*, p. 107. His own, inaccurate, return of French losses in the Battles of the Pyrenees shows the unremarkable figure of one officer to twenty-five other ranks in the casualties, although officers were much more heavily represented among those killed: one for every twelve other ranks. Oman, *History of the Peninsular War*, vol. 6, p. 774. On officer's hats see *ibid.*, vol. 6, p. 236.

43. Based on figures in Oman, *History of the Peninsular War*, vol. 2, pp. 652–3, vol. 3, pp. 552–3, vol. 4, pp. 613, 617, 630, 634–5, vol. 6, pp. 761, 774. The figures for Busaco are slightly distorted by the inclusion of II Corps' missing. British figures from Oman and WO 79/50 'Return of the Numbers killed and wounded . . .'.

44. This paragraph is based on a study of British and French cavalry casualty figures at Talavera, Albuera and Vitoria; Montbrun's at Fuentes and Le Marchant's brigade, and British as a whole, at Salamanca, and the British and their heavy cavalry in particular at Waterloo, drawing on Oman, *History of the Peninsular War*, Siborne, *History of the War in France and Belgium in 1815*, and Bowden, *Armies at Waterloo*. The only case where the officers suffered *less* than their proportion was Le Marchant's brigade at Salamanca, though Montbrun's officers lost no more than their share. In the British cavalry at Albuera, the officers amounted to 6.5 per cent of the strength, but suffered 10.4 per cent of the loss. The lack of reliable figures for strength and casualties in Napoleon's battles in central Europe is particularly frustrating when examining statistical questions such as this.

45. Hodge, 'On the Mortality Arising

from Military Operations', pp. 242–3. Although officers were much more likely to be killed or wounded in action, Hodge concludes that overall men were 60 per cent more likely to die in the course of a year's campaigning.

CHAPTER TEN: MORALE AND COHESION

1. Hennell, A *Gentleman Volunteer*, p. 102.
2. Holmes, *Firing Line*, pp. 213–20.
3. Costello, *Peninsular and Waterloo Campaigns*, p. 82; *Letters of Private Wheeler*, p. 28; Duffy, *Austerlitz*, p. 106.
4. Parquin, *Napoleon's Army*, p. 6.
5. Letter printed in *JSAHR*, June 1922, pp. 130–1.
6. Lawrence, *Autobiography of Sergeant William Lawrence*, p. 210; 'Extract of William Milne's letter', 7 March 1811, Additional Lynedoch Papers, National Library of Scotland, Ms 16, 197 ff.3–4.
7. Leaving colours at home: Rothenberg, *Art of Warfare in the Age of Napoleon*, p. 137, and Siborne, *Waterloo Letters*, p. 76; 5th Brigade at Waterloo: Maj.-Gen. G. Surtees, 'British Colours in the Waterloo Campaign', *JSAHR*, vol. 43, no. 174, June 1965, pp. 74–5. Mainwaring at Fuentes: the origin of the story is in G. C. Moore Smith, *The Life of John Colborne, Field-Marshal Lord Seaton* (New York, Dutton, 1903), p. 164, see also Lt.-Col. A. F. Mockler-Ferryman, *The Life of a Regimental Officer during the Great War, 1793–1815* (Edinburgh, Blackwood, 1913), pp. 164–9 and Frederick Mainwaring, 'Four Years of a Soldier's Life', *USJ*, 1844, Pt 2, pp. 512–22 esp. 515. The inspector's report is quoted in H. C. Wylly, *History of the King's Own Yorkshire Light Infantry*, 2 vols (London, Lund Humphries, 1926), vol. 1, p. 242. On the 2/69th at Quatre Bras: Haythornthwaite, *Armies of Wellington*, p. 80; Napier, *Life of Charles Napier*, vol. 1, p. 97.
8. Oman, *History of the Peninsular War*, vol. 5, pp. 30–45.

9. Kincaid, *Adventures in the Rifle Brigade*, p. 18; Grattan quoted in Brett-James, *Life in Wellington's Army*, p. 79; Anton in Fitchett, *Wellington's Men*, p. 274.

10. *Letters of Private Wheeler*, p. 116; for a modern view of the importance of these factors see Richardson, *Fighting Spirit*, p. 171.

11. William Windsor, 'Waterloo: Letters of a Soldier from the Peninsula and Waterloo, 1811–1815', *Cornhill Magazine*, vol. 79, June 1899, p. 742.

12. Tupper Carey, 'Waterloo: Reminiscences of a Commissariat Officer', *Cornhill Magazine*, vol. 79, June 1899, p. 729 (two quotes) – Carey served throughout the Peninsular War as well as at Waterloo, but cf. Morris, *The Napoleonic Wars*, pp. 76–7 which contradicts it; Duffy, *Austerlitz*, pp. 105–6; Holmes, *Firing Line*, pp. 244–51 has some interesting comments and examples on the effects of alcohol and drugs on soldiers in action. See also Fortescue, *History of the British Army*, vol. 8, pp. 161–2 who reports – on the evidence of two British sources – that at Fuentes de Oñoro some 'of the French [cavalry] troopers were drunk, galloping in all directions with no kind of order and under no sort of control'.

13. On the 88th see Grattan, *Adventures in the Connaught Rangers*, *passim* and Henry, *Surgeon Henry's Trifles*, p. 44; Costello, *Peninsular and Waterloo Campaigns*, p. 118; Kincaid, *Adventures in the Rifle Brigade*, pp. 272, and 273–4 on the looting; on the last point see also Atkinson (ed.), 'A Peninsular Brigadier', p. 164, and Sgt William Lawrence, *Autobiography*, p. 111.

14. *Letters of Private Wheeler*, p. 148.

15. *A Soldier of the Seventy-First*, p. 18; Anton in Fitchett, *Wellington's Men*, pp. 261–2.

16. French army: Blaze, *Recollections of an Officer of Napoleon's Army*, pp. 100, 278; Tomkinson, *Diary*, pp. 289, 318 (corporal of the Guards), 288–9 (the last quote). Not that all such cowards were tolerated, of course. For another example, which resulted in 300 lashes and disgrace, see Sgt William

Lawrence, *Autobiography*, pp. 207, 221–4.

17. George Napier, *Passages in the Early Military Life . . .*, pp. 124–5; Brotherton, *A Hawk at War*, p. 48.

18. Glover, *Wellington's Army*, p. 73; Brotherton, *A Hawk at War*, pp. 46–7.

19. Costello, *Peninsular and Waterloo Campaigns*, pp. 118–19.

20. Wood, *Subaltern Officer*, pp. 94–5; Oman, *History of the Peninsular War*, vol. 2, p. 515 and n.

21. Duffy, *Austerlitz*, p. 83 (Napoleon's proclamation), p. 129 (Suchet's claim); Rothenberg, *Art of Warfare in the Age of Napoleon*, p. 235 (Wagram); Ney, *Military Studies*, p. 87; Wellington, *General Orders*, 11 June 1813, pp. 3–4.

22. Tomkinson, *Diary*, p. 289; *Letters of Private Wheeler*, p. 28.

23. Mercer, *Journal of the Waterloo Campaign*, p. 138; 43rd: letter from Maj. Hopkins quoted in Bruce, *Life of William Napier*, vol. 1, p. 100; 95th: Costello, *Peninsular and Waterloo Campaigns*, p. 53; Ellis: Basil Jackson, *Notes and Reminiscences of a Staff Officer . . .* (London, John Murray, 1903), p. 76, but cf. *DNB*.

24. Ney, *Military Studies*, p. 87.

25. 'Captain Synge's Experiences at Salamanca', p. 59; Ardant du Picq, *Battle Studies*, p. 150; cf. Arnold, *Napoleon Conquers Austria*, pp. 155–7.

26. Brotherton, *A Hawk at War*, p. 46.

27. Siborne, *Waterloo Letters*, p. 84; Brotherton, *A Hawk at War*, pp. 69–70; Mann, *And They Rode On*, pp. 59, 72.

28. *Notebooks of Captain Coignet*, p. 176.

29. Maj. John H. Leslie, 'Some Remarks concerning the Royal Artillery at the Battle of Talavera, July 27–28, 1809', *Journal of the Royal Artillery*, vol. 34, 1907–8, p. 506n.

30. Lt. Louis Planat de la Faye quoted in Brett-James, *1812*, p. 128.

31. Dyneley, *Letters*, p. 33; Moorsom, *Historical Records of the Fifty-Second*, p. 97; Anon., 'Operations of the Fifth or Picton's Division . . .', p. 180.

32. Joseph Petit, *Marengo: or the Campaign of Italy by the Army of Reserve . . .*

(London, Jordan, 1800; anonymous reprint, n.d. *c.* 1981), pp. 54–5; Vivian, 'Reply to Major Gawler . . .', p. 319.

33. Oman, *History of the Peninsular War*, vol. 7, p. 274; Duffy, *Soldiers, Sugar and Seapower*, pp. 124–5.

34. Quoted in Bruce, *Life of William Napier*, vol. 1, pp. 55–7.

35. Seymour in Siborne, *Waterloo Letters*, pp. 18–19; see also p. 50; Mercer, *Journal of the Waterloo Campaign*, pp. 234–5; strength and losses from Bowden, *Armies at Waterloo*, p. 265; see also Anglesey, *One Leg*, p. 365.

36. Ammon and Herold, *Soldier of Freedom*, pp. 63–7, 71–2 (quotes Nagel's account); Siborne, *Waterloo Campaign*, p. 222; Bowden, *Armies at Waterloo*, p. 170. It is impossible to perfectly reconcile Nagel's and Siborne's accounts of what happened, partly at least because Nagel is intent on minimizing the misbehaviour of his regiment.

37. Blaze, *Recollections of an Officer of Napoleon's Army*, p. 121.

38. Marshall quoted in Holmes, *Firing Line*, p. 160; Clausewitz, *On War*, vol. 3, p. 203.

39. Quoted in Brett-James, *Europe Against Napoleon*, p. 145.

40. Quoted in Oman, *History of the Peninsular War*, vol. 2, p. 525 (no source given).

41. Bell, *Soldier's Glory*, p. 84.

42. Marbot, *Memoirs* vol. 2, p. 30; Marshal Macdonald, *Recollections of Marshal Macdonald Duke of Tarentum* (New York, Scribner's, 1893), pp. 150–1.

43. Verner, *Reminiscences*, pp. 46–7.

44. Kincaid, *Adventures in the Rifle Brigade*, pp. 256–8.

45. Aspern-Essling: Harold T. Parker, *Three Napoleonic Battles* (Durham, NC, Duke University Press, 1983; first published 1944), p. 72; road to Brussels (first quote) and Sir R. Hill, both Verner, *Reminiscences*, p. 47; Belgian fugitives: Carey, 'Waterloo: Reminiscences of a Commissariat Officer', p. 730. See also J. von Pflugk-Harttung, 'Front and Rear of the Battle-Line of Waterloo', *Journal of Military History*, vol. 2, Jan. 1917, pp. 19–26.

CHAPTER ELEVEN: ATTITUDES AND FEELINGS

1. Wood, *Subaltern Officer*, pp. 51–2.

2. Sherer, *Recollections of the Peninsula*, p. 113.

3. Brotherton, *A Hawk at War*, p. 11.

4. Quoted in Lt.-Gen. Laurence Shadwell, *The Life of Colin Campbell, Lord Clyde*, 2 vols (Edinburgh, Blackwood, 1881), vol. 1, pp. 4–5.

5. Napier, *Life of Charles Napier*, vol. 1, p. 101; Costello, *Peninsular and Waterloo Campaigns*, p. 143.

6. Marlots quoted in Austin, *1812: the March on Moscow*, p. 297; letter from Pte. Charles Stanley quoted in Mann, *And They Rode On*, p. 5; Nagel quoted in Ammon and Herold, *Soldier of Freedom*, p. 34.

7. Lasalle quoted in Johnson, *Napoleon's Cavalry and its Leaders*, p. 72; Kincaid, *Adventures in the Rifle Brigade*, p. 275.

8. Johnson, *Napoleon's Cavalry and its Leaders*, pp. 83–4; Harry Smith, *Autobiography*, p. 144; Kincaid, *Adventures in the Rifle Brigade*, p. 275.

9. Lemonnier-Delafosse quoted in Oman, *History of the Peninsular War*, vol. 5, p. 464; *ibid.*, vol. 1, pp. 588–9, 595 (Moore) and vol. 6, p. 401n (Cadogan).

10. Capt. Barralier, 'Adventure at the Battle of Salamanca', *USJ*, Oct. 1851, p. 274; Costello, *Peninsular and Waterloo Campaigns*, p. 95; Stevenson and Ludlam both in Haythornthwaite, *Armies of Wellington*, p. 124; Mainwaring, 'Four Years of a Soldier's Life', p. 514; Pte. John Marshall to his father, 11 July 1815, printed in *USJ*, 1831, p. 315.

11. Robinson in Atkinson, 'A Peninsular Brigadier', p. 161; Napier, *Life of Charles Napier*, vol. 1, p. 100; Colville, *Portrait of a General*, pp. 143–4 (quotes both Colville and Wellington).

12. *Recollections of Rifleman Harris*, p. 17; Rocca, *Memoirs of the War in Spain*, p. 71; Bell, *Soldier's Glory*, p. 90; Clark-Kennedy, *Attack the Colour*, p. 54 quoting from the regimental *Journal*.

13. Dalhousie quoted in Mackesy, *British Victory in Egypt*, pp. 137–8; Bruce, *Life*

of William Napier, vol. 1, p. 87 (on Macleod); Norman Scarfe (ed.), 'Letters from the Peninsula. The Freer Family Correspondence, 1807–14', *Transactions of the Leicestershire Archaeological Society*, vol. 29, 1953, pp. 42–3, 72–3; W. Napier, *History of the War in the Peninsula*, vol. 5, p. 383.

14. Santarem: Costello, *Peninsular and Waterloo Campaigns*, p. 48; Harry Smith, *Autobiography*, pp. 155–6; Oman, *History of the Peninsular War*, vol. 7, pp. 294–5 (for other stories); Gates, *British Light Infantry Arm*, pp. 150–2 (quote from Wellington).

15. George Napier, *Passages in the Early Military Life*, p. 177; original emphasis.

16. Rocca, *Memoirs of the War in Spain*, p. 153.

17. Felton Hervey: Lord William Pitt Lennox, *Celebrities I Have Known...*, 2 vols (London, Hurst & Blackett, 1876), vol. 1, p. 153, see also Moore Smith, *Life of Colborne*, p. 127; Brotherton, *A Hawk at War*, pp. 26–7 (Busaco).

18. Fuentes: Costello, *Peninsular and Waterloo Campaigns*, pp. 66–7; Vivian, 'Reply to Major Gawler...', p. 316.

19. Brotherton, *A Hawk at War*, pp. 26–7 (the quote) and 17–18.

20. Costello, *Peninsular and Waterloo Campaigns*, pp. 10–11; p. 11n quotes Cope.

21. Harry Smith, *Autobiography*, p. 46.

22. Sherer, *Recollections of the Peninsula*, p. 256.

23. Costello, *Peninsular and Waterloo Campaigns*, pp. 56–7.

24. George Napier, *Passages in the Early Military Life*, pp. 47–8.

25. Gordon, *Cavalry Officer in the Corunna Campaign*, pp. 105–6.

26. Brotherton, *A Hawk at War*, pp. 35–6, 51.

27. Levinge, *Historical Records of the 43rd Light Infantry*, p. 147.

28. Page, *Intelligence Officer in the Peninsula*, p. 145; 18th Hussars officer quoted in John Keegan, *The Face of Battle* (New York, Viking Press, 1976), p. 154; *Letters of Private Wheeler*, pp. 138, 172–3; Costello, *Peninsular and Waterloo Campaigns*, p. 51.

29. See above, Chapter 1, pp. 8–9. If an army sustained 30 per cent casualties – which was very heavy – and one fifth of these were killed – an unusually high proportion – 6 per cent were killed. This does not take into account those who subsequently died of their wounds (which will be discussed in Chapter 13), who were fewer than might be thought.

30. Costello, *Peninsular and Waterloo Campaigns*, p. 58.

31. Johnson, *Napoleon's Cavalry and its Leaders*, p. 149; Beauharnais quoted *ibid.*, p. 111.

32. Colville, *Portrait of a General*, p. 147.

33. Henry, *Surgeon Henry's Trifles*, p. 92.

CHAPTER TWELVE: VICTORY OR DEFEAT?

1. Captain Fritz ——— quoted in Brett-James, *The Hundred Days*, p. 80.

2. Quoted in Duffy, *Borodino*, p. 131.

3. Clausewitz, *On War*, vol. 1, pp. 245–6.

4. Oman, *History of the Peninsular War*, vol. 1, pp. 419–24.

5. Clausewitz, *On War*, vol. 1, pp. 244–5; Frederick the Great's losses: Duffy, *Military Experience in the Age of Reason*, p. 250.

6. Busaco figures: Oman, *History of the Peninsular War*, vol. 3, pp. 384–5: this does not include 300 or 400 French prisoners.

7. Clausewitz, *On War*, vol. 1, p. 246; on Kutusov see Josselson, *The Commander*, pp. 144–6.

8. Colonel von Reiche quoted in Brett-James, *The Hundred Days*, pp. 81–2.

9. Reuter in May, 'A Prussian Gunner's Adventures', p. 47. This passage is also quoted in Brett-James, *The Hundred Days*, p. 78.

10. Nagel quoted in Ammon and Herold, *Soldier of Freedom*, p. 66.

11. Duffy, *Austerlitz*, pp. 145–9 including the quote from Czartoryski.

12. Details of Austerlitz, *ibid.*, pp. 150–62.

13. Blücher quoted in Andrew Uffindell, *The Eagle's Last Triumph. Napoleon's Victory at Ligny, June 1815* (London, Greenhill, 1994), p. 116; Nagel in

Ammon and Herold, *Soldier of Freedom*, p. 66; Reuter in May, 'A Prussian Gunner's Adventures', pp. 47–8.

14. Duffy, *Austerlitz*, p. 150.

15. Lemmonier-Delafosse quoted in Oman, *History of the Peninsular War*, vol. 5, p. 468.

16. Lt. Julius ——— quoted in Brett-James, *The Hundred Days*, pp. 179–80.

17. *Recollections of Marshal Macdonald*, pp. 232–5.

CHAPTER THIRTEEN: AFTER THE FIGHTING

1. Gomm, *Letters and Journals*, p. 350; Costello, *Peninsular and Waterloo Campaigns*, p. 129.

2. Dr Haddy James, *Surgeon James's Journal, 1815* edited by Jane Vansittart (London, Cassell, 1964), pp. 28–9.

3. Tomkinson, *Diary*, p. 187; Kincaid, *Adventures in the Rifle Brigade*, p. 58; original emphasis.

4. Wellington to the Duke of Beaufort, 19 June 1815, *Wellington's Dispatches*, vol. 8, pp. 153–4; Frazer, *Letters*, pp. 123–4.

5. Oman, 'A Dragoon of the Legion', p. 301.

6. Kincaid, *Adventures in the Rifle Brigade*, pp. 40, 113; Costello, *Peninsular and Waterloo Campaigns*, p. 129.

7. Costello, *Peninsular and Waterloo Campaigns*, pp. 127–9.

8. Brotherton, *A Hawk at War*, p. 70; for another example of this see Sir John Fortescue, *Following the Drum* (Edinburgh, Blackwood, 1931), p. 93.

9. Kincaid, *Adventures in the Rifle Brigade*, p. 112.

10. *Recollections of Rifleman Harris*, pp. 37–8.

11. *Letters of Private Wheeler*, p. 126; Cooper, *Rough Notes*, pp. 117–18; Haythornthwaite, *Armies of Wellington*, p. 208 (for Rifleman Orr).

12. Kincaid, *Adventures in the Rifle Brigade*, p. 68; Wellington, *General Orders*, 19 May 1809 and 3 June 1811, pp. 46–7; Landmann, *Recollections of My Military Life*, vol. 2, pp. 224–7.

13. Verner, *Reminiscences*, pp. 45–6; Frazer, *Letters*, p. 159; *Surgeon James's Journal*, p. 46 (for Kelly).

14. Kincaid, *Adventures in the Rifle Brigade*, p. 56; see also Holmes, *Firing Line*, p. 382, and Keegan, *The Face of Battle*, pp. 48–51.

15. Page, *Intelligence Officer in the Peninsula*, pp. 84, 87; Mackesy, *British Victory in Egypt*, p. 122.

16. For examples see: Napier, *Life of Charles Napier*, vol. 1, p. 99; Ross-Lewin, *With the 32nd in the Peninsula*, p. 182n.

17. Dyneley, *Letters*, pp. 43–5.

18. Napier, *Life of Charles Napier*, vol. 1, pp. 103–10, 116.

19. Brotherton, *A Hawk at War*, pp. 79–82.

20. For a full account of these negotiations, see P. Coquelle, *Napoleon & England 1803–1813* (London, George Bell & Sons, 1904), pp. 237–64.

21. Mann, *And They Rode On*, pp. 79, 85–6; but cf. Brett-James, *The Hundred Days*, pp. 179–80.

22. Bragge, *Peninsular Portrait*, p. 115; Rocca, *Memoirs of the War in Spain*, p. 68.

23. Capt. Franz Roeder, *The Ordeal of Captain Roeder* translated and edited by Helen Roeder (London, Methuen, 1960), pp. 151–2.

24. Baron Boris Uxkull, *Arms and the Woman. The Diaries of Baron Boris Uxkull, 1812–1819* edited by Detlev von Uexküll (London, Secker & Warburg, 1966), pp. 91, 102, 88; see also Rothenberg, *Art of Warfare in the Age of Napoleon*, p. 90.

25. Roguet quoted in Andrew Uffindell, *The Eagle's Last Triumph*, pp. 109–11; Thiébault, *Memoirs*, vol. 2, pp. 165–6; Duffy, *Austerlitz*, pp. 156–7.

26. According to one account Offley 'lay on the ground, unable to move, but not dead' and was there murdered by a soldier's wife searching for plunder. Capt. T. H. Browne, *The Napoleonic War Journal of Captain Thomas Henry Browne 1707–1816* edited by Roger Norman Buckley (London, Bodley Head, for the Army Records Society, 1987), p. 174.

27. Barralier, 'Adventure at the Battle of Salamanca', pp. 274–7. In the course of this short article, the author's name is also spelt Barrallier and Barallier.

28. Costello, *Peninsular and Waterloo Campaigns*, p. 126 (Spanish soldier in the 95th); Frazer, *Letters*, p. 563; Brett-James, *The Hundred Days*, p. 202; Harry Smith, *Autobiography*, pp. 138–9.

29. Some use was made of brandy or derivatives of opium as an anaesthetic, and of vinegar as an antiseptic, but their effectiveness was limited.

30. George Napier quoted in Haythornthwaite, *Armies of Wellington*, p. 138.

31. François quoted in Austin, *1812. The March on Moscow*, p. 283.

32. Percy quoted in Blond, *La Grande Armée*, p. 208.

33. Percy quoted *ibid.*, p. 165.

34. Anon., *Memoir of Baron Larrey, Surgeon-in-Chief of the Grande Armée*, 2nd edition (London, Renshaw, 1862), pp. 66–7.

35. King's Dragoon Guards: Mann, *And They Rode On*, p. 101; return in *Wellington's Supplementary Despatches*, vol. 14, p. 633.

36. Hodge, 'On the Mortality arising from Military Operations', pp. 226–7. Despite all the hard fighting in 1812, with three sieges as well as Salamanca, only 905 British soldiers of Wellington's army died in hospital from their wounds; thirty-five died from gangrene and four from tetanus. This compares with typhus, which caused 999 deaths, and dysentery with 2,340. Lt.-Gen. Sir Neil Cantlie, *A History of the Army Medical Department*, vol. 1 (Edinburgh and London, Churchill Livingstone, 1974), pp. 352–4.

37. Lützen: *Notebooks of Captain Coignet*, p. 245; Brussels: Brett-James, *The Hundred Days*, pp. 196–203.

38. Letter of 22 Nov. 1813 from 'a person of great commercial eminence' in Leipzig, printed in F. Shoberl, *A Narrative of ... Events ... near Leipzig ... 1813* (London, Ackerman, 1814), pp.

x–xi. As this pamphlet was intended to raise money to relieve distress in Saxony it may have exaggerated – and some of the figures do not make sense – but there is no reason to doubt that conditions were almost as bad as described.

39. Quoted in Haythornthwaite, *Armies of Wellington*, p. 208.

40. Kincaid, *Adventures in the Rifle Brigade*, p. 42; Ross-Lewin, *With the 32nd in the Peninsula*, pp. 191–2; La-baume quoted in Duffy, *Borodino*, p. 154.

EPILOGUE

1. Lt.-Col. Charles Cadell of the 28th quoted in Brett-James, *Life in Wellington's Army*, p. 235.

2. Kincaid, *Adventures in the Rifle Brigade*, p. 285; Haythornthwaite, *Armies of Wellington*, p. 142 (John Cowley, and an excellent discussion of the subject); Costello, *Peninsular and Waterloo Campaigns*, pp. 152, 156–7.

3. Kincaid, *Adventures in the Rifle Brigade*, pp. 206–7.

4. Wood, *Subaltern Officer*, pp. 112–13.

5. Henegan, *Seven Years' Campaigning*, vol. 1, pp. 246–9.

6. *A Soldier of the Seventy-First*, pp. 111–13.

7. Costello, *Peninsular and Waterloo Campaigns*, pp. 14–16, 16n–17n.

8. *Ibid.*, pp. xii–xiv.

9. Morris, *The Napoleonic Wars*, p. 116; Brotherton, *A Hawk at War*, p. 11.

10. Norman Gash, 'After Waterloo: British Society and the Legacy of the Napoleonic Wars', *Transactions of the Royal Historical Society*, 5th series, vol. 28, 1978, pp. 147–8; Haythornthwaite, *Armies of Wellington*, p. 142.

11. Gash, 'After Waterloo', pp. 147–8; Haythornthwaite, *Armies of Wellington*, p. 74.

12. Sergeant Robertson in Mackenzie Macbride, *With Napoleon at Waterloo and other Unpublished Documents of the Waterloo and Peninsular Campaigns, also papers on Waterloo by the late Edward*

Bruce Low (Philadelphia, Lippincott, 1911), p. 166 (rumour re brass medals); Costello, *Peninsular and Waterloo Campaigns*, p. 159 (soldier of the 95th); Haythornthwaite, *Armies of Wellington*, p. 73.

13. Wood, *Subaltern Officer*, pp. 210–13; A. A. Payne, *A Handbook of British and Foreign Orders, War Medals and Decorations* (Polstead, Suffok, J. B. Hayward, 1981; first published Sheffield 1911), pp. 39–40, 54–5.

Bibliographical Essay

This study is based largely on printed primary sources – mainly the memoirs, letters and diaries of the soldiers themselves. There is such a vast and rewarding literature of this kind that it seemed superfluous to seek unpublished sources in the archives unless they provided evidence different in quality or kind from that which has been published. But such fresh material is not readily found. Having been interested in this subject for many years, I kept my eyes open for it while spending months at Southampton University working on the Wellington Papers for *Britain and the Defeat of Napoleon*, but found little that was relevant to the nature and experience of combat. At the Public Record Office I specifically looked at the full casualty returns for several regiments at Salamanca in the hope that they might give details of how individual soldiers had been wounded – whether their wounds were due to artillery, small arms fire, swords or bayonets – but found the records barren. I did, however, find a most interesting return (WO 79/50) which lists the losses of Wellington's army in action, divided by year and by rank, and I have used this extensively in Chapters 8 and 9. At the National Army Museum and several other archives I saw a number of manuscript sources which provided some interesting material, although not fundamentally different from that found in similar printed accounts. Finally, I may mention that I have read – though not principally for this work – the very extensive correspondence of Alexander Gordon, one of Wellington's aides-de-camp throughout the Peninsular and Waterloo campaigns. It is a most interesting source for Wellington's operations, but again, it has little which is relevant to this study.

Some general comments can be made about the published primary sources. Normally one would expect the works written closest to the time – particularly the letters and diaries – to be the most useful; and this rule generally holds good for discovering what happened at a particular engagement, where reminiscences have often been influenced by accounts published subsequently. But memoirs are often better at describing aspects of daily life which are taken for granted by those writing letters and diaries, while they can also be surprisingly honest in admitting to fear and misconduct.

Detailed descriptions of fighting are surprisingly rare in soldiers' accounts – there is usually much more on the joys and miseries of life on campaign and, in letters and diaries, speculation about future operations. In part this was because fighting itself was quite rare in a Napoleonic soldier's life, while battles were often followed by periods of intense activity, which left little time for writing. But it may also have been because battles were very confusing for most soldiers, so that even a few hours later they might be left with only a kaleidoscopic recollection of vivid images, but with no certainty of how they fitted together or related to the battle as a whole. Veteran troops were naturally less confused than novices, while mounted officers had a better view and wider responsibilities than subalterns; but no one – not even the commanding general – could see all of a battle, or appreciate all its facets at the time.

Almost all personal accounts therefore contain a large element of reconstructing what happened after the event. This began on the evening after the battle as the soldiers exchanged stories over their camp-fires. Striking or amusing incidents which had occurred during the fighting would gradually be smoothed into neat anecdotes which might, years later, be told with varying details in different memoirs – even being attributed to different people at different battles, though the germ of the story would still be based on an actual event. In the same way, reminiscences occasionally credit the unit with performing an action at one battle which properly belongs to another, though such gross errors are rare. More common, naturally enough, are mistakes over the strength and identity of opposing forces, and uncertainty over questions of timing, or the sequence of events, while many authors overstate – quite sincerely – the importance of their unit's part in the action.

The more detail we seek to extract from the sources the less reliable they generally become, especially when describing moments of intense combat. Some resort to stale rhetoric, others are vague, while even those which seem most plausible usually cannot be independently verified. The problem can be partly overcome by noting recurring elements in different though similar incidents, but in the end an element of uncertainty remains, which needs to be acknowledged.

Among the scores of primary sources consulted for this study, only a few can be singled out for comment, but Sir Charles Oman gives an extended and still excellent discussion of the Peninsular sources in *Wellington's Army*. Of the British memoirists, none is more lively and amusing than Kincaid, that connoisseur of a good anecdote. Less well known is Thomas Brotherton, whose stories have been collected and made more widely available by Bryan Perrett. They make only a slim volume, but are most entertaining and suggestive, while conveying a wonderful impression of Brotherton himself in later life, at ease after a good dinner, a fine port beside him and a tale to tell! But despite his jovial manner, Brotherton was no fool, and other sources confirm that he was an active, intelligent and extremely gallant soldier. Harry Smith was another serious soldier who wore his professionalism lightly, while George Bell, William Grattan, Moyle Sherer, Richard Henegan and Colonel Landmann of the Engineers all deserve mention for their entertaining personal accounts. Andrew Leith Hay's *Narrative of the Peninsular War* is less humorous, but no less valuable, as should be clear from his wonderfully detailed account of Salamanca, often quoted above. Of the 'voices from the ranks', Edward Costello's memoir has proved the richest source, with comments on a wide variety of subjects. The anonymous 'Soldier of the Seventy-First' has written a simple book of great appeal, and Thomas Morris, William Lawrence, Rifleman Harris and Private Wheeler are all useful.

The memoirs of French officers and men tend to be more extravagant and less matter-of-fact than their British counterparts, though this may partly reflect the choice made by translators, for the results are most entertaining. Marbot, Parquin and Coignet all delight in the improbable story which reflects glory on them and tests our credulity, but in between these tales they give much interesting and plausible material. Rocca is less outlandish and so more useful, while his description of Andalusia is delightful. Lejeune writes with a painter's eye for a scene, while Thiébault, though not dependable, has much of interest. Other important foreign sources include Ammon and Herold's life of Christian Nagel, and Reuter's experiences at Ligny edited by May. Two useful contemporary accounts which go beyond personal experience are Stutterheim on Austerlitz and Müller on Aspern-Essling and Wagram.

Letters and diaries tend to be less entertaining than reminiscences, though an exception must be made for Mercer's famous *Journal of the Waterloo Campaign* in which a contemporary diary has been written up for publication. The result is one of the most colourful and evocative accounts of the Hundred Days, showing considerable literary ability, and well deserving its frequent reprints. Less polished works are, however, sometimes more reliable: Captain Tomkinson's *Diary* has been recognized as a source of great importance since its first publication in 1894, and it has now been joined by the almost equally important letters and diaries of his friend Edward Charles Cocks. William Bragge's letters are quite interesting, as are those of Robert Ballard Long who commanded a brigade of British cavalry in the Peninsula, although not always to Wellington's satisfaction. Captain Dyneley's affectionate, amusing letters home were first published in the *Minutes of the Proceedings of the Royal Artillery Institution* in 1896, and have been made much more widely available by their publication in a slim volume by Ken Trotman. Less graphic and appealing, but still useful for a gunner's experiences, are Frazer's *Letters* and Swabey's *Diary*, while there is some good material buried deep in the *Dickson Manuscripts*. Comparable infantry sources abound, but it would not be unfair to single out the letters of Hennell, Aitchison and Simmons; while there is useful evidence of the attitudes of more senior officers in the lives of Colville and Uxbridge (see under Anglesey). Wellington's correspondence, however, seldom reveals much about the events of a battle, though there are some interesting reports about aspects of Busaco and Barrosa, for example, printed in the *Supplementary Despatches*.

The collection of letters produced by Captain Siborne's enquiries about Waterloo, and published by his son as *Waterloo Letters*, makes a tempting source, but one which needs to be used with caution. The letters were written twenty years or more after the battle, when memories were influenced by many accounts which had been published and some violent public controversies. They cannot resolve disputed details of the action, especially those touching on the 'Crisis', but they contain a great deal of interesting information, including excellent detail on points such as the way fresh supplies of infantry ammunition were brought up, or skirmishers were recalled.

In addition to these books, much good primary source material has been published as articles in journals. These range from specialist military publications such as the *United Service Journal*, the *Journal of the Royal Artillery*, the *Cavalry Journal*, the *Journal of the Royal United Service Institution*, and the *Journal of the Society for Army Historical Research*; through standard scholarly works such as the *English Historical Review*, to more popular serials from the *Cornhill Magazine* of the 1890s to *Country Life* and the *Listener*. Some of these articles are very brief – for example a single page printing a letter from an officer at Albuera – to much more substantial series of articles, such as the diary of Francis Hall, or the original publication of Dyneley's letters. Others which I found particularly useful include the letters of Private William Windsor, and three relating to Salamanca: Charles Synge, Norcliffe Norcliffe (see Maj.-Gen. J. C. Dalton), and Captain Barralier.

Such journals can normally only be found in a good research library; much more generally accessible are the works of Antony Brett-James and Paul Britten Austin which weave entertaining accounts of individual campaigns by a careful selection of extracts from memoirs, letters and other sources. At its best this can work very well indeed, bringing to light obscure and little-known sources, sometimes not previously available in English. It does not, of course, supersede conventional campaign histories, which provide a far better vehicle for detailed analysis and explanation, but it is a very useful supplement to them.

The sum of all these personal accounts of fighting is inevitably impressionistic, suggesting interpretations of how battles worked, rather than proving them. The relatively hard data of statistics provide a measure with which these interpretations can be tested. This is so even though the data are often less reliable than they look when neatly laid out on the printed page. Neither the 'morning states' showing the strength of an army, nor its casualty returns, are invariably accurate, and even when accurate, they can still be misleading. The morning states included men such as bandsmen and farriers who were present with the unit, but who would not take part in the fighting; while casualties were sometimes inflated by the inclusion as wounded or missing of men who had gone to the rear, or artificially reduced by commanders wishing to minimize a defeat. In general British figures seem to have been accurate, apart from minor discrepancies and mistakes. Many scholars have examined them, including some inclined to be critical, without detecting major irregularities, though it is worth adding that British estimates of French losses in battles against them – like most such estimates – were often greatly exaggerated. French figures for the Peninsula vary widely: some are good, some non-existent (e.g. Marmont's losses at Salamanca), and some wilfully inaccurate – Soult being particularly notorious in this regard. But in general, thanks above all to Sir Charles Oman, there are detailed figures for both sides for most battles involving the British in the Peninsula. Statistics for the great battles of central Europe are far inferior: we do not even know the strength of the French army at Austerlitz, let alone the breakdown of its losses. The one great standby we do have is Martinien's list of every French officer killed or wounded in any action between 1805 and 1815. Extrapolating from such a list is not without risks, but it is far better than having nothing with which to test the accounts of the likes of Marbot. (Scott Bowden's eagerly awaited *Napoleon and Austerlitz* should add greatly to our knowledge of these issues when it appears.)

Bridging the gap between primary and secondary sources are a number of books written after the war which are not personal accounts but which are informed by personal experience. Clausewitz saw extensive service in the Prussian army, and *On War* is the grandest and most far-reaching of these books. Although his main interests are broader and more theoretical, Clausewitz makes some interesting comments on tactics, and especially on the degeneration of armies during a battle of attrition. However he assumes that his own experiences had a universal relevance which was not altogether justified. Jomini's *Art of War* is also more concerned with strategic than tactical matters, but his chapter on the 'Formation and Employment of Troops for Battle' is full of interest and belies his reputation for dry, artificial abstractions. Marmont's *Spirit of Military Institutions*, Ney's *Military Studies* (written for the benefit of his corps in the Camp at Boulogne), and, although he was not born until after the war, Nolan's *Cavalry* all contain good material mixed with much which is less interesting.

Napier's famous *History* is equally the product of both research and his own experience, but his accounts of battles are seldom very long and the details are often lost in the rhetorical flourishes. His letters from the Peninsula, printed in the typically Victorian life of him compiled by H. A. Bruce, are much more interesting, though there are frustrating gaps in the sequence. Similarly, Napier's life of his brother Charles is enriched by extracts from Charles Napier's journal, and by his memorable account of his experiences at Coruña.

Napier's *History* has been largely superseded by Oman who gives very long, detailed descriptions of all the major battles in the Peninsular War. Oman writes well and quotes from a wide range of first-hand accounts to elucidate obscure points and to convey something of the atmosphere of the battle. His knowledge of the war and of sources in many languages is unrivalled; he takes great pains to ascertain what happened in as much detail as possible; he does not conceal difficulties and contradictions in the sources; and he produces a compelling narrative, while printing invaluable statistical material in his appendices.

Compared to such achievements his failings are slight: his first volume lacks some of the authority of its successors; his references are skeletal and his quotations can be disconcertingly full of trifling inaccuracies; his maps of battles have often been criticized as imprecise, though they are visually pleasing; and he is sometimes careless over details. Fortescue had the advantage of publishing most of his volumes on the Peninsular War after he had read Oman, and he can sometimes make corrections or offer alternative interpretations which are convincing. But in general the two great authorities largely agree, and of the two, Oman normally gives the greater detail while having the wider view.

No other writers in English have worked on the same scale as Oman and Fortescue, but there have been some valuable monographs and campaign histories. Busaco has been the subject of special studies by George Chambers and Donald Horward – the latter is very thorough and has the advantage of being able to draw on all previous accounts of the battle. Piers Mackesy has recently published a superb history of the British conquest of Egypt in 1801. Napoleon's campaigns have often been described, but seldom in sufficient detail to shed much light on how tactics worked in practice. Chandler writes brilliantly, but has space for only a sketch of each of the battles; Petre gives rather more detail but is sometimes confusing and often dull. The best monographs are Christopher Duffy's *Austerlitz* – shrewd, lively and with some marvellous quotations, it is much superior to his *Borodino* – and James Arnold's *Napoleon Conquers Austria*, which is less well written, but thorough, alert to tactical questions, and very useful. Robert Epstein, writing of the same campaign, makes an interesting if not altogether convincing case for regarding 1809 as marking the beginning of a new era of warfare. Strangely, despite the many books on the subject, there is no good modern history of the Hundred Days, and it may be that many of the disputed issues relating to Waterloo are so shrouded with controversy and confusion as to be insoluble.

A number of valuable studies have been published on individual armies which often shed light on tactical questions. Probably the fullest account of the French army is Elting's *Swords Around a Throne* which covers a huge range of topics in considerable detail and with great enthusiasm. Blond's *La Grande Armée* is more impressionistic and is much concerned not to forget the miseries of war. Johnson's *Napoleon's Cavalry and its Leaders* is interesting and rewarding, but ultimately fails to do its subject full justice – possibly it should have been longer. Finally Paddy Griffith's *Military Thought in the French Army, 1815–51* has a chapter on tactical training which sheds some light on the Napoleonic experience. Not surprisingly there are fewer studies of the other Continental armies. Charles Esdaile's excellent *Spanish Army in the Peninsular War* has some good comments on tactics, though its main focus is on broader questions. Gunther Rothenberg's *Napoleon's Great Adversaries* is helpful on the Austrian army, but has an enormous subject to cover in a relatively short book. The Prussian army has attracted rather more attention. Paret's *Yorck and the Era of Prussian Reform* is erudite and forceful, though his strong emphasis on light infantry and skirmishers seems excessive, even anachronistic. There are two good articles by Showalter, while Peter Hofschröer has written widely in amateur magazines and published various slight booklets – but has yet to produce the full account of the Prussian army at war which he has seemed to promise for so long.

There have been a number of important books on the British army. Oman, Michael Glover, and Philip Haythornthwaite have each published studies of Wellington's army which explore different aspects of the subject, so that they are complementary. All three are excellent in their different ways, though none gives much consideration to the allied contingents under Wellington's command. As the most recent, Haythornthwaite faced the difficulty of making his book distinct from its predecessors, and has succeeded admirably by passing lightly over familiar topics, asking interesting and novel questions, and discovering fresh material in obscure sources. His approach to tactics is sophisticated, though they do not figure very largely, and overall his book is most refreshing. So too is *Life in Wellington's Army* by Antony Brett-James. It has nothing on the fighting (though there is an excellent chapter on the wounded), but gives a vivid and interesting account of the daily life of the army both in cantonments and on campaign. Brett-James draws on a very wide range of sources and weaves quotations and paraphrases together with great skill to create an original and informative book. S. G. P. Ward's work on Wellington's headquarters is meticulous and authoritative, and he has rescued Sir George Murray from undeserved obscurity. Two important books on the background of the army also need to be mentioned: Richard Glover's *Peninsular Preparation* is a scholarly if combative account of the reforms of the British army by a great admirer of the Duke of York; while J. A. Houlding's *Fit for Service* describes the training of the army in the eighteenth century with academic authority and detail which is sometimes overwhelming, but which does not obscure its important conclusions, especially the distinction between partly and really well trained troops.

In addition to these books there are many histories of individual regiments or larger units. Regimental histories vary widely: some are quite useless; others shed just the occasional ray of fresh light on what their unit was doing; while the most useful – at least for a study like this – are those which print otherwise unpublished letters or first-hand accounts, which give new details on precisely what the regiment did in a particular battle. A good example of this last type is Levinge's *Historical Records of the 43rd Light Infantry*. Verner's *History and Campaigns of the Rifle Brigade* belongs in a class almost of its own: based on considerable original research and wide reading, it is a detailed and beautifully produced account of its subject. There have also been several important modern unit histories: Clark-Kennedy's account of the Royal Dragoons in the Peninsula and at Waterloo reveals much about the troubled inner history of the regiment and prints many extracts from its marvellously scurrilous *Journal*. Michael Mann's account of the King's Dragoon Guards at Waterloo is useful with some good new material, while Sir Neil Cantlie's *History of the Army Medical Department* is a scholarly work which sheds useful light both on the treatment of the wounded and on the constant drain which sickness caused in Wellington's army.

Light infantry of the period have always been the subject of particular interest, partly because of the outstanding performance of the British Light Division and the fondness of its members for recording their achievements in lively memoirs, and partly because, both in tactics and philosophy, it was seen to be progressive and forward-looking. David Gates has skilfully traced the origins, training and techniques of the *British Light Infantry Arm*, though he too has found it difficult to discover many good descriptions of precisely what skirmishers did – as opposed to what they were meant to do – in action. Two well-known books on the subject by J. F. C. Fuller have been discredited by more recent research: J. A. Houlding writes of *British Light Infantry in the Eighteenth Century* that it 'is to be avoided, since it is unhistorical, inaccurate, merely a vehicle for his tactical theories of the 1920s', while Gates makes even stronger criticisms of *Sir John Moore's System of Training*.

There are a number of modern studies of the art of war in the period, or of particular aspects of it. Gunther Rothenberg's *Art of Warfare in the Age of Napoleon* is wide-ranging, scholarly and authoritative; and he has also written a sensible, level-headed essay on the laws of war in the period. David Chandler includes a sparkling account of tactics and their interaction with strategy in *The Campaigns of Napoleon* but lacks the space to explore the topic fully. The technical aspects of weapons and equipment are well covered in Philip Haythornthwaite's *Weapons and Equipment of the Napoleonic Wars*, and B. P. Hughes's *Firepower* and *Open Fire*, although the latter's attempts to calculate the effectiveness of weapons in action appear simplistic and unconvincing. Jean Colin's *Transformations of War* has many interesting comments on different aspects of the subject, although his views are sometimes heavily influenced by the military debates of his time. Drill regulations are explored with baffling enthusiasm by George Nafziger and George Jeffrey, although they constantly encounter the problem of not knowing how far these regulations were applied in practice. (See also the article by John Keegan in the *Times Literary Supplement* and the interesting correspondence which it provoked.) The role of the general in action has been little explored: Vachée gives a detailed account of Napoleon on campaign and the workings of Imperial Headquarters which is most rewarding, but his account is much less effective once the battle begins. Keegan's *Mask of Command*, van Creveld's *Command in War*, and the improbably named Lt.-Col. C. O. Head's *Art of Generalship* are all most disappointing; while Wavell's *Generals and Generalship* is slight but quite interesting.

Infantry tactics have been the subject of rather more attention, although there has been much copying of dubious material from one secondary source to another. Home and Pratt's *Précis of Modern Tactics* should have been forgotten long ago, but still wields surprising influence, often at second or third hand.

Becke's *Introduction to the History of Tactics* is rather better, but is now super-seded. Ross's *Flintlock to Rifle* is a considerable improvement on these, although it still conveys a rather dry, mechanical view of tactics. Robert Quimby's *Background of Napoleonic Warfare* traces French debates about tactics during the eighteenth century. It is an important and scholarly book, but its influence has not been entirely beneficial, for it has directed attention to military writers engaged in controversies, rather than to what actually happened in battle. John Lynn avoids this pitfall in *Bayonets of the Republic* – though he takes due account of such debates. His book is based on a very detailed examination of a single army in action – the Armée du Nord in 1791–4. By trawling deep in the archives he has found a mass of fresh material that over-throws some old assumptions which had become too well established, and provides a solid basis for new argument. Some of his conclusions seem disput-able, and the general applicability of others may be doubted, but it is a most significant book.

Tactics and the Experience of Battle in the Age of Napoleon was almost com-pleted before I was able to read Brent Nosworthy's *Battle Tactics of Napoleon and his Enemies*. I approached it with some trepidation, fearing that it might pre-empt some of my own arguments; however it has a quite different approach to the subject, being more concerned with the history of tactical doctrine than how tactics worked on the battlefield. An example of the difference in perspec-tive is that Nosworthy devotes a single brief chapter (fourteen pages in a book of 516 pages) to 'the psychological basis of tactics', which I feel lies at the heart of the subject. But if there is little contact between our arguments for much of the time, there is a pleasing level of agreement when we do approach an issue in the same way. For example, we are both sceptical of the practical application of complicated drill evolutions in close proximity to the enemy, and I can heartily recommend his chapter on cavalry versus infantry.

British infantry tactics in the Peninsula have been the subject of much controversy and debate. In the 1830s and 1840s Napier and Major-General John Mitchell disputed the relative importance of firepower and bayonets (for a lively account of this quarrel see the chapter on Mitchell in Jay Luvaas's *Education of an Army*). In 1910 Oman presented his famous paper on 'Column and Line in the Peninsular War' to the British Academy, subsequently reprint-ing it with variations in both *Wellington's Army* and *Studies in the Napoleonic Wars*. Much of this essay is an original and generally convincing description of Wellington's tactics, making points which have won universal acceptance, so that they now appear commonplace and obvious, even almost trite. However he also makes one important error of fact, and two interpretations which have been challenged. The factual mistake is simple: he says that the French attacked in column at Maida where in fact they were in line, and the point is central to his argument, for he uses Maida as a case study of why line was intrinsically superior to column. The error was corrected in the version of the paper pub-lished in *Wellington's Army* but not in that in *Studies* – for which none of the obvious explanations (carelessness? pressure of other work? copyright?) provides a reasonable excuse.

The first of his interpretations which has been attacked is his statement that attacking French columns in the Peninsula had no intention of deploying into line before closely engaging the British. This contradicted both French tactical doctrine and the arguments of Oman's contemporary, the French authority Jean Colin. Their view has been revived by James Arnold in his rather bad-tempered article 'A Reappraisal of Column versus Line in the Napoleonic Wars'. However Oman's argument is more subtle than Arnold allows, and though Arnold scores some definite hits, his alternative interpretation appears unconvincing.

The second element of Oman's essay which has attracted dissent is his emphasis on British firepower as the vital point in explaining their success, shown at its crudest when he counts the number of muskets which could be brought to bear in any confrontation between troops in line and in column. Here the criticism seems well founded, for the accounts of participants usually lay at least equal stress on psychological factors – surprise, the cheering, the counter-attacking charge – as on the volley; while, as we have seen, it is not clear that the British troops always fired before the French broke (see above pp. 93, 96–7). Oman's leading critic on this ground has been Paddy Griffith, who gives an excellent account of the whole issue, and many other aspects of infantry tactics, in his *Forward Into Battle*. (This has appeared in two editions, the second having significant new material in the Napoleonic chapter, though not particularly relevant to this point.) I fully agree with the thrust of Griffith's argument and have been much influenced by his approach, though I think that he is inclined to overstate his case. (His study of tactics in the American Civil War is also very interesting, although not all readers will be convinced that it was 'the last Napoleonic War'.)

There is another ground on which Oman's essay might be criticized, although less for its content than for its immense influence. Oman concentrates on Wellington's defensive tactics, and this has been transmitted through countless popular works into an unthinking cliché that the British always stood on the defensive, in line, on the reverse slope of a ridge, and that the French always charged forward to attack them in column, never learning their lesson. In fact, of course, battles in the Peninsula took many forms, with the British often taking the offensive and the French sometimes fighting in line. Oman knew this well, and the descriptions of battles in his *History* are more subtle and careful than the disputes over his essay would suggest – although he does occasionally make sweeping statements, especially about the superiority of line over column, which now seem unwise.

Napoleonic tactics may appear an arcane subject to outsiders, but it is discussed with great enthusiasm and passion in a number of amateur journals. From the late 1970s to the mid-1980s, when I first became seriously interested in the subject, I found these magazines most stimulating and rewarding.

Empires, Eagles and Lions, the *Journal of the Napoleonic Association*, the *Courier* and *Wargamer's Newsletter* contained fresh work from writers including Paddy Griffith, Philip Haythornthwaite, James Arnold, George Nafziger, Peter Hofschröer, and Richard Riehn. Some of the pieces were distinctly amateurish, others were no more than idle thoughts tossed up for discussion, but others were quite substantial articles (often spread over a number of issues) and have since been developed at length in books. Occasionally the lively discussions led to prolonged controversies which could be exasperating to those who took part (this is said to be the reason for the tone of James Arnold's article on column and line), but in general they encouraged a cross-fertilization of ideas. I should add that I lost touch with these magazines in the mid-1980s, and do not know how they fare today, though I have seen some good articles in a similar, new journal, *The Age of Napoleon*.

A few books remain to be mentioned. John Keegan's *The Face of Battle* has had great and deserved popular success, for it developed a fresh and innovative approach to the subject by concentrating on the experience of individual soldiers in battle. The analysis of tactics is not always entirely convincing, and Waterloo is not the most typical battle of the period; but the book is well written and raises many interesting issues, often exploding previously unquestioned assumptions in the process. Keegan himself traces the origins of this approach back to Ardant du Picq who, in the mid-nineteenth century, explored what actually happened in battle with a refreshingly open mind. *Battle Studies* – Ardant du Picq's book – remains immensely stimulating, though few would doubt that he often carries his arguments too far. Both Keegan and Ardant du Picq stress the importance of psychological factors in combat, and Richard Holmes in *Firing Line* takes up this theme and explores it at length. He is particularly interested in how soldiers were trained and prepared for battle, how group loyalty sustained their morale in action, and how men dealt with their fears and reacted to the horrors of war. Although he draws examples from all periods the focus is very much on the twentieth century, but it is fascinating reading and points of comparison, similarity and difference from the Napoleonic period constantly spring to mind. My only real complaint is that his notes and references are very limited, so that it is often impossible to trace stories back to their source. More directly relevant and no less stimulating is Christopher Duffy's excellent *Military Experience in the Age of Reason*. It describes the military experience during the eighteenth century both in Europe and overseas, in cantonments, on campaign, and in battle, drawing on a remarkably wide range of sources, while remaining entertaining and enjoyable to read. The long (eighty-page) chapter on battle is perceptive and original, and it has often been the only secondary source which touched on questions which I wished to explore, suggesting lines of approach and hinting at possible answers. Duffy's book is nicely complemented by Jay Luvaas's compilation *Frederick the Great on the Art of War* which contains many relevant and suggestive comments.

Interest in military history, and in the Napoleonic Wars in particular, continues to flourish. Rare, early memoirs are keenly collected and sell for hundreds of pounds – many have been reprinted, as have Oman, Napier and numerous lesser works. New books regularly appear, and while some are slight and derivative, obviously aimed at an uncritical audience, others are more substantial, being based on painstaking research or developing original arguments. No single approach can do justice to all facets of Napoleonic warfare, and many important books have been written which have not been mentioned here because they do not relate to the details of combat. This diversity is the best and most encouraging indication of the health of the subject.

Bibliography

MANUSCRIPT SOURCES

British Library:
Add. Mss 43,217, 43,223, 43,224 Correspondence of Colonel Sir Alexander Gordon, aide-de-camp to the Duke of Wellington, with his brother Lord Aberdeen, 1809–15
Add. Ms. 44,022 Journal of Lt. Edward Macarthur, 1813–14 (39th Regiment)
National Army Museum, Chelsea:
NAM Ms 6807–123 'Memoirs of a Dragoon' – a ranker in the 5th Dragoon Guards
NAM Ms 6807–333 Unpublished letter dated 27 July 1812 from an officer engaged in the Battle of Salamanca
NAM Ms 7904–15 Lt. Donald Mackenzie, 'Narrative of Experiences in the Peninsular War and Waterloo Campaign'
NAM Ms 7912–21 Anon., Memoirs of a soldier in the 1/38th
Public Record Office, Kew:
WO 17/2470 General Returns, July–Dec. 1812
WO 25/1398 Casualty Returns for 3rd Dragoons, 1809–17
WO 25/1405 Casualty Returns for 4th Dragoons, 1809–16
WO 79/50 'Return of the Numbers of killed and wounded under the command of Lord . . . Wellington . . .'
WO 55 Ordnance Department/1194–1197 Letters from Officers on Foreign Service, 1808–18
National Library of Scotland:
Ms 16,197 Additional Lynedoch Papers

MAGAZINES

The Courier
Empires, Eagles and Lions
Journal of the Napoleonic Association
Wargamer's Newsletter
The Age of Napoleon

Articles in these magazines are too numerous and generally too brief to be listed individually, except in the few cases where they have been cited in the notes. See bibliographical essay for further comments.

PUBLISHED SOURCES

Abbott, Maj. P. E. (ed.), 'A Waterloo Letter: the Royal Artillery and its Casualties', *JSAHR*, vol. 42, Sept. 1964, pp. 113–20.

Adams, George W., *Doctors in Blue. The Medical History of the Union Army in the Civil War* (New York, Schuman, 1952).

Aitchison, John, *An Ensign in the Peninsular War. The Letters of John Aitchison* edited by W. F. K. Thompson (London, Michael Joseph, 1981).

Ammon, Friedrich von and Dr Theodor Herold, *Soldier of Freedom. The Life of Dr. Christian Nagel, 1787–1827* (Cleve, 1829; translation San Francisco, 1968).

Anderson, Lt.-Col. Joseph, *Recollections of a Peninsular Veteran* (London, Edward Arnold, 1913).

Anglesey, Marquess of, *One Leg. The Life and Letters of Henry William Paget, First Marquess of Anglesey, K.G., 1768–1854* (London, Cape, 1961).

——and F. R. Hodge, 'Correspondence concerning the Death of Major Edward Hodge', *JSAHR*, vol. 43, June 1965, pp. 80–91.

——*A History of the British Cavalry 1816 to 1919*, vol. 1 (London, Leo Cooper, 1973).

Annual Register for 1806.

Anon., 'The 29th at Rolica', *USJ*, vol. 2, Nov. 1830, pp. 745–7.

Anon., 'Charge of the 23rd Light Dragoons at Talavera', *USJ*, 1831, Pt 2, pp. 545–6.

Anon., 'General Kellermann's Charge of Cavalry at Marengo', *USJ*, vol. 3, 1831, Pt 3, pp. 216–22.

Anon., 'Cavalry Affair, 6th June 1811', *USJ*, June 1832, p. 256.

Anon., 'Operations of the Fifth or Picton's Division in the Campaign of Waterloo', *USJ*, vol. 13, no. 151, June 1841, pp. 170–203.

Anon., 'Battle of Busaco', *USJ*, vol. 16, no. 190, Sept. 1844, pp. 89–101.

Anon., 'The Column of Attack', *USJ*, 1852, Pt 2, pp. 187–200.

Anon., 'A French Infantry Officer's Account of Waterloo', Pt 2, *USJ*, Dec. 1878, pp. 453–62, Jan. 1879, pp. 66–76.

Anon., 'The Battle of Leipzig by a French Infantry Officer', *USJ*, March and April 1879, pp. 364–73, 460–74.

Anton: *see* Fitchett, *Wellington's Men*.

Ardant du Picq, Col., *Battle Studies* (New York, Macmillan, 1921).

Arnold, James R., 'A Reappraisal of Column versus Line in the Napoleonic Wars', *JSAHR*, vol. 60, Winter 1982, pp. 196–208.

——*Napoleon Conquers Austria. The 1809 Campaign for Vienna* (London, Arms & Armour, 1995).

Aspinall-Oglander, Cecil, *Freshly Remembered. The Story of Thomas Graham, Lord Lynedoch* (London, Hogarth Press, 1956).

Atkinson, C. T., *History of the Royal Dragoons, 1661–1934* (Glasgow, for the regiment, n.d. [1934]).

——'A Waterloo Journal' [Sergeant Johnston, Scots Greys], *JSAHR*, vol. 38, 1960, pp. 29–42.

——(ed.), 'A Peninsular Brigadier. Letters of Major-General Sir F. P. Robinson, K.C.B. . . .', *JSAHR*, vol. 34, no. 140, Dec. 1956, pp. 153–70.

——*Also see* Historical Manuscripts Commission.

Atteridge, A. Hilliard, *Marshal Murat* (London, Nelson, n.d. *c.* 1912).

Austin, Brig.-Gen. H. H., *Old Stick-Leg* (London, Geoffrey Bles, 1926).

Austin, Paul B., *1812. The March on Moscow* (London, Greenhill, 1993).

A.Z., 'The Heavy Cavalry at Salamanca', *USJ*, Nov. 1833, pp. 351–4.

Bacot, John, 'A Sketch of the Medical History of the First Battalion of the First Regiment of Foot Guards during the Winter of 1812–13', *Medico-Chirurgical Transactions*, vol. 7, 1816, pp. 373–86.

Badcock, Lt.-Col., 'Remarks on the Cavalry operations at Fuentes d'Oñoro', *USJ*, no. 42, May 1832, pp. 97–8.

Bainbrigge, Sir Philip, 'The Staff at Salamanca', extract from the unpublished Autobiography of Sir Philip Bainbrigge, *USJ*, Jan. 1878, pp. 72–5.

Bannatyne, Lt.-Col. Neil, *History of the Thirtieth Regiment . . .* (Liverpool, Littlebury Bros, 1923).

Barralier, Capt., 'Adventure at the Battle of Salamanca', *USJ*, Oct. 1851, pp. 274–7.

Barrès, Jean-Baptiste, *Memoirs of a Napoleonic Officer* edited by Maurice Barrès (New York, Dial Press, 1925).

Barrett, C. R. B., *History of the XIII Hussars*, vol. 1 (Edinburgh and London, Blackwood, 1911).

Battine, Capt. Cecil, 'The Charge of the 23rd Light Dragoons at Talavera', *Cavalry Journal*, vol. 5, 1910, pp. 354–7.

Batty, Capt., *An Historical Sketch of the Campaign of 1815* (London, Trotman, 1981; first published 1820).

——*Campaign of the Left Wing of the Allied Army in the Western Pyrenees . . . 1813–14 . . .* (London, Trotman, 1983; first published 1823).

Beamish, Maj. N. L., *History of the King's German Legion*, 2 vols (London, T. & W. Boone, 1832–7).

Beatson, Brig.-Gen. F. C., *With Wellington in the Pyrenees* (London, Tom Donovan, 1993; first published 1914).

Becke, Maj. A. F., 'The British Artillery at Waterloo, June 18, 1815', *Journal of the Royal Artillery*, vol. 34, 1907–8, pp. 313–28.

——*Introduction to the History of Tactics* (London, 1909).

——'The Battle of Hanau, 30 October 1813', *Journal of the Royal Artillery*, vol. 40, 1913–14, pp. 69–86.

——*Napoleon and Waterloo*, 2 vols (London, Kegan Paul, Trench, Trübner & Co., 1914).

——'Friedland, 1807', *Journal of the Royal Artillery*, vol. 44, May, June, July 1917, pp. 33–44, 81–94, 121–32.

Bell, Maj.-Gen. Sir George, *Soldier's Glory being 'Rough Notes of an Old Soldier'* edited by Brian Stuart (London, G. Bell & Sons, 1956).

Berkeley, Alison D. (ed.), *New Lights on the Peninsular War* (Lisbon, British Historical Society of Portugal, 1991).

Bird, Sir W. D., 'Wellington's Tactical Preferences?', *Army Quarterly*, July 1938, pp. 228–41.

Blakeney, R., *A Boy in the Peninsular War* (London, John Murray, 1899).

Blanco, Richard L., *Wellington's Surgeon General: Sir James McGrigor* (Durham, NC, Duke University Press, 1974).

Blaze, Capt. Elzéar, *Recollections of an Officer of Napoleon's Army* (New York, Sturgis & Walton, 1911).

Blond, Georges, *La Grande Armée* translated by Marshall May (London, Arms & Armour, 1995).

Bond, Gordon C., *The Grand Expedition* (Athens, University of Georgia Press, 1979).

Boulger, D. C., *The Belgians at Waterloo* (London, privately published, 1901).

Boulter, Samuel, 'An Eyewitness's Account of Waterloo. Letter of Samuel Boulter', *Notes & Queries*, March 1954, pp. 115–17.

Bourgogne, J., *The Memoirs of Sergeant Bourgogne* edited by David Chandler (London, Arms & Armour, 1979).

Bowden, Scott, *Armies at Waterloo* (Arlington, Empire Games, 1983).

Bowden, Scotty and Charlie Tarbox, *Armies on the Danube, 1809* (Arlington, Empire Games, 1980).

Bragge, William, *Peninsular Portrait 1811–1814. The Letters of Captain William Bragge Third (King's Own) Dragoons* edited by S. A. C. Cassels (Oxford University Press, 1963).

Brett-James, Antony (ed.), *Wellington at War, 1794–1815* (London, Macmillan, 1961).
—— *The Hundred Days* (London, Macmillan, 1964).
—— *1812* (London, Macmillan, 1966).
—— *Europe Against Napoleon* (London, Macmillan, 1970).
—— *Life in Wellington's Army* (London, Allen & Unwin, 1972).
—— *Also see* Wilson, Sir Robert.
Brotherton, Gen. Sir Thomas, *A Hawk at War. The Peninsular Reminiscences of General Sir Thomas Brotherton CB* edited by Bryan Perrett (Chippenham, Picton, 1986).
Browne, T. H., *The Napoleonic War Journal of Thomas Henry Browne, 1807–1816* edited by Roger Norman Buckley (London, Bodley Head for the Army Records Society, 1987).
Brownrigg, Beatrice, *The Life and Letters of Sir John Moore* (New York, Appleton, 1923).
Bruce, A., *A Bibliography of the British Army, 1660–1914* (London, Saur, 1985).
Bruce. H. A., *Life of General Sir William Napier*, 2 vols (London, John Murray, 1864).
Bunbury, Sir Henry, *Narratives of Some Passages in the Great War with France (1799–1810)* (London, Peter Davies, 1927).
Burne, A. H., 'The Enigma of Toulouse: a Study in Psychology', *Army Quarterly*, Jan. 1927, pp. 274–90.
Butler. Lt.-Col. Lewis, *The Annals of the King's Royal Rifle Corps*, vol. 2: *The Green Jackets* (London, John Murray, 1923).
Campbell, Col. James, *The British Army As It Was – Is – and Ought To Be* (London, T. & W. Boone, 1840).
Cantlie. Lt.-Gen. Sir Neil, *A History of the Army Medical Department*, vol. 1 (Edinburgh and London, Churchill Livingstone, 1974).
Carew, P., 'A Hussar of the Hundred Days' (letters of Capt. Taylor, 10th Hussars), *Blackwood's*, vol. 258, Nov. 1945, pp. 299–305.
Carey, Tupper, 'Waterloo: Reminiscences of a Commissariat Officer', *Cornhill Magazine*, vol. 79, June 1899, pp. 724–38.
Carnock, Lord (ed.), 'Cavalry in the Corunna Campaign: As Told in the Diary of the Adjutant of the 15th Hussars', *JSAHR*, supplement 4, 1936.
Carter, Thomas, *Historical Record of the Forty-Fourth or the East Essex Regiment* (Chatham, Gale & Polden, 1887).
Cary, A. D. L. and S. McCance (comp.), *Regimental Records of the Royal Welch Fusiliers*, vol. 1 (London, Forster, Green & Co., for the Royal United Service Institute, 1921).
Cate, Curtis, *The War of the Two Emperors* (New York, Random House, 1985).
Chambers, Lt.-Col. G. L., *Bussaco* (Felling, Worley, 1994; first published 1910).
Chandler, David, *Marlborough as a Military Commander* (London, Batsford, 1973).
—— *The Campaigns of Napoleon* (New York, Macmillan, 1974).
—— 'The Battle of Sahagun', *History Today*, vol. 24, 1974, pp. 765–72.
—— *The Art of Warfare in the Age of Marlborough* (London, Batsford, 1976).
—— *Dictionary of the Napoleonic Wars* (London, Arms & Armour Press, 1979).
—— *On the Napoleonic Wars* (London, Greenhill, n.d. [*c.* 1994]).
'C.J.T.S.': *see* 'Light Infantry'.
Clark-Kennedy, A. E., *Attack the Colour! The Royal Dragoons in the Peninsula and at Waterloo* (London, Research Publishing, 1975).
Clausewitz, Gen. Carl von, 'Clausewitz on the Defeat of Jena-Auerstädt', *Army Quarterly*, Oct. 1941, pp. 109–21.
—— *On War*, 3 vols (London, Routledge & Kegan Paul, 1949).
—— *The Campaign of 1812 in Russia* (Westport, Connecticut, Greenwood, 1977; first published 1843).
Close, E. C., *The Diary of E. C. Close* (Sydney, W. E. Smith, n.d.).
Cocks: *see* Page.
Coignet, Capt., *The Notebooks of Captain Coignet* (London, Peter Davies, 1928).
Cole., Sir Lowry, *Memoirs of Sir Lowry Cole* edited by M. L. Cole and S. Gwynn (London, Macmillan, 1934).

Colin, Commandant J., *The Transformations of War* (Westport, Connecticut, Greenwood, 1977; first published 1912).

Colville, John, *The Portrait of a General* (Salisbury, Michael Russell, 1980).

Combermere, Viscountess and Capt. W. W. Knollys, *Memoirs and Correspondence of Field Marshal Viscount Combermere* [Sir Stapleton Cotton], 2 vols (London, Hurst & Blackett, 1866).

Cooper, Capt. T. H., *A Practical Guide for the Light Infantry Officer . . .* (London, Muller, 1970; first published 1806).

Cooper, J. S., *Rough Notes of Seven Campaigns* (Staplehurst, Spellmount, 1996; first published 1869).

Coquelle, P., *Napoleon & England 1803–1813* (London, George Bell & Sons, 1904).

Costello, Edward, *The Peninsular and Waterloo Campaigns* edited by Antony Brett-James (London, Longman, 1967).

Cowper, Col. L. I. (ed.), *The King's Own. The Story of a Royal Regiment*, vol. 1 (Oxford, for the regiment, 1939).

Craufurd, Revd A. H., *General Craufurd and His Light Division* (Cambridge, Trotman, 1987; first published 1891).

Crompton, Lt. G., Letter describing Albuera, *JSAHR*, June 1922, pp. 130–1.

Dalbiac, Col. P. H., *History of the 45th: 1st Nottinghamshire Regiment* (London, Swan Sonnenschein, 1902).

Dallas, H. A., 'The Experiences of a British Commissariat Officer', *Army Quarterly*, Oct. 1926, pp. 127–37, Jan. 1927, pp. 360–7, Oct. 1927, pp. 78–90.

Dalton, Charles, *The Waterloo Roll Call* (London, Arms & Armour, 1978).

Dalton, Maj.-Gen. J. C., 'The Battle of Austerlitz Tactically Considered', *Minutes of the Proceedings of the Royal Artillery Institution*, vol. 23, 1896, pp. 205–16.

——'A Family Regiment in the Peninsular War', *The Cavalry Journal*, vol. 18, no. 68, April 1928, pp. 282–9.

Davies, D. W., *Sir John Moore's Peninsular Campaign, 1808–9* (The Hague, Martinus Nijhoff, 1974).

Davies, John Landon (ed.), *The Battle of Waterloo*, Jackdaw no. 18 (New York, Grossman, 1968).

Davson, Maj. H. M. 'Dürrenstein', *Journal of the Royal Artillery*, vol. 40, 1913–14, pp. 161–6.

De Lancey, Lady, *A Week at Waterloo* edited by Maj. B. R. Ward (London, John Murray, 1906).

Dent, William, *A Young Surgeon in Wellington's Army, being the Letters of William Dent* compiled and edited by Leonard Woodford (Old Woking, Unwin Brothers, 1976).

Dickson, Lt.-Col. Sir Alexander, *The Dickson Manuscripts* edited by Maj. John H. Leslie, 5 vols (Cambridge, Trotman, 1987–91; first published in 2 vols in 1908).

Dodge, Theodore A., *Napoleon*, 4 vols (Boston and New York, Houghton, Mifflin, 1904).

Douglas, Capt. Neil, 'The Diary of Captain Neil Douglas, 79th Foot, 1809 to 1810' edited by Antony Brett-James, *JSAHR*, vol. 41, June 1963, pp. 101–7.

Duffy, Christopher, *Borodino and the War of 1812* (London, Seeley, Service & Co., 1972).

——*Austerlitz 1805* (London, Seeley, Service & Co., 1977).

——*The Military Experience in the Age of Reason* (London, Routledge & Kegan Paul, 1987).

Duffy, Michael, *Soldiers, Sugar and Seapower. The British Expeditions to the West Indies and the War Against Revolutionary France* (Oxford, Clarendon, 1987).

Duncan, Capt., Francis *History of the Royal Regiment of Artillery*, 2 vols (London, John Murray, 1872).

D'Urban, Maj.-Gen. Sir Benjamin, *The Peninsular Journal, 1808–17* (London, Greenhill, 1988; first published 1930).

Durova, Nadezhda, *The Cavalry Maiden. Journals of a Female Russian Officer in the Napoleonic Wars* (London, Paladin, 1990).

Dutton, Geoffrey and David Elder, *Colonel William Light – Founder of a City* (Melbourne University Press, 1991).

Dyneley, Lt.-Gen. Thomas, *Letters Written by Lieut.-General Thomas Dyneley* . . . (London, Trotman, 1984).

Earle, E. M. (ed.), *Makers of Modern Strategy* (New York, Atheneum, 1966).

Eaton, Charlotte A., *Waterloo Days: the Narrative of an English Resident at Brussels in June 1815* (London, Bell, 1888).

Edmonds, T. R., 'On the Mortality and Sickness of Soldiers Engaged in War', *The Lancet*, vol. 2, 28 April 1838, pp. 143–8.

Elting, John R., *Swords Around a Throne. Napoleon's Grande Armée* (London, Weidenfeld & Nicolson, 1988).

Epstein, Robert M., 'The Viceroy at War: 1809', doctoral thesis presented to Temple University in 1981 and subseqently published as *Prince Eugene at War, 1809*.

—— 'Patterns of Change and Continuity in Nineteenth Century Warfare', *Journal of Military History*, vol. 56, July 1992, pp. 375–88.

—— *Napoleon's Last Victory and the Emergence of Modern War* (Kansas University Press, 1994).

Eques 'British Cavalry', *Royal Military Chronicle*, vol. 2, Oct. 1811, pp. 489–91.

Erckmann-Chatrian, *Waterloo* (New York, Scribner's, 1869).

—— *The Conscript* (New York, Scribner's, 1903).

Esdaile, C. J., *The Spanish Army in the Peninsular War* (Manchester University Press, 1988).

—— *The Duke of Wellington and the Command of the Spanish Army, 1812–14* (Basingstoke, Macmillan, 1990).

—— *The Wars of Napoleon* (London, Longman, 1995).

—— 'A Visit to Jena and Auerstadt', *Age of Napoleon*, no. 16, pp. 17–19.

Fenton, Capt. T. C., 'The Peninsular and Waterloo Letters of Captain Thomas Charles Fenton', *JSAHR*, vol. 53, Winter 1975, pp. 210–31.

Fitchett, W. H. (ed.), *Wellington's Men. Some Soldier Autobiographies* (London, George Bell & Sons, 1900).

—— 'One of the Fusiliers of Albuera' (extracts from Cooper's *Rough Notes of Seven Campaigns* . . .), *Cornhill*, vol. 110 (new series vol. 37), Nov. 1914, pp. 608–25.

Fletcher, Ian (ed.), *A Guards Officer in the Peninsula. The Peninsula [sic] War Letters of John Rous, Coldstream Guards, 1812–14* (Tunbridge Wells, Spellmount, 1992).

Foch, Marshal, *The Principles of War* (London, Chapman & Hall, 1918).

Forrest, Alan, *Conscripts and Deserters: The Army and French Society during the Revolution and Empire* (Oxford University Press, 1990).

Fortescue, Sir John, *A History of the British Army*, 13 vols in 20 (London, Macmillan, 1899–1930).

—— *The County Lieutenancies and the Army 1803–1814* (London, Macmillan, 1909).

—— *Historical and Military Essays* (London, Macmillan, 1928).

—— *Following the Drum* (Edinburgh, Blackwood, 1931).

Frazer, Sir Simon Augustus, *Letters of Colonel Sir Augustus Simon Frazer, K. C. B.* edited by Maj.-Gen. Edward Sabine (London, Longman, 1859).

Fyler, A. E., *History of the 50th Regiment* (London, Chapman & Hall, 1895).

Gallaher, John G., *The Iron Marshal* (Carbondale, Southern Illinois University Press, 1976).

Gardner, Dorsey, *Quatre Bras, Ligny and Waterloo: a Narrative and a Criticism* (London, Kegan Paul, Trench & Co., 1882).

Gardyne, *The Life of a Regiment. The History of the Gordon Highlanders* (Edinburgh, Douglas, 1901).

Garrett, R., 'A Subaltern in the Peninsular War: Letters of Lt Robert Garrett, 1811–13', *JSAHR*, vol. 13, 1934, pp. 3–22.

Gash, Norman, 'After Waterloo: British Society and the Legacy of the Napoleonic Wars', *Transactions of the Royal Historical Society*, 5th series, vol. 28, 1978, pp. 145–57.

Gates, David, *The Spanish Ulcer* (London, Allen & Unwin, 1986).

—— *The British Light Infantry Arm c. 1790–1815* (London, Batsford, 1987).

Gawler, Maj. George, 'The Crisis and Close of the Action at Waterloo', *USJ*, July 1833, pp. 299–310 with further correspondence *ibid.*, Pt 3, pp. 1–16, 1835, Pt 1, pp. 303–4, and 1836, Pt 2, pp. 357–8.

—— *The Essentials of Good Skirmishing*, 2nd edition (London, Parker, Furnivall and Parker, 1852).

Gilbert, Arthur N., 'A Tale of Two Regiments. Manpower and Effectiveness in British Military Units during the Napoleonic Wars', *Armed Forces and Society*, vol. 9, no. 2, Winter 1983, pp. 275–92.

Gill, J., *With the Eagles to Glory: Napoleon and his German Allies in the 1809 Campaign* (London, Greenhill, 1992).

Gleig, Revd G. R., *The Story of the Battle of Waterloo* (New York, Harper Bros, 1860).

Glover, Michael, *Wellington's Peninsular Victories* (London, Batsford, 1963).

—— *Wellington as a Military Commander* (London, Sphere, 1973).

—— *Wellingon's Army in the Peninsula, 1808–1814* (Newton Abbot, David & Charles, 1977).

—— 'Misconduct at St Pierre, 13th December 1813', *JSAHR*, vol. 55, Autumn 1977, pp. 186–7.

—— *Warfare in the Age of Bonaparte* (London, Cassell, 1980).

—— *The Velvet Glove. The Decline and Fall of Moderation in War* (London, Hodder & Stoughton, 1982).

—— *Also see* Hennell.

Glover, Richard, *Peninsular Preparation. The Reform of the British Army, 1795–1809* (Cambridge University Press, 1963).

Gomm, Sir William, Maynard *Letters and Journals of Field-Marshal Sir William Maynard Gomm, G.C.B.* edited by Francis Culling Carr-Gomm (London, John Murray, 1881).

Gordon, Capt. Alexander, *A Cavalry Officer in the Corunna Campaign 1808–9. The Journal of Captain Gordon of the 15th Hussars* (Felling, Worley, 1990; first published 1913).

Graham, Robert: *see* Historical Manuscripts Commission.

Grattan, William, *Adventures in the Connaught Rangers* edited by Charles Oman (London, Edward Arnold, 1902).

[Grattan, Lt. William], 'Reminiscences of a Subaltern', *USJ*, April, June and Sept. 1831 and June 1834.

Gray, Daniel S., 'The Services of the King's German Legion in the Army of the Duke of Wellington: 1809–15', unpublished doctoral thesis presented to Florida State University, 1970.

Gray, Ernest A., *The Trumpet of Glory: the Military Career of John Shipp, First Veterinary Surgeon to join the British Army* (London, Robert Hale, 1985).

Great Britain: War Office, *Rules and Regulations for the Formations, Field-Exercise and Movements of His Majesty's Forces* (London, T. Egerton, 1808).

Green, John, *The Vicissitudes of a Soldier's Life* (Louth, privately printed, 1827).

Green, Rifleman William, *Where My Duty Calls Me* edited by John and Dorothea Teague (West Wickham, Synjon Books, 1975).

Greenwood, Major, 'British Loss of Life in the Wars of 1794–1815 and in 1914–18', *Journal of the Royal Statistical Society*, vol. 105, 1942, pp. 1–16.

Griffith, Paddy, *French Artillery* (London, Almark, 'Nations-in-Arms' series, 1976).

—— (ed.) *Wellington Commander* (Chichester, Antony Bird, n.d. [1985]).

—— *Military Thought in the French Army, 1815–51* (Manchester University Press, 1989).

—— *Battle Tactics of the Civil War* (New Haven and London, Yale University Press, 1989).

—— *Forward Into Battle. Fighting Tactics from Waterloo to the Near Future*, 2nd edition (Swindon, Crowood Press, 1990).

—— 'Where Did Our View of Napoleonic Warfare Come From?', *Age of Napoleon*, no. 12, pp. 22–4.

Gronow, Capt., *The Reminiscences and Recollections of Captain Gronow* (Frome, Surtees Society, 1984).

Guillemard, R., *Memoirs of a French Sergeant* (London, Hutchinson, 1898).

Guy, Alan (ed.), *The Road to Waterloo* (London, National Army Museum, 1990).

Haig. D., *Cavalry Studies* (London, Hugh Rees, 1907).

Hall, Francis, 'Recollections in Portugal and Spain during 1811 and 1812', *Journal of the Royal United Services Institution*, vol. 56, 1912, pp. 1389–408, 1535–46, 1735–9 and vol. 57, 1913, pp. 1319–34.

Hamilton-Williams, David, *Waterloo: New Perspectives* (London, Arms & Armour, 1993).

Harris, Rifleman, *Recollections of Rifleman Harris* edited by Christopher Hibbert (Hamden, Connecticut, Archon, 1970).

[Hawker, Capt. Peter], *Journal of a Regimental Officer during the Recent Campaign in Portugal and Spain* . . . (London, Trotman, 1981; first published London, Johnson, 1810).

Hay: *see* Leith Hay.

Hayman, Sir Peter, *Soult. Napoleon's Maligned Marshal* (London, Arms & Armour, 1990).

Haythornthwaite, Philip J., *Weapons and Equipment of the Napoleonic Wars* (Poole, Dorset, Blandford Press, 1979).

——— *The Armies of Wellington* (London, Arms & Armour, 1994).

Head, Lt.-Col. C. O., *The Art of Generalship* (Aldershot, Gale & Polden, n.d. [1930s]).

Headlam, Sir John, 'The Duke and the Regiment', *Journal of the Royal Artillery*, Jan. 1944, pp. 1–11.

Heathcote, Ralph, *Ralph Heathcote. Letters of a Young Diplomatist and Soldier during the Time of Napoleon* edited by Countess Groben (London, John Lane, 1907).

Henderson, Col. G. F. R., *The Science of War* (London, Longman, 1919).

Henegan, Sir Richard D., *Seven Years' Campaigning*, 2 vols (London, Henry Colburn, 1846).

Hennell, George, *A Gentleman Volunteer. The Letters of George Hennell from the Peninsular War, 1812–13* edited by Michael Glover (London, Heinemann, 1979).

Henry, Walter, *Surgeon Henry's Trifles. Events of a Military Life* edited by Pat Hayward (London, Chatto & Windus, 1970).

Hervey, Sir Felton, 'A Contemporary Letter on the Battle of Waterloo', *Nineteenth Century*, vol. 33, March 1893, pp. 430–5.

Heyman, N., 'France against Prussia: The Jena Campaign, 1806', *Military Affairs*, vol. 30, 1966–7, pp. 186–98.

Hime, Lt.-Col. H. W. L., *History of the Royal Regiment of Artillery, 1815–53* (London, Longmans, Green & Co., 1908).

Historical Manuscripts Commission, *Supplementary Report on the Manuscripts of Robert Graham Esq. of Fintry* edited by C. T. Atkinson (London, HMSO, 1942).

Hocking, William E., *Morale and its Enemies* (New Haven, Yale University Press, 1918).

Hodge, W. B., 'On the Mortality Arising from Military Operations', *Quarterly Journal of the Statistical Society*, vol. 19, Sept. 1856, pp. 219–71.

Hofschröer, Peter, *Prussian Light Infantry 1792–1815* (London, Osprey 'Men-at-Arms', 1984).

——— *Prussian Line Infantry 1792–1815* (London, Osprey 'Men-at-Arms', 1984).

Holmes, Richard, *Firing Line* (London, Cape, 1985).

Home, Col. R. and Lt.-Col. S. C. Pratt, *A Précis of Modern Tactics* . . . (London, HMSO, 1896).

Horsburgh, E. L. S., *Waterloo: A Narrative and a Criticism* (London, Methuen, 1900).

Horward, Donald D., *The Battle of Bussaco: Masséna vs. Wellington* (Tallahassee, Florida State University Press, 1965).

——— *Napoleon and Iberia. The Twin Sieges of Ciudad Rodrigo and Almeida, 1810* (Tallahassee, Florida State University Press, 1984).

——— *Also see* Pelet, J. J.

Hough, Lt. H., 'The Diary of 2nd Lieutenant Henry Hough, Royal Artillery', *Journal of the Royal United Services Institution*, vol. 61, Nov. 1916, pp. 840–48.

Houlding, J. A., *Fit for Service. The Training of the British Army, 1715–1795* (Oxford, Clarendon, 1981).

Houssaye, Henry, *1815 Waterloo* (London, A. & C. Black, 1900).
——*Napoleon and the Campaign of 1814* (London, Rees, 1914).
Howard, Michael, *Studies in War and Peace* (London, Temple Smith, 1970).
Howarth, David, *Waterloo: Day of Battle* (New York, Galahad, 1968).
Hughes, Maj.-Gen. B. P., *Firepower. Weapons' Effectiveness on the Battlefield, 1630–1850* (London, Arms & Armour, 1974).
——*Open Fire: Artillery Tactics from Marlborough to Wellington* (Chichester, Antony Bird, 1983).
Ingilby, Lt., 'Diary of Lt., Ingilby R.A. in the Peninsular War and Waterloo Campaign', *Minutes of the Proceedings of the Royal Artillery Institution*, vol. 20, 1893, pp. 241–62, 315–23.
Irvine, Dallas D., 'The Origin of Capital Staffs', *Journal of Modern History*, vol. 10, June 1938, pp. 161–79.
Jackdaw: *see* Davies, John Landon.
Jackson, Basil, *Notes and Reminiscences of a Staff Officer . . .* (London, John Murray, 1903).
James, Dr Haddy, *Surgeon James's Journal, 1815* edited by Jane Vansittart (London, Cassell, 1964).
James, Lt.-Col. W. H., *The Campaign of 1815. Chiefly in Flanders* (Edinburgh and London, Blackwood, 1908).
J. B., 'Formation of a Solid Square', *Royal Military Chronicle*, vol. 3, no. 16, pp. 274–7.
Jeffrey, George, *Tactics and Grand Tactics of the Napoleonic Wars* edited by Ned Zuparko (Brockton, Massachusetts, Courier, 1982).
J.M.: *see* [Mitchell, John].
Johnson, David, *Napoleon's Cavalry and its Leaders* (London, Batsford, 1978).
Jomini, Baron de, *The Campaign of Waterloo* (New York, Redfield, 1853).
——*The Art of War* translated by Capt. G. H. Mendell and Lt. W. P. Craighill (Westport, Connecticut, Greenwood Press, 1971; first published Philadelphia, Lippincott, 1862).
Jones, J. P., *History of the South Staffordshire Regiment (1705–1923)* (Wolverhampton, Whitehead, n.d. [1923]).
Jones, Lt. Rice, *An Engineer Officer under Wellington in the Peninsula* (Cambridge, Trotman, 1986).
Josselson, Michael and Diana Josselson, *The Commander. A Life of Barclay de Tolly* (Oxford University Press, 1980).
Jourdain, Lt.-Col. H. F. N. and Edward Fraser, *The Connaught Rangers* (London, Royal United Service Institution, 1924).
Keegan, John, *The Face of Battle* (New York, Viking, 1976).
——*The Mask of Command* (London, Cape, 1987).
——'Keeping in Time. The Rise of Foot Drill and the Decline of the Minuet', *Times Literary Supplement*, 12 July 1996, pp. 3–4 and subseqent correspondence in the *TLS* of 2, 9, 16 and 23 Aug. and 6 Sept. 1996.
Kennedy, Sir James Shaw, *Notes on the Battle of Waterloo* (London, John Murray, 1865).
Kerry, Earl of, 'The Archduke Charles and the Austrian Campaign of 1809: Unpublished Letters from the Bowood Papers', *Nineteenth Century*, July 1926, pp. 110–22.
Kincaid, Capt. Sir John, *Adventures in the Rifle Brigade and Random Shots from a Rifleman* (Glasgow, Richard Drew, 1981).
Koontz, John, 'Reasons for Studying Napoleonic Drill Regulations', *Empires, Eagles and Lions*, no. 74, Sept. 1983, pp. 2–7.
Lachouque, Henry and Anne S. K. Brown, *The Anatomy of Glory* (London, Arms & Armour, 1978).
Landmann, Col., *Recollections of My Military Life*, 2 vols (London, Hurst & Blackett, 1854).
Larpent, F. Seymour, *The Private Journal of F. Seymour Larpent, Judge-Advocate General . . .* edited by Sir George Larpent, 2nd edition, 2 vols (London, Richard Bentley, 1853).

[Larrey] Anon., *Memoir of Baron Larrey, Surgeon-in-Chief of the Grande Armée*, 2nd edition (London, Renshaw, 1862).

Lawrence, Sgt William, *The Autobiography of Sergeant William Lawrence* . . . (London, Sampson Low, Marston, Searle & Rivington, 1886).

Laws, M. E. S., 'The Royal Artillery at Barrosa', *Journal of the Royal Artillery*, vol. 78, no. 3 1952, pp. 196–206.

—— 'A Waterloo Letter', *Journal of the Royal Artillery*, vol. 81, no. 4, 1954, pp. 305–7.

Lee, Nigel de, *French Lancers* (London, Almark 'Nations-in-Arms' series, 1976).

Leeke, Revd William, *The History of Lord Seaton's Regiment at the Battle of Waterloo*, 2 vols (London, Hatchard, 1866).

Leith Hay, Sir Andrew, *A Narrative of the Peninsular War*, 3rd edition (London, John Hearne, 1839).

[——], *Memoirs of the Late Lieutenant-General Sir James Leith* (Barbados, privately printed, 1817).

Lejeune, Baron, *Memoirs of Baron Lejeune*, 2 vols (London, Longmans, Green, 1897).

Le Marchant, D., *Memoir of the Late Major-General Le Marchant* (London, Bentley, 1841).

Lennox, Lord William Pitt, *Celebrities I Have Known* . . ., 2 vols (London, Hurst & Blackett, 1876).

Leslie, Maj. John H., 'Some Remarks concerning the Royal Artillery at the Battle of Talavera, July 27–28, 1809', *Journal of the Royal Artillery*, vol. 34, 1907–8, pp. 503–8.

Levinge, Sir Richard, *Historical Records of the 43rd Light Infantry* (London, Clowes, 1868).

'Light Infantry Movements' by 'C. J. T. S.', *USJ*, 1829, Pt 2, p. 601.

Lochet, Jean A., 'Some Comments and Considerations on French Tactics, Part VII', *Empires, Eagles and Lions*, no. 72, June 1983, pp. 21–34.

Long, Maj.-Gen. R. B., *Peninsular Cavalry General (1811–13) The Correspondence of Lieutenant-General Robert Ballard Long* edited by T. H. McGuffie (London, Harrap, 1951).

Longford, Elizabeth, *Wellington. The Years of the Sword* (London, Weidenfeld & Nicolson, 1969).

Longworth, Philip, *The Art of Victory. The Life and Achievements of Generalissimo Suvorov* (London, Constable, 1965).

Low, E. B.: *see* Macbride, Mackenzie.

Luvaas, Jay, *The Education of an Army. British Military Thought, 1815–1940* (University of Chicago Press, 1964).

—— *Frederick the Great on the Art of War* (New York, Free Press, 1966).

Lynn, John A., *The Bayonets of the Republic. Motivation and Tactics in the Army of Revolutionary France, 1791–94* (Urbana and Chicago, University of Illinois Press, 1984).

Macbride, Mackenzie, *With Napoleon at Waterloo and Other Unpublished Documents of the Waterloo and Peninsular Campaigns, Also Papers on Waterloo by the Late Edward Bruce Low* (Philadelphia, Lippincott, 1911).

Macdonald, Marshal, *Recollections of Marshal Macdonald Duke of Tarentum* (New York, Scribner's, 1893).

Macdonell, A. G., *Napoleon and His Marshals* (London, Macmillan, 1934).

MacGrigor, Sir James, 'Sketch of the Medical History of the British Armies in the Peninsula of Spain and Portugal during the Late Campaigns', *Transactions of the Medico-Chirurgical Society*, vol. 6, 1815, pp. 381–489.

—— *Autobiography and Services of Sir James McGrigor* (London, Longman, 1861).

McGuffie, T. H. (ed.), 'The Bingham Manuscripts', *JSAHR*, vol. 26, no. 107, 1948, pp. 106–11.

—— 'The Bingham Papers and the Peninsular War', *Army Quarterly*, vol. 58, 1949, pp. 124–8, 254–6.

—— (ed.), *Rank and File* (London, Hutchinson, 1964).

Mackenzie, Capt. T. A., *et al. Historical Records of the 79th Queen's Own Cameron Highlanders* (London, Hamilton, Adams; Devonport, A. H. Swiss, 1887).

Mackesy, Piers, *The Coward of Minden. The Affair of Lord George Sackville* (London, Allen Lane, 1979).

——*British Victory in Egypt, 1801 The End of Napoleon's Conquest* (London, Routledge, 1995).

Mackie, William, 'The Battle of Busaco and the Third Division', *USJ*, vol. 9, no. 100, March 1837, pp. 366–79.

Madden, C. D., 'The Diary of Charles Dudley Madden, 4th Dragoons, 1809–11', *Journal of the Royal United Service Institution*, vol. 58, 1914, pp. 334–59, 500–26.

Mainwaring, Frederick, 'Four Years of a Soldier's Life', *USJ*, 1844, Pt 2, pp. 512–22.

Mann, Michael, *And They Rode On. The King's Dragoon Guards at Waterloo* (Salisbury, Michael Russell, 1984).

Marbot, Baron de, *Memoirs of Baron de Marbot*, 2 vols (London, Longmans, Green, 1892).

Marmont, Marshal, *The Spirit of Military Institutions* (Westport, Connecticut, Greenwood, 1974; first published 1864).

Marshall, Pte. John, Letter to his father, 11 July 1815, *USJ*, 1831, pp. 313–17.

Marshall-Cornwall, James, *Marshal Massena* (Oxford University Press, 1965).

Martinien, A., *Tableaux par corps et par batailles des Officiers Tués et Blessés pendant les Guerres de l'Empire (1805–1815)* (Paris, Editions Militaires Européennes, n.d.).

Mathews, J. J., 'Napoleon's Military Bulletins', *Journal of Modern History*, vol. 23, 1951, pp. 137–44.

Maude, F. N., 'The Development of Napoleonic Strategical and Tactical Methods as Illustrated by the Battle of Waterloo', *Journal of the Royal United Service Institution*, vol. 52, 1908, pp. 1194–217.

——*The Jena Campaign, 1806* (London, Swan Sonnenschein, 1909).

——'Cavalry', *Encyclopedia Britannica*, 11th edition, 1910, vol. 5.

Maurice, Col. F., 'Waterloo' Pt 3: 'Charges against Wellington', *USJ*, July 1890, pp. 257–63.

——*The History of the Scots Guards*, vol. 1 (London, Chatto & Windus, 1934).

May. Capt. E. S. (ed.), 'A Prussian Gunner's Adventures in 1815', *USJ*, Oct. 1891, pp. 45–6.

Meier, Norman C., *Military Psychology* (New York, 1943).

Mercer, Gen. Cavalié, *Journal of the Waterloo Campaign* (London, Peter Davies, 1969).

Millar, C. M. H., 'The Dismissal of Colonel Duncan Macdonald of the 57th Regiment', *JSAHR*, vol. 60, no. 242, Summer 1982, pp. 71–7.

[Mitchell, Maj.-Gen. John], 'Tactics No. II Combat of Cavalry against Infantry', *USJ*, vol. 4, 1832, Pt 1, pp. 289–306.

——'Reply to the Remarks of "An Old Soldier"', *USJ*, vol. 4, 1832, Pt 2, pp. 212–19 [see under 'Old Soldier'].

——'Tactics No. IV How Should Infantry be Trained and Armed?', *USJ*, vol. 6, no. 68, July 1834, pp. 309–25.

Mockler-Ferryman, Lt.-Col. A. F., *The Life of a Regimental Officer during the Great War, 1793–1815* (Edinburgh, Blackwood, 1913).

Moore, Sir John, *The Diary of Sir John Moore* edited by Maj.-Gen. Sir J. F. Maurice, 2 vols (London, Edward Arnold, 1904).

Moore Smith, G. C., *The Life of John Colborne, Field-Marshal Lord Seaton* (New York, Dutton, 1903).

Moorsom, W. S., *Historical Record of the Fifty-Second Regiment . . . 1775–1858* (London, Richard Bentley, 1860).

Morris, Thomas, *The Napoleonic Wars* edited by John Selby (London, Longman, 1967).

Moyse-Bartlett, H., *Nolan of Balaclava. Louis Edward Nolan and His Influence on the British Cavalry* (London, Leo Cooper, 1975).

Müffling, Baron von, *Passages from My Life . . .* (London, Richard Bentley, 1853).

——Extract of a letter from Müffling to Boyen dated 24 June 1815 describing Waterloo, *Journal of the Royal United Services Institution*, vol. 36, 1892, pp. 105–6.

——*History of the Campaign of the British, Dutch, Hanoverian and Brunswick Armies . . . 1815* (London, Trotman, 1983).

Muir, R., *Britain and the Defeat of Napoleon, 1807–1815* (New Haven and London, Yale University Press, 1996).

Mullaly, Col. B. R., *The South Lancashire Regiment* (Bristol, White Swan Press, n.d.).

Müller, W., *Relation of the Operations and Battles of the Austrian and French Armies in the Year 1809* (Cambridge, Trotman, 1986; first published London, Goddard, 1810).

Myatt, Frederick, *The Soldier's Trade. British Military Developments, 1660–1914* (London, Book Club edition, 1974).

——*Peninsular General. Sir Thomas Picton, 1758–1815* (Newton Abbot, David & Charles, 1980).

Nafziger, George F., *Napoleon's Invasion of Russia* (Novato, California, Presido Press, 1988).

——*A Guide to Napoleonic Warfare. Maneuvers of the Battery, Battalion and Brigade during the First Empire as found in Contemporary Regulations* (Privately published [1996]) (This has subsequently been published by Greenhill Books as *Imperial Bayonets: Tactics of the Napoleonic Battery, Battalion and Brigade as found in Contemporary Regulations.*)

Nagel: *see* Ammon and Herold.

Napier, George, *Passages in the Early Military Life of General Sir George T. Napier* (London, John Murray, 1884).

Napier, Maj.-Gen. W. F. P., *History of the War in the Peninsula and South of France*, 6 vols (London, Boone, 1853; first published 1828–40).

——*Life and Opinions of General Sir Charles James Napier*, 4 vols (London, John Murray, 1857).

——'Letters from Col. William Napier to Sir John Colborne' [postwar] edited by Prof. Moore Smith, *English Historical Review*, vol. 18, 1903, pp. 725–53.

Nettleship, Andrew, *That Astonishing Infantry! A History of the 7th Foot (Royal Fusiliers) in the Peninsular War, 1809–14* (Sheffield, privately published, 1989).

Ney, Marshal, *Military Studies* translated by G. H. Caunter (London, Bull & Churton, 1833).

Nolan, Capt. L. E., *Cavalry: its History and Tactics* (London, Bosworth, 1853).

Norcliffe: *see* Dalton, Maj.-Gen. J. C.

Nosworthy, Brent, *The Anatomy of Victory. Battle Tactics 1689–1763* (New York, Hippocrene, 1990).

——*Battle Tactics of Napoleon and his Enemies* (London, Constable, 1995). (This has also appeared with the title: *With Musket, Cannon and Sword: Battle Tactics of Napoleon and His Enemies.*)

Oatts, L. B., *Proud Heritage: the Story of the Highland Light Infantry*, 2 vols (London, Nelson, 1952–9).

Ojala, Jeanne A., *Auguste de Colbert: Aristocratic Survival in an Era of Upheaval 1793–1809* (Salt Lake City, University of Utah Press, 1979).

'Old Soldier, An', 'Modern Troops and Tactics – Cavalry & Infantry' [reply to article by John Mitchell], *USJ*, 1832, vol. 4, Pt 2, pp. 42–9, 392–4.

Oman, Sir Charles, 'The Dutch-Belgians at Waterloo', *Nineteenth Century*, vol. 48, Oct. 1900, pp. 629–38.

——'French Losses in the Waterloo Campaign', *English Historical Review*, vol. 19, Oct. 1904, pp. 681–93, and vol. 21, Jan. 1906, pp. 132–5.

——'Column and Line in the Peninsular War', *Proceedings of the British Academy*, 1909–10, pp. 321–42.

——*Wellington's Army, 1809–1814* (London, Edward Arnold, 1913).

——'A Dragoon of the Legion' (letters of Capt. Carl von Hodenberg), *Blackwood's Magazine*, vol. 193, March 1913, pp. 293–309.

——*Studies in the Napoleonic Wars* (London, Methuen, 1929).

——'Albuera Once More' [account by A. B. D. von Schepeler, on Zaya's staff], *Army Quarterly*, July 1932, pp. 337–42.

——*A History of the Peninsular War*, 7 vols (New York, AMS Press, 1980; first published Oxford, Clarendon, 1902–30).

Ompteda, Baron, *A Hanoverian-English Officer A Hundred Years Ago. Memoirs of Baron Ompteda* translated by John Hill (London, Grevel, 1892).

Oxford Dictionary of Quotations, 3rd edition.

Page, Julia V. (ed.), *Intelligence Officer in the Peninsula. Letters and Diaries of Major the Hon. Edward Charles Cocks 1786–1812* (New York, Hippocrene, 1986).

Paret, Peter, *Yorck and the Era of Prussian Reform 1807–1815* (Princeton University Press, 1966).

——*Clausewitz and the State. The Man, his Theories and his Times* (Princeton University Press, 1985).

Park, S. J. and G. F. Nafziger, *The British Military: Its System and Organization, 1803–1815* (Cambridge, Ontario, Rafm, 1983).

Parker, Harold T., *Three Napoleonic Battles* (Durham, NC, Duke University Press, 1983; first published 1944).

Parker, Brig. James, 'Combat of Cavalry versus Cavalry', *U.S. Cavalry Journal*, 1912, pp. 768–83.

Parkinson, Roger, *Clausewitz* (London, Wayland, 1970).

——*The Hussar General* (London, Peter Davies, 1975).

——*The Fox of the North* (London, Peter Davies, 1976).

Parquin, Charles, *Napoleon's Army* translated and edited by B. T. Jones (London, Longman, 1969).

Paton, Col. George *et al.*, *Historical Records of the 24th Regiment . . .* (London, Simpkin, Marshall, 1892).

Patterson, Maj., 'On the Utility and Importance of Light Troops and Cavalry in the Field . . .', *USJ*, vol. 17, no. 194, Jan. 1845, pp. 95–101.

Payne, A. A., *A Handbook of British and Foreign Orders, War Medals and Decorations* (Polstead, Suffolk, J. B. Hayward, 1981; first published Sheffield, 1911).

Pelet, J. J., *The French Campaign in Portugal, 1810–11* edited and translated by Donald D. Horward (Minneapolis, University of Minnesota Press, 1973).

Petit, Joseph, *Marengo: or the Campaign of Italy by the Army of Reserve . . .* (London, Jordan, 1800; anonymous reprint, n.d. *c.* 1981).

Petre, F. L., *Napoleon's Campaign in Poland, 1806–7* (London, Arms & Armour, 1976; first published 1901).

——*Napoleon's Conquest of Prussia, 1806* (London, Arms & Armour, 1977; first published 1907).

——*Napoleon and the Archduke Charles* (London, Arms & Armour, 1976; first published 1909).

——*Napoleon at Bay, 1814* (London, Arms & Armour, 1977; first published 1914).

——*The History of the Norfolk Regiment, 1685–1918* (Norwich, Jarrold, 1924).

Pflugk-Harttung, J. von, 'Front and Rear of the Battle-Line of Waterloo', *Journal of Military History*, vol. 2, Jan. 1917, pp. 19–26.

Pimlott, John, *British Light Cavalry* (London, Almark 'Nations-in-Arms' series, 1977).

Pivka, Otto von, *Armies of the Napoleonic Era* (Newton Abbot, David & Charles, 1979).

Powell, Anthony, *Barnard Letters, 1778–1824* (London, Duckworth, 1928).

Priest, Guy (ed.), 'An Ensign's Dispatch from Waterloo', *Country Life*, 16 June 1950, p. 1812.

Quimby, Robert S., *The Background of Napoleonic Warfare* (New York, AMS Press, 1979; first published 1957).

Rait, R. S., *The Life and Campaigns of Hugh, first Viscount Gough, Field Marshal*, 2 vols (London, Constable, 1903).

Rapp, Gen., *Memoirs of General Count Rapp Written by Himself* (Cambridge, Trotman, 1985; first published London, Colburn, 1823).

Reuter: *see* May.

Richardson, F. M., *Fighting Spirit* (London, Leo Cooper, 1978).

Richardson, R. G., *Larrey: Surgeon to Napoleon's Imperial Guard* (London, John Murray, 1974).

Riehn, Richard, *1812. Napoleon's Russian Campaign* (New York, Wiley, 1991).

Robinson, H. B., *Memoirs of Lieutenant-General Sir Thomas Picton . . .*, 2nd edition, 2 vols (London, Bentley, 1836).

Robinson, Maj.-Gen. P. F.: *see* Atkinson.

Rocca, A. J. de, 'Memoirs of the War in Spain' in *Memorials of the Late War* vol. 2 (Edinburgh, Constable, 1828). (This is generally cited as *Memoirs of the War in Spain*.)

Roeder, Capt. Franz, *The Ordeal of Captain Roeder* translated and edited by Helen Roeder (London, Methuen, 1960).

Rogers, Col. H. C. B., *Napoleon's Army* (London, Ian Allan, 1974).

―― *Wellington's Army* (London, Ian Allan, 1979).

Ropes, J. C., *The Campaign of Waterloo* (London, Putnam's Sons, 1893).

Rose, J. H. (ed.), 'A Report on the Battles of Jena–Auerstädt and the Surrender of Prenzlau', *English Historical Review*, July 1904, pp. 550–3.

Ross, Steven T., 'The Development of the Combat Division in Eighteenth Century French Armies', *French Historical Studies*, vol. 4, 1965, pp. 84–94.

―― *From Flintlock to Rifle. Infantry Tactics, 1740–1866* (Rutherford, Fairleigh Dickinson University Press, 1979).

Ross, Sir Hew D., *Memoir of Field Marshal Sir Hew Dalrymple Ross, G.C.B.* (Woolwich, Royal Artillery Institution, 1871).

Ross-Lewin, H., *With the 32nd in the Peninsula . . .* (Dublin, Hodges, 1904).

Rothenberg, Gunther E., *The Art of Warfare in the Age of Napoleon* (London, Batsford, 1977).

―― *Napoleon's Great Adversaries. The Archduke Charles and the Austrian Army* (London, Batsford, 1982).

―― 'The Age of Napoleon' in *The Laws of War* edited by Michael Howard, George J. Andreopoulos and Mark R. Sherman (New Haven and London, Yale University Press, 1994).

Scarfe, Norman (ed.), 'Letters from the Peninsula. The Freer Family Correspondence, 1807–14', *Transactions of the Leicestershire Archaeological Society*, vol. 29, 1953, pp. 42–78.

Schaumann, A. L. F., *On the Road with Wellington* (New York, Knopf, 1925).

Scurfield, R., 'The Weapons of Wellington's Army', *JSAHR*, vol. 36, Dec. 1958, pp. 144–51.

Segur, Count Philippe de, *An Aide-de-Camp of Napoleon* (London, Hutchinson, 1895).

Shadwell, Lt.-Gen. Laurence, *The Life of Colin Campbell, Lord Clyde*, 2 vols (Edinburgh, Blackwood, 1881).

Sherer, Moyle, *Recollections of the Peninsula* (Staplehurst, Spellmount, 1996; first published 1824).

Shoberl, F., *A Narrative of . . . Events . . . near Leipzig . . . 1813* (London, Ackerman, 1814).

Showalter, Dennis E., 'The Prussian Landwehr and its Critics, 1813–19', *Central European History*, vol. 4, no. 1, March 1971, pp. 3–33.

―― 'Manifestation of Reform: The Rearmament of the Prussian Infantry, 1806–1813', *Journal of Modern History*, vol. 44, no. 4, Sept. 1972, pp. 364–80.

Siborne, Maj.-Gen. H. T. (ed.), *Waterloo Letters* (London, Cassell, 1891).

Siborne, Capt. William, *History of the War in France and Belgium in 1815 . . .*, 3rd edition (London, Boone, 1848).

―― *The Waterloo Campaign 1815*, 5th edition (Westminster, Constable, 1900; first published 1844).

Simmons, Maj. George, *A British Rifleman* (London, A. & C. Black, 1899).

Simpson, Capt. W. H. R. (ed.), 'Extracts from the Memoir of Baron Alexander de Senarmont . . .', *Minutes of the Proceedings of the Royal Artillery Institution*, vol. 1, 1858, pp. 335–44.

Smith, G. C. Moore: *see* Moore Smith, G. C.

Smith, Sir Harry, *The Autobiography of Sir Harry Smith, 1787–1819* edited by G. C. Moore Smith (London, John Murray, 1910).

Soldier [Anon.], *A Soldier of the Seventy-First* edited by Christopher Hibbert (London, Leo Cooper, 1975; first published 1819).

Steffans, Henry, *Adventures on the Road to Paris, during the Campaigns of 1813–14 extracted from the Autobiography of Henry Steffans* (London, John Murray, 1848; bound with Haygrath, *Recollections of Bush Life in Australia*).

Strachan, Hew, *European Armies and the Conduct of War* (London, Unwin Hyman, 1988).

Stutterheim, Maj.-Gen., *A Detailed Account of the Battle of Austerlitz* (Cambridge, Trotman, 1985; first published 1807).

Surtees, Maj.-Gen. G., 'British Colours in the Waterloo Campaign', *JSAHR*, vol. 43, no. 174, June 1965, pp. 73–6.

Surtees, William, *Twenty-Five Years in the Rifle Brigade* (London, Muller, 1973).

Sutcliffe, Victor, *The Sandler Collection. An Annotated Bibliography of Books relating to the Military History of the French Revolution and Empire* (Cambridge, Trotman, 1996).

Swabey, Lt. William, *Diary of Campaigns in the Peninsula for the Years 1811, 1812 and 1813* edited by Col. F. A. Whinyates (London, Trotman, 1984).

Sweetman, John, *Raglan. From the Peninsula to the Crimea* (London, Arms & Armour, 1993).

Swiney, Col. G. C., *Historical Records of the 32nd (Cornwall) Light Infantry . . .* (London, Simpkin, Marshal, Kent & Co., 1893).

Synge, Capt., 'Captain Synge's Experiences at Salamanca', edited by F. St L. Tottenham, *The Nineteenth Century*, July 1912, pp. 54–68.

Thiébault, Baron, *The Memoirs of Baron Thiébault*, 2 vols (London, Smith, Elder & Co., 1896).

Thompson, W. F. K.: *see* Aitchison.

Thomson, John, 'Extracts from his "Observations" of the Waterloo Wounded', *The Lancet*, 7 and 24 July 1915, pp. 135–6, 210–11.

Thorpe, Francis N. (ed.), 'Two Diaries of Waterloo', *English Historical Review*, vol. 3, 1888, pp. 539–52.

Thoumine, R. H., *Scientific Soldier: A Life of General Le Marchant, 1766–1812* (Oxford University Press, 1968).

Tomkinson, Lt.-Col. *The Diary of a Cavalry Officer in the Peninsular War and Waterloo Campaign, 1809–15* edited by his son James Tomkinson (London, Swan Sonnenschein & Co., 1895; first published 1894).

Towles, Louis P., 'The Battle of Ulm and the Development of the Grand Army', unpublished doctoral thesis presented to the University of South Carolina, 1977.

Uffindell, Andrew, *The Eagle's Last Triumph. Napoleon's Victory at Ligny, June 1815* (London, Greenhill, 1994).

Uxkull, Baron Boris, *Arms and the Woman. The Diaries of Baron Boris Uxkull, 1812–1819* edited by Detlev von Uexküll (London, Secker & Warburg, 1966).

Vachée, Col. A., *Napoleon at Work* (London, A. & C. Black, 1914).

Van Creveld, Martin, *Command in War* (Cambridge, Massachusetts, Harvard University Press, 1985).

Verner, William, *Reminiscences of William Verner (1782–1871) 7th Hussars* (London, Society for Army Historical Research special publication no. 8, 1965).

Verner, Col. Willoughby, *History & Campaigns of the Rifle Brigade*, 2 vols (London, John Bale, Sons & Danielsson, 1919).

Vichness, Samuel E., 'Marshal of Portugal: The Military Career of William Carr Beresford 1785–1814', unpublished PhD thesis submitted to Florida State University, 1976.

Vivian, C., *Richard Hussey Vivian, First Baron Vivian – a Memoir* (London, Isbister, 1897).

Vivian, Lt.-Gen. Sir Hussey, 'Reply to Major Gawler on his "Crisis of Waterloo"', *USJ*, July 1833, pp. 310–23, and Oct. 1833, pp. 145–9.

Vossler, H. A., *With Napoleon in Russia, 1812* (London, Folio Society, 1969).

Walker, H. M., *A History of the Northumberland Fusiliers, 1674–1902* (London, John Murray, 1919).

Walter, Jakob, *A German Conscript with Napoleon* (Kansas City, Kansas University Press, 1938).

Ward, S. G. P., *Wellington's Headquarters* (Oxford University Press, 1957).

——'General Sir George Murray', *JSAHR*, vol. 58, no. 236, 1980, pp. 191–208.

Warre, Sir William, *Letters from the Peninsula 1808–12* (London, John Murray, 1909).

Wavell, Gen. Sir Archibald, *Generals and Generalship. The Lees Knowles Lectures delivered at Trinity College, Cambridge in 1939* (Harmondsworth, Penguin, 1941).

Webb-Carter, Brig. B. W., 'A Line Regiment at Waterloo', *JSAHR*, vol. 43, no. 174, June 1965, pp. 60–6.

Webber, Capt. William, *With the Guns in the Peninsula* edited by Richard Henry Wollocombe (London, Greenhill, 1991).

Weigley, Russell F., *The Age of Battles. The Quest for Decisive Warfare from Breitenfeld to Waterloo* (London, Pimlico, 1993).

Weller, Jac, *Wellington in the Peninsula, 1808–1814* (London, Vane, 1962).

——*Wellington at Waterloo* (London, Longman, 1967).

Wellington, Duke of, *The General Orders of Field Marshal the Duke of Wellington . . .* edited by Lt.-Col. Gurwood (London, Clowes, 1837).

——*The Dispatches of Field Marshal the Duke of Wellington . . .* compiled by Col. Gurwood, 8 vols (London, Parker, Furnivall & Parker, 1844).

——*Supplementary Despatches, Correspondence and Memoranda of Field Marshal Arthur, Duke of Wellington, K.G.* edited by his son, the Duke of Wellington, 15 vols (London, John Murray, 1858–72). (The title varies slightly from volume to volume.)

Wheatley, Edmund, *The Wheatley Diary* edited by Christopher Hibbert (London, Longman, 1964).

Wheeler, William, *The Letters of Private Wheeler 1809–1828* edited by Capt. B. H. Liddell Hart (London, Michael Joseph, 1951).

Whinyates, Col. F. A., *From Coruña to Sevastapol. The History of 'C' Battery . . .* (London, Allen, 1893).

Wildman, Capt. Thomas, 'The Battle of Waterloo: a Letter . . .' edited by Sir Grimwood Mears, *The Listener*, 24 June 1954, pp. 1085–7.

Wilson, Sir Robert, *General Wilson's Journal, 1812–14* edited by Antony Brett-James (London, Kimber, 1964).

Windsor, William, 'Waterloo: Letters of a Soldier from the Peninsula and Waterloo, 1811–1815', *Cornhill Magazine*, vol. 79, June 1899, pp. 739–50.

Wood, Gen. Sir Evelyn, *The Achievements of Cavalry* (London, Bell, 1900).

Wood, Capt. George, *The Subaltern Officer* (Cambridge, Trotman, 1986; first published 1825).

Wrottesley, George, *Life and Correspondence of Field Marshal Sir John Burgoyne*, 2 vols (London, 1873).

Wylly, H. C., *History of the King's Own Yorkshire Light Infantry*, 2 vols (London, Lund Humphries, 1926).

——*History of the 1st & 2nd Battalions, The Sherwood Foresters, 1740–1914*, 2 vols (Frome, for the regiment, 1929).

Young, Brig. Peter and Lt.-Col. J. P. Lawford, *Wellington's Masterpiece. The Battle and Campaign of Salamanca* (London, Allen & Unwin, 1973).

Index

Abercromby, Lt.-Gen. Sir Ralph 74, 153
Adye, Captain (writer on artillery) 37, 38, 40;
    Bombardier and Pocket Gunner 37
aftermath of battle 83, 248–65; retreat of the
    defeated 7, 240–7; emotions of the
    victors 248–50; plundering 250–7;
    prisoners 253–8; the wounded 259–64
after the war 266–74
aides-de-camp 62, 147, 148, 158, 160–1, 162,
    166, 169, 170–4, 206, 209
Aitchison, Ensign John (3rd Foot Guards)
    95–7, 181–2, 303
Alba de Tormes, Battle of (28 Nov. 1809) 237,
    244
Albuera, Battle of (16 May 1811) 20, 115, 133,
    151, 163, 237, 244; casualties at 8, 45, 190,
    191, 267, 294n44; destruction of
    Colborne's brigade at 13, 110, 135;
    artillery at 45; Beresford's conduct at 154,
    163; Lt. G. Crompton at 196
Alburquerque, Duque de 95
alcohol 178–9, 199–200, 295n12
Alexander, Emperor of Russia 10, 151, 240,
    243, 245
Alexandria, Battle of (21 March 1801) 222
Allan, Sir William 277n16
Almeida 238
Alten General Count Charles 161, 168
Alten, General Victor 58
American Civil War 13, 46, 47
American War of Independence 51
ammunition: types of artillery ammunition
    30–1; consumption & casualties inflicted,
    artillery 31, 34–6, 40–4, 46–7, 279n23;
    infantry 82–3, 161, 283n34; resupply
    of 33, 83
anaesthetics 231, 261, 299n29
Anglesey: *see* Uxbridge
anonymous memoirist of the 71st Highland
    Light Infantry 4, 83, 268, 303

anonymous threatening letters 176
antiseptics 231, 261, 299n29
Anton, Sergeant (42nd) 23, 110, 111, 198, 201
anxiety 3–4, 6–7, 217–18, 249
Arapiles, village of 19, 159
Archduke Charles 24, 145
Archduke Ferdinand 168
Ardant du Picq, Col. C.J.J.J. (soldier and
    writer) 72, 114, 205, 311
Armée du Nord 63
Arnold, James (historian) 306, 310, 311
Artillerist's Manual 43
Artillery: equipment 14; drivers 15, 44,
    279n30; tactics 15–17, 33–5, 37–8, 40, 50,
    128–30, and close terrain 22–3, grand
    batteries 33–4, 278n9, counter-battery
    fire 35–8, 40–1, as proportion of army 29,
    33; types of 29–30, 34–5, horse
    artillery 30, 105, regimental artillery 35,
    212; range 30, 42–4; ammunition 30–1,
    consumption 31, 34–6, 40–2, 279n23;
    effectiveness 30–1, 35–6, 40–4, 46–7,
    279n27, psychological 34–5, 38, 47–50,
    95–6; command and control of 31–3, 41,
    214; supporting friendly troops 34–5, 38,
    50, 90–1, 92, 212; need support of friendly
    troops 34, 38–9, 129; casualties suffered
    by 40, 41, 45–6, 92; reluctance to fight at
    close range 44–6, 92, 129; in action: at
    Austerlitz 90–1, at Friedland 40, 44, at
    Wagram 29, 33, 278n9, at Talavera 95–6,
    at Busaco 92, at Salamanca 16, 29, 35, at
    Borodino 29, at the Huebra (17 Nov.
    1812) 36, at Bautzen 38, at Vitoria 32,
    41, 47, at Ligny 38–9, at Waterloo 29, 34,
    38, 41–4, 47–8
Aspern-Essling, Battle of (21–2 May 1809) 9,
    10, 24, 158, 172, 215, 242; Austrian orders
    for 144–5
atrocities 20, 223